Henry E. Bothin
Philanthropist of Steel

Henry E. Bothin

Henry E. Bothin
Philanthropist of Steel

Michael Casey

Copyright ©2015 by Michael Casey

Henry E. Bothin, Philanthropist of Steel

Second Edition March 2015

All rights reserved. No part of this publication may be reproduced, distributed, or transmitted in any form without the prior written permission of the publisher, except in the case of brief quotations embodied in critical reviews and certain other noncommercial uses permitted by copyright law.

ISBN 978-0-9961661-0-2

Library of Congress Control Number 2015904356

Published by Michael Casey, PO Box 526, Nicasio, CA

First Edition September 2014

Editing and book design by www.StoriesToTellBooks.com

Cover image South Side of Market Street Between 3rd and 4th Streets permission of San Francisco History Center, San Francisco Public Library

Image of Rock Island Bridge Crossing the Mississippi from 1866-1872 provided with permission by Putnam Museum of History and Natural Science.

Image of the Transbay Transit Tower courtesy of Pelli Clarke Pelli Architects and provided by Hines and Boston Properties.

Photographs of 222 Second Street artist's rendering of Foundry Square III office building provided courtesy of Tishman Speyer with the consent of Allen Palmer.

Photograph of Piranhurst permission of *Santa Barbara Magazine*, first appeared in Volume Eleven/Number 3, Summer 1985 edition.

Images of Mar Y Cel and the Cypress Stage at Piranhurst courtesy of the Montecito Association History Committee.

Image of painting *The Wreck of the Effie Afton* courtesy of the Rock Island County Historical Society. Undated, unknown artist.

Credit and thanks to Barb Von Ahsen for her sketch of the Bothin home in Portage dated June 2014.

Credit and thanks to the Fairfax Historical Society and Bill Sagar for permission to use photos of Hill Farm and Arequipa as well as the display room for ceramic tiles at the Panama Pacific Exposition.

Credit and thanks to Garrett Walkup for providing Bothin family photos.

Dedication

This book is dedicated to the following civic minded volunteers who have freely given their time and energy by serving on the Board of Trustees of what was initially the Bothin Helping Fund and is now known as the Bothin Foundation. Henry Bothin was the founder and first member, but he surrounded himself from the outset with capable and thoughtful people, family members and non-family alike. That the Foundation remains a valued part of San Francisco's philanthropic community nearly a century after its founder's death is a testament both to the careful stewardship of its assets and also to the caring way that those assets have been and continue to be distributed to the needy within our community. In dedicating this book to those trustees, both living and deceased, I am, I believe, speaking for Henry, both in recognizing their dedication and in thanking them for making the world a somewhat better place.

TRUSTEES OF THE BOTHIN HELPING FUND (NOW BOTHIN FOUNDATION)

Name	Date of Election	End of Term
Henry E. Bothin	September 29, 1917	October 14, 1923 (died)
Ellen Chabot Bothin	September 29, 1917	February 10, 1965 (died)
Genevieve Bothin Lyman	September 29, 1917 Re-elected May 4, 1942	October 30, 1935 (resigned) October 23, 1983 (died)

Name	Date of Election	End of Term
Rev. C.P. Deems	August 29, 1918	February 13, 1936 (resigned)
William Thomas	August 29, 1918	April 9, 1924 (resigned)
Robert C. Bolton	August 29, 1918	1932 (died)
Edmund F.R. Vail	July 6, 1920	January 11, 1923 (resigned)
William T. Summers	July 6, 1920	June 11, 1930 (resigned)
Ida Sutter Maas	January 11, 1923	February 18, 1952 (died)
Elizabeth Ashe	March 23, 1923	January 25, 1954 (died)
C.O.G. Miller	October 29, 1923	April 23, 1952 (died)
Edmunds Lyman	November 21, 1923	October 30, 1935 (resigned)
	Re-elected February 26, 1948	September 6, 1964 (died)
Theodore A. Maas	January 4, 1925	May 1, 1971 (died)
Edward H. Clark	February 13, 1936	1981 (died)
N.L. McLaren	February 13, 1936	April 1, 1963 (died)
Marshall P. Madison	February 13, 1936	December 18, 1968 (died)
Genevieve Lyman Casey di San Faustino	February 18, 1952	March 10, 2011 (died)
Carlos J. Maas	February 18, 1952	April 12, 1972 (died)
Edmona Lyman Miller Mansell	April 1, 1963	November 11, 1999 (died)
Ranieri di San Faustino	December 14, 1964	February 5, 1977 (died)
A. Michael Casey	April 12, 1971	
Lyman H. Casey	April 12, 1971	October 1, 1977 (resigned)
	Re-elected 1982	
Benjamin J. Henley, Jr.	February 28, 1977	1994 (died)
Rev. Canon William Geisler	August 31, 1978	1993 (termed out)
Allan V. Giannini	1982	1984 (resigned)
William W. Budge	1983	1995 (termed out)

Name	Date of Election	End of Term
Stephanie C. MacColl	1984	2003 (termed out)
Rhoda W. Schultz	1985	1997 (termed out)
Robert L. Miller	1994	1997 (resigned)
Mary Gregory	1996	1998 (resigned to join staff)
Gordon E. Miller	1997	October 10, 2006 (died)
Nancy Connor	1998	2004 (termed out)
John E. McCosker	1998	2003 (termed out)
Kimberly K. Casey	2001	2004 (Gen V termed out)
Carol K. Prince	2003	2008 (termed out)
Suzie Pollak	2003	2008 (termed out)
Jay Jacobs	2004	2010 (termed out)
Jessica Galloway	2004	2010 (termed out)
Shannon Casey Welch	2005	2008 (Gen V termed out)
Devon Mansell Laycox	2007	
Lyman R. Casey	2008	2011 (Gen V termed out)
Laura King Pfaff	2009	
Paul Sussman	2009	
Herbert Tully	2010	2013 (resigned)
Pam McCosker	2010	
Katherine Casey Joiner	2011	2014 (Gen V termed out)
Christian Miller	2011	
Theodore Griffinger	2013	
Rebecca Miller	2014	

*Note: Charlie Casey, the son of my brother, Lyman, is the President of Pacific Foundation Services, which contracts to provide grant management, accounting, and myriad other services that improve both the quality and efficiency of the work of the Board. Charlie has done a terrific job and this dedication would be severely incomplete without a recognition of his contributions and those of the PFS staff.

Contents

Preface	xi
Introduction	xxix
1. Background Roots In Europe	1
2. First Generation of Bothins in America	9
3. Early Beginnings in America	15
4. Henry's Early Life in Wisconsin	35
5. Westward Ho!	47
6. The 1870s: A Time to Be Careful	81
7. The Tea and Spice Business	89
8. Expansion and New Beginnings	103
9. Marriage to Jennie Whittier	113
10. Turning Point: Judson Manufacturing Company	123
11. Business Changes: Real Estate	159
12. Outside Business Interests and Directorships	201
13. Marin County, Across the Bay	209
14. The Fairfax Ranch and Early Philanthropy	219
15. Hemet	229
16. 1906 Earthquake and Fire	233

17. Rebuilding After the Quake — 249

18. Jennie and Henry Bothin Divorce — 259

19. Genevieve and Family — 275

20. Marriage to Ellen Chabot — 283

21. A Change in Lifestyle — 289

22. Changes in Real Estate Strategy — 295

23. Henry's Attachment to Ross — 299

24. Broadening Philanthropic Efforts — 305

25. Santa Barbara – Piranhurst — 321

26. Santa Barbara – Mar y Cel — 331

27. Permanent Philanthropy - The Bothin Helping Fund — 341

28. Commercial Real Estate in Santa Barbara — 357

29. Ongoing Business Affairs — 361

30. The Final Years — 369

31. A Life Well and Fully Lived — 373

Epilogue — 377

Endnotes — 387

Index — 449

Genevieve Bothin Lyman

Preface

My grandmother used to call her father, Henry Bothin, a horse thief. She, Genevieve Bothin Lyman, knew it wasn't a fair description of her father, but she chose to say it anyway because she didn't like him. After all, she was just twelve years old when Henry and his wife, Jennie, went through a very public divorce that deeply embarrassed Genevieve, and for which she never forgave him. In those days, divorce was a dirty word, and unfortunately the collateral damage usually fell upon the children who were taunted by classmates, ostracized by the latters' parents, and generally tormented by the community. It mattered not that divorce, back then, was often driven by the same issues and incompatibilities that today are considered reasonable and unexceptional. But such was not the case in 1907, when my great grandmother petitioned to have her marriage to Henry Bothin terminated. As she was then required to do, she claimed mental cruelty as the cause, and so set into motion the wagging tongues that maliciously circulated the Bothins' dirty laundry and traumatized twelve-year-old Genevieve by preventing her from visiting her schoolmates' homes and otherwise depriving her of the social interactions she craved.

What is most surprising is that Genevieve, who lived to the ripe old age of eighty-nine, carried her grudge against her father to her grave. Despite the absence of scandalous misbehavior or other malfeasance that might really have justified her feelings, she chose to turn her back on all the good things that her father had accomplished during his lifetime, including those that made her a wealthy and pampered woman. She chose instead, for reasons unknown, to feign ignorance about him and his background even as she served, for eighteen years, as the president of the foundation which bore his name and imprint, the foundation he had established to benefit local poor and underserved youth, which today still remains an important part of the fabric of philanthropy in San Francisco.

But this book is not about whether Henry Bothin deserved the enmity of his daughter, or, for that matter, whether Genevieve was overly spoiled and unappreciative of all that he did for her in an effort to make up for the awfulness of the divorce. Rather, this book tries to look at Henry from all sides and to present a fair picture of my very successful and quite generous great-grandfather. Despite a lack of formal education, he thrived simultaneously in not just one, but two altogether dissimilar businesses, and he was highly respected by his business peers, serving on a number of corporate boards and being called upon to help turn around the fortunes of several utilities which had, through poor management decisions, come upon hard times. Although unapologetically a capitalist, he also chose to use a significant part of his wealth for the greater good. In 1917, he set up The Bothin Helping Fund—now the Bothin Foundation—to assure funding beyond his own death for several non-profit organizations that were an important part of his later life.

In writing this biography of a man I never knew, I have necessarily come to appreciate how little I still know about this person whose blood I share. His was a life lived largely in private, and while that was undoubtedly as he wanted, its footprint has grown fainter with the passage of years, and I am left with many mysteries, most of which will probably remain forever unsolved.

But this book was also written for an altogether different reason. It is a story never before told about a relative, and in that sense it is a circumstance common to us all. We all have ancestors who lived abundant lives outside the limelight—lives full of hard work and of memorable accomplishments and disappointments alike, but lives that, for reasons both good and bad, never found their way onto the front page of a newspaper. Henry was not "everyman," but in telling his story I have felt that in some small measure I have done what we all would like to do—pay homage to someone in our family lineage whose efforts have made our own lives a bit easier and a bit more meaningful. Whether that somebody was a construction worker who helped to build the Golden Gate Bridge, or a veteran who fought for our freedom during one of too many wars, or a housewife who raised a child who became a teacher, each of those people, and many, many more who have gone before us, largely in anonymity, made things, taught people, entertained folks, performed needed services, and in their short-lived unique lives, helped others. Henry Bothin was such a person, and in telling his story I am fulfilling, in a sense, a debt of gratitude for all he did for others and for me as well.

This book began as a project intended just for the benefit of the family, and yet the deeper I dug into the life of Mr. Bothin, the more it seemed that his biography deserved to be read by a broader audience. However, because so little was written about him while he lived, and because letters both from and to him are in such short supply, there are many gaps in the story which somewhat blur the picture. Still, what little has survived, when gathered together, creates a tableau which I hope will be as interesting to the reader as it has been to me in its compilation. At the very least, it is my hope that this book will add to the base of knowledge about the blossoming of San Francisco during the last quarter of the nineteenth century and the first decades of the twentieth and about one man's role in that dynamic growth.

In the process of building this portrait of Henry, a number of conflicting facts have inevitably surfaced. In some cases, these are the result of different interpretations of a given event, while in others they arose due to a natural tendency of the truth to be corrupted in small ways every time a story is retold. Where conflicting versions of an event have surfaced, I have tried to use those tools we all have learned to use to separate truth from exaggeration or fabrication. I hope I have been successful more times than not; however, I do not claim a perfect record, and mistakes have undoubtedly been made. Any mistakes are mine, and for them I apologize.

A good example of the need to exercise judgment in reporting facts is a story, which was written as part of a brief family history by Ida Sutter Maas, Henry's favorite niece and a granddaughter of Henry's parents, Ernst and Rosa Bothin.[1] Ida's mother was Emily (Emma) Bothin Sutter, one of Henry's older sisters. In 1887, while in her forties, Emily moved back to the family home in Portage, Wisconsin to care for her parents, Ernst and Rosa, during their declining years. Ida, who would have been sixteen years old in 1887, lived with her parents in Portage and spent many hours in the company of her grandparents. One would expect her to have spoken with them, probably in German (their native tongue), about their own childhoods, how they met, and their early lives together. Although Ida was an accurate reporter of many facts and events which have become a part of this narrative, in 1940 (some fifty years after Rosa's death) she included in that short history the following story—one which she seems to have penned in all seriousness, but which has a fairy tale quality to it. It begins as follows:

> This saga begins five generations ago in an unidentified spot in rural Germany, where families were large and customs primitive. It concerns humble people with no documented evidence, only that which is remembered of storys [sic] current during

the lifetime of the granddaughter of Ernest Bothin, who is trying not to color the incidents chronicled.

A small 'goose girl' possibly ten years old is given the care of a baby brother as well as to guard a flock of geese, along with other children similarly occupied. The baby falls asleep and is carefully nested in the shade of bushes lining a country road. The sister romps with her companions far enough away so that the baby will not be disturbed.

A Mr. and Mrs. Bothin passed down the little used road on their way home from a distant village. The young wife having just lost a baby son by death is for a time mentally unbalanced, and on seeing the sleeping child insists it is the answer to her prayers, and the husband seeing no one near to question, puts the child in her arms and they drive on. Later it was understood that the neighborhood folk dragged the goose pond convinced that the child had awakened and crawled to the pond and was drowned. (At this point the narrative is weak—we must assume that later inquiries and explanations had been made resulting in the above information about the child. I confess there is little in my actual knowledge to corroborate just how conclusions were arrived at.) [Parenthetical statement is Ida's.]

The child was reared as Ernest Bothin, educated and considered the heir of the foster parents, who evidently were of good family as he fell in love with a Rosena Von Lawrence of minor nobility. All went well when lo and behold a child—a son was born to the Bothin family. This changed the status of the adopted Ernest Bothin. The Von Lawrences now cancelled the engagement of their daughter giving as a reason the assumption that the union would harden the prospects of a younger sister. Poor frustrated Rosena fell into decline with the result that the Von Lawrences reconsidered their verdict and decided to save their daughter's life and happiness by allowing the marriage of Rosena and Ernest, providing they migrate to America: thus becoming out of the picture. They came to America, settling in Ohio. For many years we hear nothing more than that...[2]

To me, Ida's story of her grandparents' early life reads like a Grimm Brothers' tale. At best it seems to be a bit of fanciful fiction rather than any accurate portrayal of events. Given that I have come to see Ida as an otherwise fair reporter of events and circumstances, I doubt this sort of romanticized tale came from her. More likely, it sprang forth either from the imagination of her aging grandmother or from the natural consequence of re-telling of stories handed down by word of mouth from generation to generation and further embellished with each iteration. Ida herself notes in the story that it has come down verbally and without written corroboration. Adding to the opportunities for exaggeration, Rosa appears (based on other research) to have been illiterate and therefore incapable of committing the story to written form when her mind was sharp. She probably also spoke halting English, while her native German would have been Ida's second tongue. So whichever language they communicated in, all the elements for misinterpretation and/or enrichment of the tale, innocent or otherwise, were present. What is most surprising to me is that Ida would have believed it and would have passed it on as family history.

In actual fact, we know little about the early years of Henry Bothin's parents. His father was Michael Ernst Boethin, Prussian by birth, and he originally spelled his surname "Boethin," an unusual name that became even more unusual when he changed its spelling to "Bothin" when he arrived in America. Research reveals absolutely no records of anyone in Prussia who carried the surname "Bothin" and scant few named "Boethin." Indeed, the very unusualness of the name turned out to be a blessing in this case since it dramatically narrowed the search parameters and enabled me to find Henry's father's actual roots. Also, his given name (the middle name which he used) was in fact Ernst, not Ernest as Ida wrote it.[3] What little we know about Ernst's ancestry and early years is largely limited to the places of his birth and marriage and the names of his father and those of his siblings who lived to adulthood and married. His father was named Johann, and he also had at least six siblings who reached adulthood and married—two (or possibly three) born before him, three (or possibly four) afterwards and one within a year on either side of his date of birth.[4] Since all of those individuals carried the name "Boethin," then it follows that either the "Mrs. Bothin" of Ida's story was in fact Ernst's true mother (in which case the story of his kidnapping unravels rather quickly) or else the names of the kidnapper and kidnappee were identical—a scenario which seems highly improbable given the rarity of the name.

There are a number of other ways to debunk Ida's story about her grandfather's supposed kidnapping; however, only one other bears mentioning. That is that Ernst's parents are known to have had two sons who were older than Ernst.[5] At least one of those sons survived to adulthood and married, thereby giving him precedence over Ernst as regards rights of succession by way of primogeniture. Another brother was born four years after Ernst; however, there are no known male siblings born after 1815, when Ernst was only four. Therefore, Ida's story's allusion to a younger brother whose apparently sudden and unexpected birth deprived Ernst of any inheritance rights completely unravels when held up to church records, which confirm the true makeup of that generation of the Boethin family.

Turning to Rosa's role in Ida's story line, it too seems replete with misinformation. Indeed the untruths in her part of the story are what are most instructive and most relevant to Henry's background, for they suggest that Rosa (or Rosena as she was called by Ida) was either addled at the time she recounted the story to Ida, or else she was given to serious exaggeration, if not outright falsehoods, and quite possibly had a very fragile ego. Rosa apparently told her teenage granddaughter that she, Rosa, was born Rosina "von Lawrence" and was of minor nobility. In fact, her maiden name was not "von Lawrence" but rather was simply "Lawrenz." Had it been "von Lawrence" she might have had a basis for her claim to minor nobility, for the term "von" was often given to highly placed civil servants and military leaders and sometimes to people with sizable landholdings, to convey respect and a privileged status. In other words, a person born with the name "von Lawrence" would have commanded a level of deference in her community, or anywhere in Prussia for that matter, simply because of the prefix "von" attached to it.

In Rosa's case, not only is it known that her maiden name was simply "Lawrenz," but, as importantly, she appears reliably to have been illiterate. This fact dispels the notion that she might have had noble roots, for the German people have a long cultural history of placing high importance on education. Indeed by the middle of the 18th century, over sixty years before Rosa was born, universal literacy, at least within the upper and middle classes, was the norm throughout Scandinavia and northern Europe.[6] In fact it was a German by the name of Friedrich Froebel who first came up with the name and idea of "kindergarten" (literally "children's garden") in the 1830s in Germany, and the first kindergarten in the United

States was begun by another German, Margarethe Schurz, who set it up in Watertown, Wisconsin in 1856.[7] So for someone who was herself apparently illiterate, it seems altogether absurd to claim a stature even approaching middle class, much less minor nobility.

At the risk of piling on, Rosa's story is also disproved in another rather obvious respect as well. Despite her telling Ida that her parents had conditioned their consent to the marriage upon the couple's agreement to leave home and emigrate to America, the fact is that Ernst and Rosa did not leave Germany any time soon after they were married. They were married on April 28, 1836, and it was not until sixteen years later, in August of 1852, that they came to the United States.[8] The 1860 census from Portage, Wisconsin (where they were living at the time of that census), notes that six of their eight children were born in Prussia, the youngest of whom, Julius, was listed in that census report as having been born in Prussia in about 1850, some fourteen years after Ernst and Rosa were married. So, assuming there was any truth at all to Ida's story, then if Rosa's parents did in fact demand, as the price of their consent to the marriage, that the couple leave Germany, the Lawrenz family either later had to have had a change of heart, or else Ernst and Rosa must have departed only far enough from her parent's home to be beyond their reach and able to settle and raise a family in anonymity. Given that we know from other sources that the children were brought up in Chodziesen (now Chodzież in modern day Poland) and that their parents were from very nearby villages if not Chodziesen itself, it seems unlikely they could have hidden their offspring from the children's grandparents for a decade and a half.

As interesting as it may be to look critically at the contrived tale told by Rosa to her granddaughter, this work is not about Ernst or Rosa Boethin, but rather about their son, Henry. Its true significance to this work lies not so much in its own words as in the fact that Henry's mother chose to misrepresent her own roots. For if Rosa was given to exaggerate her own family history in that way to her own granddaughter, that speaks volumes about her ego and about the environment in which Henry spent his formative years. And so, that story will be revisited in other contexts, as Henry's own story unfolds.

Henry's own life became important not for who he was descended from, but rather for what he accomplished on his own. It may seem unimportant, in the overall scheme of things, to spend much more time trying to understand details of his father's or mother's early lives. On the other hand, the history of the place that generations of the Boethin and Lawrenz families called home is important to an understanding of Henry's roots and upbringing. Czarnków and Chodzież, towns that lie sixteen miles apart and about fifty miles north of the far larger city of Poznan, are an integral part of the story that follows. They are the environmental backdrop against which Ernst and Rosa developed their own value systems, values that they brought with them to their newly adopted country, and by which they cast their imprints on Henry's early life, his education, his motivations, and everything else about him, which in turn are threaded through the tapestry of his life and its effect on others.

Finally, it must be pointed out that my efforts to trace Henry's parents' ancestry back beyond their own generation have borne minimal fruit. While it would have been nice to have a better sense of their backgrounds, that gap is simply one among many puzzles that must always remain when writing about someone who was not prominently in the public's eye during his lifetime and about whom few contemporary articles ever appeared in print. One can only find what is available in the historic record, and there are many, many gaps in that record. One such gap, for instance, is the birthplace of the very person about whom this book is being written. Henry Bothin always said he was born in Cleveland, Ohio, and his voting registration records and obituaries are all consistent with that assertion. Yet my request for a copy of his birth certificate at the

Probate Court of Cuyahoga County, Ohio, was fruitless; it turned out that there is no such record. Does that mean that he lived a lie about his birthplace? Absolutely not. Henry undoubtedly heard from his parents that he was born in Cleveland, and who would know better than they where he drew his first breath? The fact that the clerk's office in a large city could not find a nearly 150-year-old document does not trump the unrecorded word of the couple whose child he was, who had no reason to lie about the place of his birth.

And so it is with much of this book—it attempts to sort fact from fiction but necessarily makes judgment calls about credibility and probabilities, and does so with some frequency. What follows is simply my best effort at chronicling the full, rich, and well-lived life of my great grandfather.

Acknowledgements

This is my first effort at writing a book. That may well show in many ways; but not in the quality of help I received from a number of quarters. Without the capable and enthusiastic support from the following people, the book simply could not have been written.

Anna Mae Axness of Portage, Wisconsin was hugely helpful. She and her husband, Jim, poured through land title records, obituaries, church and cemetery records, and other materials and found for me, among other crucial nuggets, all of the records of Henry's father's property purchases in both Portage and Lewiston. It was Anna Mae who persuaded a friend, Dave Tamminga (the historian for St. John"s Lutheran Church in Portage), to review the old archives and records of the church which provided useful information on the senior Bothins. Of crucial importance, Anna Mae also uncovered the obituary of Henry's older sister, Pauline, whose birthplace was noted at "Chodusen" in Prussia. Although misspelled in the newspaper that carried the obituary, it didn't take much sleuthing thereafter to find Chodziesen and to ride that trail back to church records which opened a previously unknown generation of the Bothin (then spelled "Boethin") family in northern Europe. Anna Mae and Jim also acted as my tour guides on a trip back to Portage, showed me the location of the Bothin home and of all of Ernst's investment properties, clarified some geographic misconceptions I had, and took me to see the family headstones in the Silver Lake Cemetery, headstones which had probably not been visited, cared for, or appreciated in over a century, but headstones which aroused emotions in me which were unexpectedly strong. I can simply never thank Anna Mae enough.

Another person who was very helpful to me is Lukasz Bielecki. Lukasz is the founder of the Poznan Project, a genealogical database which contains marriage records from 1835 to 1884 within the former Prussian province of Posen, now the Polish province of Poznan. This database, compiled by volunteers under Lukasz' guidance, is of particular importance because after the end of the Second World War the Germans were largely expelled from Poland, and their Lutheran Churches (complete with all their historical records) were abandoned, demolished, or taken over by the Catholic parishes which serve the religious needs of the vast majority of Polish people. Not only did Lukasz' database enable me to find records including the marriages of Henry's parents and of a number of their siblings, but I was also able to track down the small towns where they were born, raised, and where they raised Henry's six older siblings who were born there before the family came to this country. Finally, Lukasz kindly agreed to act as my guide during the summer of 2013 when I visited Czarnkov and Chodziez, the present day Polish names of the towns where Henry's family originated.

Garrett Walkup was immensely important to my research. He is a distant cousin, descending from the line of Henry's sister, Emily and her daughter, Ida. Garrett has a treasure trove of information which clarified large gaps in my knowledge about Henry. He provided me with the short family history which had been prepared by his great grandmother, Ida Sutter Maas, and which is discussed in detail in the book. He also provided to me the photographs of Henry's parents, Ernst and Rosa, as well as Henry's sister, Emily Bothin Sutter, and two of her children, Ida and Emil Sutter, copies of which appear in the book. He also gave me copies of the collection of letters from Emil, who worked for Henry at Judson for a year in 1889 and 1890 before succumbing to tuberculosis.

Bill Sagar is an historian with the Fairfax Historical Society. Bill made available to me a wealth of material relating to Henry's life in Marin County, his purchase from Phoebe Heart of the 1,232 acre ranch which was to play such an important role in his later philanthropy, and background information which he had gathered as one of the four researchers who compiled and wrote the 1997 book entitled *Hill Farm and Arequipa*. I particularly appreciated Bill's enthusiasm for my undertaking, his review of early drafts of the book, and the fact that, quite on his own, he took the trouble to prepare an index for the book when it was a far smaller and more modest effort. Bill also arranged graciously to grant me permission to use images of Hill Farm, Arequipa, and Elizabeth Ashe.

Hattie Beresford is another person to whom I am indebted. She gave generously of her time and immense knowledge about Montecito. She also provided background on Piranhurst, the home in Montecito which Henry and his second wife, Ellen, built and enjoyed, and also on his commercial property acquisitions in Santa Barbara. Hattie, who is a journalist who writes for Montecito Magazine, has written articles about Henry and some of his interests, and she not only provided me with useful information about his life in that Southern California community, but also directed me to other sources, including the Gledhill Library of the Santa Barbara Historical Museum, The Montecito Association History Committee, and the Montecito Journal. Very, importantly to me, she also arranged two tours which took me back through memory lane. The first was a tour of Piranhurst itself which, thanks to the attention paid to it by its current owners, today remains as spectacularly beautiful and well kept up as it was during Henry's and Ellen's lifetime. The second was a memorable visit to Mar Y Cel, the mountaintop property which adjoined Piranhurst and on which Henry had been building reservoirs, buttresses, a tea house, an outdoor theatre and other improvements up to the time of his death. That property, which unfortunately was the site of the infamous Santa Barbara Tea fire in 2008, is being lovingly restored today by its current owners who graciously took me on a tour, complete with a delicious picnic lunch at the spectacular Tea House. In thanking Hattie, I also want to extend my thanks to the owners of both Piranhurst and Mar Y Cel for their kindnesses.

Terry Carter was a wonderful source of information about both Piranhurst and Ellen Bothin. Because of the scars left by the very public divorce which Henry and his first wife endured, his only child who lived to adulthood, (my grandmother, Genevieve) had an altogether different perspective on both Henry and Ellen than that which Terry recalls. Terry's family worked as groundskeepers at Piranhurst, and her recollections as a child added much needed balance to my grandmother's far less complimentary statements about both Henry and Ellen. I thank her enormously for her insights and for the efforts she went to to speak with other members of her family in order to create a mosaic which frankly rings truer than do the more vindictive utterances about her father that my grandmother unfortunately took to her grave.

Al Schreck is one of the general partners of KSW Properties, the partnership which bought the Bothin Real Estate Company's portfolio of properties in 1971. Al and his late partner, Len Kingsley, through wise and creative management decisions over a period of forty years, took what was then a stagnant collection of real estate holdings and restored them to the luster and value they had during Henry Bothin's lifetime. Al gave generously of his time to explain the wisdom of Henry's real estate decisions and the ways KSW sought to (and usually did) add value during the period of their ownership of those assets. Al also provided me with the photographs of several of those properties which appear in the book, and he is quoted several times in the text. Our family and I owe both Al and Len a huge debt of gratitude, not just for Al's insights that appear in these pages, but for his and Len's brilliant stewardship of the real estate empire Henry strove so hard to create.

John Chamberlain is a good friend and former grammar school classmate. He is in the commercial real estate leasing business and it was he who arranged contacts with both Allen Palmer of Tishman Speyer and Meredith Treaster of Hines. They in turn graciously arranged to obtain permission for me to use images and artists' renderings of the 222 Second Street, Foundry Square III, and Transbay Tower office buildings. I also want to extend my thanks to Tishman Speyer, Hines, Boston Properties and to Pelli, Clark, Pelli, the architects of the Transbay Tower.

Dewey Livingston is an historian and author several times over who knows far more about Marin County than I ever will. Dewey was very kind and supportive of this effort, and he steered me toward additional sources, particularly regarding White's Hill and West Marin which contributed greatly to my knowledge and have found their way into the book.

Gary Scales, former mayor of the Town of Ross, former President of the Lagunitas Club, highly regarded rose grower, amateur writer and photographer (although the word "amateur" hardly does him justice) is a close friend who made available to me the records of the Lagunitas Club for my research and pointed me toward a number of good sources of information, particularly regarding the history of the town of Ross. Gary has also been extremely encouraging to me in many, many aspects of this work.

Lynn Downey (the historian for Levi Strauss and Company and whose grandmother was treated at Arequipa), Barbie Geisler, Hattie Beresford, Bill Sagar, and, of course, my ever patient wife, Jeanie, reviewed early manuscripts of this book and provided help and guidance for which I am enormously grateful.

Very importantly, I want to thank Biff and Nan Barnes. When I submitted my manuscript to Biff, he told me that it was fine if what I was interested in was just family consumption, but, to my utter surprise, he told me that he thought it was a book which might have more general interest if I could expand it and add additional context. That was nearly two years ago, and both Biff and Nan have put up with many calls and e-mails since that time as I, a novice and untrained writer, struggled to place Henry into a broader historic framework which might hopefully be of interest to a wider audience. Who knows whether I have succeeded, but if I have to any extent at all it will have been because of Biff and Nan and their patience and encouragement. Nan and Biff have also done a wonderful job helping me organize photos, photoshopping them as appropriate, editing endnotes so they conform to the *Chicago Manual of Style*, creating the index, designing the look of the book, and performing all those absolutely necessary back room functions that are invisible to the reader but without which this book could not have been finished or published.

Finally, I want to thank Jeanie, who has put up with a fully distracted husband over the past several years. Re-heated meals because of my total immersion in this project became the norm for all too long, as did scintillating dinner conversations about topics ranging from skyscraper foundations to steel bridges and more. Always supportive, and always willing to critique draft manuscripts and provide helpful insights, Jeanie is the rock I rely on and love ever more as we approach a half century of marriage.

Introduction

"Go West, young man, go West and grow up with the country," said Horace Greeley in 1865, nearly seventeen years after the great California Gold Rush, an historic event which had drawn nearly three hundred thousand young men, flocking to California in search of the nineteenth century's version of a winning lottery ticket. Some had found gold and some among them had managed to keep it, others were still looking, but most of the crowd had long since dissipated and returned home by the time Mr. Greeley wrote those words.

Although the gold find at Sutter's Mill was ancient history by 1870, California, and more specifically its financial center, San Francisco, was anything but. The city, which had grown from a hamlet of less than 500 souls in 1847, had, by 1870, exploded to over 150,000, making it the tenth largest city in the country. The transcontinental railroad, completed in 1869, was disgorging, every day, new and hopeful transplants from the East Coast, the Midwest, and elsewhere throughout our young nation, and the port of San Francisco had become crowded, not only with ships bringing people and freight into the country from all over the world, but with ocean-borne vessels fueling a lively export trade as well. As though that wasn't enough, there was the draw of the Comstock Lode, a hugely rich silver find in western Nevada that had been first discovered in the late 1850s. It was still attracting people with high hopes and was also still producing millionaires well into the 1870s.

The allure of California persisted despite severe droughts in the early 1860s that had, by 1864, essentially decimated the vast herds of longhorn cattle which had come north to Alta California in 1769 with Gaspar de Portola and Father Junipero Serra and had multiplied, by the 1820s, to nearly half a million animals.. It persisted despite the "great earthquake" of 1865 that destroyed a number of buildings, and scared the wits out of a completely surprised citizenry, an event which was humorously described in *Roughing It* by eyewitness Mark Twain. In short, the San Francisco of the early 1870s was still a magnet for people seeking excitement, adventure, and success. Their enthusiasm, generated by stories of success of all kinds, spurred further growth. Indeed, few would have been surprised back then to learn that over the next twenty years the city's population would double to 300,000, thereby making it number eight on the 1890 list of most populated cities in the country.

Into that locus of optimism and the thrill of the hunt, a young man named Henry Bothin from faraway Portage, Wisconsin followed the lead of his older sisters, Otillia and Minnie, and left the miserably cold winters of the upper Midwest in favor of an unknown future in balmy San Francisco. Just eighteen years old in 1871, he, like so many other hopefuls, arrived with only the shirt on his back, an intense desire to succeed, a willingness to work hard, and—this is what set him apart from others—a generosity of soul which would, far more than the money he made, secure his legacy.

Henry had seen none of the paintings of majestic Yosemite or of the California coast, nor had he seen or likely even heard about other landmarks of the state's natural beauty that had been captured on canvas and were then being toured, displayed and sold back east by such accomplished artists as Albert Bierstadt, William Keith and Thomas Hill. Nor had he seen Timothy O'Sullivan's photographs of the spectacular scenery west of the Rockies, nor, indeed, was he much aware of anything about San Francisco other than what he had read in letters sent home by his sisters. But they were enough; they had made him yearn to come west.

During the seven years before Henry moved west he had labored without pay on his parents' farm near Portage. He had watched while his elder sisters (with whom he was far closer than he was to his German-born parents) left—one by one—to marry and start their own lives in distant places. Finally, lonely and frustrated, he made off with two of his father's horses that he reckoned were his due in return for the involuntary servitude he had given his parents, and with the proceeds of their sale, he turned west and left that chapter of his life behind forever.

John Muir, the naturalist who would become the founding President of the Sierra Club and who was most instrumental in the establishment of Yosemite as a National Park, grew up on a farm just outside Portage and not far from where young Henry spent his childhood. But Henry's interests were far different from those of Muir. Whereas Muir came to explore and to study plants, Henry came simply to escape from a life he saw as going nowhere and to embrace the freedom to pursue his natural business sense.

During his lifetime, Henry, whose formal education ended at the fifth grade, would start and successfully run two companies in the coffee, tea and spice industries, and recognizing the future of a nascent steel industry, would buy control of and head Judson Manufacturing Company, one of the largest iron and later steel producing companies in the West. In his spare time, he would also become the largest individual landowner of commercial real estate in San Francisco, a tycoon who owned 81 buildings at the time of the 1906 earthquake and fire. Seventy-nine of them were destroyed in that catastrophe, and most were rebuilt within four years thereafter.

In business, the respect he commanded extended well beyond those who worked for him. When Pacific Gas and Electric was founded in 1905, he was asked to serve on its Board, a position he continued to hold until his death seventeen years later. He also served on the Boards of the California Insurance Company, the only insurer that honored, at 100 cents on the dollar, all the claims by its policyholders for losses in the 1906 earthquake and fire; and he served, too, on the Boards of the California Wine Association, the Natomas Company, and the East Bay Water Company, as well as several smaller companies.

As important, if not far more so, Henry would also become the financial backer of Hill Farm, an outdoor respite center for needy children and their mothers, and of Arequipa, a center devoted to treating women with tuberculosis. In both cases he was reaching out to ease the suffering of others from diseases that had struck tragically in his own home or in those of close family members. His mentor in philanthropy was Elizabeth Ashe, a remarkable woman who, both before and after active service as a nurse on the European front during the First World War, devoted her life to the care of the sick and the downtrodden in and around San Francisco. To assure that her work would survive beyond his own death, Henry would set up and fund one of the earliest private foundations in the state of California, a foundation today known as the Bothin Foundation, which, by following his example, has managed for nearly one hundred years after its founding to keep Henry's name and his memory alive in the minds of generations of the less fortunate in our society and those who care deeply about them.

This story of Henry Bothin's life does not simply chronicle his successes and high points. Like all of us, Henry had his warts, and nowhere is that more evident than in the events leading up to his well-publicized divorce from his first wife, Jennie. This event would color, for the rest of her life, the way his only surviving daughter, my grandmother, felt about him. While much of that family animosity may have been deserved, this story tries to place that event into context and to recognize the real consequences of the requirement to prove fault that was necessary for a divorce in those days.

This is the story of one man's path to success as he defined it, a path that is interesting for its many turns and for the fulfillment of the legacy that survived him.

I.
Background Roots In Europe

The Great Comet of 1811, with its massive gaseous tail, was a spectacular sight in the night sky throughout the year that Henry Bothin's father, Ernst, was born. Napoleon saw it as a good omen as he prepared for his ill-fated invasion of Russia the following year, but others, the vast majority of God-fearing people all over the globe, worried that it might portend the end of the world. Residents of a seventy-five square mile radius around New Madrid, Missouri blamed it for the largest earthquake ever to be felt in the United States, one which briefly caused the Mississippi River to flow backwards and was felt as far away as Pittsburgh, Pennsylvania and Norfolk, Virginia. For farmers in Europe, however, 1811 was a very good year, one whose excellent crop-growing weather enabled vintners, in particular, to turn out one of the best vintages ever.

Far less famously, 1811 was also the year in which Ernst Boethin was born on September 22nd in or in the vicinity of the town of Chodzież (then known by its German name, Chodziesen), a small town which is located in Trzcianka County in what is today a part of northwest Poland. From what little can be derived from scant records, he apparently spent his childhood with his parents in the tiny settlement of Netzkrug which lay nearby at the edge of the

Noteć River and probably existed as a river ferry crossing point and consisted, back then, of a single building that housed a tavern and several rooms to let. Today nothing is left of Netzkrug other than hints of an old foundation or two. Even back then it seems to have been a modest enterprise meant to provide rest and food to travelers. Its permanent population consisted of just seven residents, most if not all of whom were Boethin family members. The nearby village of Chodziesen, on the other hand, was a larger town and was where Ernst and his bride, Rosa, would later raise the first six of their eight children.[9]

If the year 1811 was a year of preparations for Napoleon's ill-fated invasion of Russia, 1814 was a year for the celebration of peace. In that year, Napoleon suffered humiliation at the hands of the Russians he had hoped to conquer, and his defeat led to the re-drawing of the political map of Europe and, specifically, to the restoration of Posen Province to Prussian control. In the United States, an area of the globe that had little significance at the time to the residents of Posen Province, 1814 also marked the end of our young nation's ill-conceived war with England, a war which some say was allowed to die from lack of enthusiasm on the part of both combatants. In that year, as people returned from battlefields to reunite happily with their families, Rosa Lawrenz was born in the small village of Hammer (now Kuznica Czarnkowska) which lies just several short miles north of Czarnków.[10] Czarnków is the town where Rosa grew up and where she and Ernst were married on April 28, 1836. Rosa was the third of at least five children born to Philipp Jacob Lawrenz and Anna Rosina Schroeder Lawrenz.

Chodzież is, today, a clean and picturesque town of about 20,000 inhabitants. It sits at the edge of a tree-ringed lake and is encircled by other lakes as well as dense pine and birch forests. It lies a short drive from Poznań, an historically important city that today is the largest city in West Poland and fifth largest in the country, a city that is a major industrial center as well as a college town, proud of both its cultural and sporting traditions. The city can be reached by a scenic three-hour train ride from Berlin amid vistas of pine and birch forests interspersed with neatly manicured pastures and hay fields. The natural beauty of its surroundings has made Chodzież a tourist destination; and the combination of its scenic values, as well as the beauty of the hills which frame it, have caused the entire region, including Czarnków, to be referred to as Poland's Switzerland. However, as spectacular as the area may now seem, back in the early years of the nineteenth century tourists were few, if any, and the residents were intent more on survival than on feasting their eyes on the vistas around them. And for Chodzież, which was the administrative center for that part of Prussia, which included nearby Czarnków as well, survival meant healthy crop yields for its mostly agrarian economy.

Czarnków today has a population of approximately 11,000. It is located about sixteen miles southwest of Chodzież, and it straddles the Noteć River, a westward flowing river which meanders slowly through the town and which empties one of two major watersheds running through northwestern Poland. The Noteć river, generally speaking, demarks the southern boundary of "little Switzerland" and, specifically, of what is known as the lake region of the country. Its elevation is 125 feet above sea level, a fact that undoubtedly amuses the Swiss, who would search in vain there for Edelweiss or alpine ski runs. Instead it has a rather flat topography that, although offering little challenge to bobsledders, was perfectly suited to agriculture. In the middle of the 19th century, when Ernst and Rosa left for America, those of its residents who remained—and that was nearly everyone in town since Ernst and Rosa were not joined by either family or friends when they left—were primarily involved in farming, trading, wood production, and raising cattle. It was heavily populated by German speakers (73 percent), with the balance of its population consisting of Polish-speaking natives.

Historically, Posen (now Poznan) province (the state in which both Chodzież and Czarnków are located), along with the other provinces that together make up the land mass of modern-day Poland, has been conquered, unconquered, re-taken, freed again, and generally tossed back and forth between nations and ruling families more often than a well-used tennis ball. During the 17th century, most of northern Poland was overrun by the Swedes, and then, during a period stretching between the 1770s and the early 19th century, the internally weak provincial governments of its various regions were unable to resist being partitioned a total of three times by separate actions of Russia, Prussia, and Austria, all of which, at various times, decided among themselves how best to eliminate the Polish homeland and divide it according to their own wants and perceived needs. As a result of these partitions, the province of Posen spent most of the nineteenth century as part of Prussia. During that time Germans, including both Ernst's and Rosa's ancestors, were encouraged to settle in the lands Germany had taken, thereby, to some extent, relieving the rest of Germany from overcrowding while increasing the population density of the region Ernst and Rosa called home.

From 1815 until 1848, the region was administered as a part of the Grand Duchy of Posen, an administration that was supposed to recognize the rights of Polish peoples and to support and encourage development of the Polish language and customs. As a practical matter, none of that happened, and the Poles remained frustrated and angry, but largely helpless to do anything about the situation.[11]

With that as background, the question arises, what was it that caused Ernst and Rosa to join over one million of their fellow countrymen, who between 1840 and 1860 abandoned their German homeland in favor of an America that was being increasingly seen as a land of opportunity? Several possible answers come to mind. First, there had been a huge population surge throughout Germany after 1815, when suddenly peace replaced the bloody battles of the

Napoleonic Wars, and young men began procreating rather than dying on the battlefield. That explosive population increase had by the mid-1840s led to several tempting incentives to leave Germany. The first was a condition of dramatically increased unemployment, which, of course, created enormous obstacles to earning even a subsistence living. The second was the further dilution of family landholdings, to the point where an ever-decreasing amount of land per farmer began throwing more and more people into the ranks of the poor. This dynamic is well described by Helmut Schmahl in a self-described brief overview of his doctoral thesis *Transplanted But Not Uprooted: 19th Century Immigrants from Hesse-Darmstadt in Wisconsin*:

> As in most parts of Central Europe, population growth had been immense within the previous 25 years. The number of Rheinhessians had increased by one-quarter, which posed severe problems to an agrarian area where it was common practice among peasants to divide up their land in equal shares among their heirs [a practice of partitioned inheritance known as] *Realteilung*). Emigration was regarded by many middle class families as the only remedy against impoverishment, especially after a series of crop failures in the 1840s In 1847, the *Kolner Zeitung* reported that among the numerous families who were leaving Rheinhessen, 'there was not even one, which could be considered, poor' ... A farmer who auctioned his estate for 12,000 Gulden ($4,800) explained his decision to emigrate with the following words: '*You can call me a wealthy man, but I have nine children. After my death, each of them would not even inherit 1,500 Gulden ($600), and they would belong to the paupers in this country and could not aspire to earn as much as to live without sorrow. I therefore

> *prefer to go to North America now with the funds I have at my disposition, buy a large homestead for my family at a nominal price and thus lay the foundation for a worry free future for my descendants'.*[12]

And then, just as those dynamics were beginning to stress peoples' abilities to put food on the table, nature added its own unwelcome gift of multi-year crop failures beginning in 1846. As explained by Tyler Anbinder in *Nativism and Slavery: The Northern Know Nothings and the Politics of the 1850s*:

> ...the preponderance of Germans emigrated for many of the same reasons as their Irish counterparts. The potato crop also failed in Germany in the late 1840s, and although potatoes did not dominate the German diet, food prices and poverty rose dramatically as a result. Massive unemployment exacerbated these problems, reaching an unprecedented 17 percent by the mid-1850s....In short, most German emigration after 1848 (as before it) was for economic reasons.[13]

This combination of unfortunate events led to both agricultural and industrial depression, which greatly affected both artisans and tenant farmers[14] (of which Ernst may have been both). Bad economic news also spawned political unrest, and, in 1848, rebellion broke out. Led largely by academics and students who were long on ideals but politically inexperienced, its leaders created havoc for a time, but ultimately were unable to accomplish much other than spreading talk of individual freedoms and national unity. If that rebellious group, known as "48ers," achieved anything of lasting significance, it was probably to further the desire of many to leave a country (or more accurately a disorganized group of administrative units posing as a country) that seemed either incapable of or unwilling to deliver either freedom or national unity.

Adding fuel to the desires of Germans to leave home were letters from America written by many who had emigrated earlier.[15] Those letters, or more rightly testimonials, were numerous and were widely circulated and eagerly read by people who were becoming more desperate and looking for better futures both for themselves and their children. Indeed, the exodus from German-held territories, including Posen, had begun as early as the late 1830s when groups of Lutherans who, refusing to adhere to the demands of the Prussian Kaiser, had emigrated to America and begun sending back letters to family, friends, and fellow townspeople extolling America and, particularly, the territories around modern-day Wisconsin, where they established early Lutheran congregations.[16]

Still, it is one thing to have reason to leave one's homeland and quite another to actually do so. While it is true that literally millions of Germans left home and emigrated to America during the decade when Ernst and Rosa left, most of those who did so were far younger, had either no children to raise or at most one or two, and/or had no close family ties they were abandoning. In the case of Ernst and Rosa, they were older—Ernst north of forty and Rosa in her late thirties. Unlike the typical emigrant's profile, they also had six children who relied on their parents' ability to put food on the table, and finally, they both had nearby siblings with whom, one might imagine, they would have created a bond, an anchor to both share the pain and soften the effects of hardships endured together. One would normally have expected those factors, taken together, to have at least discouraged if not precluded the Boethins from deciding to leave.

If indeed the economic times were so dismal as to cause Ernst to lose his livelihood, then one would have expected others of his and/or Rosa's family and/or their friends and neighbors to have also suffered enough to have left with them. Yet there is no evidence that they departed in the company of any of their family members or friends. Indeed, they seem to have simply turned their backs on their former lives and left with never a communication home thereafter. Under those circumstances, an exodus from their homeland would, it seems, have been a very hard choice to make, particularly given that they were heading to a new country with a new and alien language, and unknown customs and traditions. But leave they did; so the whys must linger as one of those many enigmas that remain unsolved.

Ernst Boethin and Rosa Lawrenz Boethin

2.
First Generation of Bothins in America

In 1852, Harriet Beecher Stowe's classic anti-slavery novel *Uncle Tom's Cabin* was published and it immediately became a literary success and a political bombshell. In its first year, over 300,000 copies were sold in the United States and over one million were sold in Great Britain. It quickly became the second most widely read book of the 19th century, behind only the Bible, and, as a narrative about the plight of slaves, it strengthened the arguments of abolitionists and advanced the debate which would ultimately, less than a decade later, lead to the American Civil War. Indeed, Abraham Lincoln is reputed to have said, upon meeting Miss Stowe, "So this is the little lady who started this great war."

For Ernst and Rosa Boethin, *Uncle Tom's Cabin* was the furthest thing from their minds as they planned their exodus from their homeland. Slavery was a term they had probably never even heard, and although the plight of serfs in their own country was not that far removed from the horrors that befell blacks in the southern states of this nation, the practice of serfdom had been abolished in Prussia before either Ernst or Rosa were born. Furthermore, its end had come peacefully, the natural result of changed economic circumstances that made it impractical and outdated as a custom, rather than primarily because of moral outrage leading to hardened positions that might threaten war. So, even if it had been recognized as an issue, Prussians in general, and Ernst and Rosa in particular, would not have recognized the depth of sentiment in this country over the issue, nor would they have foreseen it as a cause of war or a reason to re-think their plans.

Rather, when Henry Bothin's parents decided to leave Prussia and relocate to the United States, they would have done so because of all the positive feedback they had heard, and almost certainly in ignorance of, surely without fear of, pressures building over abolition. As they prepared for their voyage to the new world, what most likely consumed their attention was the fact that they were wiping the slate clean on the first half of their lives. From the fact that they totally turned their backs on family, friends, and on all the traditions and comforts of home and homeland. one can only imagine that they felt that the closeness of their immediate family and the hope for new friends and a new beginning would provide them with whatever social nourishment they felt they needed. But the very sharpness of the break, combined with the absence of any evidence at all to suggest that either of them ever later communicated with family members in the old country, or, indeed, ever spoke with their own children about the latters' aunts, uncles or cousins, all suggests that they may have left Germany under a cloud or, quite possibly, at odds with family members.

Why the Boethins left Germany, and speculation about family dynamics, is not particularly important, in and of itself. However, it does merit some discussion, if for no other reason than the rather incredible story about their roots that Rosa told her granddaughter, Ida Sutter Maas, nearly forty years later and which is told in the preface to this book. That story was either fanciful exaggeration or an intentional effort by Rosa to mislead her granddaughter at just the time when most people, as they approach and enter their seventies, typically become interested in passing on knowledge about their families to the next generation and beyond. Quite apart from its creativity, what Rosa's story doesn't say is anything about where she and Ernst were born, who his and her parents and siblings really were, when, where and how they (Ernst and Rosa) met, details about their wedding, their way of life in the old country, why they remained in Germany for over fifteen years after supposedly promising to leave the country immediately after their wedding, what Ernst (and possibly Rosa as well) did for a living in Germany, what were the political and economic circumstances at home which may (and almost certainly did) play a role in their ultimate decision to abandon their homeland, why none of their extended family joined them in coming to America, how their parents and siblings weathered the storms at home and what had come of them in the forty years since they parted company, the names of family members (if any) with whom the senior Bothins remained in contact, a description of their fears and hopes as they made their trans-Atlantic voyage to a new life in America, where and when they arrived in America, what their original destination was when they arrived, why they stopped off in Cleveland for a year or more, what life for them was like when they first arrived in Portage, and on and on.

So, what do we know and what don't we know about that first generation of Boethins—the parents of the man whose life will be chronicled in this book? What we do know is that they were risk-takers. We also know that they were capable of total separation from family and friends and that they also had the capacity to never look back. They (or at least Rosa) were also willing to exaggerate family stature. Finally, we know that Rosa was illiterate and that Ernst was content to marry an uneducated woman, and from that we can suppose that, since there was nearly universal literacy in those days in Germany, it is likely that they were both from lower than middle class backgrounds.

Next, the question arises: what were the realities of Ernst's and Rosa's new life in America, and how might those realities have affected the early life of their son Henry? First, we learn from the obituary of Henry's sister, Pauline [see notes 8 and 9] that they— Ernst, Rosa, and their first six children (Otillia, Amelia, Pauline, Emily, Willimina, and Julius)—left their home in Chodziesen, Prussia, and, by some as yet unknown method, crossed the Atlantic Ocean and arrived somewhere in America in August, 1852. Unfortunately, there are no known passenger records to corroborate that date,[17] and so we are left with Pauline's recollections as passed on to the person (undoubtedly her husband, Alfred Lee) who gave the biographical information to the newspaper that published her obituary.[18]

As to Rosa, there are no known documents in America that provide information about her, other than her tombstone and census data for 1860, 1870, and 1880, all of which consistently listed simply "Prussia" as her place of birth. As vast as Prussia was in those days—and its boundaries included a good portion of modern-day Poland—the simple term "Prussia" is about as descriptive of one's roots as the word "China" would be to someone seeking his Asian ancestry.

Similarly, the records about Ernst, albeit somewhat more voluminous, provide no help about his roots. Ernst is identified in those same census records where Rosa's name appears, but his name also appears in the records of St. John's Evangelical Church in Portage (of which he was one of the founders), his Declaration of Intent to become a Citizen dated November 8, 1853, deeds to properties that he purchased and later sold in and around Portage, a short biographical sketch that was written in 1880 and appears in a work entitled *The History of Columbia County, Wisconsin*, brief reports of his second marriage following Rosa's death in 1891, his own obituary, and his tombstone at Silver Lake Cemetery in Portage. Not one of those records cites where he came from other than the word "Prussia," a generic response that subsequent generations would, but for Pauline's obituary, have been left with to describe the place of their births, their childhoods, their dreams, their marriage, the birthplace of their children, and the location of friends and family left behind. As a source document, it is hard to overstate the value of Pauline's obituary, which after many years of fruitless search for the family's Prussian roots, finally opened that door and allowed the light in.

Ernst's tombstone reads "Ernst Boethin." Despite some records that refer to him as "Ernest," and despite the fact that he did give Henry the name "Ernest" as a middle name, Ernst seems to have kept the German spelling of his birth name. However, his surname, "Boethin," was a different matter altogether. Other than Ernst's and Rosa's shared tombstone, no other record or document exists, to the best of my knowledge, in America where either Ernst or Rosa ever used or spelled their name "Boethin." Having said that, there are numerous instances (such as census records, deeds, etc.) where third parties variously (and creatively to say the least) spelled it "Buchin," "Bothier," "Botine," "Böthin" and "Bothine," to list just a few. And just as the senior Bothins do not ever seem, during the portion of their lives spent in America, to have strayed from the Americanized version of the spelling of their surname, so too their children, including Henry, appear to have adopted that spelling. Indeed, it is interesting to note that Henry's sisters, Mary and Pauline, each of whom predeceased their parents, are both buried immediately adjacent to the graves of Ernst and Rosa in the family plot in the Silver Lake Cemetery in Portage, Wisconsin, and each of those headstones—which Ernst and Rosa doubtless commissioned a stone cutter to cut—spells their surnames "Bothin." The current pronounciation of the name is \bō-'thēn\ or "Bo-**theen**".

3.
Early Beginnings in America

We don't know where Ernst and Rosa and their family first set foot on American soil, nor do we know exactly how long they stayed wherever it was that they landed. We do know that by July of 1853 (eleven months after arriving in the United States) they were in Cleveland where, on July 17th of that year, Rosa gave birth to Henry. But other than the fact of Henry's birth in Cleveland, absolutely nothing has been uncovered about the family's brief stay there. Cleveland had a number of German immigrants among its population base of 17,000 souls in 1853; however, there is no readily obvious logic to explain why Ernst and Rosa would have chosen it as a destination. Rather, Wisconsin, with its cheap and plentiful land and with a very active recruiting program by which the state aggressively solicited German, Irish, Norwegian, and other northern European immigrants to populate its territory, seems a far more likely end point from the outset. Interestingly, the normal route to Wisconsin for German immigrants who had landed in either Boston or New York (the two most likely ports of entry for the Bothins) would have been to take a steamboat up the Hudson River to Albany, then travel by canal or train to Buffalo, and, finally, by boat across Lakes Erie, Huron and Michigan, on to Milwaukee.[19] Buffalo lies at the eastern end of Lake Erie, whereas Cleveland is located near its westerly end. It is altogether possible, therefore, that the Bothin family had initially planned to travel to Wisconsin, but for any one of a number of possible reasons, the most obvious being Rosa's safety and comfort in the latter stages of her pregnancy with Henry, they were sidelined briefly in Cleveland. Since Cleveland has nothing significant to add to Henry's life, I have been content to let that remain an open question. Ultimately, the fact remains that after a year or at most fifteen months spent in Cleveland, the call of Wisconsin ultimately won out, and it was there that the senior Bothins made their home for nearly all of the rest of their lives.[20]

Why Wisconsin? Leaving aside its enterprising marketing effort to attract German settlers, it in fact shares a number of environmental similarities that would have made it feel more like their former homeland. Each is, for instance, relatively flat. They both have similar weather patterns, reaching average lows of about 10 degrees Fahrenheit or less in the months of December, January and February, and rising to highs of about 80 degrees Fahrenheit in July and August. Extreme lows and highs are not dissimilar. They have similar amounts of precipitation and snowfall. Both were, in the mid-nineteenth century, agrarian, and both relied on similar crops. As attractive as those inducements were, however, probably the clincher was the simple fact that Wisconsin had been successful in attracting large numbers of German nationals to populate the new state, and that meant that Ernst and Rosa could enjoy the company of kindred spirits who shared a native tongue and observed many of the same customs and traditions that would have been familiar to them. Indeed, by 1900, 709,909, or 34 percent, of Wisconsin's citizens were of German background.[21]

When the Bothin family settled in the town of Portage in 1853,[22] Wisconsin had been a state for just five years, and Portage had not yet even been incorporated as a city. That happened two years later, in 1855. The region was replete with available land to farm, and the town fathers had made it known that they welcomed new residents with open arms. The availability of cheap land to own and farm was the primary motivator, particularly to those of German, Norwegian and Irish descent who made up most of the population of European immigrants who were the early settlers of Portage, and more broadly, central Wisconsin. Those settlers were typically people who, historically, had worked on the land in their native countries but who, in most cases, neither owned that land nor had much hope of ever owning it. So more than anything else, the availability of decently large and inexpensive tracts of land which could be bought was the main reason that the population of Portage exploded from 909 residents in 1850 to 7,507 in 1860. So it probably was with Ernst and Rosa. Even today over 40 percent of Portage's residents report German ancestry, while 12 percent report Irish roots.

Geographically, Portage, the town where young Henry grew up, lies approximately thirty miles north of present-day Madison, Wisconsin. It is set in the south-central portion of the state and is more specifically located in the lowlands between the Fox and the Wisconsin Rivers, an area now referred to as the Wisconsin River Valley.[23] The Fox River flows north to Green Bay where it empties into Lake Michigan; however, it is a very slow moving river, and historically it has provided no obstacle to upstream shallow draft navigation. In 1673, the French explorers Louis Joliet and Father Jacques Marquette paddled up the Fox in search of an inland route connecting the St. Lawrence waterway and the Great Lakes to the Gulf of Mexico. At the site of present-day Portage, they found the Wisconsin River just two miles (or, as early explorers used to say, "2,500 paces") away. The Wisconsin River begins in the forests of northern Wisconsin and flows south, emptying into the Mississippi at the Iowa border just south of present-day Prairie du Chien, Wisconsin. Hence, from a trade perspective, the location of Portage was ideal for the transit of furs, timber, and other products and goods from the Great Lakes to the Gulf of Mexico. Indeed, well before the revolution out of which the United States was born, "the portage" was a link in the international chain of trade that sent pelts from Wisconsin, Minnesota and Iowa to Europe in exchange for tools, pots, beads, cloth, firearms and 'firewater.'"[24]

Because of its location, the town of Portage was booming when Ernst and Rosa, with baby Henry and his siblings in tow, first settled there. As reported in the *Wisconsin Gazetteer* in 1853:

> Population 2,000; with 12 [general] stores, 7 hotels, 1 steam saw mill, 2 harness makers, 4 wagon makers, 6 blacksmiths, 3 cabinet, 3 paint, 8 shoe, 3 tin and sheet iron, 3 butchers, 6 millinery, and 4 tailor's shops, 2 breweries, 2 livery stables, 2 jewelry stores, 2 drug stores, 1 brick yard, 1 iron foundry, 1 blind and sash factory, a chair factory, and 1 tannery; 12 lawyers and 5 doctors, 3 district and 2 select schools; 1 church building and 2 denominations… Two steamers ply constantly between this place and Galena during the summer… The amount of lumber sent below is almost beyond calculation… The importance of Portage City, as a commercial point, is beyond doubt very great. It commands 200 miles north where the pine forests nourish a large population, and are continually pouring their products south, and will for years to come.[25]

The attractiveness of Portage in terms of commercial location had initially focused on water transit and specifically on the hope for a canal connecting the Fox and Wisconsin rivers; however, that dream died, both because of an inability to persuade Congress to appropriate needed funds and also because of the arrival, by the late 1850s, of the railroad, which provided a more efficient method of carrying goods year round. Just at about the same time as Henry would have been starting school, Portage found itself at the center of the rail-based statewide transit hub and as a major part of the national rail network. The commerce that fed the city's growth was initially driven by agriculture, and specifically by wheat, which was the favored crop until the 1870s and was milled in Portage and sent to market by both river and railroad. As more and more farmers became aware of the need to fertilize their land and rotate their crops, wheat began to give way to other farm products, including other grains as well as hops and somewhat surprisingly, tobacco, which was widely grown in the area around Portage. Milk and cheese would later also become popular and profitable products produced by dairies that sprang up in the area; however that came later, in the 1870s after Henry had already left home for greener pastures out west.[26]

Lumber was also abundant in northern Wisconsin; indeed, the legend of Paul Bunyan took shape from stories told in the lumber camps of northern Wisconsin and Michigan, where huge forests of white pine and Norwegian pine were cleared and the logs rafted down the Wisconsin river to Portage, where they were placed on railroad cars for shipment throughout the heartland of the country. The section of the Wisconsin River between Wausau and Portage, which covered just over 100 miles, provided waterpower to an expanding number of lumber mills, which grew from 24 to 107 during the decade between 1847 and 1857.[27] Although Portage itself did not have a large milling industry, wood was plentiful and supported a number of cabinetmakers, wagon makers, furniture builders, casket makers, and of course carpenters and finish carpenters, among whom Ernst Bothin was one.[28] Perhaps the major role played by Portage in the state's lumber industry was as a supplier of wholesale grocery and mercantile products to the logging camps up north and as a stopover point where taverns and hotels provided respite and recreation for raftsmen, loggers and other people who plied the lumber trade.

A brief biography of Ernst, written in 1880 and appearing in *The History of Columbia County, Wisconsin*, reports that upon entering

Wisconsin, he and his family lived in Portage City initially and that, a short time later, he purchased a 215 acre farm in nearby Lewiston. It also mentioned that as of 1880 he had several other properties in and around Portage. In fact, that description of Ernst's real estate investments is overly modest. Ernst started buying real estate quite soon after first arriving in Portage. He had listed his profession as "carpenter/joiner," and either he was quite good at his trade and very frugal, or else, and this is highly unlikely, he and Rosa had brought some capital with them from Germany. His first purchase of property was a lot on West Cook Street (then the main street of town) that he bought in December 1855 for the then-princely sum of $250. He then built on the lot the house they were to keep and live in during all of the time thereafter, when they lived in Portage. That lot today lies two blocks from the Wisconsin River; however, back when they bought it, prior to the construction of levees that today control the river's flood plain, it would have been a riverfront lot.

In 1855, $250 was a lot of money. While precise statistics on wages are hard to find, it would appear that the most likely rate of pay for a carpenter/joiner in those days was $.30 per day on the low side, up to possibly as high as $1.00 per day. Even using the high end of that range, it becomes apparent that it would take upwards of 8 months to earn $250. So either Ernst saved his pennies frugally or he was able to obtain credit. Either way is telling, in terms of lessons learned by his son Henry, for in this respect, if no other, Ernst was a role model for the way Henry was to later conduct his own business life. First, on the issue of credit, loans were then, just as they are supposed to be today, only extended to people who were judged both creditworthy and morally fit for such advances. In the 1850s there was no federal banking system, nor, obviously, were there databases to provide credit or background checks. Indeed, in 1853 Portage didn't even have a bank, and it is unlikely one had been established in the following two years. What little money there was available to be loaned out was mostly, if not entirely, provided by private lenders who made decisions largely on their gut sense that a borrower was likely to repay the loan. So it is easy to see why a man's reputation for high moral integrity as well as a history of credit worthiness were of even greater importance than they are today as imperatives to compete successfully for the limited pot of money available for loans.[29] Furthermore, loans were generally short-term advances that were expected to be repaid within a year or less and in no case longer than five to seven years out. They often carried even shorter terms. The typical borrower was a business that could rely on turning over inventory or selling a product as the source of repayment. The idea of a 30-year home mortgage simply didn't exist, and so a loan to enable home ownership would have been a particularly difficult plum to acquire.

Thus, to have purchased the property on West Cook Street that he bought in 1855, Ernst would either have had to save the money over the two year period between 1853 when the family first arrived in Portage and 1855 when he purchased the land, or else he would have had to convince a lender (most likely the man who created the lot) not just of his talent as a carpenter/joiner but also of his character, his business acumen, and most likely his standing in the community. Such traits, as anyone knows, are generally not established overnight, but rather take hard work and time (generally measured in years) to obtain. Given his frugal nature, and also since the deed makes no mention of secured debt, I have assumed that Ernst likely saved the money—no small feat in those days, and particularly so given that he had not had much time to develop a clientele and book of business.

The fact that Ernst was able, within just two years of arriving in Portage, to purchase a well-located lot in the center of town suggests that he worked hard and was good at what he did. Since carpentry was not a unique trade requiring a special talent or for which a premium could be charged, it seems appropriate to assume that he also had the personality and character needed to compete successfully for business and that he was a competent manager of his earnings. That assumption is supported by the writings of his granddaughter, Ida Sutter Maas, who recorded that her grandfather "was a success as a cabinet maker."[30]

In that same 1880 biographical sketch of Ernst, it was also noted that in addition to living in the house on Cook Street, Ernst "also rents another house near the depot and owns other real estate in the City." More specifically, in June of 1856 he purchased two other pieces of property on Oneida Street (adjacent to the train depot) for $115 and $150 respectively, and then, in 1863, he purchased yet another double lot in Portage for $489 at a foreclosure sale. The deed reveals that he was the lender on that property and foreclosed on it after the death of the borrower. The following year, in 1864, Ernst paid $1,600 for 175.4 acres of farmland in Lewiston, ten miles west of Portage, and then, seven years later in 1871, added another forty acres to the farm. That purchase price, incidentally, works out to $9.14 per acre.

It is noteworthy that the deeds to the various properties that Ernst bought and owned show title in his name alone. Rosa's name is not included on any purchase documents, a fact that differs from many other records of real estate ownership at the time in Portage where both husband and wife are often noted on the deeds. I suspect probably that was so because Rosa was illiterate and unable to sign her name other than with an "x." Indeed, after Rosa's death in 1891, Ernst remarried a woman named Ernestine, and Ernestine's name was placed on all the deeds and other recorded transactions which followed.

It seems fair to ask how Ernst became as successful as he apparently was. The answer probably lies, to some extent at least, in his good fortune to have moved at a propitious time to a rapidly growing part of the country. Portage was, at the time the Bothins arrived, growing briskly, having added nearly 6,300 new residents and 1,389 new households in the decade of the 1850s. That represented a sevenfold increase from the town's population ten years before. As a carpenter/joiner, Ernst had opportunities to build homes as well as doors, sashes, window trimmings, furniture, and myriad other wood products. Steady employment was available in Portage to talented cabinetmakers,[31] and Ernst would seem to have fit that description.

It seems clear, too, that Ernst was a frugal manager of money as well as a man who saw the value of investing in real estate. His son Henry followed in those same footsteps when he became an adult, and, probably more than any other trait passed on to him by his father, Henry learned to appreciate the value of a dollar saved and the folly of personal spending for any but the most basic of needs.

Apart from his business, Ernst's only other known interest was his devotion to the Lutheran faith. He was a founder of St. John's Lutheran Church in Portage. The records of that church contain a note to the effect that he was one of its twelve charter members. Later, in the 1880 biographical sketch, he and Rosa were said to be members of "the Evangelical Church" which likely refers to the Methodist Episcopal Church where he was a "class leader." The change from St. John's to the Methodist Episcopal Church would explain why he, Rosa, and their daughters, Mary and Pauline, are all interred in Silver Oak cemetery rather than Oak Grove cemetery where St. John's parishioners were buried.

In the 1860 census, where their name is creatively spelled "Buchin," Ernst and Rosa are listed as living in the 4th ward of Portage City along with five of their children, Emily (age 14), Willimina (age 12), Julius (age 10), Henry (age 7) and Mary (age 1). Emily (known as Emma), Willimina (known as Minnie), and Julius are all listed, along with both parents, as having been born in Prussia, whereas Henry is shown as born in Ohio and Mary as born in Wisconsin. By then, Henry's eldest three sisters, Otillia, Amelia, and Pauline, had all married and moved away from home, although unlike the others who moved out of state, Pauline and her husband made Portage their home.

From outward appearances, Ernst's and Rosa's life in Portage suggests a success story, one that might have been expected to carry with it a sense of contentment and of belonging in the community. After all, Ernst was seemingly doing well in business, the family had a nice home in an excellent part of town, they had good investments, they were prominent leaders in their church, and they were surrounded by others of German extraction with whom they could socialize and feel comfortable. Furthermore, Portage had an excellent public school system extending from first grade all the way through high school, and so they had access to a means of educating their children to prepare them to do well in the world. For all those reasons, the expectation would seem to be that life was good. But in 1864, Ernst and Rosa chucked all that and moved away from Portage to a farm they had just bought in a small rural area ten miles away called Lewiston. In those days ten miles was really ten miles. In good weather, it would have probably taken little more than an hour by horse and buggy to cover that distance, but during the winter months (in Wisconsin, from November to May) it would have taken far longer—if indeed the trip was possible at all. By making that move, Ernst and Rosa effectively left the home Ernst had built (although they didn't sell it), left their church, turned their backs on Ernst's apparently very successful business, and uprooted their children from school, from familiar surroundings, and from the friends they had made.

Why Lewiston? In the 1860s, and still for the most part today, Lewiston was a rural farming community. Like Portage, much of it lies close to the Wisconsin River and, although its soil was never as rich as some of the better farmland in southern Wisconsin, it was, in 1877, described as having black loam soil and "representing the best farming district in [Columbia] County."[32] Lewiston had a Lutheran church (St. Michael's) in the 1860s, but it appears to have had little other infrastructure and apparently no school. It seems to have simply existed as a collection of isolated farms, and unlikely to offer much to stimulate the Bothin children still living at home. Indeed, if there was anything that Henry's generation might have benefited from in Lewiston, it was probably an ever-closer bond among siblings, simply because of the absence of other playmates. That bond between Henry and his sisters, in particular, lasted throughout his life, and it is best expressed in the generosity he later showed to his siblings and their offspring both during his lifetime and in his will.

It is noteworthy that Ernst was able to raise the funds needed to buy the farm without having to sell either the Cook Street house or any of the other investment properties he had acquired in Portage. In fact, even as the family was residing in Lewiston, he was still investing in Portage real estate. In 1874 and again in 1875, he purchased two more pieces of property in Portage. His final known property acquisition came in 1881 when, for $400, he purchased two additional lots on West Cook Street. Those properties were located squarely in the center of the commercial hub of the city. So the move to Lewiston was not made out of economic necessity.

In the context of trying to better understand Henry's formative years, numerous questions arise about his parents. The foremost question, of course, is why they decided to make that seemingly implausible move from the comforts of life in Portage to the harsher life of a farmer in an isolated locale. But one would like to know also, for instance, if they even spoke English, how and to what extent they educated their children, and whether they were strict disciplinarians or lackadaisical parents. The list goes on and on, and yet, because they didn't keep diaries, and also because they avoided being "newsworthy"—they apparently led quiet, private, and non-controversial lives—there is precious little in the public record to turn to when seeking answers to these or other questions.

As to the first question about why they left Portage to settle in Lewiston, that defies logical explanation but will be dealt with on a somewhat speculative basis shortly. As to the question of how well, if at all, they came to speak English, one must assume that Ernst, at least, attained a working vocabulary in English and probably far greater fluency than that. While he might have been able to work for wages as a carpenter/joiner without having to communicate well in English, one doubts that without a pretty solid working familiarity with the language of his adopted country, he could either have become successful operating his own finish carpentry business or have felt comfortable in the worlds of real estate acquisition and mortgage lending, with their reliance on written contracts, deeds, and recordation requirements.

It is not as clear how much English, if any, Rosa ever spoke. Clearly she could have gotten along perfectly well speaking German at home and at church, with the latter's insistence on holding services in German. Indeed, the records of St. John's church mention that services were conducted solely in German until as late as 1908, and it wasn't until 1929 that the descendants of the founders of that church began to allow services to be regularly conducted in the tongue of the country to which their forebears had pledged allegiance nearly three quarters of a century earlier.

But home and church aside, the question of learning English, at least as far as Rosa is concerned, would probably turn, in part at least, on the company they kept and whether or not they surrounded themselves by German-speaking neighbors, or expanded their horizons to include the melting pot of Portage's residents. A review of the census data from 1860, 1870, and 1880 all clearly suggest that they lived in mixed neighborhoods throughout their stays in both Portage and Lewiston. In 1860, the families whose names appear on the same census page as theirs (and therefore were presumably their neighbors in the 4th ward of Portage) included the Mitchells from New York, the Steinbachs from Austria, the Finnegans from Ireland, the Ambristers from Canada, the Beans from Vermont, the Spens family from Vermont, and the Teach family from Pennsylvania and England. In 1870 (when they were living on the farm in Lewiston) their neighbors (again according the census records) were Martin

Poulson from Norway, the Douglass family from Vermont, the Fellows family from Vermont, the Vancooens from Pennsylvania, the Cornings from New York, the Utters from New York, and Peter Lewis from Norway. Finally, in 1880 when they were back home on West Cook Street in Portage, the census record shows that their neighbors then were the St. John's family from New York, the Currys from Wales, the Owen family from Wales, the Splain family from New York, the Edwards family from Wales, the Schulze family from Prussia, the Loos family from Germany, the Sherbarts from Germany, the Ames family from New York, the Wells family from New York, and finally the Lenz and Sieverkrop families from Prussia. Simply put, the census data provide strong evidence that the Bothins were a part of the melting pot and did not limit their associations to people of German backgrounds. That evidence would suggest (but hardly conclusively) that unless Rosa shunned social interactions, she likely came to learn at least enough English to socialize with neighbors, to shop, and to participate in the community.

Furthermore, the Bothins seem to have welcomed their role in the melting pot. As an example, in 1860 at their home on West Cook Street, they hosted both the wedding and the post-wedding reception for the marriage of their daughter, Pauline, to John Harmon. John was not of German extraction, nor was Pauline's second husband, Alfred Lee, who she married after Harmon had died while a soldier in the Civil War.

Still, it is clear that the language spoken at home remained German until Ernst and Rosa's deaths—a not unexpected fact, since by the time they came to this country, they had reached an age where learning a new language would have been a far more daunting challenge than it would have been with younger brain cells. The proof comes in the form of letters home written by their grandson, Emil Sutter, who was Ida Bothin Sutter's brother and a grandson of Ernst and Rosa. Emil apologized in a letter written "To the Folks at Home" in 1889 (over 35 years and several generations after the senior

Bothins had come to America) for penning his letters in English as opposed to German. So, as much as the senior Bothins may have outwardly mingled with people of all national backgrounds, the likelihood is that at home the family still, for at least as long as Ernst and Rosa lived, communicated primarily in German.

Questions about the senior Bothins' success as parents become important mainly because they became estranged from Henry around the time he left home in about 1871. That estrangement apparently lasted for the rest of Ernst's and Rosa's lives, so it justifies a look at Ernst and Rosa in the context of their roles as heads of the family. In that regard, it is interesting that all but one of their seven children who survived to adulthood moved far away, and that none of their children or their husbands stayed to work at or ultimately inherit either Ernst's cabinetry business or the family farm. Otillia and Minnie moved to California, as did Julius and Henry. Amelia and her husband and family lived, at different times, in both Kansas and Iowa. Emily (Emma) and her family moved first to Prairie du Chien, Wisconsin and later to Eau Claire, Wisconsin, about 135 miles away from Portage. The only child of the senior Bothins who reached adulthood and remained in Portage was Pauline, who married John Harmon from nearby Lewiston and, after his death, married Alfred Lee, who was from Portage. Pauline died on February 8, 1880, leaving her husband and a ten-year-old son named Frank.

Although nearly all of Ernst's and Rosa's children ended up living far apart from their parents, that isn't really, in this case, necessarily a sound indicator of the family dynamics. When one looks closely at the flight of their children, one realizes that four of the six who moved were women who followed their husbands. Furthermore, Emma did move back to Portage in the late 1880s to look after her mother who was in failing health, although there is some evidence that she was bribed to do that by an offer of ownership of the house on Cook Street in return for her caregiving. If that promise was in fact made, it apparently was never kept, since the grantor/grantee indexes do not show any transfer of either that property or any other of Ernst's Portage properties into her name. Interesting, too, is that as soon as Rosa died in 1891, Emma and her family left Portage and moved back to Eau Claire rather than staying on to provide care to her father, who was by then eighty years old and undoubtedly could also have benefited from her continued presence and caregiving.

It is also interesting that, during the first half of the decade of the 1880s, Ernst and Rosa moved to Newton, Kansas to be near their daughter, Amelia, and her husband and ten children. As stated by Ida in the history she wrote, "…he [Ernst] built a handsome home in Newton, Kansas where the Kaufman family had settled."[33] But then, in about 1887 according to Ida, they became homesick for Portage and returned to their home on West Cook Street, and it was then that Emma and her family moved to Portage from Eau Claire to care for them. One has to wonder about this. When Ernst and Rosa moved to Kansas they would have been in their mid-to-late 60s, and probably would still have been mourning the loss of two of their children, and just as probably, would have been emotionally upset about the estrangement that had occurred with their son, Henry. Under the circumstances, it is entirely understandable that they might have sought the comfort of a closer physical tie to at least one of their children. Furthermore, they had fairly recently sold their farm in Lewiston and might not have fully re-integrated themselves back into life in Portage. So, on a number of different levels, the chance to move to Kansas to be with their daughter, Amelia, and her family would have been a welcome change. But then why move back to Portage seven years later? If anything, they would have aged further and been more in need of care, while their friends in Portage would have been dying off, and really all they had left in Portage, other than their house and their real estate investments, would have been the graves of their two daughters who had predeceased them. Perhaps that was enough, although it cannot be ruled out that they may have overstayed their welcome in Kansas.

It appears that Henry's older brother, Julius, was the senior Bothins' favorite.[34] He moved as a young man to San Francisco, where he worked for Henry for a number of years. Julius was not successful in San Francisco, and he apparently angered Henry by frittering away a good business that Henry essentially gave to him to run and that he instead wasted. Later he went to Arizona, where he was briefly married and had his only child, Lulu. If there was ever a good candidate to return home to Portage to be with his family and to possibly inherit his father's properties, it would seem to have been Julius, and yet he didn't.

What is one to make of all that? Based on the records, it would seem that whatever ties Henry's siblings had to their parents, they were not strong enough to prevent Otillia, Minnie, Julius and Henry from leaving the nest and traveling across the country to settle in faraway San Francisco. Nor were those ties strong enough to convince either Amelia or Emma or their husbands (neither of whom seem to have had particularly strong ties elsewhere) to stay in or near Portage and take advantage of either the farm or of Ernst's business acumen to help them develop careers locally. Certainly Portage, with its central location and its thriving agricultural, lumber, brickmaking, foundry and tool making, tanning, shoe manufacturing, grain milling, textile, beer brewing, and cigar manufacturing industries would have provided any young man with numerous choices—indeed more choices were there than in most other communities of its size. It may be that, just as Ernst and Rosa were seemingly able to turn their backs on their own siblings and extended families when they left the old country, and to repeat that process twelve years later when they moved to Lewiston, so, too, their own children were likewise content to sever the family apron strings and, with the exception of several finite periods of caregiving, to move on as soon as they were able and pursue their own lives in far distant places.

As to why their children all moved away, one might call it coincidence, or call it the pioneer spirit which was then enticing people west, but it just may be that Ernst and Rosa were not the sorts of people who cherished family or made their children their first priority. After all, back in 1852 they had dragged their six children away from friends and family in Prussia, and, again in 1864, they had pulled up stakes and left Portage for isolated Lewiston. If one folds into the mix the willingness to misrepresent their family history and identity to their own children and grandchildren, then one begins to see the outlines of a collage containing elements of compulsiveness, selfishness, insecurity, and a host of other traits; it seems to indicate at least a willingness to impose stress on themselves and their children.

As noted by Sarah Kershaw in an article entitled "The Psychology of Moving"[35] "[s]ome therapists…call frequent moving 'pulling a geographic,'" which means, "seeking external changes to change internal problems." Ms. Kershaw goes on to quote a psychologist who notes that "no matter how much you move, you still take yourself with you."[36] It is possible that for Ernst and Rosa, their moves reflected an inability to get along with family, neighbors or community and a compulsive need to periodically move in search of a better place and a new start.

Whatever may have been their justification for the move to Lewiston in 1864, Ernst, Rosa and five of their eight children did move there, and for the next thirteen years of their lives lived in isolation, without the schooling or vibrant culture they had known in Portage. During the first seven of those years, Henry watched as, one by one, his older siblings moved away to start new lives in distant places. Ultimately, he too moved away, in about 1871, not to return during the lifetime of the senior Bothins.

For Ernst and Rosa that lifetime would last over twenty years and ultimately include tragic circumstances. In 1877, their youngest daughter, Mary, died, leaving them alone in Lewiston to mourn her passing. They were both by then in their mid-sixties and had probably reached the age when they could no longer comfortably put in the long hours and hard work demanded of farmers While age might well have eventually caused them to sell, probably the primary motivator in the timing of their decision would have been the emotional shock of the loss of their youngest child who had, for the last six years of her life, been the sole child still living at home. So it was probably no coincidence that the year Mary died was also the year they sold the farm and moved back to Portage. The move back to Portage would have been compelling at that time in their lives not only because of Mary's death but, in a more positive vein, because Pauline, their only child who still lived in Portage, and her husband Alfred, and son Frank, could help them to weather their grief.

But then tragedy struck again. Three years after they moved back to Portage to be near Pauline and her family, Pauline, too, died.[37] Born in 1841, Pauline had lived an unhappy adult life before her death on February 8, 1880, of "consumption." She had been married, widowed, lost a child from that first marriage, and remarried, all before the age of 27. "Consumption" was the word used to describe tuberculosis, a disease that was generally fatal in those days before the discovery of antibiotics. So, just as her life seemed to be stabilizing with a lasting marriage and a ten-year-old son, she herself died at the young age of 39.[38]

It goes without saying that nothing hurts a parent more than the loss of a child. In the case of the senior Bothins, they must have been absolutely devastated to have lost not one, but two children in the space of three years. Given their history of uprooting themselves for far less important reasons, and given the apparent difficulty they had making friends and bonding with neighbors, their move to Kansas would have come as no surprise. Had it ended there, this topic would likely never have been raised, but the fact is that it didn't, and it was the move back from Kansas to Portage in their declining years that provides further evidence of their proclivity to "pull a geographic," perhaps because of a tendency to wear out their welcome even with one of their children.

On May 9, 1891, Rosa died at the age of 76. Just over a year later, and to the amazement, frustration, and chagrin of family members, Ernst, then 81 years old, married Ernestine Gloksin on or just prior to July 16, 1892. Mrs. Gloksin has been described as a woman in her sixties at the time of this marriage and as having two grown children. Nothing more is known about her background or how she met Ernst; however, it is clear from correspondence that Ernst's children were disappointed to say the least. Thus, in a letter dated November 8, 1892, Henry responded to an earlier letter from his sister, Emma, by saying "…regarding Father if you can get him to visit you and with kindness you may overlook the mistake that he has made." One can assume that Emily's letter was harsher than Henry's response in condemnation of her father's decision to marry Ernestine.

It is possible that family opposition to Ernst's remarriage reflected the natural expectation of any child that a widowed parent should spend an appropriate period in mourning, particularly if, like Ernst and Rosa, they had been married for over fifty-five years. However, on closer examination, that is less likely to have been the reason for their dismay. After all, Ernst was well past normal life expectancy at the time, and none of his children seemed willing to move back to Portage to help him as he entered his ninth decade. So, who could blame him for moving fairly quickly to find a wife who might ease his loneliness and provide care for him in his final years? He did, after all, wait fourteen months before remarrying, and given his advanced age, that timing seems unlikely to have provoked so strong a family reaction. Rather, I suspect that the reason for family chagrin had far more to do with the character of their new stepmother. Evidence suggests rather strongly that Ernestine was an opportunist. Given Ernst's age at the time, his apparently comfortable financial circumstances, his presumed need for someone to care for him, and his loneliness after having lost his soul mate of fifty-five years, he would have been understandably vulnerable to the wiles of a woman of Mrs. Glocksin's makeup.

And it does seem rather evident that Mrs. Gloksin was an ambitious and opportunistic woman. Beginning in November, 1892 (just a few months after they were married), Ernst and Ernestine began dispensing his property to people who bore no blood relation to him. The first transaction, for which $5 in consideration was recited, was a warranty deed from them both to one Theoden Steinke. That was followed three years later by another transaction whereby he gave (for stated consideration of $1.00) another property to a Mr. Gustav Fredrick, and then, six months later, he made yet another seeming gift (again for token consideration) of another of his properties to one August Bellinghausen. Whether Messrs. Steinke, Fredrick, and/or Bellinghausen were sons-in-law or otherwise related to Ernestine is not known; however, the transactions do certainly raise questions, particularly when combined with the total absence of any record of a transfer of the West Cook Street home to Emma as she had been promised. In the end, there is no evidence at all that Ernst left any investment properties or any other assets to any of his children.

Ernst lived another four years after marrying Ernestine before dying himself on March 29, 1896 at the age of 85. He and Rosa, along with both Mary and Pauline, are buried at the Boethin plot in Silver Lake Cemetery in Portage. It is not known where Ernestine might be buried.

4.
Henry's Early Life in Wisconsin

Henry was the seventh of eight children, all born over a span of nearly 20 years[39] and on two continents. He was, at most, four to five months old when his family brought him from his birthplace in Cleveland, Ohio, to Wisconsin where he grew up. His first eleven years were spent in Portage, living, as we know, in a household ruled by parents who may have had difficulties making friends and establishing relationships. More importantly for Henry, his illiterate mother seems to have been secretive about the truth of the family's background, while his father, undoubtedly a very hard worker, seems to have placed an extremely high value on money and investments, even to the detriment of his children's education and opportunities, particularly Henry's, who would clearly be disadvantaged.[40]

When Henry, as a child, was learning about the world around him, that world—Portage—was going through exciting times and rapid growth, all tempered by the agony of a war too near. It was a time when the nation, racked by long-standing animosities over the slave question, would erupt into a Civil War that turned neighbor against neighbor and, at times, family members against their own blood relatives. Although Wisconsin lay far north of the battlefields themselves, it, like all the states, sent boys off to war and mourned the loss of men who never returned. Out of a population of 775,000 people in 1860, 90,000 (about 11.5 percent) of Wisconsin's residents went off to war. Of those, 12,000 never returned, including young Henry's brother-in-law, John Harmon.

For Henry, who was far too young to face conscription, his childhood world included the same sorts of distractions and fascinations that have always provided awe and wonder for young boys. The undersized and narrow canal which had been built to link the Fox and Wisconsin Rivers may have been a disappointment to adults, for whom it was to have been the centerpiece of a waterborne transit system, but for Henry and his playmates its locks and steep walls quite probably provided jumping platforms and ideal swimming holes. The Wisconsin River itself, a high-traffic corridor for barges carrying vast quantities of cut timber from the northern reaches of the state, was treacherous yet also inviting to kids seeking fun and derring-do. Its bouldered beaches and unpredictable flows and currents were both perilous and tempting. So, too, was the ever-widening system of rail transit led by huge locomotives whose size, sounds, and majestic bearing were constant draws in Portage, as elsewhere, to kids. They could gather around and dare one another to be the last to place pennies on the rails to be crushed by clattering iron wheels, which rolled on, oblivious to these insignificant obstacles in their way. And when not obsessed by watching mankind's recent inventions, Henry and his friends would have built forts in some of the wide variety of maple, birch, basswood, elm and oak trees which populated the neighborhoods, and, of course, they would have found secret hiding places in rock outcroppings and all those other awe-inspiring places where pirates, Indians, and villains have always laid in wait to capture but ultimately be defeated by young and creative heroes.

Unlike his father, who as a youngster likely had to labor in the fields in the old country, Henry had the good fortune, while he lived in Portage, to grow up in a reasonably well-to-do family setting where his help was not needed to put food on the table. Whether he ever jumped into the canal locks, waded out into the Wisconsin River, or tried to hitch a ride on a slow-moving train car will never be known, but he was certainly not without games to play with others his age.

(left) Sketch of the original Bothin home at 508 W. Cook Street. The house fell into disrepair and was ultimately demolished in 1964. The sketch was done from a poor quality photograph taken just before it was torn down. The artist, Barb Von Ahsen, recreated the outline of the house as it would have appeared before its later owner allowed it to deteriorate.
(right) This neighboring Portage home has been restored and looks architecturally much as the Bothin home would have when new albeit with far fancier and more elaborate trim than the Bothin house would have had.

So, in blissful ignorance of the chaos and carnage farther south, Henry's childhood was much like those of other children growing up in that era. Then, kids tended to play outdoors, and they were used to far fewer toys and games than their modern-day counterparts are showered with. I am always reminded of a tailor I knew who was from Armenia, who told me that as a child he had one toy—a sardine can. He used it as a car, pushing it along sandy finger-made roads; he tied a string to it and sometimes whirled it around his head or towed it hither and yon; he filled it with stones and watched the pebbles fly out as he swung it around; he made that one toy take on as many roles as his developing mind could devise. In Henry's case, he may or may not have had a few more toys, but every one of them would have been thoroughly used and appreciated.

He would have played marbles with his friends, and he would have had his favorite "shooter" and a pocket-sized leather sack containing all the glass bead marbles that he had won by making accurate knuckle shots and knocking his playmates' marbles, one by one, out of the circle. With his sisters, he might well have learned to play "the graces," a game using dowels and hoops that were tossed from person to person. But more than any other outdoor game, he would have played "knŭrr and spells," a ball game where he and his friends, using a flat stick, would see who could hit a cloth ball (the knŭrr) the farthest. And when he wasn't playing games, he and his buddies would have run around the neighborhood finding secrets, building forts, and discovering the world around him.

The house Henry grew up in was a stone's throw from the Wisconsin River. It was located in a reasonably well-to-do neighborhood comprised of a melting pot of ethnic backgrounds ranging from Norwegian, Irish, Welsh, and Germans to American-born settlers who had moved west to Portage, mainly from the New England states, in search of cheaper land and better opportunities. Based on his lifelong attachment to his older sisters, one assumes that Henry was raised as much by them, possibly more so, than by his parents.

Young Henry attended grammar school at the public school in Ward 4, which included the neighborhood on West Cook Street where the family home was located. Wisconsin had a very good public school system back when Henry began his formal education. Under state laws then in effect, "any town with ten families or more qualified as a school district."[41] In 1859, the City of Portage established its own school district and divided itself into four wards, building a school in each. Although the following quotation related to a nearby rural school and not specifically to the school Henry would have attended, it provides a good glimpse into the day of a schoolchild back in those days:

> Although today we view them as cozy and charming, one-room country schools were not built for comfort. Appointments were sparse... Students sat two to a desk. The open shelf beneath the desktop held only a couple of books and writing slates, which filled the room with a clattering, squeaking, scratching cacophony when in use. The users were responsible for cleaning them. A woodstove was the only source of heat in cold weather, and students sitting near it roasted while those farther away were chilled to the bone—all suffering in disciplined silence. Drinking water was provided by a single pail and dipper, shared by all. Pupils had to parrot what they learned by rote at a 'recitation' bench usually located in front of the teacher's desk. All in all, the room contained little that wasn't utilitarian...[42]

The subjects that Henry would have studied as a child in elementary school would most likely have included reading, writing, arithmetic, history, geography, and grammar. Those subjects were usually taught during eight years of primary schooling; however, in Henry's case he was only able to complete five years of formal schooling because the family moved to their newly purchased farm in nearby Lewiston, which had no school. A memorandum prepared after his death by his second wife, Ellen, confirmed this as the extent of his formal schooling. His older brother, J.C., and his sisters presumably went to the same school, and would have completed their eight years of elementary education by 1864 when the family moved away from Portage. Indeed, Emma (eight years Henry's senior) may even have completed high school. Based on the close bond he had with his sisters, Emma and Minnie, one suspects that they probably helped him, to some extent at least, with some of the subjects he had to miss due to the move.

The fact that his parents felt comfortable removing him from public school after just five years attests to the fact that they did not place a high value on formal schooling, which suggests all the more strongly that they, themselves, were not well educated. But while that may be true, Ernst's success in business and real estate investing, the latter of which in particular required skills in reading, writing, grammar, and numbers, would, one would expect, have brought him to understand the value of formal learning. This, more than anything else, is what seems so surprising about his apparent lack of interest in providing Henry with the tools a formal education provides to help make possible later success.

Despite his sisters' nearly assured effort to help overcome his educational deficit, Henry's written communications throughout his life make clear the fact that he was a poor speller and was largely incapable of organizing his thoughts and putting them coherently on paper. In other words, he did not become successful due to much that he learned in school. Rather, the level of success he would ultimately attain adds his name to a long list of people, including such notables as Albert Einstein, Thomas Edison, and Leonardo Da Vinci, who succeeded in their chosen fields despite severe learning challenges or the absence entirely of any formal training. On the other hand, he did learn basic reading and writing skills that, although incomplete, left him fully capable of later starting and running several businesses and, in that context, understanding balance sheets, profit and loss statements, legal contracts, notes and mortgages, marketing techniques, pricing models, and all the myriad other areas of expertise one must master to operate, as he did, in not just one but several industries. Those few years of formal study also equipped him to buy and sell commercial real estate, to work with architects and engineers to build and renovate commercial buildings, to understand rental markets, financing arrangements, security instruments, and lines of credit, and to be comfortable dealing with escrows, regulations, legal rights and responsibilities, and other skills that he necessarily mastered and employed on the way to becoming the largest individual commercial land owner in San Francisco by the time of the 1906 earthquake and fire.

Between 1864 when the family moved to Lewiston and about 1871 (the year when he most likely left home), Henry labored on the farm and not in the schoolhouse. Meanwhile, he also watched, probably with envy and frustration, as his two elder sisters, Emma and Minnie, both moved away, followed by his older (and only) brother, J.C. By 1871, and quite possibly for a year or two before that, he would have been alone on the farm with just his parents and his baby sister to keep him company. During that time, and particularly after Minnie left for California, Henry undoubtedly also heard, in letters from both Otillia and Minnie, about the wonderful opportunities that existed in California, and one can well imagine that the grass looked a lot greener out west.

Shortly after the 1870 census that documented Henry's presence in Lewiston was completed, Henry decided to leave. Unfortunately, the way he executed his planned departure resulted in an enduring estrangement between him and his parents. The event that most likely caused the hard feelings seems to have had to do with the way Henry obtained the cash he needed to travel west to San Francisco. Just who might have been at fault, if anyone, is not known for certain; however, Ida Sutter Maas wrote in her family history, referred to earlier, that Henry funded his trip west by taking "a span" (a matched pair) of Ernst's horses that were used to pull his threshing machine. According to Ida, Henry sold those horses and, in that way, raised the cash he needed to fund his trip to San Francisco. If true, (and one suspects it probably was true), it could well explain the falling out, even though Henry may have had (indeed I would argue clearly did have) a perfectly legitimate reason for having done what he did.

Lewiston was located far enough away from Portage to have effectively isolated the family from school, friends, and familiar surroundings. Henry surely questioned the move, not only as he labored at his farm chores, but also as he watched in frustration as his siblings moved away one by one. Emma was the first to leave. She married John Sutter in early 1868, and she and her husband moved over one hundred miles away to Prairie Du Chien, Wisconsin. Then, in either that same year or possibly the next, Minnie left home and travelled to San Francisco, where she stayed with their eldest sister, Otillia, and where she shortly met and married Hermann Sadler. Julius, too, seems to have moved away prior to 1870, since the census taken in that year does not mention his name as a resident of the Bothin household. So, by 1870 the family unit living on the farm was down to just Ernst, Rosa, Henry, and young Mary. Quite possibly the only companionship close to his own age that Henry had was a hired hand by the name of Knute Holonson, who was also living and working on the farm at the time.

During this general time period, Ernst apparently made and saved enough money to be able to invest in a thresher machine that he leased out to other farmers and from which he derived profits.[43] The thresher machine was likely (due to the factory's geographic proximity) a Case Thresher made by J.I. Case Co. of nearby Racine, Wisconsin. Such a machine cost about $1,800 in the late 1870s.[44] The fact that Ernst had the ability to not just buy the farm for cash in 1864, but soon after to buy an $1,800 piece of equipment as well to help harvest his grain crops, is further evidence that he had either done extremely well in the cabinet making business or else he bought it on credit and used the income from leasing it out to local farmers as his means of managing his debt service and paying off the investment in the machine.

Whichever might have been the case, Ernst was seemingly

always interested in business opportunities that required capital and that, in turn, deprived the family of the comforts of living those dollars might otherwise have provided. That is not meant necessarily as criticism since it is obviously the right of any citizen to spend his money in any legally permissible way; however, two things do stand out about Ernst's approach to money management. First, and as will be seen shortly, it provided the catalyst for Henry's decision to leave home in the manner he left, and secondly, Ernst's frugal nature and emphasis on investing at the expense sometimes of a more comfortable lifestyle was a model that became imprinted on Henry's own personality and was to define his own approach to those same sorts of choices once he himself later married.

The 1870 census, where the family name is again creatively misspelled, this time as "Bothier," notes Ernst and Rosa living at their home in Lewiston. Ernst's occupation is listed as "farmer." Henry was listed too, but whereas often census takers of the day used words such as "son of," "student," or "living at home" to describe the roles of family members living at a given address, in Henry's case Ernst described both him and Mr. Holonson as "providing Farm labor." Henry's younger sister, on the other hand, is listed as "at home." Notably, neither twelve-year-old Mary nor Henry is accorded the title of student, and while that was not overly surprising given the lack of value the family seemed to place on education, that census report is telling for the way he is described. While it is always dangerous to read too much into several words on a census sheet, this particular document speaks loudly in several respects. First, Ernst failed to give seventeen-year-old Henry credit as a farmer in his own right, instead simply listing him in the same category as he did with the hired hand. Far more telling, however, is the fact that Ernst failed to even acknowledge Henry as a member of the family, instead just referring to him as providing labor. It doesn't take very much imagination to envision the sort of tension which likely already existed between Henry and his father as early as 1870.

As much as Henry may have felt insulted by his father's treating him as simply a laborer, as he was listed in that census, the tension between father and son would have undoubtedly had another component as well. Thus, undoubtedly Knute Holonson would have been paid wages for the farm work he did, whereas it is highly probable that Henry received no wages at all, but was expected, as a family member, to contribute his work for the good of the family. Proof of that assumption can be found in the simple fact that had he been paid wages (and given the lack of anywhere to spend wages in Lewiston) he would have had money of his own and thus no need to take and sell his father's horses to pay for his trip west.

Farming has never been thought of as an easy business; the urbanization of America is largely a story of the flight of farmers away from their rural roots and communities and into cities where they could (hopefully) obtain better paying jobs and a more stable and reliable way of life. There is hardly room here to describe all the travails and risks of farming, but suffice it to say that weather-related crop failures, tornados, grasshopper infestations, falling prices caused largely by inexpensive competing products transported by an ever wider railroad system, and the rigors of the work itself, made for an always difficult and stressful way of life; one that became increasingly less appealing to successive generations of Americans. The life of a farmer in those days required large families as an economic necessity, in order to fulfill all the daily and seasonal chores involved in clearing land, plowing and planting, growing and harvesting one's crops, constructing and repairing fences and needed farm structures, tending to livestock, and myriad other chores, which often required backbreaking work from dawn to dusk or later. And all this does not begin to describe the additional work done by women, who not only typically participated in the work of the men, but also put meals on the table, skimmed the milk, churned the butter, did the laundry, baked bread and pies, did the ironing, canned vegetables and fruit, and raised the children.[45]

The Bothin farm consisted of 175 acres in 1864. In 1871, Ernst bought another 40 acres, which simply meant more work to do. Most farms in those days in Wisconsin raised wheat as their primary crop as well as some corn, potatoes, and other crops. They also usually included a vegetable garden that provided the family's food supply, and often included a few swine, oxen, chickens, and perhaps one or two cows and calves as well. Even with Rosa's help, Ernst would have been hard-pressed to handle it all without the help provided by Henry and the farmhand, Knute Holonson. Furthermore, the economics of farming were changing with the ever-expanding railroad network. The price of wheat, once a readily marketable staple, came under pressure as more distant growers were able to compete in ever-widening markets. And so, not only would Ernst and his family have endured long hours and hard work to survive, but they would also have had to become creative with their crops and their equipment. Undoubtedly that is why Ernst bought the thresher, as an investment in equipment that could hopefully bring him a return that might help to finance the improvements and other equipment he would have needed to keep the farm profitable. But while an extra piece of equipment could be seen as a labor saver, the addition of forty more acres to farm—an increase of nearly 25 percent in the size of the property—would most likely have been looked on by Henry as an intolerable worsening of the labor expected of him.

But what were his options? Otillia and Minnie had preceded him to San Francisco and sent periodic letters home with positive and enthusiastic accounts about their newly adopted home state of California. Indeed, Otillia had married and moved to San Francisco some time prior to 1859 (the year her first child, William, was born in California), so she had had well over ten years to indoctrinate her siblings through letters sent home to her parents and sisters. Obviously she had succeeded with Minnie, who went west as a single lady and didn't meet her husband until after she had moved. That was a pretty major step, and one that tells its own story about how badly Minnie wanted to leave home and how bleak she saw her future in Lewiston and its environs to be. Minnie's trip also raises the question of how she was able to generate the cash needed to travel. She obviously had no husband to pay for her trip, and the only other obvious choice would have been to ask her father. If I am right in this assumption, then there existed precedent for one of Ernst's children to ask for and receive money with which to leave home. Her decision to travel to San Francisco by herself is also confirmation of how persuasive Otillia was, and it sets the stage for Henry's own flight west.

So, picture a very bright young man who is feeling constrained by the relative isolation and climate of central Wisconsin, not liking either its agrarian base or its limited opportunities, frustrated by hard work without pay, and wanting to go where the action was. He would have eagerly awaited and then consumed letters from his older sisters about California's phenomenal and seemingly endless growth and opportunities, tales that would have included the Gold Rush and the more recent and ongoing discovery of silver at the Comstock Lode. Henry's impatience must have become all-consuming. Indeed, Otillia must have been quite a saleslady, for ultimately four out of the seven children of Ernst and Rosa who survived to adulthood abandoned rural Wisconsin and succumbed to the excitement offered by San Francisco in the 1870s. Henry's turn was coming.

5.
Westward Ho!

It is not known exactly when Henry traveled west to California. Based on the 1870 census, which shows him still in Wisconsin, and the 1875 *San Francisco City Directory*, which lists twenty-two year old Henry as an employee of Chartres Coffee and Spice Company,[46] it obviously occurred sometime during that five-year window. We have some clues, however, from several sources. First, there is a "memorandum" about Henry that is dated March 3, 1952, which was prepared by either his second wife, Ellen, or his nephew, Ted Maas. That memorandum states that Henry "[w]orked on father's farm until 1871, then came to San Francisco."[47] Although not by any means conclusive on the topic, that memorandum was presumably based on what its author had learned from Henry during his lifetime. That information is implicitly corroborated by Ida Sutter Maas' 1940 letter about family history, which also tends to narrow the time frame and place it more toward the beginning of that date range. In her brief family history, Ida describes Henry's farewell to Wisconsin:

> At the age of 14 or 15, Henry was sent out with the threshing crew as time keeper and collector of fees, representing his father. His older sisters, Mrs.

Mau and Mrs. Sadler, had married and settled in far off California which in part explains why the lad, tiring of a hum-drum existence, decided to do something about it. What he did was to sell a span of his father's horses, leave the threshing crew, and with the money depart for California. He arrived in San Francisco one Sunday morning. Finally located the Sadler home at that time located on Van Ness at O'Farrell. A high ornamental iron fence guarded the home and Henry could not get the gate open so had to wait outside until a newsboy delivering the paper let him in. He surprised his sister "Minnie" at her breakfast table.

Aunt Minnie [Ida's aunt] herself supplied the following. 'We did not know what to do with the country boy so my husband placed him with a store keeper near Walnut Creek to learn something of business methods.' Henry had a mind of his own and in time objected when his employer insisted that he dig fence post holes when not busy in the store. Again he returned to San Francisco eventually acting as itinerant salesman of tea and spices for his brother in law, Mr. Mau's importing business.

At twenty-one he returned to Wisconsin for a visit. One of my very earliest memories is my amazement at the size and whiteness of a handkerchief he drew from his pocket to wipe my presumably runny nose. I must have been about five years old at that time. I gathered from later conversations in my presence that the handsome, dapper business man was considered a terrific success.[48]

Although this portion of Ida's family history has more credibility than the earlier romanticized tale about Ernst's and Rosa's early lives, the devil is still in the details. Henry was actually seventeen at the time of the 1870 census, and that government-generated document places him still living then at home in Lewiston. Ida's history is clearly incorrect about Henry's actual age when he let home; however, it does clearly indicate that he was a very young man—in other words undoubtedly far closer to the teenager he would have been in 1871 than a man in his twenties which would have been the case had he not come out until later in that date range. Furthermore, the description provided by his sister, Minnie, is pretty clearly of a young man presumably far closer to seventeen in age than twenty-two, and that description of a young "country boy" would not be inconsistent with the 1952 memorandum. Based on the two sources, it seems fair to place Henry's arrival in San Francisco in 1871 or very closely thereafter—at a time when he was about eighteen years old.

So, what were the circumstances of his leaving? They are important because they bear heavily on his character, and yet the details necessarily involve some speculation. While it is highly probable for a number of reasons that he did in fact take horses from his father and sell them to pay for his trip west, outright theft would have been out of character. A horse thief, family member or not, is and was then a criminal, but Henry's later life shows no signs of criminal tendencies. That said, however, it is also true that he and his parents were estranged.[49] Taking his father's horses, even as young as Henry would have been when that happened—if it did—would certainly explain the strain in the relationship. But there are always two sides to every story. For Henry's side of the story, we can start with a letter he wrote to his sister, Emma, dated July 2, 1890. Granted, that letter was written many years after Henry left home; however, its importance here is that it does not convey any sense of guilt, but rather expresses a simple desire to help his sister in her effort to care for their aging parents and to rally his two West Coast sisters to contribute because it was the right thing to do. That letter does not express remorse for past sins, nor does it suggest a willingness to shoulder the burden himself out of any sense of contrition. The letter reads, in pertinent part, as follows:

> Enclosed find $15 P.O. order. I suppose you have received some money from both Mrs. Mau and Sadler. I do not wish you to consider this as a gift from me but only as your just dues for taking care of Mother & Father. I am well aware it is not easy task. I do this as old people are peculiar and they are our Parents + we must do all we can for them… Now, if I can be of any assistance let me know. I will send you each month $15 and no doubt Mrs. Mau and Sadler will send either you or Father $20 or so each month. With this and your other income I think you can get along nicely but if you can't let me know.. As far as I am concerned & (I think I can speak for Mrs. Mau & Sadler), we will cherefully turn over our interest and rights to Father's property to the balance of our family only I hope that our Parrients may live a long time yet and I want to feel that their remaining years are free from the slightest ill feeling and that they have the best care and to that end we are willing to provide as long as they live."

Interestingly, he closed that letter by referring to the family farm, noting that his financial obligations were causing him to "not sleep as well as I used to on the old farm in Lewiston." One would imagine that if Henry were embarrassed by the way he left the farm, that would probably be a topic he would have avoided in correspondence with family members, and so the very fact that he raised the subject is compelling evidence that he never considered that his having sold his father's horses was even an issue much less something which he should feel badly about or be ashamed of.

Still, even if Henry felt no wedge, it is clear that ill feelings existed on the part of Ernst against Henry, and it seems that the animosity on the part of the elder Bothin(s) was known about and understood by at least Henry's sister, Emma, and her children. Its essence is best captured by quoting from a letter that Ida's brother, Emil, sent to the "Folks at Home" who would have included Ida and her parents, Emma and Joshua. In that undated letter,[50] Emil (who was, at the time, working in California for Henry) said the following:

> I have much to say in this letter, very much. Of course when I came here it was understood by you at home that I should serve as Portage Consul at San Francisco. Until the other day, my diplomatic qualities were not exercised, but last Tuesday, Uncle Henry asked me to come up Wednesday eve as he wished to talk with me about you folks. Well, Wednesday evening I kept my appointment and he commenced by saying that Mrs. Will Mau had answered to the question by him 'How are the old folks and are they contented'! that Grandma was low and possibly not content. He wanted [m]y statement as to how things were at Portage and here my diplomacy came in and I told him what I thought best and he thought perhaps the old folks were a little neglected and I soon put this idea out of his head and he is a reasonable man and was satisfied…What he wants is that the old folks are comfortably taken care of. I fully assured him on this point and he argues that they can have but a few more years to live and should be looked after in their declining years… Above all things don't receive the impression that Henry is dissatisfied with

Ida Sutter

Emil Sutter

things there because he isn't. He wishes however that you should bear with them while they last.

I want you should get the correct impression of this because I would not like to have you misunderstand the situation. I have a good pull here, all of course on account of Bothin and, for say a year, I would not like to see a rumpus... I am not writing this way prompted by selfish motives or any personal fear of discomfort. But when I get a start in this country I will be able to change positions if necessary, now it would be hard to break away from here... I must impress on you all not to let out at home that I have written in this manner, when they ask you what you hear from me tell them anything which would be the contents of an ordinary letter. If you ever talked where the old folks can catch a hint they would write out here and a word from them sets everyone afire. I am not so situated that I can tell Bothin what my opinions of his parents are and how much I like them, not at present at anyrate[sic]...

What is one to make of the foregoing? First, it seems clear that Emil felt uncomfortable answering Henry's questions about his parents and the care they were receiving. Second, one has to ask why Henry seemingly was not willing to communicate directly with his parents, but had to learn about their well-being through his sister, Otillia Mau, and/or through his nephew, Emil. Thirdly, Emil clearly was fearful that the senior Bothins were capable of sending a very nasty letter that would inflame someone (presumably Henry but also possibly his siblings as well). In the absence of evidence of other simmering disagreements or friction existing between Henry and his parents prior to his leaving the farm, and since there seems to have been very hard feelings on the part of the senior Bothins toward

Henry after he left, it would seem to follow that the hard feelings had to do with events close upon or connected directly to the way he left home. Stealing horses (or the belief that their son had stolen the horses) would certainly fit that description. So, even if Henry felt he had done no wrong (and it would seem he did feel that way) it appears that his parents did not share that view. As an aside, Henry's daughter, Genevieve Bothin Lyman,[51] used to say regularly (and did more than once in my presence) that her father was a horse thief. Of course, that was the statement of a woman who disliked her father; however, it also failed to give equal time to any explanation that Henry would likely have given when he was alive and able to defend himself.

And an explanation is certainly available. That argument would go thusly: When Ernst was a young man living in Prussia, it was common for families to have many children. Indeed, it was a necessity to have many hands when working the land and raising crops in order to do the work necessary for the family's survival. There were no child labor laws, and it was universally understood that children were not paid for their labor while working on the family farm. After all, they were provided with shelter, food, clothing, and the necessities of life, and so the equation seemed equal on both sides. One suspects that Ernst, whose frugal nature has already been established, probably brought with him to America that same mindset, that one's children were expected to work alongside their parents toward the common goal of survival. And if during a particular year they made a profit, Ernst would undoubtedly have felt that that profit should be put aside as a reserve against the next year, when a tornado, a grasshopper infestation, or a weather-caused crop failure could otherwise wipe the family out. So, one can well understand how Ernst would truly believe that he owed Henry nothing for the work he did on the farm.

To the contrary, from Henry's perspective, he watched his father succeed in business and put away enough in the way of profits, year after year, to be able to invest in real estate in Portage, to buy the farm even as he retained titles to his other properties, to buy an expensive thresher machine and lease it out at a profit (one that Henry was expected to collect and bring home), and then to add another forty acres to the size of his farm, all without straining financially. If Henry were not family, his father would have had to pay for the labor Henry was providing (just as Ernst undoubtedly paid their hired hand), and Ernst clearly had the wherewithal to pay for it. Survival was not an issue. Rather, Henry would have known his father was making a profit from his labor and would have felt entitled to be paid at least something for the labor he had, for a number of years, contributed to the family enterprise. Furthermore, and interestingly, Minnie had left home as a single woman several years earlier and quite probably had no cash to pay for her trip either. It is quite likely that she asked Ernst for the money to pay for that trip, and presumably (since Minnie was able to make the trip) Ernst had relented and given it to her. Assuming that to be the case, there was precedent for Henry to feel entitled to a similar response if he were to request it.

Henry was clearly not happy with life on the farm, and he wanted to leave the family nest and set off on his own. Indeed, since he was closer to his sisters than he was to his parents, that desire would have only grown stronger once Minnie left home. One can imagine Henry and his father having a conversation; Henry would have said he wanted to leave and follow Minnie to San Francisco, and then he would have asked his father for help with covering his travel expenses, quite probably just as Minnie had asked for help a year or two before. But whereas Minnie had most probably been given money to cover her trip west, when it came to Henry, whose labor on the farm was, at least to Ernst's way of seeing it, of greater need and value, his father, ever the penny-pincher, would have declined, and so the battle would have been joined. To Henry, who had no other access to cash, it might have seemed fair, and perhaps little enough compensation, to sell two horses to raise the cash he could not otherwise find. And while seventeen- or eighteen-year-old Henry would almost certainly have preferred their parting to be otherwise, he also undoubtedly felt that selling the horses and keeping the money was simply the only way he could gain access to the cash he had earned fairly and squarely through his hard labor. To him, this equation was equal on both sides. Perhaps, just as his parents had never looked back on their decision nearly twenty years earlier to leave their home in Prussia, Henry also never looked back thereafter on his decision to leave the farm for a better life out west, nor did he ever regret or feel remorse for the way he chose to raise the cash he needed to do that. Whatever the actual facts were, and I suspect my analysis is probably not far off, and whatever the means, Henry did leave home and probably never returned.

To get to California, Henry would have had a choice of railroads, and my assumptions about the routes and trains he took are just that. Certainly easier and less dangerous than the wagon trains of a generation before, nonetheless rail transit was still in its relative infancy in 1871. It had come a long way since 1828, when the Baltimore and Ohio Railroad had begun service as the first common carrier with scheduled rail service in the country; however, it was, at the time of Henry's trip west, hardly a mature industry. At that time, the railroad business was in a frenzy, with entrepreneurs competing furiously over construction of one route after another. A number of these enterprises became highly successful, but many others broke ground only to fail, be bought out by another, and to move on haphazardly from locale to locale. By 1871 over 45,000 miles of track had been laid in the United States, the vast preponderance of it east of the Mississippi, and the spider web was starting to connect most large cities in the east and the Midwest with each other.

However, the only true long distance route in existence was the transcontinental railroad, which had been completed just two years before in 1869. The word "Transcontinental" was misleading, for that route began not on the East Coast, but nearly 1,150 miles inland at Omaha, Nebraska, a town that was fully one-third of the distance from the east to the West Coast, and on the western side of two of the largest rivers crossing the continent, the Mississippi and the Missouri. But whether or not the term describing it was accurate, its completion was explosive, for it opened up the entire country to settlement and connected east and west to create a truly united set of states. The "Transcontinental" railroad was not a single company's route; it involved a trip on the Union Pacific from Omaha to Promontory Point, Utah, a change there to the Central Pacific's westward train to Sacramento, and finally a short trip on yet another train from Sacramento to Oakland. Still, it was a huge advance over what had existed previously. Five years earlier, for instance, a cross-country trip from New York to San Francisco would have cost the average traveler about $1,000 and taken two months. By 1871, Henry was looking at a trip of less than one week, and in just four of those days he would have been able to travel nearly 2,000 miles from Omaha to Sacramento at a cost of as little as $65 for a third class ticket.

But to catch the train in Omaha, Henry first had to get from Portage to Council Bluffs, Iowa, a city located on the eastern side of the Missouri River, directly across the river from Omaha. To get there he most likely took the "Milwaukee Road" the commonly used name for the Chicago, Milwaukee, St. Paul and Pacific Railroad. That train would have followed a southeasterly route to Chicago, which lies about 180 miles away from Portage, and that leg of his journey would have taken him less than a day. Assuming he traveled in the spring or summer of the year, which is likely, he would have arrived in Chicago just a few short months before the Great Chicago Fire of 1871. That calamitous fire burned most of the city, whose buildings, sidewalks, and even roads were all built of wood—wood that was, in October of that year, tinder-dry from the effects of a serious drought affecting the region. Although he could not have known it then, about fifteen years later the city of Chicago would become very important in Henry's life, precisely because of that fire and the lessons learned from it, especially the value of steel as a building material to reduce the danger of fire.

In Chicago he would have changed trains and, although he had a choice of two railroads available to get him to his destination, I assume that in all probability he boarded the Chicago, Rock Island and Pacific Railroad (the "Rock Island"), which would have taken him from Chicago west to Council Bluffs, Iowa. That trip would have taken a day, and then he would have crossed the Missouri River by boat before boarding the Union Pacific's train heading west. Meanwhile, as he rode on the Rock Island line, he would have crossed the Mississippi over a bridge at Rock Island, Illinois; a bridge whose existence had, ever since 1853 and, indeed, before then, been the subject of fierce debates, legal action, and not-so-legal activities as well. The fights over its right to be built had involved, among others, then-Lieutenant Robert E. Lee, Jefferson Davis (who was then Secretary of War in President Franklin Pierce's cabinet, and later President of the Confederate States), and the man who was at that time probably the best railroad attorney in the country, a man by the name of Abraham Lincoln.

Although Henry undoubtedly would have been oblivious to the historic importance of that bridge, his trip across it merits inclusion in this work both because of its role in the development of the west where Henry would make his home and his mark, and also, on a broader scale, because of the then-booming world of rail transit that was at the time, and for the next two years until the Panic of 1873 hit, the main topic of business conversation in America. The bridge in question was the first to span the Mississippi River and had been controversial for years. The issue first surfaced way back in 1837, when then-Lieutenant Robert E. Lee was commissioned to do surveys of various points along that major waterway, including the rapids at Rock Island as well as those near Des Moines and

St. Louis, and to come up with suggestions for ways to tame those rapids to enable commerce to flow along the river for longer than what was then an annual four month high water season. Lee's proposals for cutting channels through those several sets of rapids did in fact approximately double their usable seasons, to eight months per year, and consequently, facilitated the growth of commerce on the river to the point of creating a strong lobby of steamboat interests.[52] Those interests would collide during the 1850s with equally strong railroad interests intent on crossing the Mississippi to link East with West. Specifically, as the "Rock Island" expanded its tracks west of Chicago toward the towns of Moline and Rock Island on the easterly shore of the Mississippi, another aligned company, the Mississippi and Missouri Railroad, laid its tracks east from Council Bluffs to Davenport, Iowa, which lay on the westerly shore of the river. Then, following contentious debate, in 1853 the Illinois legislature approved the creation of a third company, the Railroad Bridge Company, to construct a bridge linking the rails on both sides of the river.

Because Rock Island—now Arsenal Island, a three-mile long and one mile wide island in the middle of the river—had been home to Fort Armstrong until it was decommissioned in 1845, the federal government claimed an interest in the debate. Jefferson Davis joined the steamboat interests and argued vociferously against the bridge. When his orders and arguments were ignored, he filed suit in the case of *United States v. The Rock Island Bridge Company*, seeking an injunction. Ultimately, Judge John MacLean of the U.S. Circuit Court for Northern Illinois ruled against Davis and the government, thereby freeing the railroads to continue construction of the bridge.

The bridge, an 1,851-foot long wooden structure with nine support piers sunk into the Mississippi riverbed, was completed in 1856 amidst much celebration in railroad circles and chagrin among the steamboat interests. The celebration was short lived however, for just fifteen days later a steamboat, the *Effie Afton*, crashed, under very

The Rock Island Bridge

This painting, The Wreck of the Effie Afton, depicts the fire that the wreck caused, which consumed the original Rock Island Bridge.

suspicious circumstances, into one of the bridge's piers and caught fire. The fire consumed not only the vessel, but ultimately the entire bridge as well, much to the delight of steamboat owners up and down the river. Because of the circumstances, including the fact that the vessel had gone through the drawbridge before allegedly becoming disabled and drifting back into the pier, as well as the intensity of the subsequent fire and its rapid spread, many people believed (and perhaps rightly so) the crash had been intentional and that the *Effie Afton* was carrying flammable fuel that was intended to create a fire large enough to engulf the entire bridge.

Whatever the facts might have been, Captain John Hurd, the owner of the *Effie Afton*, then filed suit against the railroad to recover damages for the loss of his boat and its cargo and to close down the bridge. That suit, entitled *Hurd v. Rock Island Railroad Company*, was defended by an experienced trial attorney by the name of Abraham Lincoln. Summaries of the case provide a glimpse into the thoroughness of Lincoln's preparation and the strength of his two-day closing argument, an argument that, although resulting in a hung jury, was widely considered a huge victory for his railroad client, who, by virtue of the outcome, was able to continue using the bridge. Among other arguments that Lincoln made, he pointed out the growing importance of the railroads for moving both people and freight from east to west and vice versa along tracks that were not limited by natural watercourses such as the river. He cited statistics that showed that in the year following the *Effie Afton* incident, the Rock Island Railroad had hauled 12,586 freight cars and 74,179 passengers across the hastily rebuilt bridge.[53] He also pointed out that even with Lieutenant Lee's channels through the rapids, the Mississippi was still limited to eight months of use per year due to winter weather, whereas the bridge carried products and people year round. Ultimately, the point he drove home was that "one man had as good right to cross a river as another had to sail up or down it."[54]

The battle wasn't yet over. Congress undertook an investigation to determine whether or not the bridge constituted a hazard to navigation. After determining that it did, Congress nonetheless declined to take any action. In 1858, as might have been expected, a lawsuit was filed by a steamboat owner, James Ward, in which he asked that the bridge be declared a nuisance and ordered removed. After the trial court ruled in Ward's favor, the railroad appealed the lower court's decision to the United States Supreme Court. The Supreme Court handed down its decision on January 30, 1863 in the case of *Mississippi and Missouri Railway Company v. Ward*. In that decision, which reversed the lower court's ruling, Justice John Catron, writing for the majority in a six-to-three decision, held in favor of the railroad on narrow grounds relating to how the complaint was framed; however, he also wrote that if the lower court's ruling were permitted to stand, "no lawful bridge could be built across the Mississippi anywhere; nor could the great facilities to commerce, accomplished by the invention of railroads, be made available where great rivers had to be crossed."[55] That was precisely Lincoln's point in the *Hurd* case, and so, even though Lincoln could not have become involved as defense counsel in the *Ward* case because of his run for President and his ultimate election as the country's chief executive, his arguments in the *Hurd* case lived on through the *Ward* court's decision.

So, despite the probable ignorance of eighteen-year-old Henry regarding the importance of some of the landmarks he passed on his trip west, or the significance of his even being able to board this train, the fact remains that he did travel along tracks, the planning for which, less than a decade earlier, had consumed more of President Lincoln's time and energy during his presidency than any other issue, save only the Civil War itself, and the laying of which constituted the single largest private endeavor in the history of our country up to that time.

In another context altogether, the railroad, on which he rode in relative comfort, was itself probably the most prominent tableau on which could be displayed the endgame of the concept of "westward expansionism." Although its tracks were rarely targeted by Indian raiding parties, its inexorable push west, spurred on by federal land grants and other generous motivations, had, by the time Henry rode it, largely accomplished the displacement of the Native Americans in whose trust those lands had reposed for centuries.

Henry was probably not interested in either politics or the Indian wars that had gone before. Nor was he probably much interested in the spectacular vistas he passed as he climbed through Emigrant Pass, crested Donner Summit, and then descended through the western foothills of the Sierra Nevada range toward Sacramento. Rather, the emotion which probably most drove him was that he had finally shed the family ties in Wisconsin and was about to begin a new life in a land of opportunity.

And what a land of opportunity it was. In the early 1870s San Francisco was the western center of both trade and finance. Its port (and therefore its merchants, banks, insurers and other businesses which both supported and also made their living off the port) controlled 99 percent of all imports into West Coast cities and over 80 percent of exports from them. It was the transportation hub of the western United States, and the destination of necessity both from and to virtually all of the other twenty-four western cities ranging from the Mexican border to Alaska.[56] It was well on its way to having more manufacturers, more employed personnel, and greater product valuation than all of those other western cities combined. From the standpoint of finance, it was home to ten insurance companies, several savings and loan associations, and more than ten banks—principally the Bank of California, Wells Fargo and Co., The National Gold Bank and Trust Co., Hibernia Bank (known as "the peoples' bank") and the Merchants Exchange Bank.

San Francisco, 1851

San Francisco, 1871

Although Henry could not have helped but notice the pace of business and the broad variety of enterprises in plain view everywhere he looked, one imagines that what might well have caught his immediate and rapt attention was the port itself. The Wisconsin River, for all its rapids and barge traffic, was, by comparison, a tiny sliver of water flowing in the midst of farmland that stretched as far as the eye could see, whereas San Francisco Bay, and the endless horizon of open ocean beyond its Golden Gate, would have presented an awe-inspiring vista well beyond the imagination of anyone whose life had been spent in the country's interior. If the pace on land was brisk, the movement and the loading and unloading of ocean-going vessels was even livelier. Literally hundreds of ships passed back and forth each month between San Francisco and other ports of call, which included cities along our western coast, our eastern seaboard, Latin and South America, and throughout Asia and the subcontinent.

Closer to home, Henry would have seen the vast variety of manufacturing concerns turning out everything from ships to pianos, from food products to cigars, and from carriages to fine linens. Many of those businesses catered to the shipping trade, including Coffin and Hendy, a ships chandlery, and Goodall, Nelson and Perkins, who were initially shipping agents and later the organizers of Pacific Coast Steamship Company, which provided service to over twenty ports of call along the West Coast.[57] Other new or rapidly expanding businesses were also proliferating, including Hawley Brothers Hardware, a huge hardware and agricultural products concern that filled a four story building near the waterfront and sold its products around the globe. Claus Spreckels was in the process of turning a small sugar refinery in the city into what would, within a few short years, become one of the largest beet sugar companies in the world. Even Collis Huntington and Mark Hopkins, two of the "big four" who had built the western leg of the transcontinental railroad, decided that their fortunes from the railroad were not enough and opened a branch of the hardware store they had many years earlier begun in Sacramento.[58] And they were not alone. Egged on by the city's continued relative isolation from eastern manufacturing centers and the price protection afforded by the high transit prices charged by the railroad to bring competing products to western markets, Levi Strauss, who had begun making pants for miners in 1853 out of tent canvas, was now using denim to make the product he called "blue jeans" and would shortly patent the process of using rivets to add strength. As they say, the rest is history. But for every Levi Strauss, Claus Spreckels, Domingo Ghirardelli, the chocolate magnate, Isaias Hellman, the state's leading banker of the day, and other contemporary business giants, there also existed many, many other people with ideas and ambition who, just as Henry would later, began businesses to serve a burgeoning local, regional and global marketplace. Those entrepreneurs, who were very much in evidence throughout the city, were building factories that billowed smoke and filled the air with the noise of industry. They hired workers, perfected products, established markets, advertised their wares, and looked ever forward. It was, in other words, a city on the move and very intent on its growth.

It was also a city with a broad range of cultures and a keen sense of humor, and nowhere is that latter trait better shown than in the way it treated an eccentric named Joshua Norton. Norton, who first came to San Francisco in 1849, left after a series of financial reversals that forced him to declare bankruptcy. In 1859 a different Joshua Norton returned, now mentally unbalanced and living in a fantasy world. But rather than becoming a menace or an unwanted vagabond, the new Joshua Norton was harmless and highly entertaining to an audience who came to love and support him. In 1859 he issued a proclamation declaring himself "Emperor of these United States" and for the next twenty-one years he issued periodic decrees and proclamations of various sorts, including disbanding Congress, abolishing both the Republican and Democratic parties, demanding the construction of a suspension bridge or tunnel connecting San

Francisco and Oakland, insisting that a League of Nations be created, and declaring it a high misdemeanor to utter the word "Frisco." For Henry, who arrived a dozen or so years after Emperor Norton first claimed his stage, the legend was already well established. Henry would have seen him regularly inspecting the streets of the city, including the condition of its cable cars and the appearance of his police officers, all the while resplendent in his elaborate blue uniform topped with gold epaulets and wearing a beaver cap that was decorated with a peacock feather. He always traveled with a saber safely tucked in its scabbard and with either a cane or an umbrella with which to embellish his speeches and other public utterances.

This extraordinary man was revered by the people of San Francisco, who showed their generous side to support him. Unable to afford meals at restaurants, he issued his own currency to pay his debts, and that currency was accepted by merchants citywide. Indeed, restaurants and other tradespeople erected brass plaques that they proudly displayed outside their premises, declaring their establishment to be "by appointment to his imperial majesty, Emperor Norton I of the United States." Even the 1870 census taker joined in the game, listing Norton's name, his address, his age, and noting his occupation as "Emperor."

Emperor Joshua A. Norton I

For a young man from faraway Wisconsin, the Emperor would have represented not only good theater, but also a softer side of life than Henry had probably ever witnessed while growing up. The city's residents saw Norton as a means of respite from the pace and intensity of business and as an icon for tolerance. When Emperor Norton died in 1880, the city rejected a pauper's funeral and coffin, raising money instead for a proper casket and a public farewell. It is said that 30,000 people from every walk of life, quite possibly including Henry, lined the streets, and that the funeral cortege stretched upwards of two miles long.

If Emperor Norton brought out the best in the city's citizenry, other traits showcased a darker side. Discrimination was probably an alien topic to Henry, a blight one suspects he had never witnessed. In Portage, and most assuredly in Lewiston, there had been neither the time nor the inclination to place people into categories by race or to judge them as either superior or inferior. Although he probably understood that the Civil War was being fought over the issue of slavery, and more particularly whether it was just or justifiable to treat blacks as a race of humans deserving exploitation for the sake of commercial gain, to him that could have only been an abstract concept, given that he had probably never seen a black man in the flesh. Indeed, by 1860 there were only 1,200 blacks living in all of Wisconsin, and by far their largest concentration was in Milwaukee, a city Henry had never visited. If he had any knowledge or impressions about the topic of slavery at all, they would most probably have come from abolitionists who helped in the underground railroad by which slaves were whisked through Wisconsin and elsewhere to freedom in Canada.[59] And if blacks were a rarity, it is almost certain that he had never seen or even heard of anyone from China. In rural Wisconsin, the melting pot was primarily made up of Germans, Norwegians, Poles and Irish, who typically worked side by side and without rancor or name calling, and so the Irish immigrants in San Francisco, too, would probably never have entered his mind as people to be discriminated against.

However, once having arrived in California, the ugly side of discrimination could not have escaped his notice. With respect to blacks it bears mentioning that California had, as a result of the Missouri Compromise, been granted statehood in 1850 as a free state, an action that had the support of 80 percent of the populous. After all, the region had scant history of slave ownership, in large part due to Mexico having abolished the practice in 1829. That aside, Californians seemed, at the time, to have had other reasons for wanting no part of slavery within its boundaries. Although there had been several instances of southerners bringing slaves into California to work the mines during and prior to 1849, that practice was unpopular. During the State's constitutional convention in Monterey in 1849, delegate Walter Colston put it succinctly:

> The causes which exclude slavery from California lie within a nutshell. All there are diggers, and free white diggers won't dig with slaves. They know they must dig themselves, they have come out here for that purpose, and they won't degrade their calling by associating it with slave labor. Self-preservation is the first law of nature. They have nothing to do with it in the abstract, or as it exists in other communities—they must themselves swing the pick, and they won't swing it by the side of negro slaves. That is the upshot of the whole business.[60]

Whether the reasons were as stated by Mr. Colston or not, the fact is that Californians as a group were fiercely opposed to slavery, and that fact is indelibly inscribed in Section Eight of the State's Constitution, which reads "Neither slavery nor involuntary servitude, unless for punishment for crimes, shall ever be tolerated in this state."[61]

Although officially a free state, California, during the years following statehood, was no haven for blacks. For example, the state (with a number of notable exceptions) abided by the terms of the

Fugitive Slave Law that had been passed in Washington as part of the Compromise of 1850, by whose terms law enforcement personnel and ordinary citizens alike were required, under penalty of both imprisonment and hefty fines, to return runaway slaves to their owners. In fact, in 1852 the state even adopted a fugitive slave law of its own that remained on the books for three years before lapsing and not being renewed. The State Legislature also enacted laws that prevented blacks from testifying in legal matters, and in general treated them as second-class citizens.[62] The battle over the rights of blacks (including whether or not they were even permitted to enter the state) persisted until well after Lincoln's razor-thin election victory in the state in 1860.[63] As late as 1874, California's Supreme Court decided, in the case of *Ward v. Flood*,[64] to reject the efforts of a black student to attend a white school, and thereby paved the way for the doctrine of "separate but equal" that was to become the law of the land until reversed in the 1954 landmark decision of *Brown v. Board of Education.*[65]

The irony of the state's position on slavery was that, just as the free white men of early California had declared themselves strongly opposed to blacks being held in bondage, they were nonetheless more than happy to classify blacks with the same mantle of inferiority that described their outlook and emotions about Native Americans and the Chinese.[66] In a back door sort of way, by so doing they elevated the Irish by default to a higher social order than the one that ethnic group was accorded in other parts of the country.

Just as Henry learned early in his stay in California about discrimination against blacks, so, too, he learned a great deal about an even more high-pitched and emotionally charged sense of outrage against the Chinese. Discrimination, often violent, against the Chinese began around 1850; it was still on the rise when Henry arrived in his newly adopted state over twenty years later, and remained a tinderbox issue throughout the 19th century and through the early years of the 20th century. Again, the history is instructive.

Prior to the discovery of gold there were only 54 known Chinese nationals living in California; however, by 1876 that number had skyrocketed to 116,000, many of whom had arrived during or shortly after 1850. The reasons for their rapid immigration were really no different from those that were also causing American opportunists to flock to California—greed for gold. Many Chinese, however, were also driven to flee their homeland; they faced both poverty brought about by weather-related crop failures, which had wreaked havoc particularly in the Kuangtung Province of Southern China,[67] and to escape the ravages of the Taiping Rebellion, a civil war in southern China that would ultimately claim millions of lives. Although many who fled China resettled in other parts of Asia, a large number, almost entirely made up of young, single males, made their way to California. Upon arrival, the young men, most of whom were uneducated and described themselves as koo lee ("koo" meaning "to rent" and "lee" meaning "muscle")[68] flocked to the mining fields, but were soon displaced by Americans who saw them as undeserving interlopers with no right to extract American minerals. Knowing neither the language nor the customs of this country, they typically left peacefully, but that wasn't enough. The legislature, egged on by political grandstanding by Governor Bigler, passed the Foreign Miner's License Law, which imposed a tax of $20 per month on all foreign-born miners. That tax effectively chased the Chinese back to San Francisco and other urban centers where, penniless, many started businesses including laundries and restaurants, while others took whatever work they could find at any wage they were able to negotiate.[69]

By 1854, most Caucasian miners had drifted away from the declining gold fields and had themselves returned to San Francisco looking for work. Finding that the "chinks," who typically had no family to feed and whose needs were modest, had cornered the market for cheap labor, they clamored for ways to overcome the perceived Chinese advantage. That led to grotesque rumors and ultimately to cries for action against a hardworking people whose only crime was the color of their skin.

Cartoon by George Frederick Keller for
The San Francisco Illustrated Wasp, May 11, 1878

Soon the koo lee Chinese (whose self-description had been bastardized to "coolie") were accused of unfairly undercutting wages and destroying the American labor system (when in fact there was none). But it all sounded good, and willing legislatures, made up entirely of white males, passed laws designed to harass the Chinese with the goal of convincing them to go home. The first of those laws was actually an interpretation of the original California Constitution that guaranteed the right to vote "for all adult white male citizens and male naturalized citizens from Mexico." As interpreted, that definition excluded the Chinese from the right to vote on any laws, including laws designed to harass them. Furthermore, the Chinese, just as was the case with blacks and Indians, were considered "aliens ineligible for citizenship" and thus without hope of ever gaining the right to vote or, for that matter, to own land or file mining claims.

The foregoing was followed by a California Supreme Court decision that has to be considered, even during an era where discrimination by one ethnic group towards another was commonplace, one of the most, if not the most, ill-considered and inflammatory decisions ever handed down by the State's high court. The case, entitled *The People v. George W. Hall* was decided in 1854 and can be found at 4 Cal 399. It arose as an appeal by a convicted murderer of his conviction, a conviction that had been supported by the testimony of several Chinese witnesses. Chief Justice Murray, in an opinion which would today be unthinkable, held that the Chinese were an inferior race of humans and that the precedent which might be set if they were given access to the courts might well then naturally extend to unthinkable lengths such as the right to vote, to serve as jurors, and even to sit on the bench or run for elective office. One particular paragraph of the opinion encapsulates the barbaric intolerance then prevalent, not only among ordinary citizens, but among the leaders of the state as well. In it, Chief Justice Murray stated:

> The anomalous spectacle of a distinct people… whose mendacity is proverbial; a race of people whom nature has marked as inferior, and who are incapable of progress or intellectual development beyond a certain point, as their history has shown; differing in language, opinions, color, and physical conformation; between whom and ourselves nature has placed an impassible difference, is now presented, and for them is claimed, not only the right to swear away the life of a citizen, but the further privilege of participating with us in administering the affairs of our Government.

The foregoing written opinion, short as it was and totally devoid of references to legal precedent for any of its assertions, obviously sent an electrifying message that reverberated through the Chinese community and put them on notice that the laws of this state would not offer them any protection whatsoever. It also led, as a direct consequence, to the establishment of "Tongs," secret societies which provided, among other services to their members, security and a degree of safety against white provocateurs. Although the *Hall* decision pre-dated Henry's arrival in California; it still stood as precedent and continued to be in full force and effect when he arrived. While hard to believe in this day and age, it is probably one of, if not the, best examples of legally sanctioned prejudice that can be found. The *Hall* case lends credibility to the very thought that back then the leaders of California were capable of not just what the *Hall* case stood for, but also for the passage of other laws and ordinances that further harassed the Chinese; laws on the books when Henry first arrived in San Francisco that remained there throughout most of the remainder of the 19th and early 20th centuries.

Despite the *Hall* case and laws that, for example, prevented Chinese-American children from attending public schools, required them to live only within certain geographically segregated sections of town, refused the hiring of police to patrol their neighborhoods, established special licenses, fees, and requirements designed to make them less competitive in certain industries like fishing, logging, and textiles, still, the Chinese managed to succeed in America, and, as improbable as it might seem, to continue to immigrate to this country in large numbers.[70]

Interestingly, it was Emperor Norton who found an elegant, if highly risky, way to defuse racial tension on at least one occasion. He saw a particularly ominous clash developing between some Chinese men and a riotous crowd of people intent on attacking them. By showing a side of himself that was rarely on view, in his own unique way, he was able to lower the volume of animosities. He simply placed himself between the two factions, bowed his head, and recited the Lord's Prayer over and over again, until both antagonists calmed down and dissipated. Better known for his ability to provoke laughter at the absurdities of life, Emperor Norton was nonetheless at his core a man of peace, and it was his acts, such as this one, which caused him to be widely revered.

If Emperor Norton provided the "yin," then the horrors of legally sanctioned discrimination were the "yang" of life in San Francisco at the time Henry first arrived. Those were just a few examples among the many new sights, sounds, ideas, and slices of life that would have bedazzled a young man, arriving as he did from Small Town, USA, and suddenly experiencing the size and pace of a big city on the move. Like a blind man suddenly discovering his sight, Henry's every sense must have been on constant alert, as the rube from rural Wisconsin encountered one new experience after another.

Once having arrived in California, there was much to do. Among other things, Henry obviously had to get a job in order to survive. Presumably he had expectations of help from his sisters, although Minnie's comments to Ida as recited by the latter in her family history and noted earlier do not suggest any pre-arranged offers of employment. It is likely they had sent open ended letters extolling the beauty and abundance of opportunities in California; still, Minnie's comments to Ida make clear that they never really expected Henry to suddenly show up, literally on their doorstep, without prior notice. Regardless, Henry, at his age, probably left home without much thought about what he would do when he got where he was going. We do know from Minnie that she and her husband arranged a job for Henry with a storekeeper in Walnut Creek, and we also know that he felt taken advantage of and left after a time. Thereafter, we know that Otillia and her husband gave him a job as a tea and spice salesman for the family company. Other than those two tidbits about his life during the four years between 1871 and 1875 we know virtually nothing. We don't, for instance, know where he lived, who his friends—of either sex—were, what his interests were, if any, outside of work, and we don't know if he stayed in contact with his far away siblings or how he got on with Minnie and Otillia and their spouses. In short, that four-year period of his life is a nearly blank slate.

Meanwhile, the San Francisco, which was acclaimed for its many opportunities, also had its detractors. Out-of-state newspapers warned of deadly earthquakes and fires, to the point that a *San Francisco Real Estate Circular*, printed in April 1872, responded to some particularly negative and sensationalized reporting:

> …Nevertheless, the people of the Atlantic States look upon California as one of the most dangerous earthquake countries in the world. This is due to the infernal habit of exaggeration which characterizes Eastern newspaper letter-writers and newspaper editors. The New York papers published such sensational heads as these lately: 'California Rocking from One End to the Other!', 'California's Fearful Cataclysm!, 'The Solid Earth Melting!', etc., etc. while a few correspondents here supplemented and added to the lies and excitement.[71]

Another article for the month of May, 1872, appeared in the *San Francisco Real Estate Circular*:

> These Eastern newspaper visitors, it seems, cannot come here and write of California without talking nonsense and making fools of themselves. The correspondent of the *St. Louis Republican* did not prophesy our destruction by earthquakes, that lead having been exhausted before he came here; but with

wonderful skill, he opened for himself a new vein of sensation and stuff about our danger from fire. He says: I am forced to the irresistible conclusion that San Francisco is a doomed city, and the mind cannot but paint for itself a horrible picture of the lapping flames leaping from one frail tinder-box to another until, not one-third of a thriving, prosperous city is swept from existence, but the whole. It needs no gift of prophecy to predict the future, for it is inevitable, and written so plainly, that in very truth 'he that runs may read.'[72]

The Real Estate Circular's author responded to that perceived piece of trash journalism by citing the fact that San Francisco's homes were built not of the sort of flammable woods used in construction elsewhere in the country but rather of redwood, which is far more resistant to burning and more easily extinguished, and by extolling the fire prevention systems employed locally, which far exceed those of other cities.[73]

Despite the staunch defense posted by the City's defenders, each of those eastern journalists who predicted San Francisco's ultimate destruction by natural forces would, unfortunately, be proved right some thirty-four years later in 1906; however, at the time their sensationalist hit pieces were seen as simply blathering, and, while they might have sold a few tabloids, they certainly had no effect on the continuing stampede west.

Just as the city had detractors, the very opportunities that made it famous also drew a crowd of scam artists and people intent on making their fortunes at the expense of others' greed and naiveté. No better example of this exists than the Great Diamond Hoax of 1872. The premise was that if people felt that gold and silver were laying around on western lands for the taking, then why not diamonds, rubies, emeralds and other precious stones as well? That it was so patently ridiculous an idea is precisely what made it credible when it was carefully executed by a couple of unlikely thieves. The plot was hatched in 1870 by a man named Philip Arnold and his cousin, John Slack, both poorly educated Kentuckians who had been in California for over twenty years in search of the end of the rainbow. Arnold, the more clever of the two, was in 1870 employed by the Diamond Drill Company, which used industrial diamonds for the drill bits it made. Arnold got hold of a bag of uncut industrial diamonds, and he and Slack mixed them with some semi-precious stones that Arnold had likely gotten from Indians in Arizona. They climbed into tattered clothing to assume their character roles of bedraggled, tired, and weather beaten miners, and soon approached their first mark, a man named George Roberts, who was a gullible investor with more connections than neurons. After persuading him that the sack they carried with them had valuable diamonds that they had just found in "Indian country," they swore him to secrecy and gave the diamonds to him to hold until the bank opened the next day. They then left, knowing full well that Roberts would break his vow of silence, which he did rather quickly. Roberts told William Ralston (founder and President of the Bank of California and a man known to always be hungry for his next deal) and one or two other gullible and unscrupulous capitalists, one of whom, Asbury Harpending, was then in London and immediately made his way back to San Francisco.

While Harpending was hot-footing it back to town, Arnold and Slack came back to the City themselves with a second packet of even more diamonds and "precious stones" and began tossing around values in the millions for their find. By now, the investor group had widened a bit, and together they persuaded a "reluctant" Slack to part with his share for $50,000. The pair then headed to London where, for $20,000, they bought literally thousands of additional uncut diamonds and rubies, some that they brought back to San Francisco and others that they scattered at their still secret mine location, which they fully intended should be "found" by their investor group at the right time.

At this juncture, Lady Luck made her appearance on the scene. Ralston sent some of the diamonds back to be evaluated by jeweler, Charles Lewis Tiffany, who, rather incredibly, pronounced them to be extremely valuable. (Only later would it be learned that Tiffany had little experience with uncut stones, a fact that nobody, including Arnold and Slack, had any reason to suspect.) Now suddenly the game exploded. An investment group was established, stock was issued, and Arnold got another advance, this time in the amount of $100,000. He spent less than 10 percent of it buying even more stones in London to scatter throughout their secret field. Now came the trip to the mother lode—a trek that took the investment group by train to Wyoming, followed by a round-about four day journey by horseback to the mesa where the jewels were said to have been found. After the Easter egg hunt to rival all other Easter egg hunts, lo and behold! Diamonds, rubies, sapphires and other stones just happened to be found lying around on the ground, in ant holes, and in other equally obvious spots. Even the mining engineer, a man named Henry Janin who Ralston had hired and who had accompanied them on this trip, was completely fooled and ended up staking a claim to several thousand surrounding acres of what he obviously thought might yield similar riches.

All told, Arnold and Slack made over $600,000 on this scam, but it soon unraveled when Clarence King, a Yale educated geologist, visited the site and realized that the stones were found only in areas surrounded by footprints and never in areas that were undisturbed. Other tests satisfied both him, and later, an embarrassed Janin, at which point the investors were notified, a planned stock offering was cancelled, and several millionaires, including Ralston who was said to have lost $250,000, were brought down a few pegs by unsympathetic journalists who gleefully published news of the fraud.[74]

The Great Diamond Hoax was one of many swindles and frauds that arose in a frontier town where rags to riches stories were, if not commonplace, at least not unusual. The trick was to resist the temptation to gamble and to leave one's greed at the door, and yet greed is the motive, then and still now, that lies uppermost in the minds of men whose hard work, sweat, optimism, and capital rule the marketplace.

6.
The 1870s: A Time to Be Careful

When Henry first set foot in San Francisco, he found himself in a city at the center of what has been called the Second Industrial Revolution, a city whose surroundings were awash with natural resources that had led to rapid growth that was still underway, a city built around a natural port as well as inland waterways through which its agricultural output could be easily brought to market, a city that was attracting immigrants and citizens alike, both from within the United States as well as from countries around the world, a city that had just been connected to the rest of the nation by way of a transcontinental railroad that many had said could not be built, and a city that was serious about its growth, its opportunities, its financial leadership, and its diversity.

As intriguing and as different as San Francisco was from its older and more established counterparts in the northeast and, to a lesser extent the Midwest, it was, after all, still a part of the union, and not a city state set apart from the rest of the country. It may have had advantages based on its location and on the unique wealth-producing activities that had marked its beginning and driven its growth, but at its core, it was guided by the same principals and emotions that steered the rest of our young nation.

And so, if in 1871 it seemed to have endless optimism, that was at least in part due to the nationwide exuberance which surrounded it—an exuberance which floated the spirits of its political and business leaders who saw no limits to its future, but an exuberance that, as such things always do, would ultimately self-destruct in 1873 and thereby teach Henry some timely lessons that would serve him well for the rest of his life.

We may not know much about the real-world education that Henry absorbed during those early years of the decade of the 1870s, but we do know something about the business climate that then prevailed—the canvas, if you will, whose colors and shapes reflected the palettes of its many contributors, but whose final brush strokes sullied the masterpiece that might have been.

Nationally, the disastrous Civil War had ended, and the country was finally at peace and anxious to heal the scars of war. Railroads, the darlings of both investors and lenders, were expanding at a dramatic pace, doubling their nationwide coverage by adding well over 30,000 miles of track between 1865 and 1873 and, by so doing, connecting vast areas of the country to one another, including, for instance, the industrial Northeast with the agrarian Midwest. In turn, that expansion, which resulted in a trebling of transported freight during that period, enabled the transit of goods back and forth across most of the length and width of the country and the creation of more distant markets for many high demand products. It also led to the development of mineral and natural resource industries such as coal, copper, timber, and iron,[75] all of which relied for their success on broad markets that, in turn, depended on rail transit. All this was set against a backdrop of heavy tariff protection, rising to as high as 49 percent in 1868, and thereby giving the nation's businesses tremendous security against global competition and plenty of room to grow.

Adding to the opportunities for growth were intellectual advances. The U.S. Patent Office, which had issued 7,653 patents in 1860, was suddenly, after 1865, overwhelmed by a doubling of that number to figures in excess of 15,000 new patents per year during the eight years following the end of the war. Such devices as the typewriter, barbed wire, dynamite, and the vacuum cleaner, to name just a few, were breakthroughs that appeared on the market, but of equal importance were improvements in machinery that made industry more efficient, cost effective, and usable. Even more than intellectual properties, immigration fueled a massive increase in labor resources. Between 1865 and 1873, several hundred thousand people arrived on America's shores each year, mostly from Ireland, Germany, Norway, and other European nations. In many cases, that immigration was fueled by food shortages brought on by poor harvests in Europe. This phenomenon not only helped to provide labor to meet the growing demand within the United States, but also created an export trade opportunity for agricultural products that railroads enabled producers to ship to Europe and elsewhere.

As a result of these advances and the growth of business, there arose a need for far more railroad and factory workers, and that need was met through a combination of immigrant labor and the migration of farmers to urban centers, where they found more stable employment with far fewer weather and other, crop-related risks. That growing pool of labor stabilized the supply side of the equation and kept wage inflation under control, again to the advantage of manufacturers and other employers.

But for every step forward, there looms risk of one sort or another. The dramatic post-Civil War growth in this country was necessarily accompanied by a growth in industrial plants and ever more complex machinery, all of which required manpower, and that in turn created employer/employee conflicts of a magnitude not before seen. Those same plants and equipment were also more expensive and required both investment capital and debt financing on a scale that, although also approaching uncharted waters, nonetheless became available, for several unrelated reasons. First,

American industrial growth compared favorably to the lackluster trade environment in Europe (whose citizens were, after all, abandoning their homelands to come to this country), and so foreign investment, primarily from England, flourished.[76] Second, domestic banks were flush with cash due to a savings rate among Americans that then averaged about 20 percent per year.[77] So, cash was there for the taking, and the railroads and other businesses were all too happy to sell their bonds for further expansion.

Inevitably, railroads over-expanded, often to destinations that yielded too little passenger and freight revenue to service the debt that had enabled them to grow. Also, the "railroad mania" had included long-term loans for docks, warehouses and other supporting infrastructure whose payback depended upon the growth of towns in the path of those lines; towns that sometimes failed to meet expectations and grew more slowly than projected or, for various reasons, were abandoned altogether. In the meantime, because of the emphasis by banks on making railroad related loans, many other non-railroad businesses, whose own expansion was tied to their anticipated ability to sell products to distant markets, found themselves unable to borrow needed cash to support their own growth, which in turn reduced projected rail freight revenue and hurt the railroads just that much more.

As though investment and lending excesses weren't enough to raise red flags, in October, 1871 the great Chicago fire burned a swath 4 miles long by ¾ miles wide and in the process destroyed 18,000 buildings, twenty-eight miles of wooden streets, one hundred twenty miles of wooden sidewalks, and did an estimated $200,000,000 of damage in 1871 dollars. That would equate to $3,880,000 in 2012 dollars, but it would take over $25 billion in today's dollars to replace.[78] Just 50 percent of the value of those losses was insured; however, of that 50 percent, fully half of the insurers were unable to pay off their claims and went bankrupt. Everyone—banks, insurers, and investors suffered huge losses in that fire. To add insult to injury, the following year Boston too suffered a major fire that destroyed 776 buildings and did an estimated $73.5 million in damage ($1.4 billion in 2012 dollars).[79] Again, many insurers proved unable to cover their insured claims, but those that did were stretched thin by the magnitude of the losses they absorbed, and so banks, insurers, and investors yet again took huge hits to their balance sheets. The combination of these and other unfortunate and untimely events caused bank reserves in New York City to drop from $50 million to just $17 million, which in turn placed depositor's savings accounts in jeopardy and led to the very real risk of a run on banks.

Still another event that pulled the nation ever closer to recession was a reduction in the money supply that caused interest rates to rise, thereby hurting farmers and other businesses who relied heavily on debt to carry them during seasonal lulls. That particular event had its genesis in a decision two years earlier by the German government to discontinue minting silver coins, a decision which was followed in this country by the Coinage Act of 1873, which reversed the prior policy of backing our currency with both gold and silver and, instead, placed America solidly on the gold standard. With the government no longer a buyer of silver, that fact in turn depressed the price of silver, which dealt a blow to western mining interests and western banks, many of whom suddenly found the value of their capital reserves (to the extent they were backed by silver) dramatically reduced.

The stage was set for a financial correction, but even skeptics who had warned of rough times ahead were ill prepared for the depth of the downturn that followed. Known variously at the time as "The Panic of 1873," and "the great depression," it has since 1929 generally been referred to as "the Long Depression." Its immediate cause was the collapse of Jay Cooke & Co, whose assets were heavily invested in the Northern Pacific Railway. The bank was unable, due largely to scarce money and high interest rates, to market a $300,000,000 bond offering they were underwriting and that they were relying on for liquidity. Once the first domino had fallen, it was quickly followed by a chain reaction of other bank failures, the closing of the New York Stock Exchange for ten days, the failure of fifty-five railroads (out of a total of over 100 that would ultimately collapse within the first year of the downturn), widespread factory layoffs, the halting of construction projects, falling real estate values, the failure of over 18,000 businesses, and widespread unemployment, which was normally in the 4 percent range in the years preceding 1873, and reached a high of 8.25 percent in 1878 before returning to its pre-depression level in 1880 as the country began rebounding. Overall, the country (and indeed the developed world) suffered through financial and economic chaos that lasted for six long years and didn't fully abate until the beginning of the decade of the 1880s.

Just how much all of this affected twenty-year-old Henry is not known for sure. He was, in 1873, working for his siblings, whose business was in the wholesale grocery trade and somewhat insulated from the worst excesses of the depression. However, with cost consciousness in his DNA, and with eyes that could not have helped but see the gloomy visage of a community sobered by unemployment and scarce money to spend, it seems a reasonable guess that he learned by watching and listening and was lucky not to have been more directly affected.

After a nearly five-year hiatus during which there is no information available about Henry, some knowledge about him finally surfaces in 1876. In that year he is known to have been living in a small hotel/rooming house called the Commercial Hotel, but of far greater interest is that that year's *City Directory* listed him, in bold type, as being involved on his own in the importation of coffee and spices. No company name was associated with that listing, nor was any business affiliation given for similar listings placed during the next couple of years. However, the absence of any reference to an employer would seem to make clear that, by 1876 when he was just twenty-three years old, he had decided that he understood the coffee, tea and spice business well enough to sever employment ties with the family grocery business and to go off on his own. By the same token, as we will see, the route he was beginning to take was a very conservative one—one that kept him close to the family by giving him a ready sales outlet for the products he was starting to represent. As he began to grow in his career, he would have been watching with interest the growth of the city around him, a city whose population in 1870 stood at just under 150,000 and would grow by more than half again to 234,000 by 1880.

Apparently, Henry did not have to borrow heavily to launch his business, and because his business was in the category of consumer staples, he seems likely to have come out of the recession relatively unscathed. By 1876 the young country boy from the backwoods of Wisconsin, who had arrived in San Francisco penniless, was wiser and far more experienced. He had learned from his father to be frugal, and that trait (which was on prominent display during the next quarter century of his life) was undoubtedly extremely helpful to him during those first difficult years of his career. Indeed, a number of Emil Sutter's later letters home refer to this trait of Henry's and to the advice he often gave to Emil to live modestly and to save whatever he could.

7.
The Tea and Spice Business

Clearly, by 1876 or shortly thereafter Henry was doing something right, at least according to his niece, Ida, and he had, despite the country's economic malaise, become at least moderately successful. In her 1940 memorandum Ida mentioned that when she was still a child of six or seven, Henry traveled back to Wisconsin and visited her parents—her mother was his sister, Emma—and her family. Ida's childhood recollection is that he was a "handsome, dapper business man" with a huge white handkerchief—a young man who, to her parents, seemed a "terrific success." Her language conveys a sense of confidence, perhaps even a swagger in his step, and a belief in his own abilities. So, the first half of the decade of the 1870s seems to have provided Henry with a learning experience that he took full advantage of, one that gave him a pretty clear vision of the direction he would follow and how he would succeed in business.

As a part of that learning experience, Henry seems to have evolved a sympathetic ear to the plight of workers and specifically to the issues of wages and working conditions. While there would be no public information on that topic until far later—first in conjunction with his operation of his tea and spice factory in Sacramento during the mid-1880s and then later when he took over and began operating his steel company, Judson Manufacturing Company—still that trait deserves brief mention here because it was probably instilled in him during the long depression years.. As we will see, Henry would later be labeled in newspaper accounts as a good employer, one who paid fair wages, gave his employees extra time off—particularly when holidays fell mid-week—and supported local causes. Given his own father's miserly ways, it is probably fair to assume that Henry's approach to personnel issues was not bred in his nature, but rather was a learned trait. If that is true, then, while possibly dating to his own unhappy experiences working on the family farm, more likely his learning curve on that topic would have come during those difficult years during the 1870s when joblessness was rampant and working conditions, for those fortunate enough to be working at all, often were both unhealthy and dangerous. Those years heard a tremendous clamor for workplace reform from the likes of firebrands like Denis Kearney, whose speeches called on workers to rise up against capitalists; however, more likely in Henry's case, (and this is my opinion only and is mostly based on writings in the San Francisco newspapers at a later time) he seems to have simply developed a healthy balance, on the one hand always seeking profits while at the same time recognizing that that goal could best be realized with a supportive and contented workforce.

Returning to Ida's recollections of Henry's trip to Wisconsin in the late 1870s, interestingly, nowhere does she say or infer that he went home to Portage—only that he took a trip back to Wisconsin. We know that Ida's parents were living in Prairie du Chien, Wisconsin at the time, a town that was less than two hundred miles southwest of Portage and near the Iowa border. Ida had been born in Prairie du Chien in 1871, and she lived there, where her father was a teacher and ultimately principal of the local school district, until 1878. Ida didn't describe meeting Henry as part of a larger family gathering, nor did she weave the senior Bothins into her recollections of that event. So, using 1877 or '78 (when Ida would have been six or seven years old) as a probable date for Henry's trip to his home state, it seems most likely that his sole destination (either as initially planned or as it turned out) was Emma's home.

While it is certainly understandable that he would have wanted to see Emma, with whom he had a close relationship, the fact that he traveled all that distance and didn't go on to either Lewiston or Portage is both telling and unfortunate. Of course, that may have been of his own choosing, but one suspects that it probably was not. Entering the realm of speculation, it seems curious that a son would take the trouble and expense to travel several thousand miles and then fall short by only just 200 miles or so of his parents' home. To me it makes sense that Henry would have sent letters ahead to both Emma and to his parents advising them all of his travel plans, and that either he was rebuffed directly by Ernst and Rosa or else Emma told him that an effort at reconciliation would fall on deaf ears. Either way, the son seems to have tried to come home, and blame for the failure to have at least tried to make things right falls, in my judgment, on his parents' shoulders. Right or wrong, there would never again be an effort made on Henry's part to overcome the estrangement that still persisted a decade later when Emil penned his letter home and spoke of the lingering ill will between Henry's parents and him.

Emily (Emma) Bothin

Before discussing Henry's career in the coffee and spice business, it is worthwhile to mention his older siblings, Otillia and Willimina (Minnie) with whom he always remained close. Otillia was more than fifteen years older than Henry and had moved to San

Francisco during the late 1850s. She had married Henry Mau, who was, by 1868, well established in the wholesale grocery business in San Francisco and was doing business under the name Henry Mau and Company. That company, later re-named Mau Sadler Company, continued in business well after Mr. Mau's death in the mid-to-late 1880s,[80] with Otillia remaining an active participant.

Minnie (five years older than Henry) and her husband, Hermann Sadler, came to work for the Maus shortly after she arrived in San Francisco. By 1876, Mr. Sadler had become a partner in the Mau's grocery business, and, by 1889, the company was known as Mau Sadler and Company. Hermann had, by then, become President. William Mau (Henry and Otillia's eldest son, who was just five years younger than Henry) was First Vice President, and Otillia was Second Vice President. The business was advertised as "direct wholesale importers of fancy and staple groceries, teas, cigars, cigarettes and tobacco." Their company was a food broker and acted as west coast agents for a number of brands of foods and consumable products including Horace Kelly Co's Key West Havana cigars, Franco-American soups, Richardson and Robbins canned foods, Grandma's Delight Japan Tea, Gordon and Dilworth's preserves, H.G. Wilbur and Sons chocolate and cocoa preparations and others.[81] Their business was to represent those vendors and place their products into retail grocery outlets throughout their distribution chain. As is typically the case with grocery items, theirs was a low margin business which relied on high turnover off store shelves to make up in volume the profit which their industry was typically unable to establish on per unit sales.

The reason for mentioning the Mau/Sadler connection is that coffee, tea, extracts, and baking powders were all products which sold into the grocery trade. It would make sense that Otillia and her husband, who were themselves entrepreneurial and successful, and who, by 1875, clearly understood their younger brother's drive and abilities, would have been well equipped to point Henry in the direction of a good business opportunity that might benefit not just himself but the family as well. It seems logical to assume that Henry's foray into the tea, coffee and spice business was very probably prompted by those two siblings and their husbands, whose support and encouragement would have given him a clear advantage over competitors, in that he had a ready family sales outlet for at least a portion of his product line, a fact that would have removed a lot of his business risk. While highly competitive, that business was largely immune to variances in economic conditions because of the simple fact that people have to eat no matter what the economic conditions are they face. Therefore, Henry had the good fortune to have chosen not only a good time, but a good industry as well on which to cut his teeth in business, particularly given the 1873 recession, which might have done him far greater damage had he been in a more cyclical or highly leveraged business.

The 1879/1880 *City Directory* printed a new listing for Henry, one that depicts him as a partner in the firm of Bothin Dallemand and Company, importers of baking products, coffees, and spices.[81] That business, a co-partnership that initially listed both Henry and his brother, J.C. (Julius Christopher) as partners with Albert Dallemand, was certified in a filing with the Secretary of State's office in Sacramento shortly before March 10, 1879. The certificate identified a retail outlet in San Francisco. The timing was good, for by 1878 the country was coming out of the depression and was beginning to grow again.

The Bothin brothers' partner, Albert Dallemand, was born in Germany in 1833[82] and came to San Francisco some time prior to 1868, when he was listed in the *San Francisco City Directory* as a salesman with the firm of Rosenbaum & Friedman. Although it is not known what brought Messrs. Bothin and Dallemand together, it would appear that Dallemand was entrepreneurial himself and had an interest in merchandizing. Interestingly, with Dallemand twenty years older than Henry, one would have expected that, by virtue of the age and experience differential, he might have appeared first on the firm's masthead. The fact that he didn't lends greater credence to the assumption that Henry was already set up with an established clientele, in this case his family's grocery outlet, and that, therefore, he brought more to the enterprise than did Dallemand, so that his name bore more value and justified being placed first.

Whatever might have been the internal dynamics at play in 1879, their partnership prospered. Nonetheless, within a year it became obvious that J.C. didn't have the knack for business that the others had, and he was quickly removed as a principal. Indeed, a supplemental certificate dated just seven months after the original filing listed just Henry and Mr. Dallemand as the two co-partners of the venture. The two continued successfully at their chosen business, and by December 1884, they expanded, adding both Tobias Oberfelder and his brother, Max, as co-partners in the business, which retained its original name of Bothin Dallemand & Co. These four remained in business together as importers and wholesalers of coffee, spices, baking products and extracts until May 27, 1887 when a dissolution of partnership was filed, by which Henry withdrew, leaving the other three to carry on the business under the name Dallemand and Co. The only two brand names known to have existed for Bothin Dallemand's lines of product were *Mrs. Mill's Cream Yeast Powder* and *Silver Spoon Bikini Baking Powder*, the latter being a trade name that apparently excited both Henry and Dallemand enough to warrant their application for trademark protection, as reported in a January 24, 1882 article in the *Sacramento Daily Union-Record*.[83]

Outwardly Bothin Dallemand & Co. may have been successful, but the business wasn't differentiating itself, nor were its products blossoming into household names. Indeed, searches of old product identities fail to bring up either of the company's two known brand names, and so one has to wonder if those labels were actually being marketed, as opposed to simply being used generically to identify categories of wholesale grocery goods for Mau Sadler's inventory purposes. The very lack of energetic marketing of Bothin Dallemand product lines suggests that by the mid-1880s Henry was probably losing interest in acting as just a jobber to supply a portion of the needs of his family's wholesale grocery enterprise.

If Henry was losing interest in Bothin Dallemand and its business model, what did he see in its place? The answer to that question seems to have been the Bothin Manufacturing Company, a business Henry founded in 1884 whose product lines remained in the tea, coffee and spice trade. This new company acted as a manufacturer, as opposed to an importer or jobber of other peoples' products. As an enterprise, it raises all sorts of questions, but it also provides answers to others about how he would deal with the seeming limitations of Bothin Dallemand. One question, of course, is why he didn't include either Mr. Dallemand or the Oberfelder brothers in this new opportunity. After all, the venture was proposing to do business in the same arenas already claimed by his still active and ongoing partnership with Dallemand. Assuming (as would seem to be the case) that the partners were still on friendly terms, one would expect Henry to offer his partners the chance to pool their talents and contacts and to use this new enterprise as a synergistic method to expand an already somewhat successful enterprise. The fact that he didn't suggests that other factors were in play.

First, product lines were undoubtedly of significance. When the partnership dissolved in 1887, Messrs. Dallemand and Oberfelder took the surviving company in the direction of liquor sales. In order to do that, one assumes that preparations for a total change in product lines had to have been in the works for some time, and inroads into product distribution rights had to have been underway for months and more probably several years. So, by 1884, Henry would likely have been well aware of the ultimate business goals of his partners, and for whatever the reason he had decided against participating.

Might Henry's reluctance to move in the direction of liquor sales have had anything to do with the temperance movement? I think the answer to that question would be no; however, it is worth a bit of analysis. Temperance was, of course, a social movement largely led by women in the nineteenth century who generally bore the brunt (and often the scars) of their husbands' alcohol-crazed abuses of them and their children. It was a movement that had been around a long time, but it seemed to gain traction during the antebellum years, when it was lumped in with fervent anti-slavery sentiments by reform-minded activists who saw both issues as works of the Devil. After the Civil War, those same activists were joined by churches (principally Baptist and Methodist) and to a lesser extent by some industrialists, who saw alcohol as the major cause of worker absenteeism and poor production. To the contrary, the post-Civil War years also saw large influxes of immigrants, particularly those from Ireland, Italy, and Germany, who clamored for the right to retain cherished customs of their home countries, which included the making of wine and the brewing and consumption of beer.

Meanwhile, as the 1880s approached, the Women's Christian Temperance Union (WCTU) began to gain membership, and as it grew stronger it joined with Susan B. Anthony and others who were doing battle to gain the vote for women. The Salvation Army, with its focus on temperance too, had been founded in 1864 and spread rapidly; however, neither of those groups posed a broad based threat to the liquor industry. The Anti-Saloon League, a powerhouse organization that relied on pressure politics to accomplish its goals and galvanized anti-alcohol sentiment more than any other organization, was nearly a decade away from formation, so, at the time Henry was deciding whether or not he wanted to align his future with spirits, the march toward Prohibition was still very much in its infancy and was not really being considered seriously by businessmen.

So, it seems that Henry's decision to steer clear of alcohol was not influenced by fear that the temperance movement might have a negative effect on sales. Nor have I been able to find any evidence at all that he had a personal bias against liquor. Indeed, to the contrary, later in his life he served as a director of the California Wine Association, an entity which held a near monopoly on the production and marketing of California wines. So, one has to assume his aversion to his partners' new direction probably had nothing to do with any negative sentiment, either emotional, philosophical or business based, about liquor sales. It is interesting that in all the research done on Henry's parents, there is absolutely no evidence that they were drinkers either of beer or other spirits. Their devotion to their Lutheran (and later Methodist) faith may have been the reason, although it also might have simply been that Ernst was a workaholic who derived his highs from making money as opposed to consuming liquor. That is not to say that he was a teetotaler, but it is to say that liquor did not ever, appear to enter into his value system in any significant way. It would seem that, to Henry, the liquor industry was simply one with which he had neither experience nor interest. Certainly, if he was considering how to make his next dollar, it would not have popped up anywhere close to the top of his list. Therefore, his natural conservatism and aversion to risk taking would provide ample reason for his decision to split with Dallemand and move off in his own direction, which was to maintain a tie with his family business while, at the same time, expanding his offerings in order to attract a broader clientele.

As early as 1886, Albert Dallemand had been working not only for the partnership with Henry, but also as a principal in the firm of George Simmons and Company, a company in the wholesale liquor business. That latter company also employed Tobias Oberfelder, who, as earlier noted, had been a principal of Bothin Dallemand as early as 1884. By early 1887, and certainly by the time of the filing of the partnership dissolution, Bothin Dallemand had completely transformed itself into a company whose sole reported business was wholesale liquor distribution.[84] Under the category of yesterday's news, a trade journal entitled *1887 Illustrated Review; San Francisco, Its Commercial Progress and Importance*[85] described Bothin Dallemand with the following language:

> Bothin, Dallemand & Co., Wine and Liquor Merchants, 215-217 California St. This house, which is one of the best known wholesale houses in San Francisco, was established by its present proprietors in 1879, and has attained its present prominence through their ability and excellent judgment in business affairs. The building they occupy is a three story brick...with a frontage of 35 feet and a depth extending back 109 feet. The establishment is completely stocked with a full line of choice foreign and domestic wines, brandies, whiskies, and the firm make a specialty in handling California wines and brandies of all descriptions... This house has established an enviable reputation for keeping only the best and purest articles, free from adulteration, and their trade is steadily increasing throughout the entire Pacific Coast and Eastern States. In fact their trade in the East has advanced to such proportions that some years ago the firm established a branch house in Chicago, under the name of Dallemand & Co... They ship, on average, about four car-loads of wines and brandies to the Chicago house every month. Five traveling salesmen are kept constantly on the road, operating the territory between Chicago and the Rocky Mountains, while as many more are employed on the coast... These men are enterprising, public spirited and prominent citizens, whose success in such a short period of time reflects favorably on the commerce and trade of the city... Their

establishment is justly a favorite with all those who desire brands of goods upon which they can rely.

That review was accurate enough for the Dallemand side of the arrangement. For Henry, on the other hand, it was totally inaccurate since there is no actual evidence that his name was, either within that time frame, or ever for that matter, associated with the sale of wine, beer or spirits. Henry's angel was his family grocery outlet, and given its clientele and their needs, if Henry was to continue to earn his bread and butter, he needed to keep his rudder pointed directly toward the baking powder, coffee, tea, and other products that were of interest to Mau Sadler and that had stood Bothin Dallemand in good stead earlier. By the same token, he also had to recognize that Mr. Dallemand would not have wanted so badly to change directions toward the liquor business if their coffee and spice company had been a standalone winner. Selling to a wholesale grocery business whose products were developed for high volume but low margin accounts was obviously not considered by either Dallemand or the Oberfelder brothers as a path to riches. Furthermore, the products themselves could not have been stellar consumer favorites if their ingredient cost structure was set to a level that allowed them to compete in the the low margin food sales marketplace.

One can see Henry, back as early as 1883, looking at his business opportunities in the coffee, tea and spice industry from several different directions. First, he must have realized that the profit margins would be greater if one could, by making his products himself, avoid having to pay the transit costs and manufacturing markup of others. Secondly, he would have understood that expanding his product line to target a more affluent customer base would provide the opportunity to expand his margins. Given the dynamic growth of the region, and therefore of his potential market, the business risks of such a venture would have been readily manageable. By the late 1870s and early 1880s, the City of San Francisco had become a booming metropolis in its own right, a city with a growth curve that was still pointing nearly straight up. While its population had surged by more than 50 percent during the decade of the 1870s, making it the ninth largest city in the nation by 1880, that growth showed no signs of letting up as the next decade got underway. Each year during the 1880s saw more than 5,000 new residents arriving in the city by the bay, and by 1890 San Francisco, whose population was then approaching 300,000, had overtaken Cincinnati to become the nation's 8th largest city. Furthermore, its port was thriving, with regularly scheduled commercial shipments both entering and leaving San Francisco to and from the Orient as well as Europe and the East Coast. Thus, it appears altogether reasonable to assume that there was plenty of profitable business available to both Bothin Dallemand (as importers) and Bothin Manufacturing Co. (as maker) of popular consumer products sold into the food industry.

For Henry, the allure of his own manufacturing company was the opportunity to reduce his costs by removing the middleman and also to develop a parallel product line that, untethered from Mau Sadler, could be molded into an independently successful and higher margin business in the specialty goods trade. That seems to be just what he did. He created *GIANT Baking Powder* and *Atlas Coffee*, and began to advertise them with some frequency, particularly in Sacramento, throughout 1883 and 1884.

To promote the former he hired a chemist who reported in writing that the baking powder was unadulterated. More specifically, the chemist wrote (and Henry used in his advertising):

San Francisco, September 24, 1883.
To H.E. Bothin, President, Bothin Manufacturing Co.

Dear Sir: After a careful and complete chemical analysis of a can of GIANT BAKING POWDER purchased by us in open market, we find that it does not contain alum, acid, phosphate, terra alba, or any injurious substance but is a pure, healthful Cream Tartar Baking Powder, and as such can recommend it to consumers.

Yours respectfully, Wm. T. Wenzell & Co, analytic chemists.[86]

As though the foregoing wasn't enough, he went on to publish corroborations of the findings of Wenzell and Co. through further testimonials from R. Beverly Cole, M.D., J.L. Meares, M.D., a Health Officer, and from Doctors Alfred Perry, W.A. Douglass and August Alers, all of whom signed as members of the San Francisco Board of Health.[87]

To add additional persuasion, Henry further enhanced his advertisement by obtaining from a chemist, Thomas Price, his statement that he had purchased not only GIANT brand Baking Powder but also its rivals, Royal, New England, Pioneer, Golden Gate and Dr. Price's Baking Powders and found that, whereas GIANT was tested at 196 cubic inches of gas per ounce, the others tested respectively at 139, 110, 107, 107, and 99 cubic inches of gas per ounce.[88]

Thus, Henry tried, through prominently displayed advertising throughout 1883 and 1884, to promote his baking powder product. He also tested a more subdued marketing approach for his coffee product, by buying less prominent print space for an ad that read: "*EVERYBODY* calls for *Atlas coffee. Try the Atlas coffee and be convinced. All grocers keep Atlas coffee for sale. Don't be put off by Atlas coffee. The best in the world is Atlas coffee.*"[89]

From the outset, it seems Henry was becoming more aggressive about marketing the product lines of his new enterprise and trying to differentiate them from the products that had been earlier sold by Bothin Dallemand, which may or may not have continued within the framework of the new company. In the absence of financial records we do not know which ad was more successful, but we do know that neither product became a household name. We also don't know enough about his products to know whether he began using more expensive ingredients or stuck with the low price ingredients he had earlier used with Bothin Dallemand, nor will we ever know if there were other flaws in his product that contributed to their failure to take off and become household names. However, we do know that by 1890 his business, even if not a home run, was making him a good living.

Unfortunately, there is no evidence that Henry's effort succeeded beyond a modest degree. Given his frugal nature, even modest success translated to an expanding pocketbook, with which he would soon begin making investments that were to pay off handsomely over time. Still, Henry's passion was his work, and the modest performance of the Bothin Manufacturing Company was probably due not so much to a lack of the energy required to build product identity and loyalty as it was to the result of a change in the direction of his interests.

8.
Expansion and New Beginnings

The Gold Rush had propelled San Francisco to prominence in the 1850s and had established it as a premier banking and financial center. For the next thirty years, its primacy west of Chicago was unquestioned. During those years its focus, and that of its leading businessmen, was on wealth creation based on resource extraction and processing as well as logging, agriculture, and food processing.[90] But while the timber cutting, wheat and cattle businesses, and food industry were important job and wealth creators, without question gold and silver were the driving forces in the young state's economy. For example, one of the principal uses of timber was to supply the need to support the ever deeper tunnels and shafts being dug to get to those precious metals, whereas agriculture, as well as the processing of food, were necessary to provide sustenance for the miners and all the people whose businesses supplied those miners with tools, mining equipment (including drills, rock crushers, hoists, pumps and nozzles), clothing, boots, housing, and entertainment. At its heart, California was, until the decade of the 1880s, a commercial center, not a manufacturing city, and this was so both because of a scarcity of demand beyond the mining community as well as an inadequate labor force.

Before the 1880s, the West had simply too small a population base spread over too broad a geographic area to support a thriving manufacturing environment. In 1870, Seattle was a small town of only 1,107 souls, Los Angeles had a total population of only 5,728, the whole state of Oregon had fewer than 90,000 people living in it, and San Francisco's 150,000 people represented 26 percent of the total population of the state, which was then just 560,000. Compare those statistics to 1890, when Seattle had grown to 42,000, Los Angeles to 50,000, and California to 1,213,000; and then look at those same numbers ten years later at the turn of the 20th century, when Seattle had doubled to 80,000, Los Angeles had doubled to 102,000, Oregon's population had increased by more than fourfold to 413,000, and California had continued its growth path and was now home to 1,485,000 people. In large part this epic pace of growth took place because of railroads, which transported people and freight, and gave rise to a more mobile society than had ever before existed. And those railroads were still expanding and putting down new rails in an ever-widening arc that was inexorably connecting all parts of the country to each other. Now suddenly there was adequate demand in the western United States to support a thriving manufacturing climate, and there were also plenty of people to supply the labor to build the products that a growing population required.

The sheer magnitude of the influx of people helped in another way as well, by driving down labor costs, since all of those new arrivals had to compete for jobs. That competition for jobs was made more acute when the Chinese laborers completed their work on the railroad and returned to San Francisco in droves, thereby adding even more to the supply of workers to man the factories and industrial plants of the new wave of manufacturers.

While employers welcomed that influx of inexpensive labor, it came at a tremendous cost to those who needed working wages to put food on the table. Desperation abounded, and as a result tempers flared and people expressed their frustrations, often through violence. Although efforts to organize workers had been around for decades with varying degrees of success, the Panic of 1873 and the grim years that followed for workers fanned increasingly confrontational rhetoric. In the West, a populace that was already upset at the railroads, who seemed to control not just transportation, but jobs and land prices and local politics as well, was joined by frustrated farm laborers laid off due to a severe drought in 1876 and 1877. Not only did those disgruntled workers take aim at capitalists, and the railroad barons in particular, but they also rose up even more vehemently than they had earlier against the mostly single male Chinese, who were perceived as driving down wages to the point where white working families feared they could no longer survive.

In 1877 a bloody nationwide rail strike known as "The Great Uprising" began in the East and gained sympathy among San Francisco's working class. They formed a workingman's association whose meetings were held nightly on the sandlots adjoining City Hall.

There, under the influence of a number of orators, they passed various resolutions, including supporting the striking railroad employees, calling for government to cease its subsidies of the already wealthy railroads, decrying military use of force against strikers, demanding a universal eight hour day, and imposing stiff taxes on the wealthy. More and more stridently they also demanded the expulsion of the Chinese.[91]

The sandlot protestors organized themselves and formed a

Labor organizaer Denis Kearney

political party. The initial success of the Workingmen's Party came at the ballot box. Their candidates succeeded in winning several elections in 1878 and 1879, and so they were positioned well, with delegates to a Constitutional Convention to be held in Sacramento in 1879. At that convention, the party pushed through numerous anti-Chinese recommendations to the Legislature, most of which resulted in strongly worded anti-Chinese laws being passed that essentially left the Chinese even worse off under the newly enacted laws of the state than before and without access to any means of redress, or to state licenses, or the ability to own property. While most of those laws had already been found unconstitutional or were, within a year or so, overturned for other reasons by the Courts, they nonetheless made it clear that a highly biased voice of the people against the Chinese was still powerful and would continue to be heard for many years thereafter.

By the end of 1880 the Workingmen's Party had largely collapsed under the weight of its infighting, but the voice of labor had been heard. As much as California was seemingly on the cusp of enormous growth potential, there would always be an undercurrent of labor unrest and anti-Chinese sentiment, an undercurrent that, however, at least for the decade of the 1880s, seemed to be drowned out by the sheer volume of the opportunities at hand.

San Francisco was not only looking at fulfilling regional demand. Its natural port, enhanced by the railhead in Oakland, enabled it to act as the conduit for transshipment, not just regionally and nationally, but globally, of both imports and exports and so to become an international city. Arriving as he did just two years after the completion of the transcontinental railroad, Henry, like all other San Francisco entrepreneurs, watched as those growth dynamics became apparent and as this so-called Second Industrial Revolution transformed what had, just twenty-five years earlier, been just a small, sleepy hamlet into a bustling metropolis.

And yet, as large and important as California, and specifically

San Francisco and its surroundings were becoming, in some ways the state remained nearly as insular and protected as it had been years earlier, when geography and transportation stood as obstacles in the way of even more dramatic growth than actually occurred. For instance, the high shipping rates charged by the Central Pacific Railroad made it expensive for eastern industries to penetrate the western marketplace, and this provided California's own budding manufacturing base with a tariff-like protection that enabled new local industries to gain traction while largely enjoying sanctuary from outside competition.

The combination of events and circumstances that created a sense of euphoria and of unimaginable opportunity caused San Francisco's manufacturing output to double during the 1870s, and by 1880 it accounted for one-third of all jobs, and "exceeded the output of all other western cities combined."[92] Some of the more important local industries that thrived during the 1870s and 1880s included meat packing and processing, lumber and woodworking, woolens and textiles, boot and shoe making, sugar refining, food processing, and ironworks. The first of these, which included the vertically integrated Miller and Lux empire, consisted of cattle yards, wholesale butcheries, tanneries, packing houses, glue works and tallow plants. Food processors included Ghirardelli Chocolate and Coffee works, National and Capital flour mills, Tillman-Bendels coffee and spice mill, and J.A. Folger Coffee Company, to name just a few. Within the ironworks sector were included Union Iron Works (the largest), Risden Ironworks, Pioneer Ironworks, Eureka Foundry, National Ironworks, Golden West Plating, California Engine Works, Pacific Hardware and Steel, and Judson Manufacturing Company, among others.[93] Manufactured products that emerged from these and other new manufacturing enterprises included carriages (and later cars and trucks), chemicals, ships, refined sugar, finished wood products including cabinets, furniture, pianos, paint, beer, wine, marble, and, importantly, infrastructure to support the expanding cities and new communities that were increasingly dotting the map. By the late 1880s, all those industries and many more were represented in San Francisco and its immediate neighboring towns down the Peninsula and across the bay.

Against this backdrop of burgeoning growth, Henry and his siblings began dabbling in a new direction, not initially to replace their foothold in the grocery industry, but more seemingly as a sideline investment. As early as the mid-1880s, their imaginations became captivated by a new industry altogether, one that had nothing to do with food but rather fed the needs of the iron horse, the ships that plied the seas nearby, and the infrastructure that was booming all around them. The Mau family, the Sadlers, Henry, and indeed Albert Dallemand as well, during the mid-1880s, together became the owners of a company called Pacific Iron and Nail Company. The May 3 1888 edition of the *Daily Alta California* reported that three days earlier that company had held its annual meeting, where Messrs. H.J. Sadler, P.A. Wagner, William Wright, H.E. Bothin, R. Sadler, W.F. Mau and Albert Dallemand had all been re-elected directors, with H.J. Sadler elected President, W.F. Mau Secretary, and William Wright general manager. That they were re-elected in 1888, means that they had been running the business for at least one, and probably several years before that. Although that business ultimately shut down in 1899 after a fire destroyed the plant, the fact remains that by the mid-1880s, Henry had put his toes into the water in at least one business opportunity that was totally different from the path he had trodden up to that time. While his siblings would return to their comfort zone in the world of food, Henry's interest had been piqued, and from that time forward his interest in coffees, teas and spices would give way to a fascination with and a commitment to the hardware trade, where he soon began to focus much more of his energy.

From 1884 to 1893, the *City Directory* continued to list Henry as President of Bothin Manufacturing Company. While he was clearly pondering the wisdom of remaining in that business, it is interesting to look at the positive side of the coffee and spice industry from the perspective of an insider in a competing company, one that had made a commitment to that industry and was well on the way to seeing it pay off handsomely. That company, A. Schilling and Co., was founded by two Germans, August Schilling and George Volkmann. Both had been born in Bremen, Germany in 1854, making them just a year younger than Henry. By 1879, Schilling had already risen to the position of partner in J.A. Folger Company, then the largest coffee company in the west, while Volkmann was just being recognized by Folger for his business talents. The two left Folger and, in 1881, set up their own company, which manufactured the same sorts of products that Bothin Manufacturing Company did. Coffees, spices, flavoring extracts and baking powders were in great demand, and so there was a profitable niche market within which to make a handsome living for those willing to commit themselves to it.[94] According to Daniel Volkmann, the youngest son of George and longtime Schilling executive, "many grades [of these products] were offered and, as was the custom of the time, all were adulterated in varying degrees. For example, coffee was mixed with chicory, tea was artificially colored, cinnamon was mixed with almond shells…"[95] Mr. Volkmann went on to say that "Prepared baking powder was comparatively new and its usage grew rapidly…and for many years baking powder was the backbone of the business, representing the largest portion of the sales and gross profit dollar."[96]

August Schilling proved that the manufacture and sale of coffees, teas, baking powders and other consumables could be highly profitable. What was it, then, that caused Henry's business to perform less well than Mr. Schilling's? If one were to guess (and unfortunately, the absence of records forces that), one would very likely look with hindsight at the tremendous success he was to have through hard work and dedication in a different industry, and conclude that his heart was simply no longer in the food industry. It was, after all, for him a business that had apron strings to his sisters and their husbands. They would always be his older siblings who knew more than he, and they would always offer their opinions about what would work and what wouldn't. In truth, they would have earned the right to their opinions, but still, given Henry's nature, that sort of interference would not have played well with either his ambition or his ego. Were I a betting man, I would wager money that Bothin Manufacturing Co. stagnated primarily because Henry couldn't separate it from family and because he found another industry that captivated his imagination.

Before leaving the coffee and spice business, it is interesting to note that Bothin Manufacturing Company's plant was located in Sacramento. Had the company been formed in the mid-to-late 1860s, the choice of Sacramento would have been obvious, since in those days Sacramento had been the intended western terminus of the Central Pacific Railroad. Even during the 1870s, a case might have been made for Sacramento, since that city remained a hub for transcontinental traffic as well as for north-south rail traffic between Seattle and San Diego. However, by 1883 the western terminus of the Central Pacific (by then the Southern Pacific) was Oakland (albeit by a rather circuitous and out of the way route through Stockton and Niles Canyon), and there was good north-south rail coverage out of Oakland as well. Nonetheless, and for whatever the reason, Henry located his plant in Sacramento, where he was seen as a highly respected employer. Several articles in local Sacramento newspapers of the day complimented him for giving his workers extra holidays, for contributing to city beautification projects, and for being a model employer. Although Henry lived in San Francisco, he traveled frequently to Sacramento to oversee his plant, and while there he typically stayed at the Golden Eagle Hotel, then one of Sacramento's better hotels.

While on the subject of lodging, it is clear from the hotels he frequented that Henry was, by the first half of the 1880s, living well. For example, during his early years in San Francisco he had listed his residence in several different modest hotel/rooming houses such as The Commercial Hotel (1876-1878) Holden House (1879/80), and Marlborough House (1880/81), but by 1884 (and possibly earlier) he was living, when not staying at the Golden Eagle Hotel in Sacramento, at San Francisco's finest hotel, the Palace.

The Palace Hotel viewed from Montgomery Street, 1887

The Palace Hotel is perhaps best known for the fact that Enrico Caruso, the famed tenor, was a guest there at the time of the 1906 earthquake and fire.[97] However, the Palace was an institution well before the quake that caused its destruction. The hotel, when it opened, was the largest in the world; it was built in just two years, between 1873 when ground was broken and 1875 when it opened. It was the brainchild of the banker and dreamer William Ralston, who spent over $5,000,000 of money invested by others in his Bank of California. When it was completed (several months after Ralston's death)[98], the Palace was a seven story structure that had 755 rooms, 7000 windows, 804 fireplaces, the first five hydraulic elevators in the west, air conditioning in each room, and bricks produced in a brick factory specially set up to provide materials for the hotel. Even its hardwoods came from an oak forest purchased specifically for the Hotel's construction needs.[99] Once completed, its operation was absolutely first class. It has been said that it "gave its guests apartments and a cuisine which, for comfort and luxury, are unrivaled in either hemisphere…"[100] So, while Henry seems to have lived frugally in other respects, he did not skimp when it came to his living quarters.

9.
Marriage to Jennie Whittier

Sometime during 1884, while Henry was busy operating his two businesses and trying to decide the direction he should take them, he met and wooed Lottie Jane (Jennie) Whittier, the daughter of Frank Whittier and Charlotte Robinson Whittier. Frank Whittier was an extremely successful and wealthy businessman who had made his fortune in the paint business. Jennie, ten years younger than Henry, was one of the most sought after young ladies in San Francisco at the time.

Jennie was the Whittiers' eldest daughter. She was born December 12, 1863 in San Francisco and grew up in the city, except for a year-long period early in her life when, because of a family tragedy, she spent a number of months in the care of her grandparents in Vienna (pronounced *Vye-enna*), Maine. Her parents, who had both been born in that small town, had, in early 1865, returned to their birthplace on what was planned as a short vacation to visit friends and family members. Jennie, who was then just a toddler, and her older brother, Frank, both accompanied their parents. During their stay, young Frank became ill and, on August 25th of that year, died. Jennie's mother was devastated, so much so that she spontaneously lost her hearing. In an effort to overcome their grief and also to search (unsuccessfully it would turn out) for medical specialists who might help to restore her mother's hearing, her parents traveled to Boston and New York in search of ear specialists. Finding nobody in this country who could help her, the couple continued their search abroad and spent several months traveling through England, France, Germany and elsewhere on the continent in their futile search for a cure. During that time, young Jennie was cared for by her maternal grandmother. Her parents finally came back to Maine at the end of 1865 and spent several months there before returning home to San Francisco in the spring of 1866. Once back home, Jennie attended school, ultimately graduating from Mills College in the East Bay.

Jennie had three younger siblings. Her sister, Nancy Edith, was born on December 7, 1867. She would later die in 1887 (a year after Jennie and Henry were married) of an unknown illness. The Whittier's fourth child, William Robinson Whittier, grew up to become a playboy and alcoholic whose most enduring legacy, one which persists to this day, is being known as the ghost who reportedly inhabits the basement and wine cellar of the lavish home at 2090 Jackson Street in San Francisco that Frank built later in his life. It became, for a time prior to World War II, the German Consulate, and later became, for many years, the headquarters of the California Historical Society. Jennie's youngest sibling, Martha Smith (Mattie) Whittier went on to marry well and to have a very good and full life.

Frank's wife, Charlotte, was his childhood sweetheart, and after Frank left Maine in search of a career, they kept in touch by letters. Frank's search ended up taking him to San Francisco, where he found initial success in business and came to feel confident that he would be able to support a wife and raise a family. At that point, he went back to Vienna with the intent of marrying Charlotte. They were indeed married soon thereafter, and the couple began their trip back to California just hours after the wedding. They lived happily together for twenty-seven years before Charlotte was killed tragically in 1885, in a carriage accident that occurred while she was visiting friends, just before a planned trip east. As she approached the home of a friend, the horses pulling her carriage were spooked by several children throwing a ball. Charlotte was thrown from the carriage and suffered head injuries from which she died several days later. Her death occurred just a year before Jennie and Henry were married.

Although no records survive regarding how or when Henry and Jennie met, it is known that both Henry and Jennie's father had business operations not just in San Francisco but in Sacramento as well, where the main plant of Whittier Fuller & Co. was located. Jennie herself spent time in Sacramento and had friends there. For instance, one newspaper article,[101] reported a moonlight trip that Jennie and others, including Lizzie Dillman, who was later one of Jennie's bridesmaids, took on the Sacramento River on the small steamer *Margie*. Henry's name does not appear among the party-goers on that occasion, but who knows if they met at another time while both were in the state's capital? Whether they met in San Francisco or in Sacramento, Henry and young Jennie hit it off and were soon engaged. As the wedding drew near, Jennie and her father, who was still in mourning after Charlotte's recent death, took an extended trip to Europe, returning in July, just three months prior to the wedding.

One can well imagine that Jennie might have been a spoiled young lady, and indeed all signs point in that direction. She grew up in a household where grief over the death of her older brother lingered on through her mother's lifelong deafness, where her father was a nonstop workaholic with a soft spot for family but a lack of understanding of how to be a parent, where her younger brother was an irresponsible no-good, and where her younger sister, Nancy, was sickly. Jennie herself was an avid horseback rider, having developed that interest by way of her father's passion for fast horses. She was also very much an extrovert who loved parties, games, and the social whirl.

William Franklin Whittier

Charlotte Robinson Whittier

Before delving into the marriage of Jennie to Henry it is well to remember the old wives' tale that women often tend to marry people like their father. Jennie's case would seem to prove that adage. Frank Whittier was a fascinating man who had many similarities to Henry. Frank was the youngest of twelve children, while Henry was the second youngest in his family of eight children. Each relied on siblings more than their parents, in Frank's case apprenticing himself for six years to his older brother in the wholesale paint business. Each left home at a young age and traveled several thousand miles west to San Francisco in search of wealth and financial success, and each was a hard-nosed and driven businessman who achieved that goal. In describing Frank, his biographer, Mary Whitney, has used words like "intensely ambitious," "tenacious," "stubborn," "shrewd," "dictatorial," "blunt," and "dedicated to the almighty dollar." He was tough and intensely disliked, but he was also very successful—if wealth is the criterion one uses to measure success. After initially going to work for a paint, oil and glass company, he (with two partners) bought the company three years later when he was in his mid-twenties. He and his partners expanded the company's product line, took advantage of new silvering techniques to produce better mirrors, introduced coal oil lamps, and soon became the leading paint and glass company on the West Coast. In 1868, Whittier, who had by then bought out his partners, merged his company with William Parmer Fuller's paint company, calling it Whittier Fuller and Company. The enterprise flourished, ultimately buying a fleet of twelve clipper ships to transport its products internationally to countries as far distant as Australia, Japan, China and even Siberia. Even more ships were later added in order to ship products to ports on the east coast of the United States, thereby saving on the exorbitantly high cost of rail transport charged by the monopolistic Central Pacific Railroad.[102]

Jennie Whittier Bothin, circa 1904

For all of his successes in the paint business (and the foregoing is but a brief snapshot), Frank Whittier still had enough energy left in the late 1880s to become engaged in a mammoth real estate development project that involved the construction of the 122-foot high Hemet Dam in the San Jacinto Mountains in Southern California. The purpose of the dam was to provide water with which to transform largely inhospitable desert land into arable farmland. Whittier, who essentially provided all the capital for this undertaking, purchased thousands of acres of surrounding land, created the town of Hemet, and then set about building the dam. A good deal of information about this venture can be found in the California Supreme Court case of *Allen v. Railroad Commission*, 1918, 179 Cal 68, a case which wasn't finally decided until after Whittier's death in 1917 at the age of 85.

Jennie and Henry were married in San Francisco on October 5, 1886. Their wedding was a grand event with a guest list of approximately 400 of the leading citizens of San Francisco and its surroundings.[103] The guest list included, among others, Mr. and Mrs. Charles Crocker, Mr. and Mrs. Albert Dallemand (Henry's partner), Mr. and Mrs. Timothy Hopkins (son of Mark Hopkins of the Big Four), Mr. and Mrs. Charles Lux, Mr. and Mrs. Henry Miller (who along with Charles Lux was the largest landowner in the State of California), Honorable and Mrs. J.D. Murphy, Mr. and Mrs. James Phelan (very successful banker and parents of the future mayor of San Francisco and U.S. Senator, James D. Phelan), Senator and Mrs. Leland Stanford, Mr. and Mrs. J.B. Stetson, Mr. and Mrs. Claus Spreckels (sugar magnate), Mrs. Charles McLaughlin (whose late husband was a highly successful and very wealthy railroad builder and who, coincidentally, adopted the stepdaughter of my paternal great grandfather, Maurice Casey), Mrs. W.C. Ralston (William Ralston's widow), and many, many other prominent San Franciscans of the time.

To place Henry's and Jennie's wedding year in context, it is interesting to note that 1886 was also the year that President Grover Cleveland became the first sitting President to be married while in office when he married Frances Folsom at the White House. It was also the year that Coca Cola was invented, that Karl Benz was awarded a patent for the first gasoline powered automobile, that the Statue of Liberty was dedicated, and, finally, it was the year that the Apache chief, Geronimo, surrendered, thereby ending the last major U.S. war with this country's Native Americans.

The wedding was an Episcopalian service held at the First Congregational Church, where Frank and Charlotte Whittier had been loyal parishioners and generous benefactors for many, many years. A grand reception followed at the Whittier home. The couple spent their honeymoon in Monterey and then moved into her father's home for a year while their own home, a wedding gift to them from Mr. Whittier, was being built.

By 1888 Henry was listing his address at his and Jennie's new home[104] at the corner of Jackson and Van Ness Ave. in what was then considered a very fashionable part of town.[105] The house was a grand Queen Anne style structure that was photographed often and was considered a classic example of that style of architecture, which was then becoming quite popular in San Francisco. It was a large three-story house with a typical corner tower, "ponderous" chimneys, complex rooflines, and a balcony at the front. The house was sized for a large family. Unfortunately, and despite their best efforts, Henry and Jennie were unable to have the family they had envisioned.

According to Henry's and Jennie's daughter, Genevieve, the couple had five children, of whom only Genevieve survived to adulthood. Unfortunately, birth and death certificates were consumed in the 1906 earthquake and fire, and so there are no official records of either the births or deaths of Henry's and Jennie's children; however, we know from Henry's letter to Emma dated July 2, 1890 that their first born was a girl who was born in late 1887 and who died shortly thereafter. As Henry put it in that letter, "I also lost a precious little daughter some three years ago." The second child, Frank Whittier Bothin, was born in about 1888 and died in 1901 of infantile paralysis.[106] Another son was born in about 1890 and died soon after. Genevieve, who was born on December 17, 1894, was their fourth child. An obituary appearing in *The San Francisco Call* on November 4, 1900 reported another child, the couple's fifth, a daughter, who was born in 1900 and died on November 3rd of that same year at the age of eight months. Because of the destruction of vital records in the 1906 calamity, there is very little else known about Genevieve's siblings and the tragedy of their early deaths.

The Bothin home at Jackson and Van Ness Avenue, San Francisco

Moving into their home may very well have been the high point of Henry and Jennie's marriage. Although they remained together for twenty-one years, Henry conceded publicly at the time of their divorce that only about six of their years together were happy ones. As a couple, they were like oil and water. Henry was driven by a need to succeed in business, and in that way he was much like Jennie's father, but Henry was also extremely frugal in his private life. Jennie's interests ran far more to parties and social events. While she was an excellent horse woman, a trait she came by naturally given her father's stables, private race track, and interest in race horses, Henry had no interest in horses other than as a necessary means of transportation. Where Henry wanted to live in the suburbs, Jennie was not accustomed to country life and, instead, enjoyed the social whirls of city life. But probably the most serious obstacle to a happy marriage was the devastating loss of four of their five children. Henry's outlet was to give generously to charitable causes involving children, whereas Jennie neither understood nor supported those efforts. In the end, their differences were to become irreconcilable and finally terminate in a far too public divorce. But that didn't happen until the first decade of the twentieth century, and there is much to learn about Henry before that unfortunate chapter.

10.
Turning Point: Judson Manufacturing Company

Beginning in 1887, Henry's business focus changed. That was the year he dissolved his partnership with Albert Dallemand, and although he would continue for another six years at the helm of the Bothin Manufacturing Company, clearly his heart was no longer in the grocery industry, and he was beginning to get far more excited over the future of iron and steel. By 1893, he had sold Bothin Manufacturing Company to his brother, J.C.

For what happened next, the best evidence is contained in a letter dated November 8, 1892 that Henry clumsily penned to his sister, Emma. In it he wrote the following:

> "Some two years ago, as my interests in the iron business were quite large, [and] to give Julius a chance to get up again, I sold him my manufacturing business and took his note for same, that through mismanagement and extravagance is all lost and I may still lose more coming on top of my Father's conduct at his time in life. You can imagine how I

feel. I am for the first time in fifteen years trying to economize and know what worry is."

By 1894 the Bothin Manufacturing Company seems to have totally disappeared off the radar. While no evidence has been uncovered to suggest that Henry's concern over contingent liabilities arising out of Julius' mismanagement ever actually materialized, still it is clear that he continued for some time to smart over Julius' incompetence, which ended up wasting a perfectly good business as well as years of Henry's time spent building it into a successful enterprise. Whether Henry ever forgave Julius is not known, but there is no record of any mention by him thereafter of his brother's name.

As hard as it may have been for Henry to swallow the forced closing of his manufacturing company, by then his focus had switched over to Judson Manufacturing Company, a company he had invested in heavily and over which he had gained full control by 1889. Judson made forged products out of iron and was a business of an entirely different type than the food industry where he had cut his teeth.

To understand why it made sense for Henry to change business direction and hitch his wagon to a totally new and different sort of industry, one needs first to recall that the population of the West, and more particularly San Francisco and its surroundings, had blossomed. With an explosion of new residents and a vastly enlarged labor pool had come a change in business focus, to the point that investors were beginning to seek out manufacturing opportunities to invest in and, in some cases, to operate. One of the most obvious of those opportunities was building the infrastructure needs of both the businesses and the communities that were beginning to proliferate. How better to participate in that growth than to marry one's business future to iron as well as steel, the former having obvious and well established uses and the latter being a product that, although already proven as a building material by those paying attention, was still little understood by many, particularly in the West.

Iron, of course, had been used by mankind since around 2,000 BC for the production of tools as well as weapons. It is the earth's fourth most abundant element and makes up more than 5 percent of our planet's crust.[107] For centuries mankind has created commercially useable iron by a process known as smelting, in which the ore is heated in a charcoal fire to release its oxygen, thereby creating a serviceable product called wrought iron, which typically has a carbon content in the range of .02-.08 percent. Wrought iron is malleable and can be hammered and forged into a variety of helpful tools and handiwork. Its downside is that it lacks the hardness and durability required of some tools and products. Then, four to five hundred years ago, a new alternative process was developed with the advent of blast furnaces that allow the metal ore to be heated to very high temperatures, during which the iron begins both to melt and also to rapidly absorb carbon, resulting in a hard but brittle product with a carbon content in the range of 3-5 percent. This concoction is called cast iron, a commodity that cannot be hammered lest it crack or fracture, but that can be poured into molds to make cast iron stoves, kitchen equipment, cannons, and other implements. While useful in some settings, the problems of cracking and fracturing of cast iron had been shown, through several tragic bridge collapses, to be of limited use in railroads and other heavy uses that placed a strain on joints and lengthy runs such as girders. In 1847, the bridge over the river Dee in England, whose infrastructure was largely cast iron, collapsed under the weight of the train crossing it. That event cost five lives and was followed by several other bridge collapses in England in 1860, 1861, and 1879, the latter of which, known as the Tay Bridge Disaster, cost 75 lives. In each case the bridge in question had used cast iron girders that, even though allegedly supported by wrought iron trusses, had fractured and caused the trains crossing them to fall through with disastrous results.

Given the huge importance railroads had assumed during the latter half of the 19th century, many people and companies were scrambling to figure out how to create a product using iron ore that could combine the hardness and durability of cast iron while eliminating the disadvantages caused by the latter's brittleness and tendency to crack. Clearly, it was the carbon content that controlled the outcome, and the goal was to develop a product within the carbon midrange of .2-1.5 percent. The solution to the dilemma had eluded good minds for years, until Henry Bessemer came up with his elegant process for the commercially viable creation of steel.

To appreciate what Bessemer did, it is helpful to understand a bit better how iron reacts to heat and chemicals and how steel is formed. Steel is the end product of a process in which iron is heated, impurities are removed, and carbon is added, in order to create a product containing the desired hardness and other properties. It is a complex process, involving chemical changes when certain harmful elements and minerals (sulfur, silica, nitrogen and phosphorous, for example) must be removed, whereas other elements (nickel, manganese, vanadium, and chromium, for instance) can be added to improve tensile strength, stability and hardness. Bessemer designed a device he called a "converter," a large receptacle with holes at the bottom, into which he blew cold compressed air. He found that the process removed all the carbon and silicon and yet, to his own surprise, left the iron even hotter. From there, he could add a compound consisting of carbon plus whatever other chemicals were desired as additives in order to create the specified hardness and malleability. In short, the process of turning iron into steel that had earlier taken days and required a lot of extra and expensive fuel to keep the iron molten the entire time could now be accomplished in the space of minutes and at a fraction of the cost.

Later improvements to the process overcame some initial shortcomings, and by 1876 the improved process had resulted in dramatic savings in the cost of steel production. For instance, whereas in 1867 the cost of iron rails was $83 per ton compared to $170 per ton for steel, by 1884 iron rails were no longer even being made, and steel rails were selling for $32 per ton. Not only had costs taken a nosedive, but the quality of the product had greatly improved the railroads' bottom line in other ways as well. Durability of rails had increased fivefold to as long as ten years each, and the weight those rails could support had skyrocketed from 8 tons to seventy, thereby enabling heavier and more powerful locomotives as well as far greater freight capacity.[108]

Clearly steel was coming of age as the ultimate successor to iron for many applications, but there was still a strong market for both wrought iron and cast iron, and even that market had not been well penetrated in San Francisco or in the West. A glimpse of the status of the ironworks industry in and around San Francisco in the early 1880s, some fifteen years after the Bessemer process was developed, is interesting and worth pursuing a bit. The first ironworks in San Francisco had been started by Peter Donahue in the early 1850s when he set up "... a primitive shop in a tent on Montgomery Street in which were located a blacksmith's bellow, an anvil, an old steamship funnel for a furnace, and scrap iron from the great fire of 1851."[109] Later, with advances in iron fabrication, that small venture went on to become the Union Iron Works, which would be known for decades as a well-run shipbuilding company. Still, that one business was woefully inadequate to meet the suddenly burgeoning demands for both cast iron and wrought iron that were coming largely from the railroad boom. For instance, when the Big Four began building the Central Pacific Railroad in 1863, and indeed straight through to its completion in 1869, not a single rail was built in San Francisco. Indeed, as noted by the authors of *A Romance of Steel in California*, (hereafter referred to as *ARSC*) "every scrap of iron used in the mines, used on that great railroad, and used in all building construction prior to 1866 came by ship around the Horn from the east."[110] Although too late to profit from the Central Pacific's monumental achievement, in 1866, Senator James G. Fair, who had made his fortune in the Comstock mines, William Alvord, a wholesale hardware importer and the Mayor of San Francisco from 1871 to 1873, and D.O. Mills, a railroad owner and one of the original founders of the Bank of California, founded the Pacific Rolling Mills, and with that, the iron industry in San Francisco became more firmly established.[111] Over the ensuing years, the shareholders of Pacific Rolling Mills Company (who in time included such other well-known names as John Parrott, William Ralston, Antoine Borel, George Whittell and James Rolph, among many other notables and astute investors)[112] profited greatly as that industry grew exponentially due to ever increasing demands for finished iron.

As much as the presence of Pacific Rolling Mills enabled the City to begin to satisfy its need for both cast and wrought iron, demand (particularly in the gold and silver mines in both California and the Comstock in Nevada) quickly overcame that company's capacity and created opportunities for others to develop competing ironworks. Other iron products that were in growing demand included piston rods, steamboat shafts, axles and connecting rods for locomotives, railroad spikes,

James Fair

D.O. Mills

William Alvord

and rails for the numerous narrow gauge railroads that were either being built or planned on the coast. More specifically, in 1873 alone, Pacific Rolling Mills filled orders for, among others projects, drive shafts weighing about ten tons each for both the steamers *Arizona* and *Orizaba*, iron bumpers for the cars of the Virginia and Truckee Railroad, which was owned by D.O. Mills, 150 tons of metal hardware for the Central Pacific Railroad, and many miles of rails for the Seattle Coal Mining Company, the Nevada Central narrow gauge railroad, the California Pacific Railroad, and the Stockton and Copperopolis Railroad.[113] They also filled orders for the rails, yokes, cables and other requirements of Andrew Hallidie's famed San Francisco cable cars.

While California was concentrating its efforts on the production of iron, primarily for the railroad and shipbuilding industries, Andrew Carnegie was beginning to produce steel on the East Coast and the Great Lakes regions of the country. His steel would soon replace both wrought iron and cast iron as the preferred material for rails in particular, for which there seemed to be never ending demand. Investors in San Francisco seem to have failed to appreciate the degree to which steel would improve and ultimately displace most of the products that Pacific Rolling Mills was turning out. It wasn't until 1884 that finally Pacific Rolling Mills built its first open hearth furnace and began, for the first time ever, to produce steel from scratch on the West Coast. Before that, steel products had been produced in California; however, the resource came from large blocks of steel called "blooms" that had been produced in Europe and transported to this country by ship, an obviously expensive process involving not only paying the producer his profit for the creation of the bloom, but paying the costs of transit by ship around the Horn as well. Once here, those steel blooms could be rolled into the desired shape and size; however, margins were tight and the threat from Carnegie's fierce competiveness very real.

As expensive as it was, producing steel from blooms was a money-maker while it lasted. One early example surfaced in the early 1880s when Irving Scott, of the Union Iron Works, argued that favorable West Coast weather considerations would speed construction by enabling men to work year round, and so he convinced the Department of the Navy in Washington to award his company the contract to construct the navy's newest cruiser, *Charleston*, on the West Coast. Other ship contracts followed, and they, along with ever-increasing demand from railroads and other sources that were also experiencing rapid growth, whetted the appetites of entrepreneurs and investors.

After Pacific Rolling Mills built its open hearth furnace in 1884 and began producing steel using the Bessemer process, the company enjoyed fifteen years of profitable operations. As stated by the authors of *ARSC*:

> "Nearly every great structure built on the coast from Baker City to San Diego during those years drew on the Pacific Rolling Mills for iron and steel. Railroads, cable roads, bridges, dams and skyscrapers flowed from its furnaces. The Mills Building on Montgomery Street—a distinguished office building; the first Call Building, now the reconstructed Central Tower at Third and Market—which withstood the earthquake and fire of 1906; the early Chronicle Building; the beams and dome of the original San Francisco City Hall; the Emporium with its immense dome on Market Street; the unusual underground yokes for Adolph Sutro's Omnibus Cable Company—all these were fabricated at the mill."

As useful as Bessemer's breakthrough was to many industries, ultimately, it was the railroads, whose proliferation and importance to trade were making them indispensable, that created the incentives that set the stage for the creation of Bessemer's process for creating commercially viable steel, and that in turn fueled the creation of a steel industry which, up to the late 1860s, simply did not exist.

Andrew Carnegie, a Scot by birth who began his storied career in 1853 as a telegraph operator for the Pennsylvania Railroad Company, is the man most widely credited with the development of the industry; whose growth he felt would be fed by the demand for steel rails for the rapidly expanding railroads that were proliferating across the nation. They needed not just rails and other heavy weight-bearing components, but they also needed their own infrastructure, including a means to support their passage across rivers and canyons, among other geographic obstacles. And so it was really no surprise that the first proof of the value and usefulness of steel came about with the construction of a bridge, specifically the Eads Bridge, a huge and complex river crossing project that was completed in 1874. There, steel was the primary material used, in a radical design for a 6,400 foot long arched bridge spanning the Mississippi River at St. Louis; a bridge that was widely believed to be impossible to construct. It was designed by James Buchanan Eads, a self-taught engineer who had never designed or built a bridge before.

Those naysayers who doubted the feasibility of the Eads Bridge had far more to doubt than just steel as it principal material. Indeed, the first test of Eads' design was digging the foundations for the bridge's four support piers. Because bedrock was eighty feet below the muddy river bottom, which itself began twelve feet below the river's surface, he had to design, place, and sink caissons that were 82 feet long each and were connected to a sealed ten-foot high work area below. The caissons were equipped with air locks and a system to pressurize the inside to equalize ever-increasing lateral pressure from outside as the workmen dug ever deeper through the mud down to bedrock. Essentially this process is like scuba diving: as divers descend deeper under the surface, the hydrostatic pressure (the pressure exerted by the atmosphere) doubles every thirty-three feet, and it must be offset by equal outward pressure to prevent the collapse of a person's lungs. In the caisson, the deeper the workmen descended, the more air had to be pumped into it to prevent the tube from collapsing inward. Using the same diving analogy, once a diver is at depth, he must be careful not to ascend too fast, lest the pressurized air in his blood (which is 80 percent nitrogen) releases too quickly, much in the same way air bubbles form when the cap is suddenly removed from a Coke bottle. In the case of workmen in the work area under the caisson, they would have fared far better had they known that they had to ascend slowly to allow for gradual depressurization, as when one opens that Coke bottle slowly. But, because nobody had studied this phenomenon back then, decompression chambers were unheard of, and medical science was unequipped to deal with the issue. As a result, fifteen workers died and seventy-nine others suffered serious cases of what was then called "caisson disease" and would now be called "the bends."

The Eads Bridge

As for the superstructure itself, it was built of steel that was supplied by one of Carnegie's many companies, but only after Eads was able to convince a skeptical Carnegie that the composition of the steel he had specified would work. All told, nearly 2,400 tons of steel and over 3,000 tons of wrought iron were used to build the structure. To prove its strength, Eads silenced his final critics by running 14 large locomotives out on the bridge, all at the same time, two days prior to its opening. In the end, the bridge worked and, in so doing, became the world's first steel arch bridge, the biggest bridge that had up to that day been built, and the structure that most convincingly proved the worthiness of steel as a building material.[114] Once the concept of steel as a means of construction was established, Carnegie began in earnest to capture the country's primary sources of iron ore and coal supplies and began vertically integrating his company to monopolize, as nearly as he could, the development of the steel industry from source, through production, to transportation of finished product, pricing, and sale. Largely as a result of his efforts, the industry grew from 77,000 tons of steel output in 1870 to over 10 million tons produced in 1900.[115] By 1901, Carnegie's vertically integrated steel empire was the centerpiece of a sale to a venture put together by J. Pierpont Morgan in which Carnegie himself received over $225,000,000 (which in today's dollars would be worth over $6 billion). In other words, there was money to be made in the steel industry.

At the same time that the Big Four needed iron and steel to turn out the rails, locomotives, rolling stock, and equipment for their railroad empire, and while wagon axles were in heavy demand, as were steel plate and iron for ships of every size, as well as their drive shafts, propellers, and other working parts, and while architects were just beginning to look at using steel to provide stability for large new buildings and bridges, fast-growing San Francisco hadn't yet awakened to the fact that steel was the product of the future, to provide for the needs of its own rapid expansion as well as that of other cities up and down the West Coast.

Pacific Rolling Mills was founded in 1866 as essentially the second sizable ironworks in the region after Peter Donohue's Union Ironworks, but it didn't build its own open hearth furnace to produce steel until 1884. Judson Manufacturing Company became the second steel producer in the West. The same 1887 trade publication mentioned earlier that described Bothin Dallemand & Co. also provided the following description of Judson as it existed in 1887:[116]

> Judson Manufacturing Co., Manufacturer of Files, Tacks, Hardware and Bar Iron. Factories—Oakland. Office and sales-room 8 Pine Street [San Francisco]. Among the manufacturing concerns of this city are to be found some where the manufacture of certain classes of iron materials and agricultural implements are made specialties independent of their general business of hardware work. The most prominent among such is the corporation known as the Judson Manufacturing Co... Three hundred workmen are given employment in the several departments. The specialties of manufacture are the company's own product and patent—the California Victor Mower, an implement used extensively by farmers throughout the state, and bar iron, while included in the list of productions are files, locks, all kinds of rolling-mill work and hardware of every description.... The volume of trade is very large, and is constantly increasing, extending to all parts of the Pacific Coast.

Judson had been founded just five years earlier, in July 1882, by Egbert Judson. Mr. Judson, who had for some years manufactured nails at a plant in Emeryville known as The Judson Horse Nail Company, merged that company with a new one that he named Judson Manufacturing Company. The new company's goal was to manufacture the Victor Mowing Machine and to significantly broaden his hardware product line.[117] One of Judson's earliest and largest investors was his close friend Anthony Chabot, the father of Ellen Chabot, who was later to become Henry's second wife.[118] Mr. Chabot, the company's initial Vice President, made a major investment of $55,000 in the venture. That investment would translate to $1,250,000 in 2012 dollars.[119] Other original incorporators included A.J. Snyder, a wealthy investor who had made his money in Oakland real estate, V.D. Moody, who was a very wealthy lumberman and cattle rancher as well as the President of the First National Bank of Oakland, and Charles Webb Howard, the President of the Spring Valley Water Company.

Mr. Judson was extremely creative, and one example of that was his decision to enter into a contract with the State of California for the use of convict labor (San Quentin Prison inmates) to manufacture Victor Mowing Machines, pulleys, hangers, couplings, collars, hardware, and horse nails. With the resultant reduced cost structure, his fledgling company enjoyed a distinct competitive advantage. Later, as it grew, its published list of products was expanded to include solid bar iron, bolts and spikes, nails, and other iron tools and equipment, and it also contracted to do machine and bridge work as well as railroad and cable work. Because of its carefully managed labor costs, it was able to compete successfully with eastern companies, and as a result it prospered and grew; by 1887, it employed a labor force of over 300. Its most successful products were tacks (it produced over 60 tons per month) and its famous "ABC fence," consisting of woven rolls of double strand wire that "surrounded thousands of square miles of California farm and cattle lands, notablymuch of the million acre domain of the great cattle king, Henry Miller."[120] While those might have been products for which it was seen as the industry leader, the company also offered a broad range of other metal products and was a strong and broad based local competitor in that marketplace.

Egbert Judson

Anthony Chabot

Ellen Chabot

By 1888, Henry was acquiring Judson's stock, and by 1889, he had become a Director and the Executive Vice President of Judson.[121] As a young man in his mid-thirties, he had not yet been recognized for his business acumen, and so it stands to reason that he would not have achieved those positions in management and oversight in the company without having first become a major part of its ownership group, and that would not have occurred overnight. Just when or how he began acquiring Judson stock will likely never be known, but clearly he had begun to prefer hardware over spices sometime in the mid-1880s, and, as was his custom, once he decided on a path, he put his all into it.

An obituary that was published after his death by Pacific Gas and Electric Company, where Henry had been a long-time director, stated that Henry had acquired control of Judson during the late 1880s by becoming "by far the largest stockholder."[122] Unfortunately, the corporate records, including the stock book and all other records and ledgers relating to ownership and investment in Judson, cannot be located and apparently no longer exist. Still, it is clear, not only from that obituary but also from a letter written by Emil Sutter on October 16, 1889,[123] that by 1889 and probably before then, Henry was in command of Judson. Emil's letter states "Now H.E. [Bothin] has nearly absolute control of the Judson and my interests and advancement rests with him." What the term "nearly absolute control" means exactly is not known; however, in the July 11, 1889 edition of the *Oakland Tribune* the following article appears:

> Recently several important changes have been made in the management of the Judson Manufacturing Company at Emeryville, which was caused by the change of ownership of a large block of the company's stock. Lately the works have not been as successful as some of the stockholders could desire, but the losses in the main have been due to

circumstances beyond the control of the corporation. Among these was the cut in freight, during the rate war, which enabled large Eastern manufacturers of agricultural machinery to bring their mowers to the Pacific Coast at such rates that the Judson Company could not compete, and in fact was obligated to sell its machines at an actual loss, and these, with other things, caused the stock of the corporation to depreciate in value, much to the dissatisfaction of the stockholders. The main portion of the plant, consisting of rolling mill, foundry, and tack and nail departments, however, always have paid.

Recently D. Henshaw Ward of the directors disposed of his interest in the concern, and on July 1st C.R. Morgan, the general manager resigned, and Mr. McFeeley, an experienced rolling mill man, took his place. Since then the rolling mill has virtually re-organized, the following changes being noted: In the Board of Directors are: Egbert Judson, H.E. Bothin who succeeds D. Henshaw Ward, P.A. Wagner who succeeds Henry Williams, N. Ohland, J.F. Cowdery, S.B. Cushing, and V.D. Moody. The officers are: President, Egbert Judson; Vice President, H.E. Bothin; Secretary, Charles Butler; Treasurer, V.D. Moody. Several other changes are being made of minor importance, but the company will continue to operate with its present force.

That article raises several interesting topics. First is the fact that new board member, P.A. Wagner, was also a board member of Pacific Iron and Nail Company, the hardware company mentioned earlier that Henry, as well as his brothers-in-law and his partner, Albert Dallemand, had previously invested in and of which they had become directors. Henry obviously respected Wagner since the two would later, in 1890, invest together in a small company that ultimately went nowhere, called Mead Dry Press Brick Machine Company.[124] Whether Mr. Wagner was brought onto the Judson board at Henry's suggestion or whether his experience in the iron business was known to other Judson officials is not known, but that appointment was probably not coincidental, and it quite clearly supports the suggestion that, by then, Henry was the company's majority shareholder and had the clout, as owner, to bring onto the Board people he respected. It also confirms that Wagner had Henry's trust.

The *Tribune* article also suggests that Henry was not concerned over short term fluctuations in Judson's value, but rather had spied a long term investment opportunity and was willing to gamble on the future of a company doing business in an industry in which he was neither trained nor experienced. The timing of the announcement is consistent with Emil Sutter's letter home, when he stated that Henry now "has nearly absolute control."

Although the stock ledger is not available, one can assume that if Henry had obtained solid control, he must have earlier purchased a significant block of stock from Mr. Judson himself, the founder and initially Judson's largest shareholder. Similarly, one must assume that he had also purchased stock from Mr. Judson's early investors, including Anthony Chabot, who died from liver disease in January 1888, as well as from Messrs. Moody, Snyder, Howard, and also John L. M. Shepard, who was a large landowner in Emeryville and was Judson's business partner in the San Francisco Chemical Works and Sulphur Powdering Mill. One has to wonder why those individuals (or, in Mr. Chabot's case his daughter, Ellen who was his sole heiress) would have sold their interests in the company that Judson had founded only five years before. Perhaps it had to do, in some cases at least, with the age of the individuals. Mr. Judson, who would die in 1893 while still serving, at least on a titular basis, in the capacity of President, was 76 years old in 1886. His close friend and largest investor, Anthony Chabot, had just died, and perhaps Judson was feeling his own age and sensing it was time to retire. The others, who were mainly Oakland businessmen, may well have invested out of trust and friendship with Mr. Judson, and, upon learning that Judson would sell, might themselves have been reluctant to remain shareholders of a company in which a young man named Henry Bothin, a gentleman that none of them would have known anything about, was interested and was investing heavily.

By the end of his life Henry, his real estate company, his family, and his foundation were the sole owners of over 90 percent of Judson's stock,[125] and it is believed that he had acquired nearly, if not all, of that degree of control certainly by 1895, when he succeeded to the Presidency of the company, and most likely by 1889, when the above quoted article was written.[126]

As an aside, it is interesting to note that, although Henry was not known publicly to have become President of Judson until 1895, nonetheless his name appears as President on a stock certificate that was issued in 1891 to James Rolph for fifty shares of Judson. That certificate was dated February 16, 1891.[127] Mr. Rolph, who was a savvy investor himself and was at the time heavily invested in Pacific Rolling Mills as well, is best known as the father of the man known as "Sunny Jim" Rolph, who served as Mayor of San Francisco from 1912 to 1931, when he resigned to become the Governor of the State. Two things are noteworthy about that stock certificate. The first is that although Henry had effective "absolute" control over the company, it would seem that he was not above attracting people of influence to invest in his enterprise. Secondly, and far more importantly, he could hardly have signed and transferred a stock certificate to an investor, particularly one as perceptive and sophisticated as Mr. Rolph, without in fact holding the office the certificate said he held. In other words, no matter what the newspapers might have reported, in actual fact Henry was the President of Judson no later than early 1891, four years before that fact was publicly acknowledged. If that is true, and my instincts tell me it likely is, then that would lend credence to my supposition that Mr. Judson had sold out to Henry by 1889, but with the understanding that he, Judson, would retain his position as President, at least on a titular basis, until Henry had had a chance to learn the business well enough to take over operationally.

Given that he publicly assumed the role of Executive Vice President in 1889, and particularly in light of the Rolph stock certificate, it seems odd that Henry's listings in the *City Directory* for the four years between 1889 and 1893 are totally devoid of mention of Judson. The omission could mean that he initially intended his involvement to be limited to a passive investment and only later decided to become involved operationally. However, if that were so, then one has to again ask why Messrs. Judson and others would have sold out to him. Furthermore, to speculate in that direction would assume that Henry would ever spend serious money on something he did not (or could not) control, whereas the evidence simply doesn't support that sort of inference. In any event, in either 1891, 1894 or 1895 (depending on whether you believe the *City Directory* (which says 1894), Judson's internal history (which says 1895), or the Rolph certificate (which suggests 1891), it is clear that Henry did in fact, at some time within that rather broad window of time, assume the mantle of President and General Manager,[128] and from then until about 1920, when he passed that torch to his great nephew, he served as its President and either ran it himself or was closely involved in its management. Under his leadership, Judson became a very successful business and a respected employer in the East Bay.[129]

Judson was, at the time he bought it, involved in the hardware business, and that included everything from tacks up to railroad spikes and other large iron products. It did not, however, include steel. That was the major product line that was added during Henry's tenure as President. In the meantime, the company continued to grow and to return profits just on the product lines it was manufacturing when he took it over. In other words, it was a profitable going concern from the outset, and an excellent platform from which to leap into steel production when the timing seemed right.

So what were the downside risks to the steel business, and could any of them have been foretold at the time Henry became involved in Judson? Probably the greatest threat to the business was the absence of any reliable local primary or backup sources of iron ore or coal. Given the exponential growth of the industry, from 380,000 tons of output in 1875 to more than 60 million tons in 1920,[130] it is obvious that sources of raw material were precious and needed to be lined up. Whereas iron ore was abundant in the eastern states and particularly so in the region around Lake Superior, where it could be shipped efficiently by water to Chicago, Detroit, Cleveland, and Buffalo, and then transported by rail from there to steel mills spaced throughout the Midwest, the same cannot be said for West Coast producers. And, ever true to his reputation as a hardnosed businessman, Andrew Carnegie used his ready and inexpensive supply of nearly inexhaustible amounts of iron ore to his advantage, gaining control of the mines and integrating them with his steel production plants. Ultimately, by the late 1880s, Carnegie's companies were the largest manufacturers in the world of pig iron, steel rails, and coke (fuel), capable of producing 2,000 tons of pig iron per day.[131] There is evidence that his cost of production and transportation from the mine to the steel mill was as low as $2.00 per ton.[132]

Contrast the foregoing with sources of pig iron in the West. In Utah, the Great Western Iron Works produced 415 tons of pig iron in the two-year period from 1874-1876.[133] In Oregon, total output of pig iron was approximately 95 net tons between 1874 and 1894; Washington produced 25,000 tons during the eight-year period from 1881 to 1889; and California produced just 15,000 tons between 1881 and 1886. Joseph Daniels, the author of the study that published these figures in the mid-1920s, estimated that the total production from the entire Pacific Coast during the period from 1874 through 1889 was about 175,000 net tons. In other words, it took the entire West Coast fifteen years to produce the same amount of pig iron that Carnegie was able to produce in less than three months.

In his study, Daniels, whose point in developing his information was to determine the feasibility of creating a blast furnace and mining for iron near Puget Sound, also cited a very interesting piece of information: in 1881, a company known as The California Iron and Steel Company had established an iron plant in Placer County, California, with a blast furnace rated at 12,000 net tons per year. In 1882, the plant enjoyed its best year ever, with total output for the year of 5,327 tons of pig iron. That works out to 14.6 tons per day, or less than 1/10th of one percent of Carnegie's daily production. The California Iron and Steel Company was managed by A.P. Hotaling (San Francisco's largest liquor wholesaler), Irving M. Scott (President of the Union Iron Works), and Egbert Judson, the founder of Judson Manufacturing Company.[134]

Daniels also notes that other San Francisco steel men were, at various times, interested in trying to set up iron production plants in California. For instance, Noble Electric Steel Company, presumably owned or controlled by the same Patrick Noble who managed Pacific Rolling Mills from 1868 until it was liquidated in 1898 and went on his own thereafter, tried unsuccessfully in 1906 to build a furnace for the production of pig iron in Shasta County. The project limped along until it was finally abandoned in 1914. As late as 1924, D.E. McLaughlin, Vice President of the Pacific Coast Steel Company, organized a syndicate to develop a blast furnace for the production of pig iron. That was still in the development stage as of the date of the Daniels' report. Ultimately, Daniel's conclusion was that estimates of the amount of source iron had been vastly overestimated and that, although a number of investors had put up large sums of money at various times to capitalize ventures to build blast furnaces, all had ultimately failed. Although myriad reasons are given for the failure or abandonment of each venture, the common thread is inadequate volumes of production to cover the cost of operations.

Even though West Coast steelmakers lacked access to adequate volumes of regionally produced pig iron, that fact seems not to have discouraged them, and certainly it didn't discourage Henry. In part, that was because scrap iron was readily available in sufficient quantities to be recycled to serve their needs. Scrap iron was, on the West Coast at least, actually cheaper and more efficient to melt and re-use than it was to mine the raw material. So long as scrap iron remained plentiful and reasonably priced, the West Coast producers seem to have felt reasonably safe from Carnegie's aggressive competition. However, it was a fragile situation inasmuch as the cost of alternative sources of pig iron delivered to San Francisco from Europe was prohibitive when compared to the price Carnegie was able to do it for. Indeed, the cost to purchase pig iron from the Bay Area factory with the buyer paying the shipping costs appears, from a number of sources including testimony by several witnesses before Congressional committees, to have been in the range of $14 to as high as $20 per ton.[135]

Given the downside risks, which primarily consisted of the lack of a stable source of raw materials at pricing which could withstand eastern competition, one has to wonder whether the rewards were worth the risks. Whether hindsight might suggest that it wasn't, the fact is that Pacific Rolling Mills did move forward with their plan to produce steel and ultimately paid a steep price for that decision. As will be seen, Judson, on the other hand, proceeded more cautiously and obtained a better outcome.

By the mid-1880s, Pacific Rolling Mills had been in operation for twenty years, but it had just begun making steel in 1884. As successful as the company was to become over the next fifteen years in providing steel for rails, shipbuilding, and commercial buildings up and down the coast, the business unfortunately failed. In large part that was due to what in hindsight seems to have been inevitable—the cost of raw material, which left it vulnerable to competition from the Carnegie interests, whose appetite for expansion and control proved inexhaustible. In part, too, that failure was due to the recession of 1893, which dealt the company a blow by causing the disappearance of numerous business opportunities, as banks stopped lending and businesses hunkered down and hoarded their cash. Then, just as the country was climbing out of that recession, the eastern steel companies slashed their prices down as low as $25 per ton delivered to the West Coast. That was well below Pacific Rolling Mills' breakeven point, and it drove the company into liquidation.

As much as Henry had, I believe, wanted to add steel to his product line early on, he was well advised to move slowly and, ultimately, to wait for a better opportunity. In the meantime, he didn't have to move quickly, because the products for which Judson was already known were holding up well, and the company weathered the 1893 recession well. It remained viable and profitable selling iron bar, files, tacks, nails, spikes, barbed wire, and other hardware. For instance, in 1892 the *Daily Nevada State Journal* reported that Judson's output of tacks was about one ton per day and that the company had a workforce of 150 that was expected to grow soon to over 300.[136] While the depression of 1893 had put a serious crimp in business, by 1895, the *Oakland Tribune* and the *Berkeley Gazette* reported that the plant was operating day and night, with a workforce of 250 to 300 men. This growth was reported to be based on a broad geographic spread of business throughout the Pacific Coast, as well as Hawaii, Central and South America, and, to some extent, the East Coast of the United States. In other words, it seems that Judson, by being cautious, had actually expanded its business even during the recession. The principal product remained tacks and nails, but the product line had expanded to include nails of all sizes, ranging from carpet tacks at the small end up to railroad spikes at the other extreme.[137] Indeed, an indication of the size and importance of Judson in those years came in 1896 when it was given the dubious distinction of being the sole company located west of the Rockies that was charged as a co-conspirator in a price fixing claim. As a defendant, it was lumped into that action alongside the American Wire Nail Company, the Indiana Wire Fence Company, the Consolidated Steel and Wire Company, the Illinois Nail Company, the Superior Barb Wire Company, the Brooklyn Wire Nail Company, and the Oliver Wire Company, all of them well established businesses located east of the Rockies.[138]

When did Judson finally make the plunge and begin producing steel? The answer is, unfortunately, uncertain. *ARSC* says that it was not until 1914 that the company obtained its first open hearth furnace, which was later followed by three more in 1917, 1918 and 1920. And yet, there are several good reasons to believe that it was actually producing steel more than a decade earlier. First there is the known fact that Henry built his one and only skyscraper, which he called the Atlas Building, in 1904, and the steel frame for that building, which still stands today, was provided by Judson. Furthermore, an article in the October 8, 1905 edition of the *Oakland Tribune* notes that, as of that date, the company was supplying steel for schools and that the demand for its steel had, by the date of the article, created an order backlog to the point that it had to delay delivery of steel for the Market Street School in San Francisco by over a week and a half simply because "they were working on so many schools that they had more orders than they could properly attend to."[139]

Furthermore, *ARSC* is internally inconsistent on the question, stating that during Henry's tenure as President, "...the business grew under his direction and fabricated some of the largest steel structures on the Pacific Coast—the Oakland City Hall, as an example." In fact, the Oakland City Hall was designed in 1910 and was built between 1911 and 1914. Obviously the steel would have been erected early on in the construction phase, and the vendor would have been selected far earlier than that. The *Oakland Tribune* confirmed that supposition in an article dated June 5, 1911,[140] when they wrote that Judson had just been awarded a $234,000 contract to provide the steel for the fabrication of the Oakland City Hall. Then, early in the following year, Judson took out an advertisement in the *Oakland Tribune* that described its business and growth:

> Judson Man'fg Co., Manufacturers of Bar, Plate and Structural Iron and Steel. The Judson Manufacturing Company, the oldest and best known manufacturing firm on this side of the Bay, was incorporated in 1882, and in addition to its rolling mill, which is the largest on the Pacific Coast, comprises also completely equipped shops for the fabrication of structural steel and bridgework, together with an efficient bolt manufacturing department, blacksmith shops, a factory for the manufacture of tacks and nails of every description and a foundry. All kinds of iron and steel work, from the smallest tack to the largest steel frame building are being manufactured. At present the steel for the new Oakland City Hall, the largest contract for steel ever let upon the Pacific Coast, is being fabricated. This contract was taken in direct competition against all the steel fabricating shops of the United States. Among the other large buildings constructed in Oakland are the Bacon Block, Union Savings Bank Building, Young Mens' Christian Association, C.J. Heeseman's, and the C.J. Capwell Building.
>
> Employment is given to 600 men throughout the year and a monthly payroll averaging $35,000 adds considerable to the circulation of money directly in our city.
>
> A complete stock of structural material, bar iron, steel, rivets, bolts, nuts, sash weights and reinforcing bars for prompt shipment are always on hand. Heavy blacksmithing, machine and jobbing castings, rock screens, dredges, and other classes of iron and steel industry are the specialties.

The officials of the company are:
H.E. Bothin   President
H.J. Sadler   Vice President
J.D. Osborne   Secretary
F.D. Parsons   Manager of the Plant
H.W. Gallet   General Sales Mgr.[141]

Notably, H.J. Sadler was Henry's brother-in-law, the husband of his sister, Minnie. J.D. Osborne would also become the Secretary of the Bothin Real Estate Company as well as, for a brief time before he died, the Bothin Helping Fund.

There is clearly a conflict between what several sources say regarding the date when Judson first began making steel. One of the sources consists of newspapers cited earlier, where several articles of the day place Judson's participation in the steel industry to a point in time well ahead of the date when the other source (*ARSC*) claims they got their first open hearth furnace. It is worth noting that *ARSC* is essentially a thirty-two page public relations pamphlet put together in the 1940s by management of a subsequent company called Judson Pacific-Murphy Corporation. That pamphlet focuses, in the main, on the early history of Pacific Rolling Mills, as well as more recent works undertaken long after Henry's death and following the merger between Pacific Rolling Mills and Judson in 1928 and, thereafter, the subsequent merger in 1945 of that company with the J. Philip Murphy Corporation. That pamphlet devotes a total of just over two pages to Judson, and mostly identifies the original incorporators, discusses the Victor Mowing Machine as well as Judson's early focus on tacks and files, and closes by lauding Henry for his philanthropy. To me it is a less reliable source than then current newspaper articles and other sources cited above.

Returning to what we do know about Judson, by the end of the 1893 recession, and certainly by 1895 when Henry was publicly listed as having taken over its reins, the company had become a solid player in the hardware industry and was positioned to enter the steel manufacturing business at a time of its choosing. With Pacific Rolling Mills faltering, Carnegie and the eastern steel companies trying to lock up the West Coast marketplace, and with the rapid growth of California's railroads, shipbuilding, and commercial building demand, it would seemingly have made sense to open that door sooner than later if one could have controlled the risks. However, by the same token, it seems clear that Henry worried about the supply of raw materials and was reluctant to take on too much risk too soon. Clearly he did pull that trigger at some point, and my best guess is that it happened sometime around or just prior to the construction of his Atlas Building in 1904. Fortunately, I don't have to be right about dates, since dates aren't nearly as important in this case as the fact that Henry did, in fact, guide the company into the steel industry when he felt the timing was right. However, if one were to try to make an informed guess about the date, the logic would proceed as follows: first, it is clear that Henry wanted to be in the steel business all along and that his investment in Judson was in furtherance of that goal. Second, in order to be in a position to have landed the Oakland City Hall job in June in 1911, the company would have had to have been producing steel for long enough to (1) get beyond its own learning curve, (2) establish a reputation for the quality of its product sufficient to be attractive to large commercial customers, and (3) have a long enough track record of on time delivery of properly specified steel product to give customers confidence that they wouldn't have to worry about returns. How long would that have taken? A fair guess would be 2-3 years at minimum and possibly a bit longer. So that leaves the question of what might have been the catalyst for making the plunge. If we weren't aware that Henry had specified Judson-produced steel as the construction material for the skeleton of his ten story Atlas Building in 1904, then the next obvious date would coincide with the City's rebuilding following the 1906 earthquake and fire.

Judson Manufacturing Company's San Francisco office

Loading flatcars in Emeryville

In fact, we do know (as will be discussed later) that Henry specified Judson steel for the rebuilding of his own buildings that came down in the 1906 event. Several of those buildings started going up before the end of 1906, so Judson must have had the capacity to supply steel in quite large quantities no later than 1906. Once we get back to 1906, it isn't hard to then go back two more years to 1904, when we know he called for Judson's steel for the skeleton of his Atlas Building.

Just what turned Henry toward Judson will, unfortunately, never be known for certain, but whatever might have been the catalyst, it was a brilliant stroke, coming as it did at a time when the iron industry, at least on the West Coast, was still underserved and the steel industry was barely born. The best and the brightest of San Francisco's capitalists of the day had thrown their money at Pacific Rolling Mills, and that company had, just as Henry was beginning to take interest in Judson, thrown its hat into the steel game. Henry's interest was clearly piqued; but rather than following the others, he would do it his own way.

Although Henry's interest in steel was by no means original thinking, he differed from the rest of the pack by assuming the driver's seat and by exercising leadership restraint, which kept him in the game for the rest of his life and long after those who had invested in Pacific Rolling Mills had to "cry uncle." He did it by taking over a healthy company, valuing and expanding its existing product line and book of business, following Mr. Judson's lead in holding costs in line, and, with an existing profitable bottom line, exercising patience before making his move. By doing this as he did, his dollars went farther, and he was able to control both Judson's and his own destiny to a far greater extent than would have been the case had he simply signed on as a passive investor in a larger and more established company like Pacific Rolling Mills. Yes, this passive approach would have led to personal respect as a visionary—respect he would have had to share with many other successful businessmen. However, respect was not what drove Henry. Rather, his goal was wealth and control. In the food industry, where he cut his teeth, his family members applied pressure to move in certain directions, but he was not content to let others affect his decision-making authority. So too he was not content to follow the swarm when it came to steel.

When Egbert Judson died in 1893, the public perception (if not the reality) was that L.P. Drexler succeeded him as President of Judson for the next two years until 1895. Even if the Rolph stock certificate trumps that perception, there is no doubt that, at

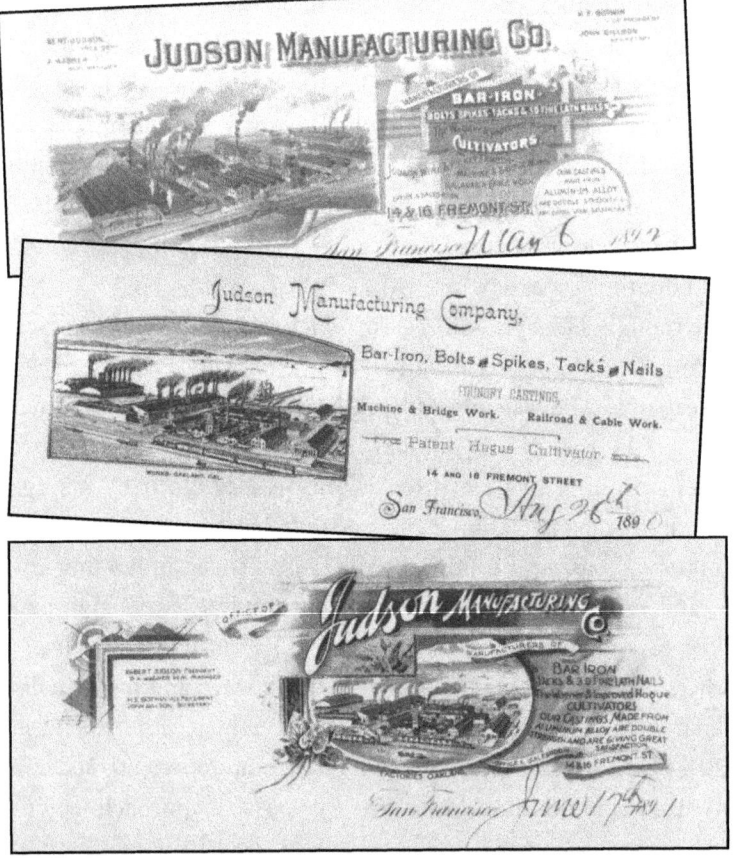

Letterheads from Judson Manufacturing Company stationary

the very least, Mr. Drexler held titular control over operations and would have been heavily involved in day-to-day decision making. Mr. Drexler was, after all, a well-respected executive in San Francisco who was also the President of the California Jute Mill Company. Although an outsider to Judson, he seems to have been brought in because of his business acumen and experience. Whether that decision was made by Henry or by the Board, it appears to have been a smart and timely decision given the rapidly escalating economic downturn as the panic of 1893 spread its tentacles throughout the business community. In point of fact Mr. Drexler (either alongside Henry or on his own) was able to navigate a careful course through the economic downturn so that, by 1895 when Henry had completed his learning curve, the company was in decent condition and ready for him to take over operational control. He was in fact elected in 1895 as its President and General Manager, positions which he retained for the next twenty-five years before handing over the company's reins to his hand-picked successor, his great nephew, Carlos Maas.[142]

Judson prospered during Henry's tenure as President, fabricating some of the largest steel structures on the West Coast, including the Oakland City Hall, the Claus Spreckels Building (later known as Central Tower), the San Francisco Hospital building and the San Francisco Public Library.

On January 16, 1913, the *Oakland Tribune* published an article about Judson's expansion. The article began with the statement that "[t]o accommodate the rapidly increasing demands for structural steel work, rolling and foundry work of all descriptions, the Judson Manufacturing Company has, within the last few months, increased its facilities for handling all work of this nature." The article went on to describe that the structural shop had a capacity of over 1,000 tons of steel per month, and that the rolling mill, foundry, machine shops and blacksmith shops were all working to capacity. That article continued by extolling the experience and credentials of the

General Manager F.M. Green and the Assistant Superintendent Edgar Burnet.

Later in April of 1913, Judson announced in a press release that it was constructing, for a hydroelectric power plant in Cascade, California, the largest cast iron sections of pipe ever built on the Pacific Coast. That pipe consisted of five pieces, the largest being 10 feet in diameter; 40-feet long; and weighing 18,000 pounds. The press release ended by noting that this job was further proof that Judson was capable of satisfying the biggest job requirements available.

One way that Judson expanded was by adding open hearth furnaces. We don't know when it got its first furnace, but if *ARSC* is to be believed, it it did bring on line a furnace in 1914 which was probably not its first. It then added to its capacity with additional furnaces in each of 1917, 1918, and 1920. Presumably those latter furnaces were brought on line because of the First World War, a global event which would have created a huge demand for steel products for use in the war effort. Each of those last four furnaces had 30 ton capacity and gave off glowing fires that were visible for miles around. In those furnaces, pig iron, limestone, and iron ore were heated to nearly 1,600 degrees Fahrenheit, at which point the limestone, excess carbon, and ore separated and collected on the surface as a waste slag. Cleaning agents were then added, and the resultant metal became carbon steel. The key to the process was to gain efficiency in the recovery of heat so as to reduce the amount of fuel needed to maintain those high temperatures. That was accomplished by pumping the exhaust gases into brick chambers that would absorb the heat and then release it slowly, thereby maintaining the required temperature for the process to continue. Each batch of steel created through this process took about eight hours from start to finish, and thereafter the raw steel could be either poured into ingots or placed in the rolling mills for continuous casting, depending on the desired product. Although this was slower than the Bessemer process, the batches created by open hearth furnaces were easier to control for quality purposes and made for a more reliable end product.

In 1916, Judson's common stock was listed on the San Francisco Stock and Bond Exchange. In an article appearing in the October 20, 1916 edition of the *Oakland Tribune*, it was reported that the stock of Judson, which had been listed approximately one week earlier, traded for the first time at $45 per share. Although its value was appraised on Henry's death seven years later at $40 per share, nothing about the company's performance during those intervening years suggests a slowdown or a disappointment in earnings.

To the contrary, in January 1923, the members of the Purchasing Agents Association of Northern California were given a tour of the Judson plant. In an article appearing several days later, on January 28, 1923, the *Oakland Tribune* reported that the campus comprising the Emeryville plant had expanded to 24 acres. Four months later, the *Tribune* reported that Judson had just been awarded the largest West Coast contract for fabricated steel ever given. This contract was for the construction of Pacific Gas and Electric's new twenty-two story headquarters building in San Francisco and called for 2,600 tons of fabricated steel. Then, in August of 1923, in another *Tribune* article, Judson stated they had just delivered steel for the Gensler-Lee jewelry store in Oakland and were in the process of fabricating and erecting steel for the East Bay Masonic Temple, the Breuner Furniture warehouse in Oakland, as well as the Awberry Plant of the Southern California Edison Company in Los Angeles. At the same time, they had enough capacity to send out daily rail carloads of structural steel for the plaster cement plant at Garlock, Nevada.

In the immediate aftermath of Henry's death on October 14, 1923, Judson continued to thrive. The first press release following his death was published on January 27, 1924 and announced that during the first week of 1924 the following new business had been brought in: Bellows Garage Building in Long Beach, Westinghouse

Factory in Emeryville, San Diego Oil Company building in San Diego, Telephone Exchange Building in Sacramento, the S. Newman building in Berkeley, and two garages in Oakland. These represented just one week's worth of sales.

Whatever might have happened to Judson after Henry's death, this much is clear: Henry took a gamble on a new and exciting industry at a time when structural steel was just becoming a viable business opportunity and was in its formative years. The gamble paid off in a big way, and he took a long and prosperous ride on the back of its success story. During that ride, he honed his management talents to the point where he became recognized by his peers among San Francisco businessmen and was invited to join a number of their boards. He also became a wealthy man, in part because of that gamble.

Because the company's records are missing, it is difficult to tell how Henry was compensated by Judson for his executive talents. Corporate executive salaries were not published in those days; however, there is some information from which reasonable estimates can be made. It is known that the average annual salary of chief executives of the country's 400 largest manufacturing businesses between 1904 and 1914 was just under $10,000 per year, and there was only one executive within the survey group who made as much as $100,000.[143] While there is evidence that some large corporations were, in that same general time frame, paying their chief executives close to $100,000 in base salary, plus bonuses, which sometimes doubled or trebled that base level of compensation,[144] obviously a company would have to earn significantly more revenue than was generated by Judson to play in that stratified arena. Hence, it is a fair bet that, at least in his early years at Judson, Henry probably was paid an annual salary in the range of $10,000. That would work out to $833 per month, not far off from what he told his sister, Emma, in a letter he sent to her on July 2, 1890. He mentioned in that letter that he was holding family expenses to $400-$500 per month because of the level of debt service he was paying "on some $90,000 of borrowed money in order to keep all [my] different business ventures going…" If one assumes he was borrowing at 6 percent, the monthly interest on that level of debt would be $450, which, when subtracted from $833, would leave $383 per month available to cover household expenses. Add to that some income Henry was still then earning from his coffee and spice business, and the total of his income would be roughly similar to what he told Emma.

Staying for a moment longer on the topic of what Henry was paid to run Judson, and assuming it was, at least during the early 1890s, something on the order of $10,000 per year, that sum would have an equivalent value in today's dollars of approximately $290,000,[145] a sum that, were it not for the amount of debt he was dealing with, would have provided a thirty-seven year old married man like Henry with a very comfortable level of income that would support quite a prosperous lifestyle, a lifestyle that his wife, Jennie, undoubtedly expected to share in. Henry lived frugally and asked his reluctant wife to do likewise, and his earnings from Judson were nowhere near the level of expendable cash he would need to support the real estate investment craze that for him was just beginning to become addictive.

II.
Business Changes: Real Estate

At the same time that Henry was whetting his appetite for steel, he was also taking his first steps into the field of real estate investment. Since most city records regarding San Francisco real estate were destroyed in the 1906 earthquake and fire, it is difficult to pin down specifics; however, some records remain that enable at least a general survey of his early acquisitions. Included among these few records are the Grantor/Grantee indices for many of the years when Henry was buying properties, and they reveal that on November 23, 1888 (while Henry was still investing in Judson) he also purchased the first of well over 200 properties that he would ultimately acquire within the city limits of San Francisco alone. That first acquisition, a property whose location is not known, was bought from a man named J.M. Byrne.[146] A second purchase followed three weeks later on December 14, 1888, and seven additional purchases in 1889 were recorded in the months of January (1), April (4), October (1), November (1) and December (1). In 1890 he purchased another seven properties; five were bought in August alone.

Unfortunately, the Deed Books for years prior to 1895 were burned in the '06 fire, so it is not possible to know where those sixteen initial parcels were located or to try to spot the beginning of a trend in Henry's mind. Similarly, it is unknown where Henry might have obtained the capital with which to make either those real estate investments or his investments in Judson. In short, many mysteries remain unsolved. However he did it, Henry had obviously mapped out a strategy in his mind to move simultaneously on both fronts, and he also had figured out a source of funds with which to execute that strategy.

The obvious connection between the two investment strategies was steel—the state of the art material that was just beginning to be recognized for its ability to significantly increase the vertical capacity of commercial buildings, and a product Judson would one day begin to produce. The advantage of steel, from a real estate investor's perspective, was, obviously, a huge increase in the usable density of a given plot of land, and a correspondingly dramatic increase in the potential yield on investment.

Until the late 19th century, the tallest buildings in the world had been churches, all of which had single stories for human use and then lofty domes and spires that soared to the heavens, but did nothing to elevate human habitation above ground level. As late as the end of the decade of the 1870s, commercial buildings rarely exceeded four stories and almost never five. They were extremely heavy buildings, using various building techniques, but almost always relying ultimately on masonry as the load bearing construction material. However, by the early 1880s, technology caught up with a demand that was fed by escalating urban commerce and a need for increased density in downtown business spaces. About that time, two innovations combined to give architects new tools with which to begin designing commercial buildings to heights never before imagined.

The first of these innovations was the passenger elevator, a lifting device that went through radical design changes between 1852 and 1887 and, in the process, was pronounced a safe (at least as that term was used back then) means of transporting people to nearly endless heights.[147] As early as 1870, passenger elevators were being installed in office buildings,[148] and by the late 1880s they were commonplace. The second innovation, which came about due to improvements in the Bessemer process, was the discovery that steel could be used instead of masonry to provide the skeletal framework to build ever-taller buildings. The Home Insurance Building in Chicago, a ten story commercial structure that was initially built in 1884 and then expanded to twelve stories six years later, is generally credited with being the first tall building to use steel in its frame, and, accordingly, it is considered by many experts to have been the first "skyscraper" in the world.[149]

The design for the Home Insurance Building, created by architect and engineer William Le Baron Jenney, was prompted by the Great Chicago Fire of 1871. Before that devastating fire, wood was the preferred building material throughout Chicago; however, in the fire's aftermath and during the city's rebuilding process, city leaders promoted the use of iron, masonry, and a new product called steel to rebuild. The ensuing building boom fueled demand for more buildings in the downtown "Loop" district, which in turn led to an effort to increase the height of the new commercial structures in order to accommodate escalating demand for office space. Masonry was thick, heavy, unattractive for interior spaces, and limited in the height it could achieve. Cast iron had no tensile strength, was brittle, and was prone to failure under the sorts of extreme heat generated by fires of the kind Chicago had just come through. Steel, on the other hand, had none of those disadvantages, which is why Mr. Jenney, whose expertise lay more in his engineering talent than in his aesthetic design credentials, created a design that used steel for the load bearing skeleton of the building and to support the walls, floor, and roof of the structure. Interestingly, the building as designed weighed only about one third of what a similar building constructed of masonry would have. It was so revolutionary that city inspectors halted construction while they researched and tested the material in order to satisfy themselves that such a relatively light weight building could be safe.[150] When completed, the Home Insurance Company building contained 235 offices, four passenger elevators, and a population of 1,250 people who inhabited it each working day.[151]

The Home Insurance Company Building touched off a race to achieve ever taller buildings. In 1888 Minnesota architect, Leroy Buffington, proposed (and was later granted a patent for) a 28-story building design which he called a cloud scraper.[152] Initially mocked for his "impractical and ludicrous" idea, the publicity surrounding his concept of a steel skeletal frame for buildings brought it to the attention of the national architectural and building communities. The idea caught on, and by the late 1880s other steel framed buildings, including the Tower Building in New York, the Rand McNally Building in Chicago, The Tacoma Building in Chicago, The Wilder Building in Rochester, New York, and other tall, steel framed structures in Kansas City, Pittsburgh, and elsewhere around the country were on the drawing boards and under construction.

Why would all of this have intrigued Henry? With no known background in the fields of either building design or construction, what might have made him think he could utilize to his advantage a cutting edge technology with which he was totally untrained and unfamiliar? The answer to that riddle would seem to be his utter self-confidence and his entrepreneurial streak. Henry never lacked for confidence, and undoubtedly it was that self-assurance that propelled him to suddenly and passionately plunge headlong into his vision of the future. He was a risk taker, albeit one who was willing to be patient and cautious before jumping. As such, it was entirely within character for him to have tried to arm himself with an arsenal of property with which to profit from the use of this new building technique.

The next question that comes to mind is why a young man, recently married and planning to start a family, would chuck aside a perfectly profitable coffee and spice company, leave the comfort of a secure and successful stream of income, and take a flyer in not one but two totally new directions nearly simultaneously? Again, Henry's self-confidence would provide a part of the answer to that question. Another part of that answer might well lie in the similarity between Henry and his father in law, Frank Whittier, who, just thirty years before, had proven his own willingness to gamble and dream big about creating a worldwide enterprise out of what had begun as a local paint company. Jennie Whittier Bothin grew up in a home where no business challenge was too big, no goal too far out of reach. She also grew up spoiled and the center of attention. Given that background, it does not seem unreasonable to assume, just two years or so into their marriage, that she might have been happier as the bride of a real estate magnate and a man on the cutting edge of high-rise steel construction than as the wife of a spice merchant. After all, nearly every successful businessman in San Francisco, many of whom had been guests at hers and Henry's wedding, had invested in the stock of Pacific Rolling Mills, the only then existing steel company in the City.[153] The flip side for Jennie, of course, would have been the troublesome fact of Henry's obstinate insistence on frugal living in order to set aside roughly 50 percent (and later even more) of his monthly income to cover debt service on his real estate acquisitions. So on balance, she might well, as a new, young, and naive bride, have supported his exit from the merchandising trade and encouraged his boldness, only to later realize just how stifling to her own dreams and ambitions that path would become.

In the context of this topic, the letter Henry wrote on July 2, 1890 to his sister, Emma, provides additional insights. Substantively, the letter expresses chagrin and frustration about their brother Julius's lack of business sense, to the point that Julius was now relegated to working for Henry in a rather menial capacity, handling collections at their retail outlet on Market Street. Henry doesn't seem to be blowing his own horn, but he does acknowledge that certain people have the ability to succeed in business while others don't, and by that acknowledgement, he expresses, without bragging, his own self-confidence even in the absence of formal business training.

That letter to Emma also contains some interesting observations by Henry about himself. For instance, he noted that he had been fortunate in that "matters that I ventured into in most cases have provided successful so far," but that only time would tell if he could keep his empire afloat, humorously suggesting that the consequence of failure might include one day having to work for Julius. He wrote that, despite outward appearances of wealth, he was carefully managing his money such that "my personal and family expenses average from [$]400 to [$]500 per month," noting that "I am paying interest on some $90,000 of borrowed money in order to keep most of my business ventures going…"

At this point, it seems helpful to explore a topic that is obvious to those in the real estate business, but perhaps less so to others. The fact is that a building is far more than just a structure. It is a series of systems, including a foundation, an exterior shell, plumbing runs, sources of heat and of lighting, interior finishes, and many more aspects, all of which must be understood by the owner in order to assure that good business judgments can be made regarding maintenance, capital reserves, financing and refinancing, allocations of responsibility between landlord and tenant, and for many other reasons as well. Just as every business comes with its own set of issues that must be mastered in order to be successful, real estate ownership is no different. Many of the issues that are unique to the world of real estate are hidden below ground or behind walls. Buying improved real estate is not just buying what is visible, but also buying that which is invisible to the naked eye, and that often has the capacity to deliver either an efficient experience or a nightmare to the owner. So, by committing himself to the purchase of commercial real estate, Henry was not only investing in an illiquid asset, but he was also exposing himself to risks that, had he not understood them, might well come back to haunt him later. Fortunately, this was an area where his father's experience probably trickled down to Henry, providing him with early training and understanding.

While a working knowledge of building systems was (and is) imperative to the purchaser and owner of commercial property, it is also noteworthy to realize that for Henry and others engaged in that industry at the time, that issue was becoming ever more complex due to the fact that many of the major systems in buildings were going through dramatic changes at about the time he was beginning his plunge. Take foundations as an example. Historically, and really extending up to the mid-1850s, commercial building foundations often consisted simply of rubble underpinnings over which the building would be erected. That worked adequately when dealing with heavy masonry structures set upon level and stable ground; however, one can well imagine that it was an archaic and problematic system of supporting a tall structure or one built on a grade. Over time, rubble was replaced by dimension stone footings of equal size and width upon which the bearing walls would be placed. But the idea of designing each footing as a separately engineered load-bearing unit, based not only on the load it would bear but also the condition of the soil beneath it, was a concept that would not even be thought of until the latter years of the 19th century. As a result, differential settlement was common over time, as were cracks and distortion in structures. For instance, the Jayne Building, a then nine-story ultramodern building built in 1850 in Philadelphia, was at the time of its construction the tallest building in the country. It was a masonry building with unreinforced brick load-bearing sidewalls. When describing it, architect and author Joseph Korom Jr. stated, "[f]rom an engineering perspective the Jayne Building broke no new ground, advanced no new theories…[154]" Mr. Korom didn't even comment on its foundation, so it, presumably, followed the pattern he had described for other buildings of the time, which, as he noted, often consisted of four of five layers of oak ties set upon a bed of sand; atop which were placed several layers of stone of different dimensions, and on top of them a rock wall was constructed, above which the building itself rose.[155] Although suggestive of beefiness, that description hardly begins to meet foundation standards which later began to be developed to properly anchor and support the highrise structures which would begin to proliferate during the middle and later years of the decade of the 1880s. It wasn't until 1873 that architect Frederick Baumann, of Chicago, published a thirty-eight page pamphlet[156] that, for the first time, laid out "rules" that essentially called for buildings to be broken down into sections, with the weight of each section to determine the size of its own supporting footing(s). These footings, which he called isolated piers, would provide a more evenly laid out system to build on. Although not entirely new thinking, Baumann's pamphlet appears to have been the first effort to argue successfully that foundations were engineering problems that needed mathematically generated solutions by appropriately trained architects and/or engineers.

Even so, the science of designing foundations, particularly those involving tall buildings, was still a long way from where it needed to be to provide the sort of stability for such buildings that we consider essential today. It would be many years, for instance, before advancements such as steel reinforced concrete would provide tensile strength to concrete, to give buildings underpinnings that could be relied upon to prevent differential settlement and other distortions from occurring, and so to enable structures to be built "safely," as that term is used in this day and age.[157] Today, after all, we ride elevators ever higher, in buildings that are laser straight and supported in ways that no one would have dreamed possible a hundred years ago. When today we enter that elevator cage, we take for granted that all the many systems of the building we are in, including its foundation, will work together in a way that lets us safely arrive at our destination. Back in Henry's day, a ride in an elevator to the tenth floor of a then-modern skyscraper was far more of an adventure than the everyday experience it is today. In that respect, we live in a different world than Henry did. For him, the properties he bought would have had a variety of different substructures, each presenting its own challenges and realities. And nowhere was there a more critical need for science regarding foundations than in earthquake zones such as San Francisco, where specially designed foundation systems were to become so important during the post-1906 reconstruction efforts. Recognizing the limitations of engineering knowledge back when Henry was inspecting properties prior to purchase, it was important that he understand load bearing issues well enough to at least make intelligent judgments about whether the building was, at its core, stable as opposed to a risky prospect to avoid no matter its cost.

Another example of a building system that was undergoing rapid changes during the time of Henry's initial foray into the industry was lighting. This is a particularly interesting topic for two reasons. First, Henry was to become a founding director of Pacific Gas and Electric Company, a position he held from 1905 until his death in 1923, and, secondly, his closest friend—the man who would ultimately stand next to him as a witness at his second marriage, and who replaced him as a director of his foundation after his death—was C.O.G. Miller, whose family founded Pacific Lighting Corporation. Founded in San Francisco in 1886, Pacific Lighting had been an early competitor in the city's gas lighting business, but improvements to the use of electricity made gas obsolete for that purpose. So Mr. Miller's company reoriented its business model and ultimately became extremely successful in the delivery of gas for other purposes, such as heating and cooking. So, not only were advances in the uses for electric generation and distribution of particular interest to him for those reasons, they were also crucial to him from the perspective of his own real estate involvements.

Historically, by the mid-1850s, San Francisco's streets and buildings were lit by manufactured gas that was initially provided by San Francisco Gas Company, a corporation formed in 1852 by Peter Donahue (who had earlier set up Union Iron Works) and his brothers, James and Michael. The brothers obtained a franchise from the City of San Francisco to set up a gasworks and ultimately became the first gas utility on the West Coast. Manufactured gas, which has been defined as "a mixture of gases obtained by thermal decomposition of oil" (among other means)[158] was a product that, in the case of San Francisco and many other western communities as well, was produced primarily by superheating asphaltum (a heavy gravity grade of crude oil found in abundance in Southern California) and subsequently treating and cleansing it in plants before delivering it through pipelines to the end customers. The product, considered a marvel of its day, was used for heating, cooking, and providing artificial light, which made the streets safer and homes more comfortable. It caught on with the public and was an immediate success, so much so that within two years of its initial startup, the San Francisco Gas Company had laid over six miles of pipe, had over 500 customers, and had lit over 150 streetlamps. As the company grew and acquired lesser rivals, and as other companies introduced improvements (primarily petroleum-based water gas, which was promoted by the competing Pacific Gas Improvement Company), gas as a source of artificial lighting continued to add customers and to expand in popularity until the late 1870s, when electric lighting was introduced as a cleaner, brighter and less costly alternative to gas for lighting purposes. For Henry, any older buildings he might have acquired, particularly in the early years, might well have been set up to use gas for lighting, in which case issues involving retrofitting to electric lighting would have been important to understand.

Electricity was hardly a new phenomenon. Today it is defined as "a form of energy resulting from the existence of charged particles,"[159] but its physical manifestations, such as lightning, static electricity, shocks from electric eels, etc., have all been known to exist from almost the beginning of time. Ben Franklin's experiment in 1752, when he flew a kite with a metal key attached into a thunderstorm, while a part of American folklore that every child is familiar with, was also a scientific experiment which advanced mankind's knowledge about the topic. By the early to mid-1800s mathematicians and scientists had reached the point of understanding the science of electricity and the formulae by which its charge (electromagnetic force) could be quantified, moved, and measured; and by then some initial (but very important) applications had been developed, including Alessandro Volta's copper and zinc battery as well as Michael Faraday's electric motor. However, the uses that harnessed electricity would soon fulfill, including lighting systems, trolley lines, factory motors and others, were still either unknown or impractical due to various obstacles that stood in the way of commercially viable advances. These obstacles were removed, one by one, during the mid-to-latter part of the century. Numerous commentators have opined that the harnessing of electricity is the greatest discovery in the history of the world. Whether one agrees with that statement or not, it is hard to argue with the National Academy of Engineering, which called electricity "the workhorse of the modern world"[160] and named electrification as the greatest engineering achievement of the 20th century. In order to arrive at that lofty status, many advancements were necessary, including those that enabled the incandescent light bulb to be invented, and in time, to displace manufactured gas as the method of choice for street and household lighting.

    Thomas Edison, like Henry Bothin, had very little formal education, but he had the advantage of a mother who home-schooled him and encouraged his intellectual curiosity. During his eighty-four year life span, he was issued 1,093 patents, a record that stood until 2003 as the most patents issued to any one individual. Of all of them, he considered his incandescent light bulb the most challenging, not because it was a novel idea, (it was not), but because it required the invention or improvement of so many other component parts to fulfill its intended goal as an efficient and affordable lighting system for use by the public at large. In other words, the incandescent bulb was only one cog in a far more elaborate system that included standardizing voltage, creating a delivery system, and, only once that infrastructure was available, having a product at the consumer end that could be bought and used at a reasonable price. To do all that, Edison first had to improve upon Alessandro Volta's invention of the parallel circuit in order to allow each bulb to be separately controlled and turned off and on. Otherwise, if the circuit was in series, every light would go on or off when the switch was thrown, and every time one bulb burned out, all lights on the circuit would also go out. He also had to develop a bulb that was durable and long lasting, a process that consumed several years of testing over six thousand different carbonized plant-based fibers as well as numerous metallic strands, before finally settling on a bamboo filament that, when placed in a vacuum tube, (the bulb) gave about twelve hundred hours of use before failing. Next he had to improve upon the "dynamos," or engines, then in use, to assure consistency when producing the proper voltage, from the central plant, out through his transmission lines, on to the end user. Also required were safety fuses to eliminate loss of bulbs due to spiking voltage, should it occur, as well as insulators to protect people and property against electric shock. Finally, he had to design on/off switches for the end user.

As much as Edison was properly lauded and rewarded for all the work that went into the creation of his lighting system, it was ultimately based on the faulty premise that direct current (DC) was the appropriate type of transmission environment. It soon became apparent that alternating current (AC) was preferable for many reasons. Edison, whose patent royalties were based on DC, fought hard (and unfairly) to demonize AC as an allegedly highly dangerous and inappropriate transmission medium. Ultimately, AC won out for a number of reasons, including the capability of transmission at far higher voltages and longer distances, with far more efficiency and with less power loss per unit of distance, as well as ease of changing voltages by the use of transformers.[161]

Obviously, Henry didn't have to become an expert in or

understand foundations, electricity, lighting, heating, roofing, plumbing or other systems to the extent several are described here; however, he certainly had to understand them well enough to know when they were defective or on the verge of failing, what the dangers were in the event of failure, how inherently stable or unstable they were, what sorts of useful life each had, and what maintenance plans were needed in order to protect his investment and prevent tenant complaints and turnover. He also had to understand, before purchasing a property, whether its various systems were outmoded or still appropriate for the use intended.

By 1890, Henry was no longer involved in Bothin, Dallemand & Co, and he was essentially done with Bothin Manufacturing Company as well. His attention was, instead by then completely absorbed by Judson and by his newly found compunction for commercial real estate. Accordingly, when he mentioned in his July 1890 letter to Emily that he was heavily in debt to "keep all my different business ventures going," one can assume that he was referring to financing his budding real estate empire, consisting at the time of the first eleven properties he had by then acquired. Those "business ventures" would not have included the five other commercial properties he was then in the process of acquiring, which would likely have added another 50 percent to his debt burden just months after he wrote that letter. So although he may have paid lip service to emotions of fear, they didn't stop him from his forward charge.

Can one say for certain that the debt he claimed was so worrisome was related to his real estate acquisitions? The answer seems to be yes. If his debts were related to his coffee and spice manufacturing company, one would expect his creditors would have prevented him from distancing himself from ownership or operational control over those entities. As for Judson, in those days (just as it is today) it would have been highly unusual, if not unheard of, for a banker to lend money to someone with no experience in the steel business in order to finance his investment (be it active or passive) in what was still a largely unproven industry. Indeed, one can just imagine how a banker might have reacted had Henry asked for a line of credit to finance a sizable investment (essentially, a takeover) in a business where he had never held a management position, much less worked in any capacity. No, it can be said with near certainty that the debt he spoke about in that letter must have been secured debt on the commercial real estate he was starting to accumulate.

From what he wrote to Emily, it is apparent that Henry needed help from bankers and other lenders to feed his real estate appetite. In fact, if one divides his $90,000 in debt by eleven (the number of properties that debt load covered) then it is apparent that he borrowed, on average, $8,200 per parcel. If the next five properties (those that he had in escrow as of the date of that letter) cost, on average, the same as the first eleven, then his debt load would have increased to a bit over $130,000 by the time he completed those acquisitions. And if his statement to Emma was accurate to the effect that he was holding his and Jennie's living expenses down to $400 to $500 per month to service his debt before those last five properties were acquired, then clearly those additional acquisitions would have brought the spendable household budget to nearly zero, a fact that could not have set well with Jennie. Indeed, if one is looking for a reason why Henry brought his purchases to a total halt after August of 1890—a hiatus that would last for five years—one really needs to look no farther than domestic issues, and Henry's recognition that controlling, and indeed corralling, his burgeoning real estate habit was the best way to keep peace in the family.

If one is to believe Henry's statements to his sister, then the debt service on his first sixteen real estate acquisitions essentially gobbled up all the couple's spendable income. This leads one to ask whether or not he or they might have turned to other sources for help. For instance, one might wonder whether Henry's father-in-law might have contributed to the cost of acquiring these properties or, if not that, might have made them gifts or loans to help the couple out. The answer to that must assuredly be no. Frank Whittier kept records of all of his financial transactions, and his biographer, Mary Whitney, would surely have discovered loans to his son-in-law. There is nothing in any of her writings about Mr. Whittier to suggest loans or gifts to either Jennie or Jennie's husband. Furthermore, the deeds to Henry's properties showed they were purchased by him alone and without any partners or co-venturers. Indeed, Jennie's name doesn't appear on any of the deeds either. Furthermore, as successful as Frank Whittier was, he needed every bit of the money he had made in the paint business to fund the huge new land venture he was embarking on in Southern California at about the same time as Henry was making his moves with both Judson and San Francisco commercial real estate.

The other possibility, of course, might well be that the properties Henry purchased were income-producing from the outset. A newspaper article mentions that Henry's start came from buying properties at foreclosure sales held by Hibernia Bank on properties whose former owners had defaulted on their loans.[162] That is an age-old problem which is no different today than it was in Henry's time—either the borrower (and bank) miscalculated the true income stream needed to service the debt or else there were problems with the building or its location which had not been anticipated. Either way, the solution was to obtain the property at a lesser cost which would enable its restructured debt obligations to be met. Henry's strength as a real estate investor was always, as will be demonstrated later, as a highly disciplined buyer. If he could selectively purchase well located and structurally sound pieces of property on terms to his liking, he did, but he never overpaid. Many were the debtors who chafed at being involuntarily subjected to a forced foreclosure sale at which Henry was the high bidder at a price well below market. The lowball offers he made led, on several occasions, to lawsuits, but the flip side was if he could acquire a property at a cost below his predecessor's, then he didn't need as much revenue as the former owner did to service whatever debt he needed to place on the property. That differential could make the difference between whether Jennie's household budget had to be further strained or not. Indeed, rental income from his real estate acquisitions could well have augmented his salary at Judson, to the point that servicing the debt he wrote about to Emma might have been an exaggerated liability. Unfortunately, the absence of records puts all of this into the realm of speculation, although it does provide a ready explanation for how Henry, who was not known to make rash decisions where it came to money, would have been able to close escrow on those five properties he was in the process of acquiring at the time he wrote to Emma.

Henry's daughter, Genevieve, always used to say that her father was well known for being heartless when it came to business, and although "heartless" may not be the most accurate term to describe this side of his personality, it certainly appears that he drove hard bargains, watched his expenses extremely closely, and was at all times opportunistic. An example (albeit occurring some ten years later) is found in a letter written in 1911 by a woman named Nellie Calloway to a San Francisco attorney, William Herron.[163] In that letter, Ms. Callaway is said to have expressed her belief that her late husband's inheritance had been absconded with through the fraudulent actions of his uncle's executor. She claimed, among other things, that the executor, a Mr. Poppe, had colluded with Henry Bothin to arrange a sale, in 1902, of a parcel of land in downtown San Francisco for $75. She went on to claim that the sale was made to a Mr. W.B. Waldron, "who was merely a tool for Mr. Bothin," and that, after the expenses of the sale had been paid, there remained only $0.85 to be distributed among the heirs. As an aside, the property in question is now a portion of the site of Embarcadero 3, a well-known and hugely valuable downtown high-rise office building in a prime commercial location in San Francisco. While Nellie Calloway may have exaggerated the facts a bit, the thrust of her complaint is consistent with other contemporary accounts, all of which confirm his attention to the cost side of any transaction. It is also true that among the properties owned by Henry at the time of his death is one whose address matches Mrs. Calloway's story exactly.[164]

Another example of Henry's attention to costs is found in a case entitled *Dunn v Dunn*.[165] There, as reported by the Court, in 1898, Henry purchased a parcel of land in San Francisco (exact location unknown) at an auction. The case arose because the sellers were dissatisfied with his winning bid of $15,500. They went to court to object to confirmation of the sale. In court, several real estate experts testified that the actual value of the lot he bought was between $22,500 and $25,000 (to wit, more than 50 percent over what he paid). Ultimately, the Supreme Court confirmed the sale, concluding that just because Henry had reaped a financial windfall, there were no grounds for setting aside the sale.

Furthermore, Henry knew more than one way to maximize return. Another California Supreme Court case is illustrative. In *Bancroft Whitney Co v McHugh*[166] Henry is reported to have been the owner, at the time of the 1906 earthquake, of a single story brick building with a basement in a prime downtown location (612-622 California Street). Bancroft Whitney Co., publishers of law books, was the tenant until the building was consumed in the fire; in its aftermath, Bancroft Whitney decided to move. Henry entered into a ground lease with W.R. Grace Company, the understanding being that Grace would build its own building on the site for its use. The case turned on issues that are not relevant to Henry's ownership, but it illustrates another side to Henry's creativity. Rather than incur the expense of rebuilding on the lot, he simply entered into a ground lease and thereby retained ownership of the valuable location. He found a way to have it generate income, and left it to others to bear the construction cost and risk.

While the point of Henry's tight fisted approach to buying and holding real estate has been adequately driven home, it is also worth noting that even a man as astute and disciplined as Henry could not anticipate everything that can go wrong with a real estate acquisition. In *Henry Bothin v Cal Title Insurance and Trust Co*, a case that was decided in 1908 by California's Supreme Court (153 Cal 718) the court ruled that, despite Henry's reasonable reliance on a title report that failed to show an obvious defect, the title insurance policy nonetheless did not provide coverage. Henry had purchased, from the Sharon Estate, two waterfront lots that had apparently been erroneously surveyed, such that both his side boundaries were off by 14'. As a result of that error, which was not picked up by the title company, Henry ultimately was involved in five separate lawsuits wherein he was either defending or prosecuting claims for encroachment and/or adverse possession. Ultimately he was awarded title to the square footage he had paid for, but the property lines ended up at angles rather than straight lines, which diminished its value by about 10 percent. In 1900, Henry filed suit against the title company to reimburse him for his legal costs and damages. The title company defended itself based on a clause in the fine print of the policy, which essentially allowed it to avoid its insurance obligation. Despite widespread criticism of the insurer, including a scathing front page newspaper article that suggested the carrier was dishonest and should not be permitted to write policies,the California Supreme Court upheld the lower court's ruling in favor of the title insurer.[167]

Returning now to the hiatus in effect between December, 1890 and February, 1895 during which Henry did not purchase any known real estate, there are a number of reasons which seem to make sense. The question of domestic pressure has already been raised; however, from a purely business perspective, it has to be recognized that he had his plate full on several fronts. Although he had sold Bothin Manufacturing to Julius during that period, it would have taken time to unwind relationships, to mentor Julius in the business, and to tie up other loose ends. Far more important, however, is that he was just settling into his role as controlling owner of Judson, as well as beginning his learning curve toward operational control. That curve began in 1889 when, as majority owner, he was elected Executive Vice President, and it continued, presumably under the tutelage first of Egbert Judson and, after his death, L.P. Drexler, until 1895 when he formally and publicly took over the company's helm. No matter how confident Henry might have been of his abilities, the very fact that he stood back for six years and essentially immersed himself in a high stakes real-world business education at Judson shows that he was also very much a realist. Although there was probably little doubt in his mind that he would, when he was ready, assume operational control, he showed patience and good business judgment. Undoubtedly, he spent most of his days during those six years between 1889 and 1895 at Judson absorbing all there was to learn about the hardware and construction-grade iron business, and that would have left him with very little, if any, time to concentrate on real estate accumulation. Finally, another consideration was no doubt at play, and that was his financial capacity. Even if he had been willing to buck Jennie's undoubted frustration over his tight control over the household budget, the likelihood is that he had reached the upper limit of available credit with which to finance further real estate acquisitions. Hence, even if he had wanted to stay active as a real estate investor, he might have been constrained by credit limitations.

The year 1890 also saw Henry busy in another way altogether. In August of that year he was one of nineteen citizens selected for the Civil Grand Jury.[168] In California and Nevada, Grand Juries serve a completely different role than the petit juries that people normally associate with the word "jury." The latter serve for a specific time and purpose, and they deal with a single event—either a charged crime or a civil dispute, both requiring resolution by a jury of one's peers. The former, on the other hand, are a group of citizens who generally apply for the position of Grand Juror and are impanelled for up to a year to provide oversight of local government. While they also can and often do decide whether or not to indict accused criminals, their main focus is to investigate abuses and inefficiencies in government and to generally oversee the usefulness and effectiveness of taxpayer expenditures. They have the right to require governmental workers to testify under oath with respect to the issues they choose to investigate, and they submit a report at the end of their term.[169] In the case of the Grand Jury on which Henry served, it did return eleven criminal indictments, but more importantly it also examined the books of the various municipal departments of the City; concluded that the tax burden on the citizens was overly onerous; questioned the manner by which the City and County of San Francisco granted railroad franchises and the specific terms of those grants; suggested ordinances requiring undergrounding of electric lines; suggested the elimination of burial grounds within the city proper; emphatically condemned the Board of Supervisors for overpaying various commissioners, particularly those charged with oversight over the widening of streets; condemned the purchase of a pest house that had been protested by the Board of Health as unfit for the purpose intended; and, on a positive note, complimented certain city officers for doing their jobs well, including the City and County Treasurer, Auditor, Tax Collector, Assessor, Sheriff, Recorder, and the Clerk's office of the Board of Supervisors. It also congratulated the Health Board, while at the same time deploring the run down and unsanitary conditions present in the morgue. In addition, it echoed the sentiment of prior grand juries in criticizing the jail as being too small, overcrowded, unsafe, unsanitary and badly in need to being enlarged or replaced altogether. Finally, it took the Fire Department to task for the inadequate size of its water mains and the woeful shortage of hydrants.[170] This work has been presented in some detail to provide the reader with an understanding of the time commitment and the amount of work done by members of the Grand Jury, including Henry. Undoubtedly the commitment of time he made to serve on that body left him with little free time to pursue sideline business issues, or even pleasure, during the six months of his service.

Then came 1892. In his letter dated November 8, 1892, to his sister, Emma, Henry, quite possibly for the first time in his business life, expressed fear. Specifically, he wrote:

> "...Some two years ago as my interests in the iron business were quite large, to give Julius a chance to get up again, I sold him my manufacturing business and took back his note for same, that through mismanagement and extravagance is all lost and I may still lose more coming on top of my Father's conduct at his time in life. You can imagine how I feel. I am for the first time in fifteen years trying to economize and know what worry is. I do not blame anyone but myself in this matter..."

The fear of the unknown Henry described, albeit briefly, in that letter would be enough to cause anyone to trim expenses and to hoard cash to protect himself, his family, and his other investments from the claims of creditors.

If 1892 was a bad year for Henry, 1893 was worse. In that year the country fell into the worst economic depression it had ever suffered. The 1880s had been a period of rapid growth and expansion of the economy, a time when people exuded confidence and when markets overheated. Railroads were overbuilt, silver was plentiful with more being discovered daily, San Francisco passed Cincinnati to become the eighth largest city in the country, and there seemed to be no stopping its outward expansion to markets opening in the Orient and elsewhere. Times were too good; and then, on February 23, 1893, the Philadelphia and Reading Railroad declared bankruptcy. Washington overreacted, with the result that the economy worsened quickly. People rushed to withdraw money from banks, bank runs followed, more railroads failed (specifically the Northern Pacific, The Union Pacific, and the Atchison, Topeka and Santa Fe), and ultimately over 15,000 companies and 500 banks (many in the West) went under. The corporate failures brought with them massive job layoffs to the point where, at its worst, the country had nearly 19 percent unemployment.[171] In that time of financial crisis, no banks were lending, and Henry probably could not have borrowed to buy more real estate even if he wanted to.

As if the Panic of 1893 hadn't brought enough bad news, on January 9, 1893 Egbert Judson, the founder of the company and its president since 1882, died. Henry was wise enough to understand that he was not ready to assume the reins at that time, and L.P. Drexler was brought in from outside to become the caretaker president.[172] Again, it is unfortunate that no records remain of Judson during this period, but it is a safe bet to assume that Mr. Drexler's management skills were tested to their limit just to keep the company from going under, and to prevent Henry's loss of his entire investment. Apparently Mr. Drexler did a superb job. Judson remained in business, and, in 1895, Henry took over the reins of a reasonably healthy company and remained president until about 1920, when he resigned in favor of his great nephew, Carlos Maas.

Although the depression of 1893 did not formally end until 1897, seemingly Judson had either remained healthy or had resumed profitable operations before then. Meanwhile, Henry had completed his learning curve to the point of feeling comfortable in his role as its president. Under the circumstances, he seems to have felt secure enough financially to be able to tiptoe back into his passion for accumulating San Francisco commercial real estate. Specifically, he bought two properties in February 1895, three more in 1896, and then two more in 1897. Then, as the country came roaring back to economic health, he bought four more properties in 1898, and then went into overdrive, buying twenty-seven in 1899, thirty-six in 1900, forty-four in 1901, fifty-eight as of October 8 1902 (when a gap appears in the Index through January of 1903), and finally, twenty-four more properties in 1903.

This manuscript is not meant as an exhaustive re-creation of Henry's real estate portfolio, and with 200 acquisitions confirmed, the point has been made—Henry E. Bothin had become a man obsessed, and a property owner of serious magnitude. It is also obvious that he had demonstrated his business acumen and had found lenders willing to advance credit in rather enormous quantities for the purchase of upwards of four, and sometimes five, parcels of commercial real estate per month. These were not insignificant parcels either. Although in the *Deed Book* many simply recite token consideration, actual purchase prices in the $20,000 to $50,000 range are not uncommon. If Henry felt nervous back in 1890 with $90,000 in debt, or if he felt fear in 1892 over uncertainties arising out of his brother's mismanagement of his manufacturing company, he did not seem nervous at all at the turn of the century when he was sitting on well over 200 parcels of valuable real estate and trying to keep track of them, manage their debt load, oversee the collection of rent and outflow of expenses, see to their physical condition and improvement where appropriate, and tend to the myriad other operational issues confronting the business of owning an empire of that magnitude.

However he was able to make the finances work, it must be remembered that Henry's bottom line goal was to position his real estate acquisitions in the path of growth and the demand for steel. Yet, it is also notable that he, himself, actually only built one building of ten or more stories. That was the Atlas Building, a building he constructed in 1904, which was one of only two out of the 81 buildings Henry owned on April 18, 1906 to survive that catastrophic earthquake and fire. Located at 604 Mission Street, the Atlas Building still stands tall today. Designed by architect Frank Van Trees, it was a ten story, steel framed building, which housed Henry's offices from the time of its completion until his death nineteen years later.

Of Henry's other commercial properties, most were improved with small structures generally ranging from one to three stories in height, and, almost without exception, they had a rental revenue

The Atlas Building at 604 Mission Street, the tallest building Henry built, survived the 1906 earthquake.

stream already in place. Many of his properties were adjacent to one another and were presumably purchased in order to aggregate larger bundles of square footage, which he would have expected to have become dramatically more valuable once the direction of downtown growth began moving south of Market Street. His property acquisitions seem to have been part of a long-term plan to accumulate income-producing land in the path of progress and to patiently wait for his properties to appreciate for a while; in the meantime, he collected rents in the short-to-intermediate time frames. That sort of plan rewarded patience over instant gratification, but it was not at all inconsistent with Henry's nature, which was to buy cheap and hold. As stated by Al Schreck, one of the partners in KSW Partners who purchased the Bothin Real Estate Company's portfolio in 1970— and a man who spent over forty years managing those properties, Henry's purchases seem not so much rifle shots into a specifically targeted location, as they were wise purchases of properties with underlying location values in different parts of town. In other words, he hedged his bets, always buying as advantageously as possible (witness the number of probate sales he attended) and also always bearing in mind the limited supply of real estate in San Francisco which, after all, was and is surrounded on three sides by water.

Looking at Henry's acquisitions through the filter of the old real estate adage of "location, location, location," it would seem, from Al Schreck's perspective, that he must have viewed the entire city as a prime location, quite possibly due to its geographical limitations and small size as compared to the magnitude of its brief but impressive history of dramatic growth and promise of greater expansion to come. However, even if the City taken as an entirety warranted that broad of a brushstroke in terms of location value, it is interesting to take a closer look in that context at some of his decisions. For instance, the inventory of properties owned at his death shows that, of 84 described properties located within San Francisco, 48 (or 57 percent) were located south of Market Street. Another 23 (27 percent) were in the vicinity of the northern waterfront. Only four (5 percent) were located within the boundary of what was considered "downtown" at the time of his death in 1923.

2240 Polk Street (at the intersection of Polk and Green Streets) was positioned near the northern waterfront area.

John's Restaurant at 63 Ellis St.
One of San Francisco's oldest restaurants, it has been in business since 1908. Best known as a setting in Dashiell Hammett's The Maltese Falcon.

Clearly Henry was willing to bet heavily that the direction of the City's future commercial expansion would be south of Market Street. He was right, although it would take nearly a century from the date of his first acquisition to prove that assessment correct. Perhaps a factor in the intensity with which Henry pursued South of Market properties was the paucity of demand for properties in that part of town and his resulting ability to buy there advantageously. Still, lower purchase costs can often translate into lower rental income and reduced resale value, thereby proving the truth of the adage. The trick is to be farsighted, to anticipate valuable locations before others do, and to buy opportunistically only in locations that will reward your prescience. Events would suggest that Henry was, indeed, astute. For, in 1985, following several years of study by planners and much vocal public debate, the City's Board of Supervisors adopted the "Downtown Plan" as part of the City's Master Plan. This plan was designed to provide developers with incentives to locate office buildings, retail, and residential construction in the South of Market (SoMa) district.[173] Between 1985 and 2009, 26.2 million square feet of commercial space was built in the area designated in the plan as "C-3," the "downtown zone," and much of that growth occurred in locations where Henry had invested. For example, one modern highrise, commonly known as 333 Market Street, is bounded on the north, east and west by Market, Beale and Fremont Streets respectively. The developer of 333 Market Street had to acquire an aggregation of lots in order to site and construct that building. Henry owned four parcels within that property envelope.

In addition, he built a commercial structure at 500 Howard Street, which has since gone through several renovations and remains an integral and central part of downtown today. He also owned the property at 615 Mission Street which became the headquarters of Owl Drug Store, known for delicious milkshakes and other soda fountain treats and also for its colorful and distinctive pill bottles which remain in great demand today as collectors' items.

Inset photo is the old headquarters of the Owl Drug Store. Main photo is the same building, renovated and as it appears in 2014.

500 Howard St (2014)
500 Howard St (1986)
500 Howard St (as constructed
after the 1906 earthquake)

This office highrise at 333 Market Street is bounded by Market, Fremont and Beale streets. Henry Bothin owned several properties on that land, including 341 Market Street (inset photo), 19-21 Fremont, 25 Fremont, and 30 Beale Street.

222 Second Street, a Tishman Speyer highrise office building under construction. Some of the land was owned by Bothin Real Estate Co.

Foundry Square III is another Tishman Speyer office building that covers land once owned by the Bothin Real Estate Co., in this case 206 1st Street.

The Transit Tower shown on the facing page is the jewel of the San Francisco Transit Center District Plan, and a key component of the City's Downtown Plan, which was adopted in 1985. The Downtown Plan, intended to serve over 20,000,000 users annually, envisioned the future growth of the downtown area as being south of Market Street and surrounding what was then the old Transbay Bus Terminal. Many of the properties Henry Bothin owned, and specifically those listed below, were located on land directly under or in the immediate zone of impact of this project.

30-40 Natoma Street (between 1st and 2nd Street)
39 Natoma Street
42 Natoma Street
46 Natoma Street
48 Natoma Street
54 Natoma Street
60 Natoma Street
61 Natoma Street
67 Natoma Street
63-67 Minna Street
39-41 Tehama Street
37 Clementina Street
57-65 Clementina Street
79 Clementina Street
144 Second Street
228-234 Fremont Street
236 Fremont Street
500 Howard Street
546-550 Howard Street
552-554 Howard Street
580 Folsom Street

The Transbay Project Transit Tower

Henry's gamble about the direction of growth was obviously tied inextricably to his quest for a burgeoning market for steel, but it was underlain also by a core belief that San Francisco would continue to grow and become not just a west coast metropolis, but indeed a global center of commerce and trade. Travel and transportation would be the key underpinnings of that vision, and while the railroad was fulfilling a part of that destiny, there was another mode of transit which was also very much on the minds of the businessmen of the day. From the time gold was first discovered in California, pressure had grown for a canal that would dramatically reduce the time it would take to travel by sea between the two coasts of North America.

In 1878 the Columbian government (of which Panama was then a part) granted approval to a French company, La Société Internationale du Canal Interocéanique, to dig a canal across the Isthmus of Panama. The French, under the direction of Ferdinand Marie de Lesseps, the man who had, in 1869, built the Suez Canal, began construction in 1881 of a sea level canal and almost immediately realized that, unlike the relative ease of digging through sand in Suez, here they would have to excavate through the hard rock spine of Central America, whose ridge at that point rose about 360 feet above sea level. While that and other engineering obstacles made progress difficult, the barrier that ultimately proved insurmountable for them was the death, due to malaria and yellow fever, of nearly 22,000 workmen. By 1889, just as Henry was beginning to acquire his initial properties in San Francisco, the French abandoned their project after completing only 40 percent of the work at a cost of nearly $235,000,000.

Nonetheless, the writing was on the wall, and it was clear that, despite fierce opposition from railroad interests whose high-priced monopolies were threatened by a canal, at some point the commercial and strategic interests of the United States to minimize the time delays between its two coasts for both passenger and freight traffic would result in a canal becoming a reality. Indeed, in 1887, even as the French were struggling to build their canal through Panama, the United States began studying an alternative route through Nicaragua. Although that study's funding fell victim to the recession in 1893, the effort regained traction in 1897, and ground was actually broken on some preliminary construction in Nicaragua. The work was discontinued when the United States acquired the assets of the defunct French company and began talks with Columbia to gain permission to complete that earlier effort. Although those discussions dragged on and ultimately involved some creative, if not questionable, diplomatic maneuvering, including President Roosevelt's decision to back Panamanian rebels in their successful quest for independence from Columbia, ultimately in 1904 the United States gained control of the Canal Zone and, over the next ten years, was able to complete the job.

The Panamanian government was understandably grateful, and with that in mind, the United States was able to come to terms on a perpetual lease of the ten mile wide Canal Zone for an initial payment of $10,000,000 plus a lease fee of $250,000 per year. For that, our nation gained a hugely valuable asset that was to change worldwide shipping patterns forever and, in the process, save about 7,800 miles of transit distance between New York and San Francisco by way of the dangerous Cape Horn.

So, to a patient man, the combination of the transcontinental railroad, which was already in place, and the promise of a dramatically improved route by sea, would have proved highly enticing as a rationale for owning real estate in California's then-principal business center.

Obviously, an effort to fully understand Henry's motivations and approach to real estate risk-taking is like seeking the deep inner meaning of a deceased artist's expression on canvas. The discussion is always interesting but ultimately entirely speculative. Perhaps the easiest way to understand what was going on in Henry's mind when he began to accumulate his real estate empire is to read an article written in the *San Francisco Call* on April 15, 1906—just three days before the horrendous earthquake and fire which so devastated the City and nearly every structure in it. The reporter stated:

> It is said of H.E Bothin that he has bought the greatest number of properties of any man in San Francisco. He buys for investment and not for speculation. He started in about ten years ago when times were dull and bought many Hibernia Bank properties acquired through foreclosure. He also bought heavily south of Market Street and in the wholesale district north of Market Street at a time when nobody else was very much interested in them and has extensive holdings in North Beach. As most of these properties have increased from 33 1-3 to 50 percent, some idea can be gained of the value of Mr. Bothin's holdings at the present time. It is said he owns several hundred pieces of property.

That reporter presumably interviewed Henry for his article and, assuming he accurately reported that conversation, it would seem Henry was simply trying to be opportunistic, a result he accomplished brilliantly. Even so, there remain a number of questions. For instance, why did he suddenly wake up one day and decide that buying distressed properties made sense? What made Henry feel he was qualified to decide whether a distressed property was really a jewel, as opposed to a repeat of the same poor decision his predecessor in title probably had made earlier? Why would a man with a family decide to go on the sort of buying spree Henry did without any formal training or experience in the field he was embarking upon? How was Henry able to convince lenders that he was any better as a risk than the person before him who had defaulted on his Hibernia mortgage? What criteria did Henry use in evaluating location values, income potential, or any of the other considerations a real estate professional would use before making a buy/no buy decision? Ultimately, we still have to return to the same place and the same questions that persist despite the April 15, 1906 article.

It has been virtually impossible to learn what sorts of properties Henry had acquired by 1890; however, it does seem clear that all were bought using financing and that undoubtedly his access to lenders put him in an advantageous position when negotiating terms. Therefore, it seems appropriate to discuss the financing options he then had available. First, one has to assume that Henry's track record at Bothin Dallemand was reasonably impressive. One comes to that conclusion for several reasons. The first involves the luck of simply being in the right place at the right time. For instance, as was stated in a 1947 publication from the National Bureau of Economic Research,[174] in those days near the end of the 19th century "business operations were extremely profitable, and vendors had alternative employments for their funds which were very remunerative." So, Henry had the good fortune of acting on his entrepreneurial instincts in the midst of a rapidly expanding and highly profitable economy, and in a city that was growing as fast as any in the nation. Secondly, by 1888 when he made his first purchase, he would have been able to document twelve years of business success with Bothin Dallemand, and that undoubtedly would have qualified him as a decent banking risk. Still, bank loans were altogether different in those days than they are today. Banking relationships were typically governed by the "classical theory," meaning short term advances (generally ranging from 30 days up to one year) which, although often rolled over, were expected to be repaid at least annually,[175] even if the payment was arranged by another loan from a different lender, a strategy which was looked on favorably as evidence that the borrower could convince more than one lender of his credit worthiness.

No matter what the terms were of any credit facility Henry was working with, it is clear that he would have had to prove his capacity not only to repay his loans but to service the debt as well. While his salary at Judson might have provided him with the ability to service debt on the eleven properties he owned as of the date of his 1890 letter to Emma, clearly the next five properties, which he was already at that time in the midst of buying, would have taken him beyond his means unless the properties themselves generated their own income streams to provide the needed cash flow. Since he did in fact close escrow on those other five properties and then, after a five year hiatus, resumed his buying thereafter, it follows that one of Henry's requirements must have been that any property he bought would carry its own weight. That pretty much eliminates raw land, at least for his initial purchases. The terms of the debt instruments he signed, and even the sources of his early financing, will probably never be known; however, we do know that short term interest rates in San Francisco in the late 1880s were within the range of 4.5-6 percent per annum. Thus, he was likely paying something near $350 to $400 per month to his bank to finance his ownership of those first eleven properties. To put that into proper perspective, the average weekly income earned by a family of four during this general period was $14.

This biography is not intended to include an exhaustive look at all of Henry Bothin's properties. Given the reality of poor record survival after the '06 fire, plus the complexity of piecing together over 220 deeds, with their metes and bounds descriptions, into a huge jigsaw puzzle, it would simply be beyond both the purpose and the scope of this undertaking. The task at hand is not to re-create his empire, but to preserve a sense of the man, his motivations, his accomplishments, and the environment in which he lived. That said, the general locations and the timing of his acquisitions do tend to place his talents into proper context.

Neither Henry's initial purchases, nor those bought later, are described in the Grantor/Grantee indices, which simply provide dates of purchase or sale, the identity of the other party to the transactions, and a reference to the book and page number in the

Deed Book. Nor are the *Deed Books* themselves particularly helpful. They do sometimes recite consideration paid (although often a token consideration of $10 or a similar sum is used in the public record), and they describe the parcel; however, they don't indicate whether the property was or was not improved and, if so, by what. Nor do they reference the source of funds used in the acquisition or any security interests taken by a lender.

About the only source for information about what improvements may have been located on a given parcel at the time of purchase are the hookup records of the San Francisco Water Company, which did survive the 1906 conflagration. However, even those are sketchy, in part since many of the addresses of buildings changed as new structures replaced the old, destroyed buildings in the aftermath and reconstruction of the city. Many, indeed most, of San Francisco's buildings were rebuilt after the fire with different entry positions, and therefore different street numbers for addresses, and since the Water Company's records are kept by address, most of the pre-fire addresses no longer exist in their records. Furthermore, most of their records have been expunged over time, and, as they relate to Henry's properties, only a handful of records remain. For those reasons, the Water Company is at best a somewhat helpful resource with obvious limitations.

With these limitations in mind, the Water Company's files do include records showing that at least three of Henry's properties (530 Folsom St., 554 Howard St., and 225-227 Sacramento St.) had had buildings on them where water service was provided, before Henry even arrived in San Francisco—two in 1862 and one in 1865—thus establishing that he purchased them as improved (and presumably income-producing) properties. Another (63-67 Minna St.) was given a water hookup in August, 1906 and can be assumed, therefore, to have been one of his earlier post-fire restorations. Another, at 546 Howard St., appears to have first applied for service in August, 1937; however, a note indicates that as of January, 1905 it had a structure on it. Henry's flagship building, the one he called the "Atlas Building" where he located his offices and presumably kept all his files and records, obtained its initial water service in 1905. Given that it survived the fire, it is not clear why the Water Company records show it was given a new water hookup in September 1907. A number of other buildings are included in the Water Company records; however, they are all later records, typically showing initial entries during the 1920s and 1930s.

As to real estate values, one assumes, if for no other reason than that Henry became extremely wealthy through his ownership of real estate, that he bought and managed his properties very well. Still, it is helpful to understand a bit about the values of real estate in San Francisco around the time he was making his acquisitions. Fortunately, an article appearing in the February 23, 1902 edition of the *San Francisco Call* provides a glimpse at then-current values. That article, which reported on recent sales closed by several real estate firms, reads as follows:

> Southwest corner of Sutter and Powell Streets, with frontage of 100 feet on Sutter and 75 feet on Powell, with frame building improvements renting for $4,200 per annum...for $125,000. Northeast corner of Lombard and Taylor streets, 137'6" x 132'6," with frame buildings, to Henry E. Bothin for $15,000; ... the southeast corner of Sutter and Taylor streets, 45'8" x 81'8" for $50,000; ...southeast corner of Vallejo and Pierce streets for $12,500; ...six flats and lot, 50' x 112' on the westerly line of Larkin between Jackson and Pacific for $23,500; northeast corner of Pacific Avenue and Scott street for $25,000 [the price to include an adjacent lot]...

That same article provides information also regarding construction costs:

> The building contracts filed during the week just passed numbered thirty and represented the total of $204,422.20 [for an average cost of $6,814 per contract] ...five story apartment house...at Bush and Powell streets indicate a cost of $30,900; erection of a two story brick building to be used as an oyster depot on the north line of Brannan street, east from Third, to cost $12,450; ...three story frame building with basement [at Bush near Divisadero] at a cost of $12,000; ...two story and attic and basement frame residence on the southwest corner of Fell and Steiner streets to cost about $17,000; ...twenty-six apartments of four and five rooms each [on Eddy street near Gough] the total cost being about $60,000; ...three flats on the north line of Pacific avenue between Larkin and Polk to cost $10,000; seven flats...on the west line of Masonic avenue near Waller, the aggregate cost of which will be $17,000; flats will be erected by Henry E. Bothin on the southwest corner of Van Ness avenue and Bay street (no cost given)...

From the foregoing, it becomes clear that buying, owning, and improving real estate was neither inexpensive nor a job for amateurs. As an example, the property that sold for $125,000 at Sutter and Powell streets sold at a 3.5 cap rate based on $4,200 in annual rental income. That means that a person buying for all cash was willing to accept a 3.5 percent annual yield for the privilege of owning the parcel. If borrowed dollars were involved in the purchase, a yield as low as that would have been eaten up by debt service and would have put the property into a negative cash flow situation, an obviously dangerous situation and one which would have scared any potential lender away. That building represented far greater risk to its owner than do most of today's purchases when cap rates typically range from 6-10 percent or more, depending on location, zoning, condition, and other considerations. Although the foregoing is just a snapshot of one transaction, and not a particularly clear picture either, it does reveal that the same risks and attention to location, to highest and best use, to financing options, to construction costs and techniques, to maximizing rental income, and to preserving value that are so important today were really no different 110 years ago. Today the only reason one would buy at a 3.5 cap rate would be if he expected to raze the existing improvements and re-build for a higher and better use, which would command far greater rental income. The point is that real estate, particularly commercial real estate, is a complex business that is best left to experts. The fact that Henry was able to find as many parcels to buy as he did, and that his empire was as profitable as it was, is a testament to an expertise he either learned on the job or, more probably, was innate in his genetic makeup. This is particularly so given that his day job lay elsewhere and had nothing to do with the commercial real estate marketplace. In short, Henry's success was as much driven by talent and hard work as would be the case today.. Now (and then), there are too few hours in a day for most people to stay on top of the dynamic and ever-changing informational databases, techniques, rule changes, competitive factors, and everything else needed to succeed both as the CEO of a steel company and, at the same time, as a professional in the commercial real estate marketplace. To have had those talents and to have been willing to commit the time necessary to apply them simultaneously to both the steel and real estate marketplaces was remarkable.

12.
Outside Business Interests and Directorships

Henry's engine was always working. Not only did he find time to run Judson and to make his name in the local real estate world, but he was also active in other pursuits as well. For instance, in 1890, he was one of the originators of a company called Mead Dry Press Brick Machine Company. The Articles of Incorporation, which were reported in the October 7, 1890 edition of the *Sacramento Daily Record-Union*, revealed that he was a founding director of the company, whose capitalization was set at $100,000. On the face of it, a brick manufacturing company would seem to be a complementary business venture; however, for whatever the reason, the venture appears to have failed within about three years.

On January 10, 1903 Henry showed a hitherto unseen side of his character. Until then, he seems to have stayed completely out of the limelight and out of politics, but on that date he appeared before the San Francisco Board of Supervisors, stating that he was prepared to invest $20,000 or more in a franchise to run a bus service along those of the city's major boulevards that were not already served by streetcars. He proposed charging no more than five cents per rider and indicated he would be up and running within four months of approval of his franchise. His primary objective was to serve the Van Ness corridor, from Market Street to the Bay.[176] Although there is nothing further stated in the public record about why the franchise was not approved, the politics of the day provide ample reason, and that reason is personified in Abe Ruef.

Born in 1864, Abraham Rueff (who later dropped the last "f" off his name) was a brilliant and hugely controversial man who in effect ruled San Francisco as the force behind the Mayor's office from 1901 until his criminal trial in 1906. He was brilliant, a childhood prodigy who spoke eight languages, a graduate of the University of California at the age of eighteen, and at the age of twenty-one a graduate of law school and a member of the State Bar of California. His passion was politics. Ruef had studied San Francisco's political past, when corporate graft predominated and the Southern Pacific Railroad controlled both political parties. Corruption was rife, and the city's moneyed interests controlled the public purse strings. Ruef first joined the Republican Party in the late 1880s, but by 1901 he had become disappointed at his lack of progress within that machine. His chance to grab power presented itself when, in 1901, waterfront workers and teamsters struck but were beaten back by Mayor Phelan and his police department. Angry and frustrated, many of the city's over 65 different unions came together to form the Union Labor Party (ULP). Sensing an opportunity, Ruef used his legal talents to write the new party's platform, used his contacts and persuasive powers to bring saloon keepers and bartenders into the fold, and in general injected himself into the center of the fray. He then persuaded one of his law clients, Eugene Schmitz, the head of the musician's union, to run as the party's candidate for mayor, and he taught Schmitz the political skills he would need to win. When Schmitz won election, Ruef was firmly entrenched as the power broker behind the scenes.

In reality, Schmitz's election changed nothing fundamentally. City Hall remained as corrupt as ever; however, now the favors were handed out by a new and different organization, one that paid lip service to the working class but in fact sold patronage favors to the highest bidder, just as before. In the midst of all this, Abe Ruef signed on as unpaid counsel to the mayor's office and used that role to expand his own client base and to dole out favors. He would collect monthly legal fees from individuals and corporations, pocket half, and spread the other half among the mayor's office and his allies on the Board of Supervisors. But it wasn't just payoffs that Ruef specialized in. He would meet with supervisors behind closed doors and coach them, both individually and collectively, on how to speak publicly on issues as well as on the desired outcome of the vote on a particular issue.

How did all this impact Henry? During the time that Henry became interested in establishing a bus line, the whole issue of trolleys and busses was a hot political issue. By 1900, horse-drawn streetcars and cable-powered cable cars were being rapidly replaced by electric powered trolleys that had been first introduced in 1892, and which were being installed and operated by by United Railroads. The electric power for these trolleys was delivered via overhead power lines that were seen by many, and in particular by Rudolph Spreckles, as ugly and a blight that reduced the property value of the houses that had to look out on them. United Railroads had been, since 1902, paying Ruef regular "consulting fees," whose obvious purpose was to maintain political support for the overhead lines, which they claimed were dramatically less expensive to install than the underground conduits that Spreckles, former Mayor Phelan, and others were clamoring for.[177]

The fact that Henry's proposal was not approved clearly suggests that either he was unwilling to pay Ruef under the table or, more likely, United Railroads saw his proposal as unwanted competition and bought the votes needed to reject the franchise proposal.

Turning back to other business involvements, in 1903, and undoubtedly owing to his involvement in Judson (whose manufacturing plant was located in Emeryville), Henry became one of five founding directors of The Syndicate Bank, an East Bay based bank that was incorporated in July of that year.[178]

Also in 1903, Henry joined several well-respected Bay Area businessmen in becoming a director of the San Francisco Gas and Electric Company. They included William Bourn (owner of the Empire Gold Mine and President of Spring Valley Water Company); Albert Payson (Officer of the Spring Valley Water Company); William J. Dutton (President of Firemans Fund Insurance Co.); J. Downey Harvey (President of the Shore Valley Railway Company); Osgood Hooker (a director of Spring Valley Water Company); Homer S. King (Treasurer and a Director of Wells Fargo Company as well as a Director of the Southern Pacific Railroad Company); Edward J. McCutchen (senior partner of the highly respected law firm of McCutchen, Olney & Willard); Louis F. Monteagle (a director of numerous public companies); Daniel T. Murphy (senior partner in the dry goods firm of Murphy, Grant & Co); and Rudolph Spreckles (heir to the Spreckles Sugar fortune).[179] Although SFG&E was ultimately merged into Pacific Gas and Electric Co., it was still providing power to San Francisco when, in the 1906 earthquake and fire, its main gas plant, a brick structure at the foot of Fillmore Street in North Beach, was very badly damaged by the quake.[180] Although no major gas leaks materialized, its pressurized lines were compromised, leaving it unable, for some time, to provide gas for either heating or lighting.

Less than three years after Henry had joined the S.F. Gas and Electric Board, on March 1, 1906 at the time of consolidation of many of the independent power and lighting companies into the new Pacific Gas and Electric Company (commonly referred to as PG&E),

Henry and Louis Monteagle were together elected to PG&E's Board and, in so doing, become the last of what PG&E still calls its group of "founding directors." PG&E had been initially formed in 1905 as the final step in amalgamating most of the various independent utility companies operating throughout Northern California and establishing an integrated area-wide power grid and distribution system. It had an initial capitalization of $45 million and had the backing of major New York financiers. Over the next few years, it completed its takeover of the independents, including San Francisco Gas and Electric Co, and, by 1914, it had become one of the five largest utilities in the United States and was supplying over 1.3 million people with their power needs. Henry remained an active director of this rapidly expanding public utility up to the time of his death in 1923. During his tenure, PG&E suffered enormous losses to its infrastructure as a result of the 1906 disaster, rebuilt, changed over from an outmoded flat rate billing system to one based on metered usage (and, in the process, installed 116,000 meters by 1912), and greatly expanded both its power generating capacity and the size of its customer base. The fact that he was not just a founding director, but he also continued on as a director for the eighteen years left of his life, suggests the level of respect he had come to be accorded by his business peers.

Sometime during the period prior to the 1906 earthquake and fire, Henry also became a director of The California Insurance Company of San Francisco, an insurer whose directors included, besides Henry, a number of other wealthy and highly regarded local businessmen including Charles Holbrook (of Holbrook, Merrill and Stetson, manufacturer of stoves and other metal products); D. Ghirardelli (founder of Ghirardelli Chocolate Company); George L. Payne (Payne Bolt Works); and A.D. Cutler and E.A. Denicke (who were both well-known local "capitalists.") This insurance company was one of the few insurers that would earn a good reputation for claims payments following the earthquake and fire. Indeed, having lost all its records in the inferno, it nonetheless paid 100 cents on the dollar on all claims presented to it (some of which were undoubtedly Henry's.)[181] Those claims were paid by money raised through assessments on shareholders. As a result of the way it conducted itself after the earthquake and fire, the company received accolades from the press and others.[182]

Finally, sometime prior to 1904 Henry became a director of the Oceanic Steamship Company, a company owned by the Spreckles family, which itself owned a number of seagoing vessels that plied the Pacific Ocean between California, Hawaii, Australia and New Zealand. Henry was one of two non-family directors, and this experience must have been both frustrating and educational for him, for the company was not doing well, and he seemed powerless to improve its plight. On January 22, 1904 the *San Francisco Call* reported on the company's annual meeting, where operating losses were announced for both 1903 (a loss of about $234,000) and 1902 (a loss of nearly $350,000.) Still, management was optimistic that, with renewed contracts for mail delivery to and from both Australia and New Zealand, 1904 would show a profit. Unfortunately, the March 22, 1907 edition of the *Hawaiian Gazette* reported that the company was still going through hard times, which were now blamed largely on disruptions caused by the 1906 earthquake and fire. Both Australia and New Zealand had pulled their mail contracts, which put the company on very precarious footing. Although the article suggested that it was about to default on bond interest payments and would likely not survive long, it turns out the company did in fact survive until 1926, when it was sold to Matson Lines. Since that company was not listed in his obituary, it is assumed Henry resigned his board position, although just when that happened is not known.

So, by the time of the devastating 1906 earthquake and fire, Henry was the President of Judson Manufacturing Co., was a director of Pacific Gas and Electric Co, was a founding director of the Syndicate Bank in Emeryville, was a director of the California

Insurance Co, was a director of Oceanic Steamship Company, and had accumulated over 200 commercial properties in San Francisco, many, if not all, with buildings on them. When one looks at the caliber of the businessmen who had become his peers, it is apparent that Henry had, by the time of the 1906 disaster, become one of the more respected citizens of the City and a person whose views and opinions were highly sought after.

13.
Marin County, Across the Bay

During the last decade of the 19th century and the first few years of the 20th, Henry became increasingly interested in moving out of San Francisco and moving to Marin County, just north of the Golden Gate. It was also during that period that he first became interested in philanthropy. Unfortunately, both those interests contributed (probably unwittingly and almost certainly unintentionally) to the breakup of his marriage to Jennie.

As to the first of those interests, in 1896 Henry and Jennie began spending summers in the Ross Valley—he enthusiastically and she reluctantly. Although Henry came to love the serenity of Marin, it would appear that Jennie was a reticent and unhappy participant. Either she didn't object loudly enough, or he wasn't listening, for in 1898 Henry purchased and built the first of three different homes he would eventually construct on land in the town of Ross.

What caused Henry to become infatuated with Marin County is not known; however, the fact that he did is telling in many ways about his nature and his priorities. Unlike Burlingame, Woodside and other communities that were located an easy train ride south of the city and were then attracting many of its well-to-do citizens, who were building ever grander estates and trying to outspend one another as though their lives and social status depended on it, Marin County was remote and accessible only by ferries, followed by a train ride to one's ultimate destination. But while it may have been less easily accessible, the draw of Marin was its natural beauty, which was centered around Mt. Tamalpais, whose three 2,500-foot peaks would have been plainly visible and inviting from the Bothins' San Francisco home.

Marin County's 828 square miles are surrounded on three sides by water. Even today over 50 percent of its rolling hills, oak covered woodlands, majestic redwood stands, and rugged coastline are dedicated as permanent open space, a testament to the importance placed by its residents on protecting its scenic values for future generations to enjoy. In Henry's day, getting there required a water crossing over a bay that can often be shrouded by fog and buffeted by heavy currents and swiftly changing tidal action. An article appearing in the *New York Times* on January 24, 1891 reported:

> The Bay of San Francisco is noted for the fierceness and swiftness of its tides as well as for the endless number of rips and eddies which make the passage of a ship through them extremely dangerous. The United States Board of Engineers made a number of observations not long ago which showed that approximately 110,000,000,000 feet of water runs out past Fort Point in seven hours, which is over six times as much as passes New Orleans in the swift flowing Mississippi River during the same time. Such a tremendous body of water passing through such a narrow channel as the Golden Gate naturally produces a current fierce, swift and dangerous.

When looked at from a present-day perspective, the article exaggerated the dangers of the Bay, at least to those riding on large ferries, however, even today all too many swimmers, wind surfers, and sailboaters have come to grief by underestimating the treacherousness of its temperature and tides. Furthermore, the danger of fog could not and cannot be overstated. Indeed, in 1901, two ferries, the *Sausalito* and the *San Rafael*, the latter with 200 passengers aboard, did indeed collide near Alcatraz Island; the *San Rafael* sank and suffered a loss of life of at least one and possibly as many as five passengers.[183]

So, even if today a commute between San Francisco and Marin is commonplace and certainly not considered dangerous, when looked at through a nineteenth century lens, a decision to build a home in Marin, which carried with it the implicit recognition of a daily train ride and ferry crossing, was one not taken lightly. That Henry so clearly favored Marin over the Peninsula speaks to his lack of interest in "running with the pack" and also reveals an appreciation for the natural world that is not otherwise much visible in the small universe of information known about him.

In the late 1890s, Marin County was a pastoral paradise, a mere seventeen minutes by ferry from San Francisco and yet a world away from the pace of city life. Its leading citizens were farmers and ranchers, while those with connections to San Francisco were few. That is not to say that Henry was a pioneer in choosing Marin, or more specifically the Ross Valley, for his second home, but the others who had, including wholesale merchant Edward Schmiedell; Judge Hall McAllister; attorney Alexander Morrison; banker James Coffin; Alaska fishing tycoon Capt. Millen Griffith; attorney George Butler; railroad and energy innovator John Martin; and others, do not appear in any records as being among Henry's friends, social acquaintances, or business contacts. Nor do any of them appear among the guests at his and Jennie's wedding, and none of their wives appear among the women with whom Jennie was known to play bridge or otherwise keep company. So it seems Henry was interested in Marin County for reasons that had nothing to do with friendships or relationships with people he and Jennie spent time with.[184]

Not only was Marin County devoid of old friends of the Bothins, but it attracted an entirely different group of people than those who would normally have traveled to the Peninsula for weekends. Marin was (and is) a hiker's destination, a place for active people who enjoy strenuous exercise, birding, wildflowers, and the natural world and Mt. Tamalpais was and is the centerpiece of their lifestyle, providing an almost Mecca-like attraction to those who crave it. As early as 1884, a register maintained by the Tamalpais Club shows that 850 men, women and children, including poet Joaquin Miller, and future San Francisco mayor Eugene Schmitz, had hiked to the summit of the East Peak during the previous four years, and that doesn't count ascents to either of the other two peaks. Nor does it include hikers who belonged to other clubs, which included the Cross Country Club, the Sightseers Club, the Columbia Park Boys Club, the Sempervirens Club, and the California Camera Club. Many of the routes to one of the three summits of the mountain, including Shaver's Grade and Eldridge Grade, began at the Sunnyside train station in Ross, and hikers would have walked from there up Lagunitas Road directly in front of Henry's property to the trailheads that were within easy walking distance of the land he was to buy.[185]

Mt. Tamalpais is also the site of the annual Dipsea Race, the oldest cross-country race on the West Coast. Although the first running of that race occurred in 1904, six years after Henry bought his first piece of property in Marin County, it is included here because it further describes the sorts of people who were attracted to Marin. That first race was set on a grueling course, which begins with 676 steps—as high as a fifty story building—and has a net elevation gain of just over 2,000 feet over the length of its 6.8 mile course. It connects Mill Valley (near the shoreline of Richardson Bay) with Stinson Beach (a small town on the Pacific Ocean.) The fact that 90 runners finished that first race is a testament to the physical and mental toughness of those who ran it. This is particularly so when one considers that running shoes as we know them didn't exist in those days and that exercise as a form of preventative medicine would not be even thought of by the medical community for well over half a century.[186]

Access to central Marin was via the North Pacific Coast Railroad (NPC) that had begun construction in 1873 of a line extending from its ferry terminal in Sausalito north to the Ross Valley, and from there, west through Kentfield, Ross, San Anselmo, Fairfax, and on out to West Marin and beyond.[187] In time, Henry would become a director of the company that later purchased NPC, but that is another story.

The railroad brought not only hikers and runners to the region, but picnickers and ordinary people looking for a bucolic spot to spend their Sundays and holidays as well. And, as central as Mt. Tamalpais was to Marin County in those days, it was not the only attraction. For example, in its issue dated June 2, 1900, the *Marin County Tocsin* reported that 5,000 people had visited the Fairfax picnic grounds in a single day. In his book *Marin, a History*, Barry Spitz noted that by 1901 passenger traffic had increased to the point that the railroad added a second set of parallel tracks between the towns of Corte Madera and San Anselmo to increase the number of daily train trips.[188] Within five years, that level of traffic had grown on peak summer days to 20,000.[189]

There is no known evidence that Henry was himself a hiker, nor was he a runner. Nonetheless, he was attracted to Marin County, and more specifically to the town of Ross, which lies in the shadow of Mt. Tam. His first Ross purchase, on February 1, 1898, was a 2.8-acre parcel, for which he paid $1,250 (less than $1/1000^{th}$ of what the same parcel would sell for today). The parcel was purchased from the estate of Albert Dibblee, a pioneer San Francisco merchant who had, in about 1870, purchased 78 acres in the town of Ross from the estate of the town's founder, James Ross. The parcel Henry bought was located at the southern end of Mr. Dibblee's holdings and bordered the north side of Lagunitas Road, just west of Glenwood

Ave. At that time, Glenwood Ave.[190] was a private road—presumably part of Mr. Dibblee's driveway—and in the deed the Dibblee estate reserved the right to erect a gate at its terminus at Lagunitas Road. The lot was also located across the street from the present day Lagunitas Club; of which his daughter, Genevieve, always said her mother, Jennie, was one of the founders.[191] According to Genevieve, Henry and Jennie built a modest shingle house located in a redwood grove on that property, and the family came over to live there during the summer.[192] They were at that house when, in July 1901, Henry's son, Frank, died.[193] Although Frank Bothin didn't live long enough to make an imprint of his own, his death from polio (then known as infantile paralysis) was the cause of what would shortly thereafter blossom into Henry's commitment to philanthropy, which is his enduring legacy.

Across the street on the south side of Lagunitas Road, there had, years before, existed a roadhouse called the Pink Saloon.[194] Lagunitas Road had originally been the main artery from the Ross Valley to Bolinas and the coast. Not only was it a road well-traveled by hikers climbing Mt. Tamalpais, it was also a logging road over which loggers hauled the trunks of giant redwoods, cut in the hills to the west, over to a saw mill located near what is today the campus of the College of Marin. William Kent, descendent of a Chicago meat packing family, a successful three term member of Congress in his own right, and the man who purchased and gave to the federal government the landmark redwood grove that we know as Muir Woods, described the Pink Saloon in his book, *Reminiscences of the Outdoor Life*, as "a rough and ready place where booze and the company of women could be had after a hard day's work."[195] For obvious reasons, the good citizens of Ross, preferring other uses for the property near where they were raising their children, wanted to see the roadhouse gone. Sometime during the 1880s, a group of Ross residents[196] formed the Ross Improvement Company and in that name purchased the land and evicted the tenants. In 1901 at least two residents, S.B.

McNear and Mrs. E.G. Schmeidell, persuaded the owners of the property to lease it to them for a social club. Thus was born the Lagunitas Club. The club was formally incorporated on October 13, 1904, and Henry was one of its founding directors.

Unfortunately, the records of the Lagunitas Club between 1904 and 1916 are missing. It is known that Henry remained a member for the rest of his life, and as its President during the period 1919-1921. Unlike many of the club's neighbors today who complain about noise, traffic and anything else which might disturb their tranquility, Henry, then the club's nearest neighbor, appears to have enjoyed a good relationship with it during his lifetime.

On December 31, 1902, nearly five years after purchasing his first property in Ross, Henry purchased a second piece of property directly across Glenwood Ave from his initial home site. From the standpoint of his marriage, both the timing and the location of that purchase could not have been worse. This property, a 5.8-acre level lot with a creek running through it, was and is still a magnificent piece of property; however, its location was within a block of the place where Jennie had, just eighteen months before, lost her son Frank. Whether she might ever again have consented to live anywhere in Marin County, much less Ross with all its sad memories of young Frank, is not known, but certainly one would think that a husband with any sense and sensitivity would have waited longer than eighteen months before asking her to return to live in a place in plain view of and located less than a block away from the home where Frank died.

Despite the utter thoughtlessness of buying where he did, the lot itself and its surroundings were, and are still, magnificent. It was (and is still) covered with elms and oaks, and it has a small creek running through it. Further enhancing its natural beauty was a pond, nearly an acre in size, that he built just in front of the large home he planned to build. Then, in November 1904, Henry purchased an additional 1.12 acres adjacent to and east of the big lot, which expanded the total lot size to nearly 7 acres. His daughter, Genevieve, said that after the earthquake, but before Henry and Jennie went through their divorce, Henry built a house on that lot; Genevieve called it "hideous" and "the ugliest house you've probably ever seen in the world," adding that Henry "had no taste."

Bothin Ross residence viewed from the lake

I believe Henry built that home to try to rekindle Jennie's interest in Ross, and to entice her to move out of their home on Jackson Street in San Francisco and over to Ross on a year-round basis. If that was his goal, he failed completely. In the first place, Jennie was too attached to her life in San Francisco to consider a move to Ross. Second, he should have known that his timing and the location of this property were such that he was destined not only to fail, but to flop miserably.

Jennie Bothin driving in Ross, 1904

There is much more to be said about Henry's connections with the town of Ross, a town he would call home for the rest of his life; but most of those connections arose after his marriage to his second wife, the former Ellen Chabot. However, Marin County was also extremely important to Henry during the time he and Jennie were together. It was, after all, there where he bought the ranch that would ultimately be inextricably connected to his interest in philanthropy; his interest in Marin County lives on to this day in the form of the foundation he and Ellen would later create.

14.
The Fairfax Ranch and Early Philanthropy

Henry's passion for helping the less fortunate, which would one day consume a major part of his life, began inauspiciously enough in February 1903 with his purchase of a 1,232 acre ranch in Fairfax from Phoebe Hearst, the widow of U.S. Senator George Hearst and mother of newspaper mogul William Randolph Hearst. The ranch was a portion of Rancho Canada de Herrera (also sometimes known as "La Divina Providencia.") As a portion of an earlier Mexican land grant to Domingo Sais, the ranch had gone through a number of prior ownerships,[197] including being the subject of two gold mining claims in the 1870s. Its barn had been the intended site of an illegal boxing match in 1889 pitting "Gentleman Jim" Corbett against Olympic Club boxer Joe Choynsky.[198]

Rancho Canada de Herrera extended from the town of Fairfax out to the ridgeline atop White's Hill. The portion Henry purchased was but a fraction of the original land grant, and its easterly boundary was pegged to the right of way for the old road that ran west out of Fairfax and extended steeply up the eastern toe of White's Hill, and ultimately across the summit and into the San Geronimo

Valley beyond. To say that old road was steep is a serious understatement. It was described in detail in a book authored by Jack Mason and Helen Van Cleave Park, and entitled *The Making of Marin*. They wrote:

> White's Hill intimidated travelers for a century. The wagon road Jesse Colwell built over it in 1865 with coolie labor was so steep folks got down and walked to give their horses a rest.[199] ...The notorious grade was off limits to the first horseless carriages. E.A. Langford made it across in 1905 despite the warning sign but was arrested on his return and fined $10. O.D. Huntsman of Olema recalls backing his Model T Ford all the way up the hill to get gasoline into his updraft carburetor.

Steep though the road grade may have been along his easterly boundary, this new ranch of Henry's also contained oak lined meadows, creeks, and rolling hills and was a spectacular piece of land. It was also strategically located along the main route from Fairfax to Pt. Reyes Station via the beautiful San Geronimo and Nicasio valleys. These bucolic valleys, at that time populated by more dairy cattle than people, were being slated for future development. Indeed, in 1863 the little town of Nicasio had been laid out in anticipation of becoming the county seat for Marin County, an event which although it never never materialized,[200] is nonetheless an example of the expectations of the day for the projected direction of growth. Perhaps an even better example of the degree of anticipated population growth throughout western Marin County was the fact that, despite the difficulties presented by White's Hill, the railroads were busy creating a means of rail transit, either across or by tunnel, through that natural obstacle. Mason and Park wrote:

> The North Pacific Coast Railroad faced its biggest test here in 1873, but—again using coolie

muscle—accomplished the near impossible. The imperturbable Chinese hacked at hillsides with pick and shovel. Charges of giant powder—an innovation then—sent rocks flying. Ox teams from Ross Landing pulled trestle timbers up the ravines. Near the summit hardrock men drilled and blasted a 1,200 foot tunnel, while a shorter one was punched through below. Passengers on the first run, January 7, 1875, were astounded at how the tracks twisted and turned to gain altitude; curves so sharp they 'could see their locomotive headed in the opposite direction from themselves...'

The North Pacific Coast Railroad did in fact overcome White's Hill and managed to run its tracks through the San Geronimo Valley beyond and along Lagunitas Creek out to Olema and Pt. Reyes Station. Until 1930 it carried lumber, local dairy and agricultural products, as well as passengers between Sausalito (where it connected by ferry to San Francisco), through the Ross Valley to Fairfax, over White's Hill, west to Pt. Reyes Station, and then along the east shore of Tomales Bay up to Duncan Mills and Cazadero in Sonoma County. The North Pacific was sold in 1902 to new owners who renamed it the North Shore Railroad. Those new owners took steps in 1903 and 1904 to greatly simplify the route by building a new tunnel through White's Hill. As stated by Mason and Park:

> The railroad took matters in hand in 1903. By now it was the North Shore [Railroad]... The North Shore got permission from Phoebe Apperson Hearst, owner of 1,230 acres of the hillside, to bore a new tunnel 3,190 feet long. The re-routed tracks, opened to traffic on December 4, 1904, came out at what was to be Woodacre, and eliminated a 4.7 mile climb. Tunnel and cut-off were named for Henry E. Bothin

of Ross, who had bought Mrs. Hearst's ranch on February 4, 1903.[201]

As with most of his involvements, Henry didn't sit idly by and watch passively as the railroad wound around the edges of his ranch. He became a director of the North Shore Railroad shortly after he bought the ranch, and, as reported in the August 15, 1904 edition of the *San Francisco Call*, when management of that railroad was taken over by A.W. Foster, who was also the President of the California Northwestern Railroad, Henry was the only member of the prior board who was kept on as a director under the new management.

The land was located strategically. Rumors abounded over Henry's intentions for that property, it being suggested at various times that he intended to build a large home for himself, that he intended to subdivide the ranch into residential home sites, and, lastly, that his ultimate intention was to capture the drainage from its watershed and channel it into a water system to supply the Ross Valley with water in competition with the Marin County Water Company (the predecessor of today's Marin Municipal Water District.)[202] That latter rumor is interesting and was based on speculation, supposedly from "many" people, who wondered if his announced intent of spending up to $100,000 to build a reservoir on the property might have translated into an intent to create a competitive water company, whose purpose might have been to break the MCWC water monopoly and thereby cause its largely absentee British investors to sell their holdings to Henry at a bargain price. This rumor suggests that Henry's reputation as a crafty businessman was by then quite well established, but rumors aside, there is no evidence that Henry ever did in fact even design, much less build, a large reservoir on the property. Ultimately, he did subdivide a portion of the property near the Fairfax train station, a neighborhood now known as Bothin Manor, and he also split the remainder of the property (those parts not included in either the Bothin Manor subdivision or the property he later gave to support charities) into two parcels, one of 482 acres and one of 570 acres. Both properties were listed as part of his estate at the time of his death.

Whatever he might have initially intended to do with the property became irrelevant when Henry met Elizabeth Ashe. Miss Ashe was the daughter of a prominent San Franciscan, Doctor Richard Porter Ashe, who was descended from a long line of Ashe family members who had distinguished themselves in medicine, law and government, and had been the namesakes of the city of Asheville, North Carolina. She was also the niece of Admiral David Glasgow Farragut, the commander-in-chief of the U.S. Navy during the Civil War. He is the naval hero who is said to have coined the phrase "Damn the torpedoes! Full steam ahead!" as he led his convoy of eighteen ships to victory at the Battle of Mobile Bay, a major turning point in the War Between the States.[203]

Born in 1869 in San Francisco and raised in well-to-do circumstances, Elizabeth Haywood Ashe began her early adult life as a Sunday school teacher at Grace Cathedral in San Francisco. In 1890 she and a fellow teacher, Alice Griffith, began to look seriously at the unhealthy conditions affecting many poor and mostly immigrant children and their parents who lived in the northeast quadrant of the city. The two budding community activists formed an organization known as "The Willing Circle" with a goal to improve the health, welfare and living conditions of the poor.

Elizabeth Haywood Ashe

The first target of their organization was the Gray brothers, who had for years been making a living dynamiting and quarrying the eastern slope of Telegraph Hill, occasionally toppling the shanties where many of those Italian and Irish immigrant families lived at their peril. Young though they were, the two women were undaunted by the battles they knew lay ahead. They declared war on the Gray brothers and fought with them in court, ultimately doing battle for thirteen years before a court order finally began to turn the tide in favor of the tenants. By then both Miss Ashe and Miss Griffith had expanded their horizons and grown well beyond whatever fight was still left in the Gray brothers.

Through sheer force of personality and an obvious caring attitude, Miss Ashe and Miss Griffith quickly gained the trust of the area's immigrant communities. In 1890, they created a boys club and also classes for girls in sewing, reading, gardening, cooking and other skills. In time they also set up a health clinic for neighborhood children, provided supervised recreation to keep children off the streets, brought in nurses to educate immigrant mothers in basic health and hygiene, and otherwise dedicated themselves to improving the lot of the city's underserved. Along the way, the two young and energetic women became aware of the largely windowless basement spaces where women toiled indoors, under conditions of poor light and air, and where tuberculosis was fast becoming a deadly byproduct of those unhealthy working circumstances.

Recognizing that she needed greater medical skills in order to fulfill her goals of improving the health and well-being of San Francisco's poor and vulnerable, Miss Ashe left San Francisco to attend classes at Presbyterian Hospital in New York, graduating in 1902 as a nurse. She then spent the next several months at the Henry Street Settlement House in New York before returning to San Francisco with the goal of creating an educational and respite center for the poor, patterned after the Hull House model, which was then successfully in place in Chicago. She and Miss Griffith soon established the Telegraph Hill Neighborhood House (THNH), an institution that remains in existence today under the name Telegraph Hill Neighborhood Center. Nurse Ashe used THNH as a base, where in 1903 she began a Dispensary Clinic and what would now be called a visiting nurses program, offering nursing care and information about sanitation and hygiene.

Mrs. John Kittle (a member of a well-known pioneer family in the town of Ross) made available to the "visiting nurses of the Telegraph Hill Association" a small cottage on her husband's property (now the Marin Art and Garden Center), and Miss Ashe traveled back and forth on the ferry to and from the cottage with her sick children. She later described her chance meeting with Henry Bothin on one of those ferryboat crossings, a meeting that would change both of their lives:

> In the summer of 1903 much of my time was spent traveling back and forth on the Sausalito Ferry conducting children to the Ross home. On one of these trips, I was seen carrying a small boy in my arms by Mr. Henry Bothin, who sought an introduction to me. He sat beside me to the journey's end, asking me innumerable questions. He learned from me that my little patient was a victim of infantile paralysis. It was not very much later that he confided in me that his only son had died from that dread disease. Mr. Bothin's interest continued to develop and before the summer was over, he promised to place at my disposal a tract of land in Marin County two miles from Fairfax. I drove out with him in his buggy to see the place and was entranced by the possibilities. It was an ideal site for our needs.[204]

In short order Henry had made available to Miss Ashe the use of a portion of the Fairfax ranch. He then delighted in seeing what she did with it for the sake of her young patients and charges. Miss Ashe said that Henry drove his buggy out to Fairfax every Sunday to see the children she was caring for. By the spring of 1905, an old farmhouse on the ranch was renovated, and on June 1st the first of twelve ill children arrived at the newly named "Hill Farm" and were cared for all summer long. Miss Ashe wrote, in an undated memo, about Henry's interest in the children:

> Mr. Bothin's interest increased daily. He spent every Sunday morning at Hill Farm with the children. He learned to know each child and his little history. Tony Garcia, aged six, particularly appealed to him.[205]

After closing for the winter, Hill Farm was then re-opened unexpectedly and hurriedly on April 22, 1906, four days after the disastrous earthquake and fire. It quickly became a sanctuary for initially about twenty people, most being mothers with infants and small children in their arms. Then, as spring turned to summer that year, Hill Farm ultimately came to be a refugee camp for 263 displaced souls. It was staffed by two doctors, three nurses and two teachers who opened a school for the children.

It is not clear just what the initial financial arrangement was between Henry and Miss Ashe; however, all that would change in about five years when Henry would take steps to assure Hill Farm's permanent financial stability.

Elizabeth Ashe and the children at Hill Farm

Children at Hill Farm

Hill Farm

Children at Hill Farm

15.
Hemet

Jennie's father's ambitious project in Hemet, in Southern California, was briefly mentioned earlier. Although Henry was not directly involved in the project, he did invest in the town, and he also built a large home there. The reason for his decision to invest—and rather heavily, it turns out—in his father-in-law's venture is not at all clear. Certainly Henry owed Frank Whittier at least a debt of gratitude for having given Jennie and him their large and comfortable home in San Francisco as a wedding present; however, Frank had more than enough money to cover his Hemet investment and certainly didn't need help from his son-in-law. Furthermore, Jennie's differences with Henry were about the way he spent their money, and so, knowing her father's comfortable financial position well, she would most assuredly have had the same objections to Henry's buying property in Hemet as when he did so in San Francisco.

No matter the motive or the folly, the fact remains that Henry did invest substantial capital in Hemet. His first involvement appears to have been an interest, probably developed sometime during 1905, in embarking on a co-venture with his father-in-law to build an electric railroad line from Redlands in Southern California out to Hemet.[206] That endeavor was ultimately abandoned; however, before that happened, he bought land in Moreno (a town along the proposed route of the railroad line) and he also began buying property in Hemet. Specifically, he purchased a large lot in the center of town at the corner of Harvard and Florida Avenue, and on it he built a two-story brick office building called the Bothin Building.[207] He then made that site an immediately popular landmark by erecting a flagpole in the middle of the intersection that he dedicated to the honor of the people of Hemet.[208] One can only assume that his intent was to enhance the image of the intersection and to thereby increase the value of the location. In 1907, he installed a vault on the ground floor of the building and leased it to The Farmers and Merchants Bank of Los Angeles, which was probably at that time the largest and best run bank in Southern California, having been started by Elias Hellman who went on to buy The Nevada Bank in San Francisco and then merged it into Wells Fargo Bank.

Also during 1905, Henry purchased 26 lots (comprising 85 acres) on Park Hill, the highest location in Hemet and an area that had been slated to be the center of its best neighborhood. He immediately began the construction there of a twenty-one room mansion. In so doing, he made two mistakes. First, he paid his father-in-law $12,610.40 for the land, but failed to buy any water right certificates. By the time he got around to recognizing the need for water, he was in the middle of his divorce, and his father-in-law refused to grant him any favors. Later, after buying water certificates at a higher price than he would have gotten them for initially, he sued Whittier, claiming unsuccessfully that his ornamental trees had been stunted by the lack of water.[209] His second mistake with regard to the Park Hill property was his assumption that Jennie would like it. Although apparently it was patterned after a house that both he and Jennie had liked while on a European tour, either the timing or the location was bad, for the Bothins never occupied that huge house.[210] Later it was leased for various purposes, including uses as a hotel and as a hospital. It remained in Henry's ownership until his death and was finally sold by his estate. The mansion was a single story colonnaded structure sitting atop a stark and barren hill, and it resembled more a mausoleum than a residence. Had his daughter, Genevieve, been asked about it, she would probably have said that, like the house in Ross, it too was "perfectly horrid."

Hemet mansion, front (above) and back (below)

Perhaps it would have been spruced up by well-designed landscaping and by a lady's touch; however, from the looks of it, one would have to say that Jennie cannot be faulted for shunning it and refusing to take on the daunting task of trying to improve that unsightly blight on the horizon.

Yet despite its ugliness, Henry must have had a reason for building that house. The only reason that makes sense is that he did it for Jennie, in the belief, albeit naively mistaken, that investing in her family's project would be appreciated and might help to salvage what was by then a sour marriage. As such, Henry's involvements in Hemet seem to simply affirm his lack of understanding of what motivated Jennie and the breadth of the chasm that was dividing them.

By the time Henry began his accumulation of properties in and around Hemet, he and Jennie were no longer living together and were married in name only. He was in the midst of improving the parcels he bought in Hemet when Jennie filed for divorce, and there is no indication he spent much money or effort there once those legal papers had been filed. Accordingly, this chapter, although highly relevant to the story of his life, is, of necessity and circumstance, rather brief.

16.
1906 Earthquake and Fire

Just when all of his various business, personal, and philanthropic endeavors were whirling around and needing stability, Henry was rocked to the core by the great San Francisco Earthquake and Fire. Historically, neither earthquakes nor devastating fires were new to San Franciscans. Indeed, no fewer than 344 noticeable tremors had been reported in San Francisco between July 28, 1769 and March 5, 1906,[211] and earthquakes occurring in 1856, 1865, 1868, and 1898 had left significant damage in their wake, including loss of life and property, prompting forewarnings of more and bigger shakers to come.[212]

Still, no amount of prior warning could have prepared the citizens of the city by the bay for what was to happen in the early morning hours of April 18, 1906. At approximately 5:12 a.m., as early risers were just starting to greet the new day and as most others lay asleep in their beds, the whole city suddenly felt the foreshock that was shortly to be followed by 40 to 60 seconds of shaking and rolling that would change their lives forever. The event began about ten miles below the crust of the earth as the Pacific Plate and the North American Plate, having pushed in opposite directions alongside one another for decades, finally reached the break point at their boundaries along the San Andreas fault line and snapped back, releasing built up pressure, much like an elastic band does as it snaps.[213] The plates snapped back, indifferent to the mayhem the resulting release of pressure caused at the earth's surface far above them.

It is one thing to mouth the word "earthquake," but it is quite another to experience one, and yet another still to adequately describe the experience. Notable contemporary authors Mark Twain and John Muir both wrote about other large quakes they had lived through, and Jack London wrote about the 1906 event. Mark Twain was in San Francisco on October 8, 1865 when the city was hit by a large tremor. He wrote:

> As I turned the corner, around a frame house, there was a great rattle and jar, and it occurred to me that here was an item!—no doubt a fight in that house. Before I could turn and seek the door, there came a terrific shock; the ground seemed to roll under me as waves, interrupted by a violent juggling up and down, and there was a heavy grinding noise as of brick houses rubbing together. I fell up against the frame house and hurt my elbow. I knew what it was now…a third and still severer shock came, and as I reeled about on the pavement trying to keep my footing, I saw a sight! The entire front of a tall four-story brick building on Third Street sprung outward like a door and fell sprawling across the street, raising a great dust-like volume of smoke!
>
> And here came the buggy—overboard went the man, and in less time than I can tell it the vehicle was distributed in small fragments along three hundred yards of street… The streetcar had stopped, the horses were rearing and plunging, the passengers were pouring out at both ends, and one fat man had crashed halfway through a glass window on one

side of the car, got wedged fast, and was squirming and screaming like an impaled madman. Every door of every house, as far as the eye could reach, was vomiting a stream of human beings; and almost before one could execute a wink and begin another, there was a massed multitude of people stretching in endless procession down every street my position commanded. Never was a solemn solitude turned into teeming life quicker.[214]

John Muir wrote from his cabin in Yosemite Valley about the March 26, 1872 earthquake in the Owens Valley. Muir, like Twain—but from a different perspective, and quite probably because he saw it from a mostly unpopulated vantage point—was enthralled by the power and the wonder of nature displayed in this quake. He wrote:

> At half past two o'clock of a moonlit morning in March, I was awakened by a tremendous earthquake, and though I had never before enjoyed a storm of this sort, the strange thrilling motion could not be mistaken, and I ran out of my cabin, both glad and frightened, shouting, 'A noble earthquake!' feeling sure I was going to learn something.
>
> The shocks were so violent and varied, and succeeded one another so closely, that I had to balance myself carefully in walking as if on the deck of a ship among waves, and it seemed impossible that the high cliffs of the Valley could escape being shattered. In particular, I feared that the sheer-fronted Sentinel Rock, towering above my cabin, would be shaken down, and I took shelter back of a large yellow pine, hoping that it might protect me from at least the smaller outbounding boulders.

> For a minute or two the shocks became more and more violent—flashing horizontal thrusts mixed with a few twists and battering, explosive, upheaving jolts—as if Nature were wrecking her Yosemite temple, and getting ready to build a still better one.
>
> ...It was a calm moonlit night, and no sound was heard for the first minute or so [after the earthquake], save low, muffled, underground, bubbling rumblings, and the whispering and rustling of the agitated trees, as if Nature were holding her breath. Then, suddenly, out of the strange silence and strange motion there came a tremendous roar. The Eagle Rock on the south wall, about a half mile up the valley, gave way and I saw it falling in thousands of the great boulders I had so long been studying, pouring to the Valley floor in a free curve luminous from friction, making a terribly sublime spectacle—an arc of glowing passionate fire, fifteen hundred feet span, as true in form and as serene in beauty as a rainbow in the midst of the stupendous, roaring rockstorm.[215]

Even those descriptions, being mere words, cannot truly convey a sense of the surreal experience one feels when surrounded by a force of nature that in the space of seconds can humble the strongest man with a display of force beyond imagination. If nothing else, it truly shows us all how insignificant we are in the overall scope of planetary events. Hurricanes, tornados, tsunamis and other hugely impactful events provide the same feeling of helplessness, but earthquakes, because they provide no warning and because they literally arise from the ground beneath us, are particularly awesome and terrifying.

Jack London described the scene the 1906 earthquake left behind in San Francisco in an article in *Collier's, the National Weekly* on May 5, 1906:

> Not in history has a modern imperial city been so completely destroyed. San Francisco is gone... On Wednesday morning at a quarter past five came the earthquake. A minute later the flames were leaping upward. In a dozen different quarters south of Market Street, in the working-class ghetto, and in the factories, fires started. There was no opposing the flames. There was no organization, no communication. All the cunning adjustments of a twentieth century city had been smashed by the earthquake. The streets were humped into ridges and depressions, and piled with the debris of fallen walls. The steel rails were twisted into perpendicular and horizontal angles. The telephone and telegraph systems were disrupted. And the great water-mains had burst. All the shrewd contrivances and safeguards of man had been thrown out of gear by thirty seconds' twitching of the earth-crust.

In the case of the 1906 earthquake, it was not only fearsome for the devastation it wreaked by itself, but it also destroyed the city's defenses against fire, and by doing that, it magnified many times the overall devastation that it caused.

Just as San Francisco had faced earthquakes before, the city was also no stranger to cataclysmic fires, having endured not one but six major fires during just its first two years of existence.[216] Because of that history, the Fire Department was well equipped. Indeed, the day before the disaster began, it had 584 firemen deployed in 38 steam fire engine companies, 10 hook and ladder truck companies, 8 chemical engine companies, one water tower company and two monitor batteries, all housed in forty-four fire stations spread throughout the city, which altogether held 14 steam fire engines, 16 hose wagons, 4 hook and ladder trucks and a significant number of other pieces of fire support apparatus.

Yet all that manpower and equipment, used to its fullest, was unable to prevent the 1906 fire from becoming "the greatest conflagration humans have ever witnessed."[217] Why? To begin with, the city's main reservoirs (Crystal Springs and Pilarcitas) were located over twenty miles away and connected to the city by pipelines, six miles of which were located directly on the fault line and were destroyed in the quake. Thus, from the outset, the city had no reservoir capacity to provide water for firefighting purposes. Other pipelines were laid in filled ground and were broken when the fill turned to mush and failed due to liquefaction. And, as it turned out, the city's failure to have any fireboats was also nearly fatal, although ultimately fireboats and other vessels provided by the U.S. Navy made up for that deficiency. Other than what the Navy provided, the city's own supply of water was quickly depleted, and that became depressingly obvious as firefighters tried to hook up to one hydrant after another, only to realize that the fireplugs contained just trickles of water and were absolutely useless. What water was readily available was limited, for the most part, to what could be gotten from cisterns and the sewer system as well as the fireboats, without which the fires would, if one could believe it possible, have been far worse.[218] Furthermore, Dennis T. Sullivan, the popular Fire Chief, lay mortally wounded from injuries he suffered when a chimney from the neighboring California Theatre crashed into the firehouse where he was living. His death left the department leaderless.

Within several hours of the earthquake, approximately fifty-two fires broke out in different parts of the city. Given the magnitude of the trembler that had just occurred, that wasn't surprising. Stoves toppled, chimneys collapsed, lanterns overturned, electric wires broke and touched other live wires, causing shorts, and anything else that could become a fire hazard seemed to find a way to go wrong. Had there been water to fight those fires, many, indeed perhaps most, would likely never have gotten out of control or posed the threat to the community that they did. Unfortunately, those small, medium sized and large fires simply overwhelmed the firefighters despite their nearly Herculean and round the clock efforts.

Furthermore, there was a failure of leadership. With the Fire Chief dead, and Mayor Schmitz about to be indicted for corruption and extortion, and with the commanding officer of the army garrison in the Presidio out of town, the ingredients for turning what was already a disaster into a major catastrophe were at hand. Indeed, had it not been for heroic action on the part of the U.S. Navy, and specifically Lieutenant Frederick N. Freeman, matters might have been decidedly worse.

Lieutenant Freeman's report of naval assistance, dated April 30, 1906, was ordered classified by the Navy (apparently because the Navy had not been appropriately asked to render assistance by the state and so was not following proper protocols). Therefore, the report was not made available to researchers until sometime during the 1980s. It is a fascinating document, explaining on the one hand what federal assets he brought to bear in trying to help save a city on fire, while, on the other, diplomatically avoiding casting blame for some very questionable decisions made by both the acting commandant of the army's base at the Presidio, Brigadier General Frederick Funston, and Mayor Schmitz.

As to Schmitz, his incompetence was not unexpected. He never had been a natural leader and was generally considered a pawn in the political arsenal of Boss Abe Ruef. Whatever skills Schmitz might have at one time been able to muster were being eroded by a series of strongly worded articles that appeared in the *San Francisco Bulletin*, written by investigative journalist Fremont Older, that were exposing Schmitz, Ruef, and their cronies for their corruption and deceit. Indeed, within a matter of months, Schmitz would be tried, convicted, and sentenced to prison for his wrongdoing. Although Schmitz would have loved to find a crisis he could deal with honorably and capably, if for no other reason than to restore a bit of credibility, it seems the only memorable contribution he made to the effort to save the city during this crisis was to issue a highly controversial edict that purportedly gave, not only to the police but also to federal troops from the Presidio, the right to shoot and kill looters on sight.

Mayor Eugene Schmitz

General Funston's role was more complex. Determined to save the city, Funston ordered the troops at the Presidio to report to the Chief of Police, which they did. In many respects their presence (and also the presence of members of the California National Guard) was helpful, as they pitched in to restore order, prevent looting, and stand guard at damaged buildings. They also played an import-

General Frederick Funston

ant role in the search for survivors, and they provided medical treatment, food, temporary shelter, and sanitation. However, untrained as they were in the roles they were playing, the troops also frequently acted heavy handedly, and, in many cases prematurely, by forcibly evacuating people too soon from their dwellings, and thereby prevented many residents from being able to defend and save their homes. General Funston has also come under criticism from some for advocating and perhaps overzealously using dynamite to destroy houses in the path of fires in an effort to create firebreaks. On the other hand, he was acting in the moment, and, with water scarce, hose limited, strong winds pushing the flames ever farther inland, and few other options available, it is difficult to find fault, particularly when the damage caused by dynamite might equally well have occurred had the flames been allowed to continue unchecked. In that regard, at least one marine, Private William P. Burton, USMC, was singled out for special praise by Lieutenant Freeman for his skill and bravery in connection with using dynamite while working with Freeman's own naval personnel.

For his part, Lt. Freeman, who was stationed at nearby Mare Island Naval Base, took command of the destroyer, *Preble*, and left the base bound for San Francisco within four hours after the quake occurred. Accompanying him was the fireboat *Leslie*, and the fire tug *Active*. Those three ships and crew arrived within 30 minutes, and for the next five days they plus the Navy's tug *Sotomoyo*, and several other vessels (a couple privately owned and others belonging to the army) combined, under Freeman's direction, to stream water to the city's fire engines and to support the city's firemen in any way possible. Freeman also set up a makeshift hospital for the injured; traveled back and forth between the City and Goat Island (now known as Yerba Buena Island) for water and supplies; frequently assumed charge of local fire stations when their exhausted chiefs needed sleep; directed where hose lines should be placed or changed; supplied fresh water to many refugees who had none; dealt with looters; handled drunken civilians who were half-crazed; forcibly closed saloons; persuaded the captains and crew of several foreign ships in port to assist in humanitarian aid; turned back ferry boats loaded with gawkers from the East Bay who were getting in the way of relief efforts; and in general provided both leadership and assets without which matters would have been far worse.

People resting in Union Square after fleeing the flames. All the buildings shown here were burned down later.

The Mission District burning, as seen from Market Street

As it was, during the four horrific days before the fires were brought under control, 514 city blocks were consumed by fire, an estimated 28,000 buildings were destroyed, and property damages were estimated up to $500,000,000. Out of a population of 410,000 people, between 225,000 and 300,000 were left homeless, and, for as long as two years after the fire, makeshift tents still dotted Golden Gate Park, the Presidio, and various beaches and other public places. In short, it was a catastrophe of a magnitude never before seen or imagined by Californians.[219]

The recollections of James B. Stetson are very helpful in bringing a human perspective to the enormity of the calamity. Mr. Stetson was the father of one of Henry's groomsmen at his and Jennie's wedding, and he and his wife were guests at that wedding. He lived across the street from the Bothin home on Jackson and Van Ness. His 18-page diary[220] provides a colorful and poignant glimpse of the catastrophe as it was unfolding. Mr. Stetson was awakened by a "very severe shock [which] was so violent that it nearly threw [him] out of bed." Once on his feet, he looked out his window and saw that the roof and the points of the gables, as well as the stonework, of St. Luke's Church had fallen to the street and lay piled up against the sides of the building to a depth of eight to ten feet. The Claus Spreckels mansion, also within his view, had lost its chimneys as well as its stone balustrade and all its carved work. At 7:00 a.m. Mr. Stetson began walking east toward the city's downtown area, and, as he topped Nob Hill and was able to see downtown, he noticed 10-12 fires burning. After wandering around most of the morning, he concluded, "the city was doomed to destruction, and that we couldn't do anything to save it…"

After returning to his home, Mr. Stetson remarked that on that first night "the fire made it as light as day." Later that evening he walked downtown again, and then after returning home to get about three hours sleep, got up and retraced his steps downtown. During all of the various treks he made on foot around the town during the several days following the quake, his memory and attention to details are astounding—from noting which buildings were burning, which had been damaged by the quake and which had not, to describing the moods of the people on the street as, in many cases, they pulled all their earthly belongings, usually packed into a single suitcase, along behind them. He noted, "[t]he throng of moving people, men and women with babies and bird cages, and everything which they held most valuable on earth, began early Wednesday morning [April 18th] and continued until the afternoon of Thursday." As he watched the fire's ever westward march, he concluded that it was burning at a rate of about $6.5 million per hour (in 1906 dollar terms). He went on to say that, as of mid-afternoon on Thursday, the firefighters began torching and dynamiting all the homes and structures on the east side of Van Ness Avenue as a backfire in order to hopefully stop the spread beyond that 125-foot wide thoroughfare.

As for the destruction of Henry Bothin's house, the family has always been of the impression that the house was dynamited. That impression came from Genevieve's consistent statements to that effect all during her life, and, indeed, is contained not only in the oral history she gave, but also appears in an account she gave to Windgate Press, the re-publishers of the book *Victorian Classics* where the following quote appears:

> "Genevieve Bothin deLimur would tell her grandchildren [of whom I am one] how the family home was dynamited to break the progress of the 1906 fire and how she had used the occasion to get rid of a hated black dress by leaving it behind in the doomed house."[221]

Stetson's account says otherwise. First, he says that the dynamiters and torchers apparently stopped their work at Clay Street, and it appeared, as of the early evening hours on Thursday, April 19th, that possibly the fire would not get as far west as Van Ness or any farther north than Clay Street, which was two blocks south of the Bothin

Map indicates the city blocks burned in the fire

home. However, at about 10:15 pm, "another tier of blocks, from Leavenworth to Van Ness, between Jackson and Pacific, had taken fire....At 11:15 it had got to Van Ness, and Bothin's house, which was at the corner of Van Ness and Jackson, was fully on fire, but although it was fully consumed, the fire did not cross to the west side of Van Ness."

For Mr. Stetson (whose house was on the west side of Van Ness and did not burn) the next few days were harrowing, with fires cropping up all around of sufficient size to "light up [his] room so [he] could see to read." All were extinguished in relatively quick order. As

View of the destruction up California Street from Sansone

The destruction of San Francisco's business district

he said, however, for those many, many unfortunate souls who had lost their homes, the parks and the Presidio became poor substitute places to sleep and call home for days, weeks, months and even years. Some people who hadn't lost their homes actually stayed in the parks for a few days, out of fear that another earthquake or fire could catch them unaware in their homes.[222]

The Bothin family—Henry, Jennie, and my grandmother, Genevieve—were far more fortunate than most, for although Henry lost nearly all his commercial properties as well as their home, the family had options. My grandmother recalled that for the first few days after the event, they stayed in one of her father's apartments on Lombard St. in the Marina.[223] They also had a house in Ross to go home to, although given Jennie's aversion to Ross, it is not clear whether or not they did.

From the perspective of business, the earthquake and fire have been said to have marked the end of San Francisco's position as the state's largest and fastest growing city. The proponents of that theory suggest that although the City rebuilt quickly, "the disaster would divert trade, industry, and population growth south to Los Angeles, which, during the twentieth century, would become the largest and most important urban area in the West."[224] While many would argue with the thesis that the earthquake was responsible for the demographic changes between Northern and Southern California, the fact is that, for whatever the reason, it is true that the day prior to April 18, 1906 was probably the high point in the city's business dominance.[225]

This earthquake would become the most studied of all major quakes in history, but what science cannot quantify is the sheer horror and the physical and emotional damage it left in its aftermath. Nonetheless, some scientific insights are valuable to know. For instance, had the Richter Scale been invented (it wasn't until nearly thirty years later), the quake would have recorded a magnitude somewhere between 7.7 and 8.3 on that scale. It was felt strongly as far north as Eureka, as far south as King City, and as far inland as central Nevada. Even as the fires were still burning in the city, California's Governor, George Pardee, appointed a State Earthquake Investigation Committee under the chairmanship of Professor Andrew C. Lawson of the University of California at Berkeley. That commission spent the next two years studying literally every angle they could think of and then submitted its report in 1908. Known as the Lawson Report, it was an exhaustive look at earthquakes in general, the geology of California, the details of the quake itself and of the San Andreas Fault as well, and provided a great deal of other data that remains important to this day in understanding the causes of this quake, the areas of vulnerability in the future, the sorts of geologic formations that perform both well and poorly in different sorts of earthquakes, the sorts of engineering solutions that might minimize future risks, and other data of interest to historians, scientists, planners, professionals, and others.[226]

17.
Rebuilding After the Quake

When all was said and done, the property damage estimates for the quake and fire totaled approximately $500,000,000 (in 1906 dollars). In today's dollars, that sum would equal no less than 11 billion dollars based on the consumer price index. (The CPI is the most conservative method of measuring comparative value.)[227] Henry's share of that loss was just a small fraction; however, even a tiny portion of such a number is still a huge loss for an individual to absorb. What was his loss? The obituary published by PG&E said that at the time of the earthquake and fire Henry owned "no less than 79 pieces of real estate in the stricken city;" all were destroyed. His own statement, contained in an article appearing in the June 2, 1906 edition of the *San Francisco Chronicle*, puts it in slightly different terms, but both the PG&E obituary and the *Chronicle* story make clear that, despite his losses, Henry, like most other San Franciscans, never lost heart:

> Yes, it is true that out of eighty-one buildings I owned before the fire seventy-nine of them were destroyed… and it is also true that every one of the seventy-nine is going to be rebuilt as expeditiously

as possible. This is no time to regret what has been lost! The only thing to do is to gracefully accept the situation and get down to hard work and rehabilitate things as quickly as possible. That is the way I view the situation and thousands more are like me in that respect.

One of the two structures owned by Henry that survived the earthquake and fire was his flagship, the Atlas Building, which was his sole skyscraper. It was (and is) located at 604 Mission Street, a ten story building he had built in 1904 using Judson steel for its load bearing core. Henry maintained his own office on the third floor, and the building had many other tenants who were also among the lucky few whose offices and records were not destroyed in the conflagration. Not only did the Atlas Building escape destruction, but its elevators were not even damaged.[228]

Henry said he was going to rebuild, and indeed, rebuild he did. Insurance was the key. If he had insurance, he had the ability to at least partially recoup his losses. There were 105 insurance companies that had written fire insurance policies on San Francisco properties, and altogether they had underwritten risks totaling approximately $234,000,000.[229] All of the policies contained the typical exclusion for earthquake damage, and none covered loss by dynamite damage either. So, the trick was to convince the carrier that your building had not suffered damage from either earthquake or dynamite, and that the sole cause of the loss was from fire. As might have been expected, 100 percent of the first 2,000 claims presented argued exactly that.[230] Ensuing litigation tied some claims up in court for years. Some insurers went bankrupt, others delayed payments for as long as they could, and most property owners turned out to have had far too little insurance. In all, there were 90,000 claims presented, and most of the claimants ended up losing heavily, many recovering as little as ten cents on the dollar.[231]

Henry appears to have been one of the lucky ones, and that seems to be due in very large part to his involvement with the California Insurance Company, on whose Board he served. That company drew accolades for the responsible way they responded to the insurance claims they were presented with; however, there is more to that story than just their claims handling decisions. Clearly this did set them apart as a role model, but the way their decisions were made is also an example of the caliber of people Henry surrounded himself with. For evidence we turn to the brief memoirs of George W. Brooks, one of the founders of the company as re-organized in 1905.[232] Mr. Brooks reported that the initial post-catastrophe meeting of the Board occurred shortly after the event, when the directors were informed that the Company was "heavily involved in the conflagration," that the amount of obligations that would be incurred was unknown but that they "overshadowed the resources of the company," and "that ways and means would have to be devised to finance [the company] through this crisis." He went on to say that Director W.E. Dean "offered a resolution that has passed into history as being, possibly, the most noticeable ever adopted by the directors of a fire insurance company. His motion was seconded by Director Mark L. Gerstle, and passed unanimously (which obviously means that Henry, too, voted in favor.) It read:

> That the action of the President of this corporation in publicly announcing that the California Insurance Company would pay all its losses in full as ascertained and adjusted, be, that the same is hereby confirmed and ratified, provided that each of the directors of the corporation affixes his signature to the matters of this meeting.[233]

Indeed, the signatures of each director were obtained, and the motion's effect carried out. The total obligations of the company turned out to be $1,840,000 net, after offsetting $900,000 in re-insurance claims (these were difficult to find, since all those policies had been lost when their company's safe was destroyed by falling building walls that exposed the contents to fire.) In order to underwrite the losses, shareholders were assessed, not once, but eight times in all, up to a total of $305 per share for each of the 6,000 shares of stock outstanding. In that way a total of $1,830,000 was raised from shareholders to cover the claims.[234]

Later, the California Insurance Co. proudly took out a ¼ page ad in the December 22, 1906 edition of the *Oakland Tribune* (and undoubtedly in other newspapers as well) congratulating itself for having honored all 505 of its claims without discount or compromise and despite having lost all its records.

It is not known how many shares of stock Henry owned in the California Insurance Company. It was undoubtedly a sufficiently large holding to justify his position on the Board, but, by the same token, he was in the company of a number of other wealthy investors who also would have held large blocks of stock. On a net basis, he would certainly have had significant dollars to pay out in order to fulfill his assessment responsibilities, but those assessments probably were significantly less than the moneys he collected back from the insurer, in satisfaction of his own claims for the cost to rebuild the seventy-nine of his own buildings which had been destroyed. However those numbers worked out, Henry seems to have been one of the lucky property owners for whom insurance did what it was supposed to do, and he was certainly one of the quickest to begin the rebuilding process. Quite apart from his good fortune in terms of who he was insured by, another factor that would have been of enormous benefit to him was that, since his offices escaped destruction in the earthquake and fire, he still had all his records intact and could provide precise information to the insurance adjusters.

The first glimpse of Henry's reaction to the catastrophe comes from letters he sent to Hemet regarding his investments in that community. Hemet historian Mary Whitney has collected copious documents regarding Frank Whittier's investments in Hemet, and a number of them are letters to and from Henry regarding his office building (then under construction) and the mansion on Park Hill (later locally referred to as Bothin Heights) which he was also then in the midst of building:

On May 2, 1906 (two weeks after the earthquake and fire—and at a time when, it should be noted, San Franciscans were not even yet able to get food staples and were, for the most part, relying on relief committees to supply necessities) Henry wrote to Whittier's manager, P.N. Myers, in response to a number of Myers' communications regarding the construction of his commercial building. In an obvious reference to the devastation he had suffered in the San Francisco calamity, Henry stated, "I will have to go slow for a while until I am on my feet. There is no money to be had at any of the banks yet, and I will have to depend on the bank at Hemet to pay for the balance of my building."[235]

Eight days later, on May 10, 1906, (at a time when he was undoubtedly still trying to grasp the enormity of his San Francisco losses) Henry still found time to concentrate on Hemet and to send a follow up letter to Myers that indicates that he was, by then, sufficiently back on his feet to demand detailed statements on all the work done on the [Hemet] building, including "the different contracts, the material that was furnished by the lumber company, and the freight paid on same." His letter goes on to say, "I want to find out how much the building is going to cost and whether it is going to run over the estimate."[236]

By June 2, 1906, Henry was already contemplating a trip down to Hemet, which he ultimately had to call off due to the press of business in San Francisco (specifically working to get insurance recovery for his building losses from the fire.) Still, he had time to attend to details of his Hemet investments, including minutiae such as selling a small construction tent that had outlived its usefulness, and dealing with a tenant who complained about some shelves and partitions, he wanted to have the landlord pay for.. Interestingly, the marital friction between Henry and Jennie was, at that point in time at least, seemingly not affecting his relationship with his father-in-law, as he says in that letter that he and Whittier planned to travel to Hemet together.

Correspondence during the next several months shows Henry paying close attention to costs, including discussions with Mr. Myers about such details as janitorial service, preventing tenants from tacking signs on their doors, making certain that a tenant's shed be built of corrugated iron rather than wood for the sake of reducing the cost of insurance, and dealing with title defects on a piece of property he held an option on located in the town of Moreno.

So, the financial side of Henry's life had started coming together scant weeks after the catastrophe and while the city's ashes were still hot. Indeed, just three months after the earthquake and fire, Henry created and incorporated the Bothin Real Estate Co. and, within fourteen months thereafter, he had conveyed all his commercial properties in San Francisco and Marin Counties to that entity. In return, he was issued 4,996 shares of stock of the company (out of 5,000 shares authorized at a par value of $100 each). Four others were each provided one share. The four others were Messrs. J.D. Osborne, his secretary,[237] Hugh T. Roberts, apparently his bookkeeper, Harry J. Kaufman, his 27 year-old nephew, and George D. Squires, his attorney.[238] From the backgrounds of those individuals, it is quite apparent that Henry had acted alone in accumulating his real estate and had no silent partners or co-investors. Also, it is noteworthy that none of the founding directors were actively involved in his real estate activities.

The Bothin Real Estate Company's charter was rather broad and included, under the heading "purposes," the right to "acquire, buy, sell, hold, mortgage, lease [real and personal property], ...act as broker or agent, ...engage in the manufacture, sale and disposition of all kinds of articles of commerce, …create bonded indebtedness, to buy and sell stocks, and to issue other bonds, notes and evidence of debt…" Clearly, this corporation was not set up to be just a passive investor in real estate.

The company was active and healthy during Henry's lifetime; however, it languished after his death, and was finally liquidated in 1971 after having sold its then-remaining 70 properties to a consortium headed by Leonard Kingsley and including as limited partners the Bothin heirs (his daughter, Genevieve, and her daughters, Genie [my mother] and Mona) as well as a number of other investors. During his lifetime, Henry purchased far more than he sold. At the date of his death, he (or the Bothin Real Estate Company) held title to more than 100 pieces of real estate throughout the state of California; well over half of them were commercial properties in downtown San Francisco.[239]

At the same time he was organizing the legal affairs of his real estate empire, Henry's correspondence with P.N. Myers, Frank Whittier's manager in Hemet, suggested he was also working with his insurer to recoup his losses. While nothing is known about details of his insurance claims, he undoubtedly benefited by having his own claims favorably adjusted. Had that not been so, it is difficult to imagine that Henry would have been able to rebuild as quickly or as completely as he did, or to continue living the lifestyle he enjoyed.

Henry was also apparently undaunted, as shown by three separate news stories written in June, July, and August of 1906. The first article was entitled "To Rebuild 79 Structures He Lost By the Fire." In that article, it was reported that Henry had already prepared plans for a new four story building on Folsom Street between First and Second—a building he had already pre-leased to "a large coffee company" (which turns out to have been the George Caswell Company.) The article went on to say that, "a dozen or more plans for other buildings are in the formative state, and his architects are working day and night on them."[240] In that same article, Henry is quoted as saying:

> I cannot at present… tell just the character or the height of the principal buildings I will erect. The architects are working on my ideas and then I will be able to make a final decision. The city will rebuild practically on the same old retail and wholesale lines. What it wants is better and more durable structures and in my field of operation I will contribute to that desired end.

Indeed, Henry's plans for his replacement buildings did show that he had learned his lesson. The second press story, published July 10, 1906, was entitled "H.E. Bothin to Erect a Four Story Building." It described his plans (with a photo) to erect a large, 4 story with basement, fireproof building on Howard St. between 4th and 5th Streets. The building had already been designed by architect, John A. Ettler, and featured a patented process of steel and reinforced concrete construction designed to brace and distribute loads evenly throughout the structure, thereby intending to protect it from future earthquakes. It had a planned completion date of November 30, 1906—just seven months after the earthquake and fire.

The third press story, bearing a date of August 7, 1906, is entitled "Henry A.[sic] Bothin Plans to Erect Building Downtown Immediately." That article described a two story with basement structure to be built on a lot he owned at Sacramento and Liedesdorf Streets. It had been designed by architect Frank S. Van Trees, (the same architect who had designed the Atlas Building for him several years earlier) and featured brick and cement construction. Construction was slated to be commenced immediately. One of those two projects was probably the building referred to in Henry's obituary in the PG&E monthly magazine as "one of the first business buildings erected [after the earthquake and fire.]"[241]

It is obvious that moss wasn't growing under Henry's feet. Imagine first the amount of time needed to process the horror of his losses, then add to that the time and effort to calculate the amount of the losses on 79 buildings for the insurance adjusters. Add to that the time needed to feel comfortable with rebuilding in an area where such unavoidable devastation could reoccur at any time, and then add time on top of that for the mental exercise of determining one's priorities going forward. Whatever timeline you come up with, you have to marvel at both the strength of Henry's conviction to rebuild and at his strategy, which seems to have been to retain as many top architects as he could, put each to work designing a building, and then set about constructing it. Given Henry's hands-on style of management, one can see that sleep would have been relegated to a rather low priority for him during those early days after the destruction of the city.

Not only was Henry undaunted, but it appears he also made certain his architects were as energetic and energized as he. For instance, one assumes that it would have taken any architect a week or more after the earthquake and fire to just find a space to work and the requisite paper and pencils (remember that one couldn't even get staple groceries in San Francisco until early May.) It seems too that the drafting portion of the architectural process, following the creative aspect, would have taken several weeks at the very least (and more likely a month or more.) Now, recall that the first published account of Henry's post-earthquake plans was published less than two months after the event, and it indicated that he already had plans prepared for his first building and also had it pre-leased. The second account, published less than three months after April 18th, noted, with respect to a completely different building, that the structure had already received a building permit and that construction was about to start. The third newspaper account, dated less than three months post-quake, revealed that all contracts had been signed for the construction of a third building, and that work was scheduled to commence at once. This means that from the first time Henry sat down in the office of each architect and began a two-way conversation about ideas for reconstruction, to the completion of the design phase, the total time could not have been more than five to six weeks. In this day of environmental impact reports, zoning regulations, citizen oversight, and public meetings, it is simply not possible to even dream of that sort of turnaround time. Even in those days when people could get work done, the schedule is simply mind-boggling. Yet the fact of the matter is that the buildings were rebuilt—all of them, and Henry barely missed a step.

18.
Jennie and Henry Bothin Divorce

For all of his business acumen, Henry seems to have had a blind spot when it came to understanding Jennie and making his marriage work. His driving ambition for financial success left few hours in his day to pay attention to the domestic side of his life, and that domestic side was full of complexities and unmet needs. Jennie was a spoiled young lady who grew up in a home with a father who, like Henry, was consumed by his work and driven to succeed, and with a mother who lived with a permanent loss of hearing as one of the emotional scars caused by the loss of her first child. The Whittier household of Jennie's youth exemplified the gender roles of the day—a father providing for the family's financial needs and a mother contentedly staying at home and providing the love and emotional support for the children. The major difference was that, for all of Frank Whittier's tough and uncompromising business side, he also idolized his wife, Charlotte, and he gave freely of the time and energy needed to assure that their relationship flourished. They had been childhood sweethearts, had grown closer during the years of separation they endured while Frank learned a business and achieved the initial success he felt he needed in order to ask Charlotte to marry him, and then Frank had traveled all the way back across the country to Maine to woo and wed the woman he loved. Later they had together mourned the loss of their first child and together traveled throughout Europe seeking in vain to find a cure for Charlotte's deafness. They shared deep religious convictions and devoutly attended church together. In short, Frank and Charlotte had a marriage of mutual respect: the gender roles might have been stereotypical, but there was a deeply seated underlying love.

So, for Jennie, the role model for a life partner was clearly imprinted, and while she undoubtedly encouraged Henry's work ethic and his drive for financial success, she also would, by virtue of her upbringing and the example set by her parents, have expected a loving and attentive home life. That was not to be. Henry was the product of a rather dysfunctional family, one in which his parents seem to have had a compunction to periodically uproot their children, to leave family and friends (if they truly had any) behind, and to seek new beginnings in new locations. After being pulled out of school following fifth grade, Henry's formative years were spent largely in isolation on a farm, surrounded only by his siblings and largely deprived of social relationships with peers. As role models, Henry's parents left him unprepared for any sort of social interaction, much less the ability to understand Jennie's tastes and needs, which were many. One has to wonder if, before Jennie, he ever had any close childhood friends of either sex, much less girlfriends, or if he knew what it was to love or be loved. None of those components of Henry's background and upbringing, taken individually, would necessarily have doomed a successful marriage; however, taken together they would arguably have made it far more difficult for him to understand and appreciate what Jennie would have expected when they exchanged their vows.

If Henry was ill-prepared for marriage by both background and inexperience, Jennie was also ill-prepared for this union. She was 20 years old and a social extrovert who chose a man ten years her senior; a man whose entire adult life had been spent trying to climb from nothing toward financial success.

Even given all the reasons why they perhaps should never have married in the first place, the fact is that theirs was not the first union of dissimilar personalities and backgrounds, and many such marriages thrive. Of course, in order for that to have happened, both parties would have had to grow in their love for each other and to want to make the marriage work. In Henry's and Jennie's case, and for whatever the reason, they seem not to have been able to come to that state. Undoubtedly there were many factors that came into play and that caused them to grow apart rather than together as the years passed, but one cause, more than any others, was probably most to blame—the untimely and tragic deaths of four of their five children, and their inability to give each other the strength to deal with their grief in a common and supportive way. Jennie's parents had mourned the loss of their child and they came closer together from the experience, but in the case of Henry and Jennie, that seems not to have happened. It goes without saying that for any parent, the loss of a child is devastating, and even though it was more commonplace back in those days, the scars left from that sort of loss were, just as they are today, never far from the surface. One can well imagine Jennie being emotionally distraught and quite possibly blaming herself for the deaths of the three babies her family lost in infancy. It would be natural for her to need an attentive husband, one who would express love, devotion and compassion. In Henry, she had a husband who seems to have been either unwilling or, more probably, simply not equipped to either feel or express those emotions, and so, as a couple, they seem not to have weathered those storms well together.

There would have had to be other causes too, some peculiar to their own personalities, and others forced on them by circumstances. For instance, Jennie was a lively woman who loved city life. She was one of the first women, perhaps even the first, to get a driver's license in California, and her love of driving even made the newspapers. On August 19, 1906 the *San Francisco Call* reported, "Mrs. Henry Bothin was also among the first to drive her own motor, having first one of the smaller cars, but later Mr. Bothin procured from the East one of the large touring cars, and this Mrs. Bothin drives either here or in town or over the roads near her pretty country home in Ross Valley." She was also apparently a good bridge player and enjoyed that pastime with other women.[242] Henry, on the other hand, was seemingly all business and had no interest whatever in social life. His was a constant quest for material gain, and his only outlets seem to have been his desire for quiet country living during non-business hours, and his private philanthropy. Henry's granddaughter (my mother, who was also named Genevieve, but who is referred to as Genie) recalls Jennie as vivacious and a "naughty" lady. But while that evidence of differences in personality might reinforce the thesis of basic incompatibility, it doesn't come close, by itself, to explaining why Jennie would have taken the rather rare step of seeking a court order to terminate the marriage. For that there must have been a great deal more boiling beneath the surface.

The very act of resorting to the courts, with all the public scrutiny that entails (as it did in fact occur in this case) is a step that was not taken lightly in those days, and divorce was resorted to only in the severest of cases. Today some fifty percent of marriages end up in divorce, but during the first decade of the twentieth century that statistic was just eight percent. One reason, and a very good one, why divorce was so rarely sought was that to obtain the judgment, one had to prove adultery, abandonment, or significant abuse or cruelty. In addition, the very word "divorce" carried with it a stigma that typically fell hardest on the woman, who was often vilified for not doing more to hold the marriage together for the sake of the children. So for Jennie to have begun such proceedings she must have reached the point of feeling that, on balance, she would rather accept the social stigma, both for herself and for Genevieve, than continue what had to have become an unbearable existence with Henry. She also must have decided that that outcome was worth the foreseeable side effect of publicly airing the family's dirty laundry.

Henry's first statement after the filing is instructive.[243] As reported in the newspaper, his initial comment was to the effect that, of their twenty-one years of marriage, only five or six were happy. Five to six years into the marriage would have taken them to 1891 or 1892, when their worlds would have started to come apart. What was happening in those years? To start with, in the latter part of 1890, Henry had gone rather deeply in debt through his initial acquisitions of sixteen parcels of real estate. That indebtedness would have caused a very uncomfortable belt tightening in an already closely managed domestic budget, and even though Henry was no longer actively buying properties during 1891 or 1892, the debt service from his earlier purchases would still have been a drag on available free cash. To his friends and acquaintances in those years, Henry must have appeared to be highly successful—he was the principal owner and Executive Vice President of a major company that was involved in the booming iron industry, and he had become something of a property baron, owning by then more commercial real estate than most of his and Jennie's friends and acquaintances would ever own in their lifetimes. Jennie would have wanted to show off their successes at just the same time her Germanic husband was applying the brakes on their household spending, so that he could buy properties in an industrial and largely unattractive part of town. So, as they entered the decade of the 1890s, they were two strong-willed individuals at odds; one wanted to spend his money placing bets on the future of commercial real estate in San Francisco, and the other wanted to enjoy the trappings of wealth that were within her grasp.

Then, after being reasonably in check for nearly five years, in 1895 Henry accelerated his real estate purchases. Yet as he added properties to his portfolio at the rate of four to five per month, Henry's financial position also improved quite dramatically. Yes, he had substantial debt to contend with; however, by the mid to late

1890s he also had enough free cash flow to purchase a nice second home in Marin County and, by 1903, a 1,230 acre ranch. He had found a way, undoubtedly because his properties were throwing off positive cash flow from rental income, to begin to show a very healthy balance sheet. Therefore, whatever anger Jennie might once have had about Henry's gambling away of household income on an unproven real estate passion should long since have dissipated.

So, one must assume that the ultimate cause of the divorce was most likely due to factors other than Henry's addiction to San Francisco commercial real estate. Yet it might still have had to do in some way with real estate, in a different way. Remember that Jennie loved the city, and if she were to be talked into a country home, she would have undoubtedly vastly preferred that it be down the Peninsula in Burlingame, Atherton, or Woodside, where prominent San Franciscans including the Crockers, Grants, Scotts, Tobins, Fagans, de Sablas, Popes, and Babcocks, to name just a few, all had homes. Those Peninsula destinations were easily and quickly reached by train, and they had the further advantage of having clubs such as the Burlingame Country Club and the San Mateo Polo Club, which focused on equestrian events,[244] and would have appealed immensely to Jennie Probably the best evidence of Jennie's preference for the Peninsula is that once the divorce was finalized, she moved to Burlingame and remained there for the rest of her life.

But instead of offering her a house on the Peninsula and a chance to pursue her social and equestrian interests, Henry unilaterally decided to buy property and build not one but two homes in Ross, which then was a small town populated by an entirely different group of people whose interests were more geared to hiking and outdoor living than to fine clothes, elegant parties and equestrian activities. Interestingly, Marin had more opportunities for horseback riding through the surrounding countryside than did the peninsula, and indeed Jennie did enjoy her horses there;[245] however, for Marinites, such interests generally gravitated more to riding for the sheer joy of being in the scenic outdoors than to hunts, jumping contests, and other events that appealed to Jennie and other women of her stature and background at the turn of the 20th century.

Under normal circumstances, a simple dispute among spouses about where to have a second home would fall far short of grounds to end a marriage. In this case, it went quite a bit further than that. Recall that in late December 1902, just eighteen months after their thirteen-year-old son succumbed to polio, Henry bought the 5.8 acre piece of property in Ross just across the street from the house where Frank had died. And on that site he built a large house, where he wanted them both to live as their principal residence. Although I can't prove it, I believe Jennie might not have had any input into that land purchase or the design of the house—a house Genevieve termed "horrid." If I am correct, then that was a real mistake on Henry's part, one that showed a total lack of empathy for Jennie's grief over Frank's death. If he truly thought she would move out of the City she loved and into a house across the street from the spot where her only son had so recently died, then he really didn't understand Jennie, and that lack of understanding or sympathy might well have served as another strike against him. Indeed, so incensed was she with the very idea that I believe she simply refused to move into that home, whereupon they began living separate and apart as early as 1903 or 1904.

Then there is the question of their San Francisco home that was destroyed in the earthquake and fire. There is absolutely no evidence anywhere of any effort on Henry's part to rebuild that home. Rather, it would seem that Henry wanted to live full time in Marin and wished no part of living in the city, as witnessed by the fact that after his marriage to Ellen several years later the couple immediately moved full time to Ross and never kept a home or even an apartment in the city. Further proof of that assumption can be found in newspaper stories (see infra) which include reference to the fact that Henry and Jennie had separated as early as 1904. Assuming I am correct, that would mean Henry lived alone in the home he had built on the 5.8 acre lot he had purchased in Ross, while Jennie and young Genevieve remained living in their home in San Francisco by themselves until it was consumed by fire in April 1906. Once that home went up in smoke, Jennie was left with nowhere to live unless one of two things occurred—either she agreed to move over to Marin with Henry or else he agreed to rebuild the home in the city. If he thought the destruction of the San Francisco house gave him leverage, Henry miscalculated. He failed to appreciate that to Jennie, the house on the corner of Jackson and Van Ness in the city was of far greater importance than probably anything else that needed rebuilding. After all, it had been a gift from her father, and it represented her family's contribution to the marriage. It was also the center of her life, the place where she entertained friends and was near the various homes where she in turn was entertained. As much as its location may have played a role in Jennie's social world, it also served as her anchor. But, as important as that home was to Jennie, it had little allure for Henry, nor did he appreciate the importance Jennie placed on it. That misjudgment on Henry's part, given its timing, may have been the straw that finally broke his marriage.

Admittedly, I have speculated about the final cause of the divorce; yet whatever may have been the immediate catalyst, the fact remains that in October 1907, Jennie took the then highly unusual step of filing for divorce. In those days, in order to obtain a divorce it was necessary to prove fault in a court of law that was open to the public and to reporters. That requirement of proving fault was an archaic practice, but one that had successfully advanced the paramount goal of discouraging people from doing exactly what Jennie had set in motion.

The following excerpt from an article that appeared in the *San Francisco Examiner* on January 11, 1908 (the day after the uncontested trial) illustrates the conundrum. That article recounts, for all the world to see, specific instances of misconduct that, in and of themselves, don't appear all that traumatic or dramatic, but that nonetheless were very private matters that should never have had to see the light of day, if only for Genevieve's sake. In order to prove fault and thereby meet the burden of proof required of her to receive the interlocutory decree of divorce, Jennie is reported to have said:

> I was forced to leave my husband on account of his insults before the servants and my friends. His constant attacks caused me to place myself under the care of a doctor. My physician advised me it was necessary for my health to leave my husband. Once he ordered me to leave the room in the presence of the servants, and at another time he pinched my arm until it was black and blue. This was about seven years ago.

That same day, the *San Francisco Chronicle* reported:

> Mrs. Bothin …charged her husband with technical desertion three years ago by forcing her to leave him through cruel conduct. She said that he frequently insulted her in the presence of servants and friends and made it impossible for her to live with him… At one time she suffered from nervous prostration as the result of his acts… Once when they went to Pastori's with some friends as guests, Bothin became angry at something and ordered her to go home, breaking up the party.

Those are interesting words, but a close look at them doesn't suggest much of substance, and certainly, given the social stigma in those days of divorce, does not begin to rise to the level of the extraordinary behavior that must have underlain the filing of such a radical court proceeding. Indeed, it is apparent that the parties agreed to water down the testimony to just the barest of necessary proof. For instance, when testifying to what her doctor advised, Jennie was allowed to offer hearsay evidence which, had this been a truly adversarial contest, would have been hearsay and inadmissible other than through direct testimony by her doctor. By streamlining the process and reducing the numbers of witnesses, the attorneys probably shortened the ordeal and eliminated the risk of more revelations that might have surfaced if more people had to be examined and cross-examined. But even if the image of Henry that Jennie painted was less villainous than might otherwise have been the case, for a teenage daughter to hear even those toned down words expressed in public would have been devastating.

Looking beyond the words uttered at the divorce hearing, ultimately the divorce, although undoubtedly triggered by some particularly unpleasant event, probably ultimately came about because of the simple fact that the couple was so incompatible and had grown so far apart that Jennie had just tired of trying to hold it together. Consider some of the articles that surfaced during the proceedings. First (although it was not first to appear) consider an interesting article from the *Oakland Tribune* dated June 12, 1909, which was shortly after Henry married his second wife, Ellen. It reported, among other things, under the heading "Philanthropists Wed" that "When his former wife, who was Miss Jennie Whittier, daughter of William F. Whittier, the paint man, made her application for divorce, she based her complaint largely on Mr. Bothin's propensity to dissipate his fortune in charity and philanthropy."[246] Another article in the same paper stated the following:

> Mrs. Lottie Bothin, wife of the millionaire philanthropist, Henry E. Bothin, has filed suit for divorce on the grounds of desertion, but it is said that the socialistic tendencies and democracy of the defendant jarred on his aristocratic, society loving wife

and that the real cause of their difficulties lies in that fact.

Friends of Bothin say that he wanted to establish a home in the country for poor children and that his wife opposed the plan because of her love for society life.[247]

The *San Francisco Examiner* article cited earlier also contained a similar statement about the lifestyles of the two parties in the divorce. That article concluded:

In the trial there was no reference to the social fads of the defendant, but when the suit was begun it was freely stated that it was the desire of the husband to live in the country where he could take their children, that led to the final separation.[248] ...It is said that the underlying ground of disagreement between Bothin and his wife was his desire for quiet country life and her wish to mingle more in society.

Jennie never was one to back away from confrontation. That character trait is too well documented in descriptions by both Genevieve and Genie to be discounted. So one must assume that in the years, and certainly in the months, that preceded the filing, she and Henry would have argued—probably quite often and probably loudly. As those arguments reached ever-louder crescendos, the earthquake and fire would have served to make Henry's temper just that much shorter. Given the elevated level of stress both were under just prior to the filing, it would have taken a couple of people who really wanted their marriage to survive to make that happen, whereas in this case, one suspects they were both simply too tired after years spent trying to make an incompatible marriage work. If that was true, then Jennie did well to concentrate her public utterances and testimony in court on more stereotypical misconduct and to leave the more personal, but undoubtedly far more strongly felt, emotions out of the proceedings.

Before leaving the topic of the divorce, one quote I find difficult to swallow is the statement published in the *Oakland Tribune* that a major cause of the divorce was "he [Henry] wanted to establish a home in the country for poor children and that his wife opposed the plan because of her love for society life." That is a rather callous statement for even a newspaper reporter to make and, in any case, it needs context. For all of their differences, I simply do not believe that Jennie would have condemned her husband for preferring the well-being of underprivileged children to her social life. In that regard, Jennie was very active in the hospital which was at that time formally known as the Hospital for Children and Training School for Nurses—commonly called Children's Hospital in San Francisco. There are numerous references in newspapers of the day, the earliest appearing in the November 29, 1896 edition of the *San Francisco Call*, that refer to her dedication to and involvement in the affairs of that hospital. In 1901 (and perhaps during other years as well) she served as the Treasurer of the hospital's Board of Managers, and several newspaper accounts chronicle her involvements, which included fundraising and collecting gifts during the Christmas season for indigent young patients at the hospital. Her daughter, Genevieve, always said that her mother was one of the founders of Children's Hospital, and while that was not, in fact, the case,[249] it remained a family priority all the way up to 1991, when the hospital merged with California Pacific Medical Center. During the period of more than a century of Children's Hospital's existence, not only was it a priority initially with Jennie, but later Genevieve, and later still Genevieve's daughter, Genie—all served at one time or another on the Board of the institution.

It is also instructive to note an article appearing in the January 11, 1901 edition of the *San Francisco Call*. That article celebrated the twenty-fifth anniversary of the founding of Children's Hospital, and it mentioned that during those first twenty-five years the hospital had grown from a small and poorly financed clinic to a large and well-funded hospital that had just finished building a new wing, which was to be used to expand its surgery and to house up to 45 nursing students. During the previous twelve months the hospital was reported to have treated over 10,000 patients, of whom 601 were children. Of those children, over half were indigent, and the article cited the policy of the hospital against turning down for treatment any person who had need for medical services.

Furthermore, it was also inaccurate for the newspapers to imply that Jennie was completely disinterested in Henry's philanthropic efforts. While she was probably jealous of the amount of his commitment to Hill Farm, she was not insensitive to Elizabeth Ashe's efforts on behalf of indigent youth in San Francisco. Indeed, as late as 1905 (when she and Henry were apparently informally separated) Jennie was one of the patronesses of a fundraiser put together by Miss Ashe to raise money for the free dispensary of the Telegraph Hill Neighborhood Association.[250]

So, to say that Jennie cared little about children or the poor is not only an overly broad statement, it is simply not true. In the final analysis, it probably is fair to say that, by the time of their divorce, Jennie had had, for fifteen years or more, an ongoing problem with Henry's priorities and stubbornness, and the longer that frustration brewed, the more difficult it became for her to live with it. She undoubtedly felt that he placed his incessant craving for more and more real estate higher on the priority scale than the lifestyle to which she aspired and felt was her due. One suspects that Jennie didn't prefer her own social desires over the needs of the poor, as much as she was objecting to yet further dilution of their community income, which was already, in her mind, far too unbalanced in favor of Henry's interests, be they business or philanthropy. If Jennie had been asked her preference, she would probably have said that Henry's interest in philanthropy should come out of the pot that was currently devoted to his investments, rather than out of the portion which, in her mind, should have supported the wants and needs which she felt were important for herself, Genevieve, and the family unit as a whole.

In the end, whoever tried the hardest to save the marriage is not really relevant. The fact is that Jennie was the one who initiated the divorce. Henry is on record as opposing the breakup and publicly stating his preference to hold the marriage together despite admitted unhappiness during all but the first six years of their life together. And yet were it not for appearances and quite probably his concern about the effect of a divorce on his daughter, Genevieve, one can hardly understand why he felt as he did. The lack of communication between husband and wife that had led Henry to build palatial structures for a wife who wasn't in the slightest bit interested in them suggests a blind spot and a total lack of understanding of what Jennie considered important, and what truly was needed to make her happy.

Another interesting note on the divorce is that Jennie was independently wealthy herself, and, therefore, unlike many women, she could afford to end their marriage without losing her ability to pursue her own interests. As stated in the January 11, 1908 edition of the *San Francisco Chronicle*, "Mrs. Bothin is a daughter of W.F. Whittier of Whittier Coburn & Co. and is wealthy in her own right." That same theme was repeated five years later when Jennie announced her intention to remarry. In the announcement of her engagement to Leigh Sypher, the February 19, 1913 edition of the *San Francisco Examiner's* headline read "Wealthy San Francisco Society Woman to Wed Leigh Sypher at Quiet Ceremony." That article said:

> Mrs. Bothin has been making her home at the Fairmont this winter, although she has homes both in town and in the country, one in Burlingame and

one in Marin County... Mrs. Bothin is the possessor of a fortune in her own right and has dispensed of it liberally, though in a quiet way, to charities here and there.

As for the divorce proceedings themselves, despite Henry's initial threats to contest them, it would appear from the actual record that their legal advisors prevailed upon them to tone down the rhetoric and to take the high road. Indeed, when called upon from time to time to make public statements about the pending divorce, Henry declined to say anything negative about Jennie. In fact, he went out of his way to defuse any public spectacle, saying "I regret the proceeding, but I will not contest it. My wife is a good person. I have nothing but the highest regard for her."[251] As a result, the actual divorce itself was, to all outward appearances, handled professionally and as amicably as might reasonably be expected. Very early on the two reached a property settlement agreement as well as concurrence on custody issues. Jennie was given a piece of downtown property as well as alimony of $500 per month rising to $1,000 per month after two years. She was also given $200 per month as child support for Genevieve. Custody was awarded to Jennie but with very fair visitation rights provided to Henry. An interlocutory decree of divorce was entered on January 10, 1908, and the divorce was finalized a year later on January 14, 1909.

Genevieve and Genie

19.
Genevieve and Family

Henry and Jennie might have severed their marital ties, but Henry still had visitation rights to see his daughter, Genevieve. While he may not have had a clue how to express his love for her in ways that would convince her he cared, there is no question that he loved her deeply and wanted her to be a part of his life after the divorce. He was obviously challenged by both Jennie's and Genevieve's attitudes, which had developed over a period of years and would not be overcome in short order, but he was also hampered by his own lack of understanding of women in general and, more specifically, by how to communicate with his own family members. In part that was his own fault and due to his own personality, but also to a large degree it would have been based on the way children were raised in those days—an altogether different style of parenting than is the norm today.

Indeed, as late as 1928, the behaviorist John Broadus Watson, in his treatise, *Psychological Care of Infant and Child*, advised parents on how to treat their children in the following words:

> Treat them as though they are young adults. Dress them, bathe them with care and circumspection. Let

your behavior always be objective and kindly firm. Never hug and kiss them, never let them sit on your lap… shake hands with them in the morning…[252]

If those words seem odd and incredible today, they seem even more alien when one realizes that they were directed not to fathers in general but rather to mothers, for it was women who raised the children while the role of men was to be breadwinners rather than active parents. If even mothers in those days were being advised to withhold emotional attachment and to treat their children as objects to be seen but not heard, then it is hardly surprising that fathers would be expected to do likewise and, if anything, to maintain greater distance and formality. Looked at under that sort of lens, Henry's conduct, unfortunate as it turned out to be, seems far less unusual or unexpected.

Nowhere is there a better illustration of Henry's good intentions but poor execution than in the way he chose to honor the memory of his son, Frank. Thus, it seems clear that, in providing the help he did to Nurse Ashe, Henry was showing, in possibly the only way he knew how, his love for Frank and grief over Frank's death. By taking his buggy rides out to Fairfax, he was grieving in his own way by watching children at play, and quite probably seeing in them a vision of his own children who had so tragically died far too soon. That he drove his buggy to Fairfax nearly every Sunday shows he cared deeply, but the flip side of that is Sunday was also Henry's only day off work, and he chose to spend it away from home rather than with his wife and daughter. Furthermore, as much as Miss Ashe obviously appreciated Henry's generosity and the time he spent watching the children his money was able to help, there is no record of his ever having joined in their play or otherwise warmed to them. Rather, Henry seems to have been comfortable expressing both grief and love through gifts of money and/or by somewhat distant and impersonal contact, but it is not evident that he cared to or even knew how to relate to or engage emotionally with the objects of his affection.

For Genevieve, on the other hand, the social stigma and related emotional issues brought about by the divorce were hugely greater than they would be today. As she said in her oral history, "…divorce was really tough in those years."[253] And Genevieve was right. The publicity surrounding her parents' divorce affected her far more deeply than it would have her parents, who had at least some ability to speak out and to defend themselves. Furthermore, since it was Jennie who bore the burden of proving cruelty against Henry, it follows that it was his conduct that was being judged and that Genevieve had to live with. If that, in and of itself, was not enough to turn away his daughter, those charges against Henry were also ammunition for Genevieve's peers. As any parent knows, children can be very cruel to one another, and when, as here, they were armed with the kind of provocation provided by the newspapers their parents read and undoubtedly talked about at home, it is easy to see how a twelve-year-old girl could be emotionally crushed, not only by what she may well have read herself, but also by the taunts and unkind comments of her peers. Even if Henry had been a warm and openly loving father, he still would have, in Genevieve's mind, two strikes against him when it came time to try to resurrect family ties in the aftermath of the public spectacle they had all just gone through.

Although Henry saw Genevieve as often as he imagined he could, and although he several times brought her to Santa Barbara for extended visits, nothing in those efforts on his part ever came close to breaking down the barriers created between them by that unfortunate legal proceeding. Realistically, only Jennie could have helped Genevieve to find a neutral place and to understand that her father was not the monster she clearly came to believe he was. However, there is no evidence that Jennie even tried at all to mend the rift. Given all that, it is not surprising that Henry's efforts were largely if not completely ineffective in mending fences with his only child.

What is surprising, however, is that Genevieve never outgrew her enmity toward her father, nor did she ever bother to try to understand him or to learn anything at all about him or his roots.[254] The few letters written between father and daughter are all written by Genevieve as brief thank you notes for this or that. They do not express love—rather they impart an obvious sense of formality, distance, and discomfort. Even as late in life as her oral history interview,[255] which was conducted when she was nearly eighty-eight years old, Genevieve was still smarting and still unwilling to bend much when it came to her father. She did go so far as to say he was "attractive" and "full of charm," and she also was willing to say her relationship with him after the divorce was "very nice," but in both cases those were platitudes delivered with little emotion. Elsewhere in that oral history, Genevieve also said that following the divorce, she would only come over to Ross to visit Henry twice or three times a year, and then mostly because he gave her a dollar when she came. She rarely went to Montecito to visit, largely because of Ellen, Henry's second wife, who Genevieve didn't care for. As she said, "It wasn't her [Ellen's] fault she never had children, she was an old maid and she just—she didn't…but she just wasn't used to children…"

As a child, or even as a young adult, one could easily understand and empathize with Genevieve's feelings about her father. What is not understandable is how she could have reached the ripe old age of 88,[256] as she did, and still never acknowledge the good her father had done in the community through his philanthropy. Nor, in fact, is it really understandable how she could have served for over eighteen years as the president of the foundation he established and still not have had any interest whatsoever in his accomplishments and his background. The Bothin Helping Fund—now the Bothin Foundation—has been in continuous existence since 1917 and is still a vibrant community resource and a part of the family heritage in which his descendants take great pride. Yet the founder has always remained a mystery largely because his daughter would never talk about him and relegated him to anonymity. For Genevieve to have sat for so long on the board of an entity named after her father and yet to have professed to know so little about him speaks volumes about the rift between daughter and father. As spoiled as Genevieve was—and she was always the first to admit she was—the fact that she held that level of grudge against him is an unfortunate legacy for which they both must assume blame.

In addition to efforts at generosity directed toward Genevieve directly, Henry also hired Genevieve's husband, Edmunds, to work for him at "The Judson" (the name the family used to refer to Judson Manufacturing Company.) Unfortunately, Edmunds was both incompetent and disinterested. One has to assume Henry recognized that; nonetheless, he kept Edmunds on anyway simply because he was "family." For example, in 1920 Edmunds was asked by a Judson manager, a man named Booth, to write a letter to Henry and in it explain why he had failed to show up for work on several successive Saturdays. Edmunds did so, and in the letter he excused his work absence by claiming that it was more important for him to stay home than to do the work he was hired to do at Judson:

> For several Saturdays past I have stayed down in the country mornings and have not come to town to the office for the reason that both Genevieve and myself determined that Saturday was the best day to have certain work done on this place, such as gravelling and some transplanting, etc., that we have to do. It was necessary, for this purpose, to hire a couple of men, and without proper supervision as you know, they would not have done the amount of work possible for them to do, and I felt that when I was paying them as much as $4.50 and $5.00 a day, I had best

get the work done as quickly as possible. For this reason I have stayed down in order to superintend them myself, and chose Saturday as that day, as I considered I was only losing half a day instead of a whole....Another Saturday I stayed down in order to help Genevieve get in readiness her mother's house for her return. So that you see I felt fully justified in taking those Saturdays off, and in fact I intend, if possible, and if I can clear up my work this afternoon, to remain down tomorrow morning, as I still have some work to do.

Edmunds went on to attack Mr. Booth himself for dereliction of duty and then closed that portion of his letter by stating "I would not mention any of these facts if it were not that I feel that I have been spied on and do not care, at my age, to be treated as a bad little boy, who plays hookey [sic] from school."

The fact that Henry didn't fire Edmunds on the spot once he received that letter is a testament to the fact that Henry always put family first and was, one might suggest, overly tolerant of behavior on the part of family members that, in any other employee, would have led to a speedy sacking.

In a further display of Henry's generosity toward family members, he set up a trust for Genevieve's daughter, Genie (referred to later as "the baby trust") that he funded with the title to a piece of property at 112 Fremont Street in downtown San Francisco and the building that stood upon it. That trust was to pay income to Genie until her 20th birthday, after which she was to receive outright ownership of the building. It ended up being a major bone of contention in an estate tax contest after he died, but more importantly, in a further display of Edmunds' incompetence, it was ultimately lost to foreclosure when Edmunds, long after Henry's death, failed to make timely mortgage payments to the Bank of Italy (the predecessor of

Bank of America.)

In fact, for all his apparently tough business side, Henry appears to have been a rather gentle and caring man, at least as it relates to family and children in general, a fact that even Genevieve readily conceded in her oral history. He made numerous gifts and loans to members of his extended family. Those included gifts to Julius' daughter, Lulu, gifts to Hattie Hoover (Amelia's daughter who, in 1912-1914, badgered him brazenly, asking for loans of up to $10,000 to help out their failing business in Kansas,) reimbursement to his sister, Minnie, for an investment she made in Amelia's son Frank's failed mining venture in Nevada (a venture where he and Ellen also lost about $4,000,) using his own crew to repaint the home of his niece, Julia, deeding some land to members of the Mau family, and paying the costs of his niece, Alice Mau's, medical bills in 1922. Those are just the gifts I have become aware of, and I have no doubt they were just a few among far more gifts that he made regularly to his siblings and their offspring.

Henry and Genie

In addition to these instances of family generosity, Henry provided employment to a number of his extended family members, including three of the four Maas brothers (children of his sister, Emily.) Even Hermann Sadler, the husband of his sister, Minnie and a successful grocer, was listed at one time as Vice President of Judson Mfg. Co, and Harry Kaufman, his nephew, was one of the founding directors of Bothin Real Estate Company.

Henry also maintained some ties to Jennie's family. After the divorce, Henry held onto his investments in Hemet and the surrounding areas. Correspondence during 1907 and 1908, after Jennie had filed for divorce, reveals that Henry was still working on the irrigation systems for the house on Park Hill and was frustrated over the issues of water rights as well as the cost of irrigation pipe. One interesting communication from P.N. Myers (Whittier's manager in Hemet) to Frank Whittier reveals that Myers felt Whittier was unreasonably assuming business risks for Henry by guaranteeing their irrigation pipe against leaks despite Henry's property's rough terrain, and the fact that Henry was insisting on using inferior rivet joints as opposed to the preferable cast screw joints. Whittier's reply was that he wished to honor his contracts "to the letter."[257]

In 1919, several years after Frank Whittier's death, William Weir (the husband of Jennie's younger sister, Mattie and one of the executors of Whittier's estate) sent a letter to Will Whittier, Frank's son, and stated for the first time that Henry Bothin "would like to cash in on his Hemet holdings."[258] While that may have been the case, Henry in fact held on to all his properties in Hemet and elsewhere in Riverside County, and they were a part of his own estate when he died four years after the date of that letter. The holdings Weir described included four parcels of land in Hemet (two were improved with commercial buildings,) 157 acres of ranchlands near Hemet with apricot, peach and orange orchards, and about 430 acres of land on and around Park Hill (comprising 29 lots of nearly 15 acres each.)[259]

20.
Marriage to Ellen Chabot

On June 3, 1909, six months after his divorce from Jennie became final, Henry married Ellen Chabot. Where Jennie was elegant, flamboyant, athletic, and outgoing, Ellen was modest, quiet, bright, and rather shy. She was forty-four years old at the time of this, her first and only marriage, and it turned out to be a perfect match, for they thrived as a couple.

Ellen's father, Anthony Chabot, had made a name for himself and a large fortune as a hydrologist and, later, as an investor. Born in Quebec in 1813 to a farming family, Chabot had early on become fascinated with rivers and flowing water. Even more than water, however, he had a thirst for wealth, and upon learning of the Gold Rush in California, he came west, arriving in July of 1849. He found a way, through a combination of water flumes, sluice boxes, hoses, and crude nozzles, to blast away whole hillsides[260] with water under high pressure and thereby expose ore, and he put a lot of gold into his pockets. Arriving in San Francisco in 1856, he and several partners formed the San Francisco City Water Works and created the first water system for the city. Ultimately, it was his recognition of the growth potential of Oakland, and his development of its municipal water system, that made him his reputation and his fortune.

Ellen's mother, Ellen Hasty, was one of twin girls who were the youngest of six children born to William Hasty and Betsy Fitch Hasty. William Hasty had come from a long line of Hastys where the family resided in Standish, Maine.[261] He died in 1837, when the twins were just four years old. Betsy, also a Maine native, was from Baldwin. Their daughter Ellen, a pianist, was the only Hasty child still living at home when Anthony Chabot accompanied his business partner, Henry Pierce (a native of Standish) on a visit to Pierce's home town. Upon meeting Ellen, Anthony was immediately smitten. After a brief romance, the then fifty-one year old Anthony Chabot and his thirty-one year old fiancée, Ellen Hasty, were married in Standish on March 10, 1864. Tragically, Ellen died a year later, on October 18, 1865, while in labor giving birth to their only child, Henry Bothin's future second wife, Ellen.[262] In his grief, and knowing that he would not be able to raise a small child by himself, Anthony returned to San Francisco, leaving Ellen to be raised for the next five years by her grandmother and by her mother's twin sister, Emily, and her family.[263]

It was while he was in San Francisco grieving his wife's death that Anthony Chabot became aware of plans to extend the western terminus of the Transcontinental Railroad, from Sacramento, to Oakland. He recognized immediately that, by virtue of that fact alone, Oakland would attract business and huge growth. As he drove his buggy around the hills behind Oakland, he saw the possibilities for several sources of water for Oakland, and immediately applied for and was given a franchise. During the next three years his company, the Contra Costa Water Company, built a 105 foot high dam and captured the watershed drainage for Temescal Creek, creating Lake Temescal with its nearly 200,000,000 gallon storage capacity. He also created an elaborate pipeline system, and, with it, he ultimately successfully replaced the numerous small wells that had once haphazardly provided water to the residents of Oakland and its surroundings. His timing was perfect, but he had underestimated the speed of Oakland's growth. The population explosion was so quick that within four years he had to build an even larger dam on San Leandro Creek to feed Lake Chabot, his crown jewel.[264]

Having completed the Temescal project, and with water systems in both Vallejo and San Jose under way as well, Chabot turned his attention to bringing his young daughter, Ellen, out to San Francisco. To do this, he arranged a marriage of convenience to Mary Ann Batcheller, a young woman he had met while in Maine courting Ellen's mother. So it was that, in the summer of 1870, Anthony Chabot returned to Standish, Maine to retrieve his nearly five-year-old daughter, Ellen, who had heard of him but had never met him. He immediately took her to nearby Lynn, Massachusetts, where he married Mary Ann, a "plain, thin faced woman, who apparently had no marriage prospects at home."[265] Mary Ann quickly warmed to the prospect of her life as a surrogate mother (which was, in truth, the only reason Anthony had married her), and she and Ellen quickly bonded and established a very close relationship that was to last throughout Mary Ann's life. Anthony, on the other hand, was a workaholic and was only very rarely at home (home being first the Eureka Hotel and later the Tubbs Hotel, both in Oakland.) Such was Ellen's (by now nicknamed "Nellie") childhood, surrounded by well-kept hotel grounds and an attentive staff at the Tubbs Hotel (Oakland's most luxurious hotel) but largely starved for paternal affection and children of her own age to play with. It wasn't until 1882 that Mr. Chabot finally bought a house for his family to live in, and it was never a lively home. Mary Ann was a reader but not an entertainer. Ellen (Nellie) has been described as growing into "a spindly, wiry, gray-eyed towhead [with] a quick mind…"[266]

After completing the dam on San Leandro Creek, in the mid-1870s Anthony lapsed into semi-retirement and turned his energies to investments and philanthropy. His investments included an 1885 investment of $55,000 in the Judson Manufacturing Company, a company recently founded by his old friend, Egbert Judson. He also correctly anticipated the direction of growth of downtown Oakland and bought large plots of land, including several ranches, lying in the path of that growth. One such ranch was a profitable 1,200 acre ranch in the Livermore Valley and another included 160 acres adjoining Lake Temescal. He also bought the first commercial cranberry bog in the United States, a 1600 acre plot of land in Washington State where descendants of his in-laws were still growing cranberries as late as 1983.[267]

But it was his charitable bent that Anthony Chabot was best known for in his later years, and remains revered for to this day. In his lifetime he made large donations to a number of churches (even though he was a member of none); to the Veterans Home in Yountville (where Chabot Cottage still exists); to the Fabiola Hospital (Oakland's first major hospital—where Kaiser Hospital stands today); to the San Francisco Opera House; to the Ladies' Relief Society; and to the Women's' Sheltering and Protection Home of Oakland (which he started, and then donated the land where the home was built, as well as $25,000 in cash). Indeed, the breadth and extent of his generosity are well illustrated by some of the institutions that bear his name: Chabot College in Hayward, Chabot Observatory in Oakland, Lake Chabot in San Leandro, Anthony Chabot Regional Park, and Lake Chabot in Vallejo.

To provide some sense of the admiration and respect his community had for Mr. Chabot, when he died on January 6, 1888, the Mayor of Oakland declared that January 9th would be a day of mourning. Oakland city flags were flown at half mast, and the city's schools and most businesses were closed for the day. Thousands of people are said to have packed the route of his funeral cortege from the First Congregational Church to the Mountain View Cemetery where he was laid to rest.[268]

Anthony Chabot left an estate worth $1,400,000. A substantial sum was given to his various charitable interests and the rest was left to Ellen. So, Ellen became a very wealthy 22-year-old heiress with almost unlimited income and, at the time, no place she knew of to spend or invest it. Instead of traveling broadly, buying fancy things, or otherwise spending her inheritance, Ellen elected to remain quietly at home with her stepmother for the next seventeen years.[269] The people she met and spent time with were typically business people who were involved in ventures that she needed to attend to in her capacity as her father's executrix. Although after her stepmother's death she became interested in fine clothes, she

Ellen Chabot

was never depicted, prior to her marriage to Henry, as a naturally extroverted hostess or a person given to lavish expenditures.

Henry's daughter, Genevieve, used to often say that what excited her father the most about Ellen was that "she had a million dollars," but it has to be remembered that Genevieve never liked either her father or Ellen, so, just as calling her father a horse thief didn't make that true, so too anything she ever said about Ellen has to be taken with a grain of salt. On the other hand, their marriage did seem to create changes in both of them, and it may well be that Ellen's inheritance did allow Henry to relax and take his mind off business.

In terms of assessing Ellen's character, Genevieve described her often as an old maid, and as someone who had never raised a child and had no idea how to relate to children. Genevieve's daughter Genie would say much the same about Ellen, referring to the times Ellen visited her while Genie was in high school in Santa Barbara. To the contrary, however, Terry Carter, the granddaughter of the head groundskeeper at Piranhurst (the Bothins' home in Montecito) paints a completely different picture. Terry, who used to play on the property as a young child, says that she recalls Ellen as a kind and generous woman. More than that, she recalls that her grandfather, Felix Rubalcava, always heaped praise on Ellen for her generosity, for her willingness (so long as guests were not present) to let the children of her groundskeepers have the run of Piranhurst, and for being a trusting and gracious employer. Terry mentioned how appreciative the Rubalcava family was for Ellen's donation to them of her World War II ration cards and food coupons. Ellen was a stickler for detail when it came to the condition she expected for the estate's grounds, yet she also maintained a loose and quite cordial relationship with Felix.[270]

Henry's and Ellen's marital plans were kept a closely guarded secret, so much that they didn't even apply for their license until the morning of the ceremony. The ceremony was conducted in Ellen's home with only six witnesses in attendance. Those present were the Honorable and Mrs. Victor Metcalf (a former secretary of the Navy), Mr. and Mrs. C.O.G. Miller (Henry's closest friend), Miss Bessie McNear, and Mr. Harry Miller. Shortly after the wedding, Ellen sold her Oakland home, and she never thereafter had much more to do with that community.

21.
A Change in Lifestyle

Although in her earlier life Ellen had been somewhat of a recluse, it appears that, after her marriage, she, and Henry as well, blossomed and began enjoying life. Before, Henry had spent his days engrossed in his business interests and rarely surfaced for fun; now suddenly life took a different turn for him. Together, they lived in Henry's large and well-staffed home in Ross, and they traveled extensively, both within the United States and abroad.

Regarding their home in Ross, it is interesting to note that even Genevieve, who never got along with Ellen, did say, in her oral history, that Ellen had excellent taste. Describing the home in Ross that she had earlier called "horrid" when first built, she said that Ellen brought in a well-known interior decorator, added nice awnings, created a "lovely garden," and made it "a perfectly lovely house."[271] That home in Ross remained Henry's and Ellen's primary residence for the rest of his life and, indeed, remained in the family until Ellen finally sold it in 1945.

Noting their interest in travel and leisure, an article appearing in "Suzette's Letter" in the January 19, 1913 edition of the *Oakland Tribune* noted that "...the Bothins will be leaving in the near future for New York, after which they plan to sail to Bermuda, Havana, the West Indies, and Panama on a trip which will keep them away until the early summer (presumably a four to six month trip in total)." In fact, the manifest list for the ship *Victoria Luise* ,which sailed from New York on February 8, 1913 on a cruise, returning to New York on March 8, 1913 confirms that they did indeed take that trip, traveling in the company of Louise Boyd (of San Rafael) and William and Julia Babcock (from San Francisco.)

Another mention in "Suzette's Letter" in the February 9, 1913 edition of the *Oakland Tribune* states that Mr. and Mrs. Henry Bothin were then on their way to Europe. The following year, the manifest list for the ship *Aquitania* includes the Bothins on its list of passengers for an Atlantic Ocean crossing that left Liverpool on May 30, 1914 and arrived in New York on June 5, 1914.

The October 10, 1910 edition of the *Oakland Tribune* (in the "Society News of the Week" section) notes that the Bothins were then in New York "selecting her winter wardrobe and also the furnishings for her charming new Santa Barbara home which will be finished, furnished, and ready for occupancy sometime in the Spring."

Those are just a few salient news items that appeared about the Bothins and their travels during the decade of the 1910s. There are others as well that talk about trips to Canada, other trips back east, and many, many trips to Montecito, the suburb of Santa Barbara where they would ultimately build a grand home on a property they bought, named Piranhurst by its prior owners. Suffice it to say that, if separately they had money, together they had just that much more, and they seemed to have learned rather quickly how to enjoy it.

The 1910 census, for instance, reveals that Henry and Ellen surrounded themselves, at their home in Ross, with a housekeeper, a seamstress, a butler, a chauffeur, and a gardener. Similarly, the later 1920 census (taken while they were living at Piranhurst) reveals that during that ten-year span the requirements for household help had remained much the same (although different people were involved).

Henry and Ellen

Thus, their Santa Barbara household in 1920 included a housekeeper, a chambermaid, a cook, a butler, and a chauffeur. Family lore has it that Henry also employed over 100 gardeners at Piranhurst, a number that is, according to Terry Carter, highly inflated for the estate's gardeners, but that number may not be too far off the mark if it includes the stone masons Henry used for the 320 acre mountaintop retreat that lay directly above Piranhurst, which they bought soon after they acquired Piranhurst. They named the mountaintop property *Mar y Cel*. It was a lavish and ambitious project he undertook to transform the mountain into a series of cascading waterfalls surrounding a 200 seat amphitheater.

All told, the *Oakland Tribune*, the *San Francisco Chronicle*, the *San Francisco Examiner*, and the *San Francisco Call Bulletin* together published in their society pages well over 200 articles about the couple during the period between 1909 and 1923. Those stories covered topics that included travel, parties they hosted, parties they attended, and many other tidbits consistent with being highly regarded members of the Bay Area's social scene.

One question that is posed by Henry and Ellen's obvious lifestyle change is whether or not it represented a dramatic change in their individual personalities. Remember that, prior to his divorce from Jennie, Henry had been portrayed as one who shunned the glitter of social events, who preferred the quiet of country life to the bustle of the city, who was moody and easily angered, and who was inattentive to family needs. For instance, the January 15, 1909 edition of the *San Francisco Call* summarized testimony given by Jennie and also her brother, William Whittier, at the trial of the divorce case. Among other things, Whittier described Henry as a man of whims who "broke or kept engagements just as the notion took him." He said that Henry would sometimes, at the last minute, refuse to accompany his wife to pre-arranged outings, and that Jennie had gone to Europe at one point in an unsuccessful attempt to have a cooling off period, only to find him unchanged upon her return. While that may have accurately described the Henry who was unhappily married to Jennie, it certainly doesn't seem to fit the image of the new Henry after his marriage to Ellen.

Ellen had, before the marriage, been known as a quiet, introverted girl, and her lady friends in Oakland thought she was destined to remain a spinster. That may have accurately portrayed the unmarried Ellen, but it too seems to bear no resemblance to the new Ellen after she and Henry had wed.

I believe that the answer to that rhetorical question is that their new lifestyle probably did not reflect a change in their personalities. Rather, it is far more likely that Henry and Ellen were simply too wealthy to avoid some notoriety, and they were a happy couple beginning a new life together and trying to find ways to cast off the shackles of their less satisfying pasts and to achieve a sort of happiness that had eluded each prior to their marriage. However, social interactions aside, both Henry and Ellen were still, in essence, private people who preferred life in the country to the glitter of the city. Although Henry's business life remained centered in San Francisco and Emeryville, he and Ellen lived for the rest of his life in Ross and Montecito. His primary residence was the home on Lagunitas Road in Ross, and he still commuted long distances to San Francisco and Emeryville to attend intently to his business interests, which continued to thrive under his management. Furthermore, his attention to philanthropy blossomed.

However, there is also another answer to that rhetorical question—an answer that may or may not be correct, but which certainly could have occurred to his daughter, Genevieve. She, a twelve-year-old adolescent at the time her mother filed for divorce, and one who had suffered through years of rarely seeing her workaholic father, might understandably have felt that, whereas *she* wasn't good enough to command his attention before, suddenly this same man, who had never had time for either her or her mother, was finding lots of time to spare with another woman and enjoying life to the fullest. In that regard, Jennie, too, could not have helped but wonder if this was the same man she had married. If that was Genevieve's perception, and one has to believe, given a lifetime of bitterness toward her father, that it was, then it really doesn't matter whether or not Henry had actually changed. It was enough that his actions gave the perception of deep changes, and that perception was, arguably, another contributing factor that resulted in Genevieve's diminished self-confidence and led to deep feelings of insecurity that lasted throughout her life.[272]

Whether or not Jennie and Genevieve read the social columns and spoke bitterly about the man they had earlier shared their lives with, clearly Ellen had, in several short months, accomplished what Jennie had tried, unsuccessfully, to do over a twenty year period. And while one hesitates to feel too sorry for Jennie, one does tend to understand a bit better why Genevieve might have harbored resentment and, indeed, why that resentment might well have affected whether or not she wanted to spend the time with him that, under the negotiated custody arrangements, he was entitled to. And not only would those feelings have affected the way Genevieve saw her father, but it also probably colored her perceptions of Ellen as well. Indeed, Genevieve's claim that she didn't like Ellen because Ellen didn't know how to relate to children was probably a subterfuge that hid the real reason she disliked her, which had more to do with jealousy over Ellen's success in claiming Henry's attention, something neither Jennie nor Genevieve had been able to do.

22.
Changes in Real Estate Strategy

Another indicator that Henry underwent a fundamental change in his approach to life following his marriage to Ellen can be found in the minutes of the Bothin Real Estate Company. Within three months of the 1906 earthquake and fire, Henry had formed the Real Estate Company and placed all of his commercial properties in San Francisco and Marin Counties into that entity. Initially, the company's Articles of Incorporation were extremely broad. However, in point of fact, a reading of those Minutes reveals that, as often happens in the aftermath of a life changing event—which the quake and fire certainly were—Henry seems to have made a rather abrupt turn in the way he viewed his real estate empire.

As broad as the powers of the Real Estate Company were, it seems that the company's focus, with Henry at its head from the outset, was to consolidate the Bothin properties, to prioritize them in terms of strategic importance, and to create and execute a plan for selling off less desirable holdings and managing the rest. In that regard, during 1907 the minutes reflect that the company approved the sale of a total of eight properties and no purchases. In 1908, the company sold eighteen properties and, again, purchased none. Similarly, between 1909 and 1914, approximately 20 additional properties were sold, and there is not a single record of the Board approving the purchase of any property. There are records of secured loans being approved in amounts ranging from $15,000 to $375,000, most of them single year term loans at rates varying from 5.5 percent to 7 percent. It seems the company had a sound credit record from the outset since those loans were taken out from, and later renewed by, at least seven lenders, including San Francisco Savings Union, The Savings and Loan Society, German Savings and Loan Society, California Insurance Company, Hibernia Savings and Loan Society, French American Bank of Savings, Mercantile Trust Co., and West Coast Life Insurance Company. That excellent credit rating would, of course, have come about because Henry had established good banking relationships with all of those same lenders in his individual capacity during the nearly twenty years when he was accumulating his properties prior to the formation of the company.

What does all that mean? The fact that all the business transacted by the Real Estate Company after the earthquake and fire was entirely on the sell side suggests that Henry needed to rest and to focus on what he already had as he set about rebuilding. Cash would be needed to meet not only the non-insured expenses of day to day operations, but also the money required to support his other investments in Hemet and elsewhere, not to mention the cost, after 1910, of running not one but two households—his primary residence in Ross and the rather spectacular masterpiece he and Ellen were creating in Montecito.

But might the minutes of the Bothin Real Estate Company actually tell a deeper story as well? It could be argued that the earthquake and fire actually had a cathartic effect on Henry. It forced him into acquisition withdrawal, and the longer he went without buying, the less all-consuming his prior drive to collect would have become. Yes, it is speculation to suggest that no acquisitions during that three year period between the earthquake and his marriage to Ellen might have represented a transformation in Henry's thinking. However, that speculation gains credibility when one looks at the minutes of 1909. For on July 26th of that year, just one and a half months after he and Ellen were married, the Board elected Ellen as a director. The very spike that had driven one of the deepest wedges between Henry and Jennie had suddenly, less than two months after he and Ellen were married, been not just vanquished, but had been sanctified by a seemingly transformed Henry who saw Ellen as his equal and as his partner rather than the person who had before questioned him and fought him where she could in his pursuit of his real estate investments.

If I am correct, Henry's transformation from an addicted collector to an executive manager didn't happen overnight. The fact that he made no purchases between the earthquake and his marriage to Ellen three years later offered time for a soft landing, a change in perspective that he probably didn't even recognize was occurring until it would have been too late to make any difference in his first marriage, but one that had largely been completed in his mind by the time of his second. In other words, I don't suggest that Ellen was the catalyst for change; rather that she benefited from the timing of something already destined to occur. But no matter the cause, it seems clear that Henry's maturation following the earthquake made it far easier for him to relax and to enjoy all the travel, entertainment, and other changed circumstances he and Ellen seem to have embarked on as a couple.

Henry and Ellen's Ross home

23.
Henry's Attachment to Ross

Henry's attachment to the Marin County town of Ross began with his purchase of two different lots in Ross. During his first marriage that attachment was mired in domestic conflict, but after his marriage to Ellen, that fondness for the town and its surroundings became a shared interest, and one they both enjoyed for the rest of his life. Even though he had bought the large lot in 1902, Henry had never sold the smaller one where Frank had been taken by infantile paralysis. And despite all the improvements they made to the home they lived in, they still valued the other property enough that it was still owned in his name when Henry died, and it was a part of his probated estate. Both properties were corner lots in a very nice neighborhood of Ross, and both provided the serenity and privacy that he and Ellen craved. Indeed, although Ellen resided primarily in Montecito after Henry's death, she continued to spend some time at least in their home in Ross for another twenty-two years after his death, only finally selling it in 1945.

Within a month after Henry and Ellen were married, on July 26, 1909, fire destroyed that first house that Henry had built on the smaller lot. The house was occupied at the time by people named LaBoyteaux who were almost assuredly renters. The fire was apparently caused by a defective flue and left a "heap of ruins."[273] An article that appeared less than two months after the fire in the September 18, 1909 issue of *Marin County Tocsin* indicated that Henry was by then already rebuilding the house that had burned and that all traces of the fire would shortly be removed.[274] That same article also noted that new additions to the Bothins' large home were nearly completed. When one combines that date with Genevieve's recollection that the improvements to the big house were Ellen's doing, it follows that Ellen, who had then been married to Henry for less than three months, was also not one to let moss grow under her feet.

Interestingly, Henry sent a check and a letter of thanks to the firemen who put out the fire. Unfortunately, it seems to have been sent to the wrong fire department and to have become contentious, thereby proving the old adage that good deeds rarely go unpunished. As reported in the *San Francisco Call* on August 16, 1909, the first firemen to respond to the fire came from the San Anselmo Fire Department. They had mistakenly understood that it was a grass fire and so had come ill-equipped to fight a structure fire. Meanwhile, the San Rafael fire chief and one of his fire fighters arrived in an unequipped buggy and pitched in to save some furniture while he waited for his department to arrive with proper firefighting apparatus. Unfortunately, they were not able to save the house. Nonetheless, Henry greatly appreciated the efforts made by the firefighters and particularly by the San Anselmo Fire Department, and it was that department to whom the check was intended to be delivered. Due to a clerical error, the check ended up in the hands of the San Rafael Department. Henry then sent a letter to San Rafael asking for return of his check, and he made out a new one to San Anselmo. Who knows why Henry felt that San Anselmo deserved the credit, but the fact is that both Fire Departments felt that they were the proper recipient. As Chief Fonnesbeck of the San Anselmo Fire Department said, "San Rafael got the check that was meant for us in the first place. Bothin intended to send the check to us, not to San Rafael, as their men did nothing at the fire to speak of." Chief Schneider of the San Rafael Fire Department responded, "We hope San Anselmo enjoys our check. We don't need it and they do."

More importantly, the fire did in fact teach a valuable lesson, and to that extent it may have served the public good. As reported in the July 31, 1909 edition of the *Marin County Tocsin*, San Rafael's fire hose was the standard size, whereas San Anselmo used hose that was ¼" smaller in diameter. That fact prevented one department (presumably San Rafael's since Henry was far more grateful to San Anselmo's unit) from being able to lend meaningful assistance. The author of the newspaper article called for all fire departments to become standardized and equipped with the same size hose in order to be able to provide mutual response to fires that cross department lines. It would be presumptive to suggest that this episode led to the standardization of firefighting equipment, but certainly it added to the wealth of evidence that such a policy was needed.

Although Santa Barbara, and specifically Piranhurst, became an ever-increasing draw for Henry and Ellen, who spent progressively more and more time there, Henry never seems to have lost his attachment to Ross. As an example of Henry's ongoing commitment to the town, in 1913 he purchased, for $2,000, another large parcel of land across Lagunitas Road and directly south of his home. That piece, bought from a man named Carl S. Plant, was nine acres in size. Although it had no frontage on Lagunitas, it was extremely important to both Henry and to the Lagunitas Club. To Henry, it included the entirety of his main southern view corridor, measuring as it did 500 feet wide by 1,800 feet deep and extending from near the valley floor all the way to the top of the ridge some 400 feet above Lagunitas Road. That property was not just directly across the street from Henry's and Ellen's home, but it was also immediately adjacent to and east of the Lagunitas Club. As such, it was also valuable to the club as protection for its privacy. Whether he purchased that parcel in order to protect his own property and views, or whether he purchased it to protect the Lagunitas Club, is not known. What is known is that it was still in his name at the time of his death.

At his death, Henry also still owned most of the ranch he had bought in 1902 from Phoebe Apperson Hearst—then referred to as a part of Rancho Canada de Herrera, but known by Henry as the "Marin Ranch."[275] He had, as earlier mentioned, given 157 acres of that property to support Elizabeth Ashe's charitable endeavors; however, the rest, totaling 1,052 acres, he still owned, along with 28 unsold lots in his Manor Subdivision in Fairfax. His estate also included the original 2.8 acre parcel he and Jennie had purchased and where he had built the house where they spent their summers during Genevieve's childhood.

In addition to those properties in Ross, in 1916 Henry purchased 152 acres in Sausalito, another community in Marin County. This property adjoined Richardson Bay and was a part of the tidelands that extend from that bay toward Mill Valley. It is now owned by the Marin County Open Space District and is known as "Bothin Marsh." Undoubtedly when he bought it he planned to develop it, but he simply ran out of time. In any case, that land was also in his estate and was not sold until more than fifty years after his death.[276] It has been restored and is today prized for its tidal wetlands, its birdlife, and its running and biking trails.

Henry was also active in the Lagunitas Tennis Club. The records of that club, although not as complete as one would like, bear interesting testimony to his generosity and also, as it relates to his later terms as president of the club, to his financial acumen on the one hand and, on the other, his apparent inability to work by consensus.

Speaking first to the issue of his generosity, the club minutes in 1916 refer to a serious drought in the community that had caused the authorities to decide to discontinue water service "for all uses other than residential." Henry, whose home was directly across the street and who had his own cistern, offered to share his water with the club. When he learned that the club could not afford the cost of running the connections, he agreed to and did in fact pay the entire cost himself.[277]

Three years later, in 1919, the club, whose minutes reflect that it had a fall-off in membership and was known as a "late pay" by most of its creditors, was quite clearly in financial doldrums.[278] It was under those circumstances that the club drafted Henry to be its president. Specifically, on August 15, 1919, the then-president of the club, W.W. Thurston, resigned, and Henry (up to then apparently a rather inactive member) was asked to take Mr. Thurston's seat on the board. During that same meeting, in what looks suspiciously like a coup, Henry was elected by the other directors to serve out the remainder of Mr. Thurston's term as president. He did in fact serve out that term, and he was re-elected in June 1920 to a second term. Just as he had done with his commercial property in downtown Hemet, Henry immediately tried to instill a positive impression on club members, this time by announcing, just as soon as he had been elected president, that he was donating a tennis trophy to the club.[279] In return, however, he asked the members to help him put the Club's financial house in order, a goal he was unfortunately unable to bring to fruition. He attempted to secure passage of motions to set new policy on several fronts at once; first to get the members to approve a $10 per head assessment; second, to establish a guest fee for the use of the Club's tennis courts by non-member guests; and third, to pass a resolution increasing dues. All those proposals were met by furious debate and all failed.[280] After failing to achieve change by positive action, he ultimately tried to accomplish at least some financial improvements through embarrassing scofflaws, by securing the passage of a resolution that approved the posting of members' names who were delinquent in their dues.

Although Henry's tenure at the helm of the Lagunitas Club cannot be called altogether successful, his efforts did prime the pump and led to hard decisions made in ensuing years. In the meantime, however, the Lagunitas Club was at that time renowned for the beauty of its setting and the quality of its oyster shell courts, where many of the finest tennis players of the time played, including Maurice MacLaughlin, Helen Wills, and William Johnston.

Henry and granddaughter Genie with Ellen

24.
Broadening Philanthropic Efforts

Prior to his divorce, Henry had taken buggy rides alone out to Fairfax every Sunday to visit the children under Nurse Ashe's care. Meanwhile, Miss Ashe was using Hill Farm to continue her good works, and those tireless efforts were gaining interest not only among a large number of influential and wealthy donors, but with Henry's new bride, Ellen, as well. It was reported in the June 26, 1909 edition of the *Marin County Tocsin*, that during the previous week, the Telegraph Hill Neighborhood Association had given a benefit for Hill Farm at the Lagunitas Country Club (undoubtedly hosted by Ellen, who now lived across the street from and was a member of the club). It was reported in that article:

> The Misses and matrons of society lent their aid with the result that it was a social and financial success. Some eighty little ones came over from the city and carried through a fine program including songs and music by their band. The boys were bareheaded and were dressed in blue overalls and jumpers. Many visitors took the little fellows for automobile and carriage rides and thus gave them the time of their lives.

The article went on to list thirty-one ladies who participated in the gathering, including patronesses Mrs. R. Porter Ashe (either the mother of Elizabeth Ashe or her sister-in-law), Mrs. Henry Bothin, Mrs. James Coffin, Miss Coppee, Mrs. M. Esberg, Mrs. Edwin L. Griffith, Mrs. John Martin, Mrs. H.M.A. Iller, Mrs. Seward McNear, Mrs. E. Remington, Mrs. George Pinkard, Mrs. George Page, and Mrs. Samuel Wormser.

In 1910, presumably with Ellen's full concurrence, Henry put his second foot into the world of charitable endeavors. He met with Miss Ashe in Fairfax one day and informed her that he was so impressed with the value of the work she had done at Hill Farm that he intended to incorporate it under the name "Bothin Convalescent Home for Women and Children." He asked her how much land she would need to fulfill her dream and told her he was prepared to donate what she needed. Miss Ashe is reported to have said, "I looked to the hills 'from whence cometh my help' and said, 'I would like to have as much as I can see.'"[281]

If Henry was taken aback by Miss Ashe's request, he didn't show it, and the following Sunday he told her that he had had the tops of the hills within her line of sight surveyed and that he was preparing to donate the resultant 122 acres to Hill Farm. With that gift of land, Miss Ashe made certain that Hill Farm continued to flourish, with an expanded mission to serve as a convalescent home for children, ages six to sixteen, convalescing from illness or surgery. Its continuing importance was emphasized when, in 1919, Henry further improved the site with the construction of the Women's Building, known as "Stone House." With that, the mission of Hill Farm was further broadened to include treatment of business and professional women needing complete bed rest, sun baths, and the same healthy diet offered to children.

On September 23, 1910, Henry formalized his promise by establishing and later filing Articles of Incorporation for The Bothin Convalescent Home, whose stated purpose was "To establish, conduct and maintain, in the County of Marin, State of California, hospitals, sanitoriums, convalescent homes, farms and camps, and to this end to acquire, by purchase, lease, gift, devise, bequest, or otherwise...such real and personal property as may be necessary or proper for carrying said objects into effect." The number of directors was set at 14, and the first directors were identified as Elizabeth H. Ashe, Alice S. Griffith, Harriette de Witt Kittle, Elizabeth J. Anderson, Ellen Chabot Bothin, C.O.G. Miller, William Kent, Thomas C. Berry, Henry E. Bothin, Frank S. Johnson, John F. Boyd, Frank D. Madison, Philp King Brown, and J.J. Kaufman.

With a board consisting of the people it did, it was now clear that his and Miss Ashe's dream was not only a reality but a well-established charitable organization whose solvency and goals could reasonably be expected to be met for the foreseeable future (as indeed they turned out to be).

In 1922 the facilities at Hill Farm were further enlarged by construction of Manor/Lyman House. A rather lengthy article appearing in the May 1938 issue of the *San Rafael Independent* provides a very helpful description:

> In a setting of natural beauty, amid pleasant surroundings, with good food, nursing, and care, weak, thin little bodies grow strong at Hill Farm at Bothin Convalescent Home, near Manor. To the home come undernourished children, sick children from city tenements and from poverty stricken country dwellings, children of all races and creeds to find an amazing and very wonderful new life. In surroundings so vastly different from which they have come, these children regain their strength in a vacation land— that is what the home seems to be to the casual visitor, an attractive vacation resort for children.

It was about thirty-five years ago that the Bothins established this wonderful home for children, and since then so great a want has it filled, that it has grown extensively and its range extended.

That article went on to describe the age and conditioning requirements of patients, the daily routines, the types of cases treated, and the fact that the care is supervised by the Pediatric Department of the University of California, with two registered nurses in regular attendance. It also described some of the special events put on by the children as well as identifying some of the other people and organizations, other than Henry, who supported its mission financially and/or by volunteering time, visiting, or otherwise delivering gifts to the children as well as good cheer to all the patients. Finally, the article reported on Stone House and its parallel mission to provide similar services to business and professional women.

As much as Hill Farm (now Bothin Convalescent Home) was continuing to flourish under Miss Ashe's guidance, she still had energy left to convince Henry to back still another important project, this one being an effort that Dr. Philip King Brown was attempting to undertake to provide a new treatment for tuberculosis. Tuberculosis was a terrible disease, and Henry had seen firsthand the awful way it consumed its victims before finally proving fatal. He had lost his sister, Pauline, to tuberculosis at the age of thirty-nine back in 1880, and both sons of his sister, Emily, had died of that dread disease; one (Emil) dying while in Henry's employ in the Emeryville shipping office of The Judson back in 1890. For that reason he wanted, just as badly as Miss Ashe did, to see advances made in its treatment and, hopefully, eradication.

Dr. Brown was a highly respected pulmonary specialist and a member of a family of well-regarded physicians.[282] It was his view that the widespread outbreak of tuberculosis, which had gripped San

Francisco in the aftermath of the earthquake and fire, had its genesis in the dusty and ash filled landscape and in the dingy working conditions where women too often toiled in those days.

Whatever its cause, mortality numbers in San Francisco were then approaching 205 per 100,000 people. Dr. Brown (who had co-founded the San Francisco Boys Club and was well known and respected by Miss Ashe) believed the reason working women were more than twice as likely as men to come down with the disease was that, as dressmakers, clerks, factory workers, and the like, they labored in windowless basements and in far more unsanitary conditions than did most men. He believed that rest and fresh air were most likely the best forms of treatment, and he was searching for a place to put that theory to the test.

Dr. Philip King Brown

Henry knew Dr. Brown, who was one of the incorporators of Bothin Convalescent Home, and he recognized in him the sort of competent medical mind whose treatment plan made sense and was worthwhile to pursue. So Henry was receptive when Miss Ashe asked him to consider a further gift of land adjacent to Hill Farm to undertake the effort. More specifically, she asked for and was given an additional 35 acres for the site of a new sort of tubercular sanitarium to be named Arequipa.[283] That gift brought to 157 acres the amount of land he gave for her charitable purposes.

Miss Ashe wasted no time putting the second gift of land to use. By January 24, 1911, it was reported[284] that ground would shortly be broken on the sanatorium, to provide a restful place for the care and treatment of people with incipient stage tuberculosis.

There was broad-based support in the community for this undertaking, and, by April 6, 1911, it was reported in the *San Francisco Chronicle* that, of the approximately $15,000 needed to be raised to erect the building, $5,000 had been committed and the rest was expected soon. Major donors to the construction project included Mrs. Francis J. Carolan ($5,000), Mrs. L.H. Holton ($2,000), Mrs. J.C. Jordan ($2,000), Mrs. W.H. Crocker ($1,375), and Mrs. James Moffitt ($1,000).[285] In addition the following contributors were also identified in a later newspaper article:[286] Mesdames Joseph D. Grant, Joseph C. Chamberlain, Mr. John C. Coleman, Mr. Edward Coleman, Miss Persis Coleman, Mrs. J.C. Coffin, Mrs. Frederick Kohl, Marcus F. Koshland, John Martin, John Kittle, M. Sussman, Moses Gunst and Miss Fanny Levy.

Arequipa was a distinct entity, having a separate purpose, clientele, and property from that of Hill Farm. Its formal name was The Arequipa Tuberculosis Sanatorium for Working Women. By the same token, its mission was consistent with that of Bothin Convalescent Home, and the fact that Dr. Brown was among the original incorporators of that entity, as well as the closeness in time when both the Bothin Convalescent Home was incorporated and the launching of Arequipa, it seems likely that Arequipa was intended all along to be included within the Convalescent Home umbrella.

The name Arequipa, \a-re-ˈqēp-ə\ (or "a-re-**keep**-a") is Peruvian and was thought (apparently inaccurately) to mean "a place of peace."[287] Whether accurate or not, that was the meaning ascribed to it, and that very well described the environment they sought to create. With Miss Ashe's nursing support, Henry's gift of property, and financial contributions from many of San Francisco's leading citizens, including Phoebe Apperson Hearst, from whom Henry had purchased the Fairfax property and after whom Dr. Brown's daughter was named, Arequipa opened on September 4, 1911.

Arequipa was not only supported financially by prominent citizens in the community, it also had not one or two, but three boards overseeing it. The first was the Board of the Bothin Convalescent Home that has already been described. The second was a blue ribbon medical board consisting of Drs. Louis Howe, R.G. Brodrick, Louis S. Mace and Harry P. Viel in addition to Dr. Brown. Finally, it also had a Board of Managers whose members included James C. Jordan, Mrs. Luther J. Holton, Mrs. Benjamin Dibblee, Miss Ashe and Dr. Brown. By involving prominent citizens as well as widely respected doctors, Henry and Miss Ashe had assured the continuing support and interest of local community leaders in both Marin and San Francisco. Its opening was widely reported in the *San Francisco Chronicle* (in articles published in both the September 1st and 3rd editions), *The Marin Journal* (in an article dated September 4th), and in an unknown San Francisco newspaper on September 3rd.[288]

Probably the reason that Arequipa most excited donors and doctors alike was the ingenuity of its program, for Dr. King and his medical board sought to combine rest along with light work in the open air as a means not only of providing a more healthy environment to clear the lungs of the disease, but also as a way to bring in revenue and thereby provide value to the institution to help cover its operating costs. To Dr. Brown, the beauty of this approach was not only that it could help provide the funds needed to make the institution self-supporting, but also it would give the patients a sense that they were contributing to their own care and not accepting the charity of others. The way it proposed to do that was to ask the patients to learn the art of pottery and to spend a few hours each day utilizing the unique clay found on the property to make ceramics which might then be sold as artwork. In furtherance of that goal, Dr. Brown and Miss Ashe hired a master potter named Frederick Rhead, set him up with potter's wheels, kilns, and other needed equipment, and then let the program run itself under the frequent supervision of Dr. Brown and the medical board.

In October 1912 a reporter named Ida L. Brooks wrote a lengthy article about Arequipa. The article explains the value of the

Arequipa experience to its patients and the emerging importance of its emphasis on pottery to both the patient's recovery and sense of self-worth. Overall it is a most impressive article, and it makes the case very well for the success of both Henry's philanthropic efforts and the use to which they were put.[289] That article, titled "Wooing Life Anew at the Potter's Wheel," says in the introduction "At this Marin County Sanitarium, women forget that they have

Arequipa, showing some of the Sanatorium and related structures

been touched by one of the world's oldest diseases by becoming engrossed in one of the world's oldest arts." The article goes on to say, "The pottery wouldn't be there if it weren't for the sanatorium, and if it weren't for the pottery the sanatorium couldn't possibly be the success it is, for it would completely lose its claim to distinctiveness." The writer, Ms. Brooks, noted:

> ...There are at least five direct objects that the pottery is designed to accomplish—primarily it

provides a means of diverting the mind of the patient from her physical condition and keeps her in the open air while at work; it makes possible for her to earn enough each day to pay her expenses at the sanatorium; it provides her with a new craft, whereby, after being cured, she may find more remunerative and healthful employment than that in which she was formerly engaged; for, being an art as well as an industry, it gives her soul a chance to develop and beautify her life; lastly it helps the institution financially.

The article also compliments the chief potter, Frederick Rhead, by calling him, in addition to a master potter, a teacher who "has rare powers of imparting knowledge"—so much so, indeed, that by and large the patients consider that they are at play all day. And that is called the "secret and charm of the whole thing."

Then, on December 12, 1912, another article was written about Arequipa, this time by Richard C. Cabot, M.D. The piece was entitled "Arequipa Sanatorium, Where a Tuberculosis Patient Can Be Cured Without Expense to Himself or Anyone Else."[290] That article explains, from a medical standpoint, the genius of Dr. Brown's idea. Essentially, and as the author emphasizes:

> ...the "curse" of tuberculosis "is not the physical suffering it entails, but the serious expense of so long and wearing an illness stretching over months and years, and the way the long idleness ravishes the patient's character. Despondency does as much damage to some patients as the disease itself...To conquer these evils through work, and still more through the encouragement given patients by the money which they earn, is Dr. Brown's great achievement."

Dr. Cabot went on to say that, based on the first years' experience, the cost of care at Arequipa is $7 per week, which was the lowest figure he was aware of for institutions providing the high level of care provided by Arequipa. He noted that there was no endowment or income other than the sale of pottery and what small amounts came in from friends of patients too ill to work. Still, after one year, there was no deficit and no debt. From a health perspective, the dangers of clay dust and lead poisoning were avoided by cleanliness and an abundance of fresh air.

In the same article, speaking of Henry Bothin, Dr. Cabot mentioned his understanding of the source of Henry's interest and involvement. He wrote:

> Through the good offices of Miss Elizabeth Ashe who is carrying on in the same neighborhood a home for sickly children, thirty-five acres of land for the sanatorium were given to Dr. Brown by Henry E. Bothin of Ross, a neighboring town. Mr. Bothin heard of Dr. Brown's project and was so much impressed by it that he called upon him and offered the land quite unsolicited.

Dr. Cabot then compared Arequipa to the tubercular ward at the City and County Hospital of San Francisco, whose records revealed that their death rate was about 20 percent of patients per month. Certainly that statistic recognizes that the County hospital admitted many advanced stage patients; however, as he noted, "A hospital where one-fifth of your companions die each month is not an inviting place to go for treatment and in fact few go there if they can possibly help it." Obviously, Dr. Brown felt that that statistic proved the need for Arequipa and attested to the huge benefit it provided to the community, and it is quite clear that he had a large following of generous donors, including Henry, who agreed and were prepared to back him financially.

As depressing as a diagnosis of tuberculosis was at the time, Dr. Cabot stated that he had spent about three days at Arequipa and, during that time, never heard a patient cough. He found the patients cheerful and lively (more so than in any other sanatorium he had visited), and he was taken by the beauty of the pottery to the point of remarking that he could not believe that "these unskilled girls could produce it." He went on to say that he had seen a letter from a dealer requesting a contract for a larger allotment of the output. Finally, Dr. Cabot mentioned that the facility was flourishing to the point that "cured" patients didn't want to leave but rather wanted to stay and to make their living permanently making pottery at the sanatorium. Based on that, Dr. Brown was considering building a large but separate pottery (which was planned but then never actually undertaken) under the same management to enable cured tubercular patients and also deaf, crippled and otherwise handicapped people to supply the labor to make pottery and reap the benefits.

Later articles followed, bearing dates during 1913, 1914, and 1915 and published in the *Los Angeles Times*, *The Independent*, and the *Marin Journal* . They all cover much of the same ground, updating the information and remaining enthusiastic about the activities at Arequipa.[291] Each of the articles seems to focus on a different point, ranging from the human interest side, to the technical specifications of the kilns and other equipment, to the constant need to train new patients as the more highly experienced women become cured and move on. Ultimately, the pottery captured the imagination of the broad press, and its popularity and nationwide appeal soared. It was sold at the finest stores in San Francisco, Chicago, New York, Boston, and other large cities, and, in 1915 it was prominently displayed at the Panama-Pacific Exposition in San Francisco.[292] Arequipa continued to flourish during World War I (despite Nurse Ashe's absence in France where she trained nurses during the war) and beyond.

One suspects Henry was rightly proud of both Arequipa and Hill Farm, although there is no indication he was ever interviewed

Patients engaged in making pottery

The dining room

The sleeping area

about his role in enabling either of them to become a reality. Rather he seems to have preferred that his philanthropy remain in the background. Lest there be any question about his ongoing personal interest (over and above his financial support) it is instructive to point out that, in her oral history Genevieve spoke of a little seven or eight year old girl in nurse Ashe's care who Henry became extremely fond of. Her name was Vivian Goff. Genevieve said that she was always surprised that Henry didn't adopt her.

Later, after Henry's death in 1923, articles about both Arequipa and Hill Farm continued to be written. For example, in 1928 an article appeared in the *San Francisco Chronicle*[293] where it was noted that Hill Farm (by then renamed Bothin Convalescent Home) accommodated 600 children at a time and had a long waiting list for what was typically a two week stay, which "is usually long enough to bring back the bloom of health to young cheeks…"

Another article, written by Mrs. Jefferson Doolittle, a member of San Francisco's Junior League, appeared in the *San Francisco Chronicle* in its August 24, 1930 edition. That article began with an anecdote about "Bobby," described as the "most pathetic case at Hill Farm" who was both physically and socially maladjusted after spending months hospitalized and in a cast. A search party had gone looking for him and found him down at the creek, "his limp completely forgotten, chasing water dogs." She went on to describe the mission (as it was at that time) to take children in need of sunshine and fresh air following serious illnesses, and her article ended with the following:

> Bobby's case is typical. The afternoon I went to Hill Farm the older children were away on a beach picnic, the strongest young ones, such as Marianne and Betty Ann, had taken their supper up the hill, and the rest were happy playing at home, knowing that there was a freezer of ice cream for their dinner.

> In this happy atmosphere children and adults forget themselves quickly and have just a wonderful vacation, at the end of which, completely healed in mind and body, they are able to go home and assume their normal places in society.

In September 1936, Arequipa celebrated its twenty-fifth birthday. Dr. Brown spoke, and poignantly noted that since opening, 1,750 girls (an average of about 70 per year) had stayed at the sanatorium and had been successfully treated. Comparing that phenomenal outcome against a statistical overall death rate in 1911 of 205 per 100,000 of population, and still as of 1936 a death rate of 72 per 100,000, it was and is readily apparent that Arequipa had saved many lives. Doctors were still giving freely of their time, and, as of 1936, the facility was taking on ever more serious cases.

On April 15, 1940, the *San Francisco Examiner* published an article entitled "2,000 girls aided by Arequipa Sanatorium." The article began:

> There are broad porches overlooking the hillside, and the green velvet meadows beyond... Girls, hardly more than children, and young, frail women rest on those porches, waiting for care and time to make them strong again—waiting for long months, sometimes the years, that tuberculosis exacts as ransom for the lives of its young victims.
>
> Other girls—2,000 of them—have rested on these porches since Arequipa Sanatorium was founded thirty years ago. By far the great majority of them have returned to the world, fit to work, to bear children, and to take their places as strong women, useful to society.

Unfortunately, the article focused more on deferred maintenance than anything else. By 1940 the buildings, still needed for the care being provided to Arequipa's tubercular patients, were falling apart. Although he was never once mentioned in the article, the overall impression one came away with after reading it, was that Arequipa was crying out for another benefactor and was ruing the fact that Henry was gone.

The Arequipa tile display booth at the Panama Pacific Exposition

Arequipa tile

25.
Santa Barbara – Piranhurst

I n early 1910, just months after Henry and Ellen were married, they travelled to Santa Barbara, then a rather small town on the coast of Southern California whose main claim to fame was its balmy weather. Santa Barbara County, during the early days of the 19th century, had been the site of three out of the twenty-one missions built by Franciscan missionaries, each spaced a day's horseback ride apart as they wended their way north through what was then known as Alta California until finally arriving at the San Francisco Bay Area. But it wasn't until after the railroad arrived in the 1880s that the town began to grow and to attract visitors from all around the country. Writer Charles Nordhoff described it as "the pleasantest" spot in California and said that its agreeable year-round weather was particularly inviting for those suffering from "health ills."[294] His book attracted many wealthy visitors, and some of them stayed on and built expansive Victorian estates. By the early 1900s, a number of pre-Hollywood studios had also descended upon the town with their stars, including actors Douglas Fairbanks Jr. and Mary Pickford, among many others,[295] and made more than 1,200 silent movies there during a span of ten years.[296]

By the middle of the first decade of the 20th century, Santa Barbara had come to be recognized as a destination resort town and an altogether delightful place to visit. As a result of the large influx of wealthy tourists, in 1903 the luxurious Potter Hotel opened and proclaimed itself to be "Where the Elite Retreat." The Potter, set on thirty acres of prime waterfront land, was a huge hotel that rose six and a half stories tall and boasted 390 guest rooms. It had its own post office, water system, and power plant. It was staffed by over 500 people (out of a total population in Santa Barbara of approximately 7,000) and its main dining room held over 700 guests.[297] It attracted a clientele from all over the world, many of whom stayed for a month or longer. Among its many visitors in 1910 were Henry and Ellen who found Santa Barbara very much to their liking. While they were enjoying their visit, they came upon a piece of property in nearby Montecito which was for sale. It was called Piranhurst, and its size was variously estimated at anywhere from 36 to 42 acres.

The Bothins would ultimately buy Piranhurst, but before that story unfolds it is worthwhile to provide some background. The property was then owned by Julia M. Richardson, the widow of Daniel Richardson, a wealthy grain merchant from Chicago. The Richardsons bought the property in 1901 from William Gillette, one of the more popular of the silent film actors, whose specialty was playing Sherlock Holmes on the silent screen. He had enlarged the property by adding parcels that he bought from longtime residents Lucy Stevens (whose late husband was involved in local water development) and Edward F.R. Vail (a local banker who was to become one of the early outside directors of the Bothin Helping Fund.)[298] Mr. and Mrs. Richardson, who intended in time to build a large winter home on the property, initially built a modest shingled cottage and then embarked on the landscaping, which was Mrs. Richardson's passion. They hired landscape architect John Whipple, who had worked on their home in Illinois, giving him a three year contract to develop the gardens,[299] and they also hired J. Wilkinson Elliott, a noted Pittsburgh landscape architect.[300] In addition, they drew plans for a 500,000 gallon reservoir for irrigating their gardens and orchards. When, in 1903, a drought threatened the investment they had made in their landscaping, they successfully drilled a well that produced about thirty-five gallons per minute and was considered the best well in Montecito.[301] Unfortunately for the Richardsons, they never saw their project completed, for in 1903 Mr. Richardson became ill and died at the age of fifty-four. His widow, Julia, continued to come out periodically to work on the gardens that were by then renowned locally as "one of the best planted places in Montecito."[302] Ironically, Andrew Carnegie, whose fortune from steel far outstripped Henry's, and who also visited Montecito often with his wife, is said to have told a reporter that "Mrs. Carnegie fell in love with the Richardson place."[303]

Ultimately, Mrs. Richardson decided to sell Piranhurst. The Bothins bought it, and the story of their purchase provides a textbook example of Henry's approach to business in general and to the purchase of real estate in particular. The description of what happened comes largely from the appellate decision decided in 1912 in a lawsuit known as *Dreyfus v Richardson* which can be found at 20 Cal App Reports, beginning at page 800.[304] According to the court's recitation of facts, Mrs. Richardson had hired Louis Dreyfus, a local Realtor, to represent her and to try to sell the property for the then astronomical price of $75,000. The property languished for over a year without any offers under Mr. Dreyfus' passive marketing style. Then, in 1909, Dreyfus suggested that Mrs. Richardson lower the price to $45,000, to which she agreed, and he asked for and received an exclusive listing. He hung out a sign, took out some advertising, and otherwise waited patiently for a buyer to come along.

In February 1910, the property was still on the market when the Bothins took their vacation trip to Santa Barbara, whereupon they learned of it from a Mrs. Biddle, who was also a guest at the Potter Hotel. Henry and Ellen went out to see the property, but decided the price was too high. They completed their stay in Santa Barbara and returned home to Ross without having made contact with the Realtor, Dreyfus, or taking any steps to show interest. Despite the appearance of disinterest, nonetheless, one month later, they returned to Santa Barbara and at some point met Mrs. Charles Eaton, who was the wife of a very highly respected local landscape architect and who, therefore, had an appreciation for the gardens at Piranhurst. Talk turned to Piranhurst, and Mrs. Eaton encouraged the Bothins to purchase it. Henry, in his typical style, explained to Mrs. Eaton that he was not interested in dealing through a broker, but that if she could locate a friend of the owner who would be willing to convey their interest in making an all-cash offer of $35,000, they would make such an offer directly to Mrs. Richardson. A Mr. Ripley was found who met the criteria and who agreed to communicate the verbal offer to the owner, and a deal was struck. The result: The Bothins (or more correctly, Ellen)[305] bought Piranhurst for $35,000, and the Realtor sued Mrs. Richardson (unsuccessfully) for a commission.[306]

Once hooked, Henry and Ellen ultimately came to fall in love with the property they had bought, and they decided to make it into a showplace not only for themselves but also for the many friends they would soon entertain on its grounds. In 1913, Henry and Ellen hired New York architect, F. Garvin Hudson, to design "an Italian style mansion on a knoll with outstanding views of the ocean and countryside."[307] Hudson did just that, and the resulting twenty room Mediterranean style masterpiece, set on gently sloping hills and featuring spectacular faraway views of the ocean, was completed in 1916. As described in David Myrick's book about the great Montecito estates being built around that time:

> The three story house was built of concrete with a plaster exterior and contained 20 rooms, including seven for the staff. The stone entrance hall contained

a curving stairway with a wrought-iron balustrade and a balcony for musicians. A black and white marble floor led from the entrance into the oval garden room, which opened to the spacious grass terrace. From the terrace, steps swept toward the formal gardens below.

A belvedere, in the form of a circular pergola, was planned at the bottom of this garden to serve as a teahouse by the Greek Theater. There was also a glass enclosed swimming pool and conservatories with a heating plant.[308]

But it was the landscaping above all that has always put Piranhurst upon a pedestal. The property boasted many mature live oaks, and under and in the midst of them the Bothins placed manicured lawns—enough, according to journalist David Brainard, "for four or five hundred simultaneous croquet games," and they planted gardens of flowers, as well as cypress hedges. These cypress hedges both encircled and created an outdoor theatre, one that has been written about in numerous magazines and journals, which included separate box seating areas carved entirely from heavily pruned cypress hedging. The topography, the views, the landscaping, and the magnificence of the home all combined to make Piranhurst one of the the most spectacular homes in a community where incredible estates were, and still remain, almost commonplace.

People often ask where the name "Piranhurst" came from. Although we cannot go back into the minds of either Daniel or Julia Richardson, it is generally thought that the name derives from St. Piran, the patron saint of Cornwall who, legend has it, was captured by heathens and thrown into the ocean with a weighted stone around his neck. Immediately, the ocean became calm, and Piran floated safely onto the beach.[309] The story of St. Piran has come to be associated with calmness and serenity, and in that regard the

Cypress Stage

Cypress Stage box seating

breathtaking photographs that appear in Masson and Chen's coffee table book, *Santa Barbara Style*, show Piranhurst in all its splendor, and they do in fact convey that sense of calmness and serenity.

One of the first articles published about Piranhurst appeared in *Harper's Bazarr*, and reveals the pride with which Henry and Ellen cared for this jewel. It described, in the following words, the open air theatre that was a part of the landscaping and became a favorite of their many guests:

> ...there is a theatre, very new in comparative point of years, but more beautiful, if that were possible, than the famed one of the Villa Gregoria. The stage occupies a slight elevation and is grass carpeted, with a low stone wall across the front, gracefully curved and ivy covered. There are ten wings, and a screen at the back where they meet, of perfectly clipped Monterey Cypress which stand out like rolls of green velvet. At each end of the front of the stage a Cypress tree has been allowed to grow tall, the tops diverted and brought together to form a proscenium arch.
>
> And quite as charming as the stage itself are the boxes. These too have been whittled out of cypress in the most ingenious manner. There are six in number, three on each side of the stone steps leading from the open space immediately in front of the stage and designed for part of the audience as in any theatre. Each box seats from four to six people comfortably. Beyond the boxes, the native trees, lighter and greyer than the cypress, are apparently painted in to the blue sky, so gradually do they tone into it in perspective.

> The electric lights are so cleverly hidden in among the trees that the effect at night is rather like brilliant moonlight than artificial light. Matinees are, however, the order rather than evening affairs on account of the distance of the estate from other estates. But when a play is on, and both players and audience are in gala dress with all the lovely color of the costumes showing against the rich green of the stage and boxes, the scene presented is very like some very rare and lovely old print come to life.[310]

Since Ellen's death in 1965 at the age of ninety-nine, the property has gone through several ownerships, each time fortunately falling into the hands of owners who cherish and respect it for what it is. As an indication of the quantity of landscaping that continues to thrive and the care with which it is tended, in 1989 the City of Montecito, upon learning that the owner had used 10 million gallons of water (enough to supply the needs of more than 150 families for a year) threatened to turn off their water.[311] But if the owners can be faulted for water usage, they should be praised and congratulated for the care they have taken to preserve the elegance and sheer beauty of this estate. The current owners graciously allowed me to visit Piranhurst in November of 2012, after an absence of 45 years. While memories will tend to fade with the passage of time, they came flooding back the moment I stepped through the front door. Back I went in time, to visualize and be captivated by a home which, while possessing all the conveniences of modern living, harkens, through its furnishings, decorative highlights, and artwork, back to a quieter and more tranquil time. It is, in short, a masterpiece, and far from feeling remorse for the fact that it is no longer a part of our family, my immediate and lasting emotion was gratitude for the fact that it is being so ardently cared for.

26.
Santa Barbara – *Mar y Cel*

As spectacular as Piranhurst may have been, the project that consumed Henry's interest and imagination almost from the moment he and Ellen arrived in Montecito lay just above its walled perimeter and across Mountain Drive. Just six months after they bought Piranhurst, and well before they had even planned the home they would build, on November 22, 1910, Henry purchased the first 119 acres of what would eventually become 340 acres of land leading up from Piranhurst to the summit of the mountain behind them. He and Ellen then hired an army of Italian stone masons to cut huge native limestone boulders into blocks, with which he created retaining walls, drainage channels, and other features to support the steeply winding, one mile long road to the top. That rockwork was also used for an aesthetic outer coating for concrete dams, several of them as high as 30 feet tall, that captured the water he stored for use in his ornamental watercourses. The watercourses included channels of gently flowing water that lined the outer edges of the roadway, as well as cascading waterfalls that ran down the hillside, from one shell-shaped catch basin to the next, and ultimately, through the use of large capacity recycling pumps, from the bottom of the mountain back up to the top—from which point the water would then cascade back down again. In all, he built a steeply graded one mile road cut into the hillside, five reservoirs, a two-hundred seat amphitheater, numerous lengths of ornamental watercourses, numerous catch basins, and then, to top it all off, at the very top of the mountain he built a teahouse, which commanded spectacular views in every direction.

Henry and Ellen called this perch of theirs *"Mar y Cel,"* seemingly intending to mean "sea and sky." But it is not as simple as that. As anyone who speaks Spanish knows, the word *mar* does in fact mean "sea"; however, the Spanish word for sky is *cielo*. The word *cel* can be found in the Catalan language, where it means "sky" or "heaven." However, in Catalan, the word "mar" translates to "march" in English, and not "sea" (the Catalan word for "sea" being "dim.") Thus, the name the Bothins gave to their heavenly outpost appears not to have come from any one language but, rather, represented an amalgam of two distinct tongues. Whether they meant it that way or not isn't really important. Suffice it to say that they seemed to have enjoyed using unusual words, and, when looked at that way, *Mar y Cel* has a nice ring to it, as do the names "Arequipa" and "Piranhurst."

It is one thing to decide to tame a mountain, as the Bothins certainly attempted with *Mar y Cel*; but what was most critical to that undertaking was water. Henry knew this from the outset, and so the creation of *Mar y Cel* came only after he had obtained the sources of water he would need. But wanting or needing water is not the same as having access to it, so the question arises, how did he get the water he would need? *Mar y Cel* was a hugely thirsty endeavor, yet as everyone in the community knew, Santa Barbara's average annual rainfall is 18.5 inches, and can easily vacillate to as low as 5 inches in a poor rainfall year. The community has always teetered on the brink of drought, and, as more and more people began to populate its lands, the problem of water became ever more acute. Charles Eaton (the husband of the woman who convinced the Bothins to buy Piranhurst) was one of the first to study new efforts being tested in

Los Angeles during the 1890s to tunnel horizontally into mountains in order to tap aquifers before their water content leaked out and became springs and streams. The proper term for these horizontal cuts is *adit*; the difference being that tunnels go all the way through a mountain, whereas an adit is a cave-like hole that is dug only as deep as needed to capture the vein or veins of water being sought. During the latter few years of the nineteenth century Mr. Eaton and others drilled a number of such adits (commonly referred to in the vernacular as "tunnels") into the mountains above Montecito, ultimately completing ten of them, of which several, including the City tunnel, the Barker tunnel, the Eaton tunnel, and the Stevens tunnel, were quite successful and transported large volumes of water to contracted destinations. In the case of the Barker tunnel, one of the clients with rights to its water was Lucy Stevens, from whose assignee, Minnie Anderson, Henry purchased rights in 1915 to 1,000 gallons per day.

Although records have not been found to substantiate additional water rights purchased, Henry obviously did acquire the rights to many thousands of additional gallons per day, and the proof of that becomes obvious when one considers the five reservoirs he built on the property to store the water he used for his ornamental watercourses. As an indication of just how much water Henry had acquired rights to, in 1924 his widow and the Helping Fund (both held title to portions of the property) donated a portion of the *Mar Y Cel* property to the Montecito County Water District, so that the District could construct a reservoir to its specifications that would become a part of the town's water storage and delivery system.[312] That reservoir was initially called the Bothin Reservoir and was later renamed the Cold Springs Reservoir, and it was specifically intended to be used to capture the flows from the "City Tunnel," which had been drilled in 1900 into the West Fork of Cold Spring Canyon,[313] and which constituted just one portion of Henry's water rights.

Originally the Tea House was a complete structure.

Three of its walls were destroyed in the 1925 earthquake, 2 years after Henry's death. Ellen never rebuilt it, seemingly preferring an open landscaped appearance.

Later, in 1947, another reservoir, which held the flows from still other water rights, and that was located on the easterly end of the property, was added to the town's water system, and became known as the Henry P. Drake Reservoir.

Visitors in the distance are seated in the Mar y Cel ampitheater

So, Henry figured out a way to solve his need for water, but the next question has to be why Henry even felt the urge to undertake a challenge of the magnitude of *Mar y Cel*. He was, after all, nearly 57 years old when he and Ellen bought Piranhurst, and the design and construction of a magnificent home on that approximately 40 acre site would consume much of his spare time for the next several years. Also, it must be remembered that he and Ellen were, after all, primarily residents of Marin County in Northern California, a long eight hour train ride away. Montecito was for them, in 1910, a winter place where they would build a vacation house, but not a community they intended to call home. It was a village where they had few friends as yet and where neither Henry nor Ellen had any roots. Furthermore, Henry was still at the helm of both his real estate company and also Judson Manufacturing Company, each located in the Bay Area and each requiring access to good and reliable communications as well as the ability to stay current on active issues and to be able to make and execute on frequently important decisions. Also, as a couple they had taken a liking to traveling; witness the many trips to Europe and elsewhere they took during the first few years of their marriage. And to all of those seemingly sensible reasons why the *Mar y Cel* undertaking seemed illogical must be added the fact that Henry was neither a trained engineer nor a hydrologist, both talents he would have to have in abundance to achieve what he set out to create on that property.

All of that logic seems either never to have occurred to Henry or, far more likely, to him it was simply irrelevant. For whatever the reason, *Mar y Cel* became an irresistible challenge. Just as he could have been accused of incredible naïveté to think, thirty years before when he was a spice merchant, that he was equipped to enter the cutthroat world of commercial real estate, and just as a similar skeptic could have accused him of lacking a full deck when he decided to bet all his chips on an iron and nascent steel industry where he had no background, his accusers and doubters would have been very wrong to underestimate him here. Each and every one of those early obstacles, which were in their time real head scratchers, were just the sorts of challenges on which he thrived. Looked at that way, *Mar y Cel* was simply another Rubik's cube to master. Henry never lacked for self-confidence, nor did he ever shy away from a challenge, and those traits probably had more to do with his moving forward than anything else.

Whether Henry ever thought he could complete *Mar y Cel* in his lifetime is not known. Certainly he had picked his parents well in terms of genes for longevity, and with their example, he had no reason to suspect an early demise. He was also not known to have had health issues, which might have given him pause. But even so, the published life expectancy tables for white men in 1915 suggested that 52 years was average. Henry didn't even start this project until he was sixty-two years old, and he couldn't have realistically expected it to be completed in less than five years at minimum, and more likely ten.

Whatever Henry's expectations might have been, he died before *Mar y Cel* was completed—indeed, his participation in the moving of a particularly large boulder on the mountain was believed by his doctors to have been the primary cause of the heart condition that would ultimately cause his death in 1923. Still, by the time of his death, the project was far enough along that it could be enjoyed by Ellen, and indeed it was. Ellen continued for many years to entertain guests at the Tea House. She often hosted luncheons, and Elizabeth DeForest, wife of their landscape architect, recalled one she attended in 1940. She wrote, "It was really quite formal. Everyone wore their best sports attire. There were fancy tablecloths, vases of flowers and beautiful silver. The young, red haired butler brought each course up from Mrs. Bothin's house, one at a time, in the Model-T Ford."[314] Even after she had aged to the point of having to move into El Mirasol, a residence for seniors, Ellen was still picked up at precisely 3:00 pm every day in her 1934 Buick by her chauffeur, Louie, and driven up to *Mar y Cel* for afternoon tea.[315]

Unfortunately, the story of *Mar y Cel* has a tragic ending. After Ellen died, the parcel where the Tea House was located was sold off and it ultimately went through several ownerships. It fell progressively into ever greater disrepair and became a haven for trespassers who, at first, were mainly hikers intent on seeing the spectacular views. Later, skateboarders were drawn to the concrete bowls of the pools and reservoirs, and that started an onslaught of kids as well as students from nearby Westmont College and elsewhere. David

Brainard, who skateboarded and otherwise cavorted at *Mary Cel* as a youngster, later wrote:

> And we skateboarded at the Tea Gardens, a wonderland of archeology rivaling anything we had ever seen in the pages of National Geographic.
>
> You may never have the opportunity to see the remains of this wondrous garden from Montecito's golden era. It is, after all, private property and full time security guards watch the gate from Mountain Drive… I haven't been back myself for some time, but I remember the layout as if it were my own back yard, which, of course, in many ways it was.
>
> … [A]bove sandstone-columned gates on Mountain Drive, a pot-holed asphalt road begins winding its way up the mountain with huge Canary Island Date Palms standing as sentinels. Fifty meters up on your left is a large, deep reservoir, once fed by fifty sequential scallop shells, each about four feet in circumference and fluted to spill into its next identical counterpart downhill. All those beautiful bowls now lie broken and abandoned, as if felled by some magnificent catastrophe.
>
> When the road reaches the top sea shell, it joins a narrow aqueduct that shames the Mission garden ruins. It was, in its heyday, a kinetic bannister of sandstone and flowing water, caught along the way in decorative basins or diverted to fill a small swimming pool.
>
> Continuing up a wide, left turn along the east side of the hill you reach a pump house from which Mr.

Bothin pumped water back up the hill to circulate in his elaborate water works. Adjoining the pump house is a reservoir, shallower than the large one below, damned on its south side and stretching some 300 feet across. We skaters called this the "Mogul Bowl" for its lumpy, challenging concrete surface.[316]

Mr. Brainard went on to describe how *Mary Cel* became a testing zone for skateboarders, along with kids on BMX bicycles and roller skates. Teenagers, including one particularly talented skateboarder named Ricky Hyde, would use its reservoirs to amaze their peers with their daring and the tricks they devised. As could be expected, ultimately one kid broke his leg, and the family had the audacity to sue the then owner of the property who, after settling the claim, jackhammered all the reservoirs to the point that even teenagers couldn't use them.

But the final insult came on November 12, 2008 when a group of students from a nearby college apparently got past the guards, walked up to the Tea House, set a bonfire, and proceeded to party all night. Whether it was the ten who have been accused, or others, the fact is that whoever the partiers were, they left the next day and despite heavy winds that were howling down the canyon above them, apparently failed to properly put out their fire. A wildfire began that, over the ensuing four days before it was finally brought under control, consumed nearly 2,000 acres, including some of the most valuable residential real estate in the country. It caused at least one known death and forced over 4,500 people to be evacuated from their homes, destroyed 210 residences, and damaged nine others.[317] Amazingly, Piranhurst itself survived the fire.

27.
Permanent Philanthropy - The Bothin Helping Fund

Henry Bothin's enduring legacy was the Bothin Helping Fund (which has since been renamed The Bothin Foundation.) The Helping Fund was incorporated on September 27, 1917 as a "benevolent corporation" under the provisions of Title XII, Part IV and Division First of the California Civil Code then in effect. At the time, Henry was sixty-four years old and prosperous. As much as his genetic background suggested the possibility that he might live into his eighties, he was also a realist. Life expectancy tables had turned against him, and he was fully aware of the passage of years. He had no intention of seeing all that he had accomplished philanthropically fail after his death. The principal objects of his philanthropic efforts had been Hill Farm and Arequipa, both included within the mantle of the Bothin Convalescent Home. Not only did they have operational needs, but they also had infrastructure, and Henry wanted to assure their ongoing existence long after his own death.

The Helping Fund's charter was quite broad, allowing it, among other things, to "buy, rent or receive donations of real and personal property... and to hold... manage, transfer or convey, lease, encumber by mortgage, or... dispose of such real estate and personal property, and [to] borrow money..." Having thus given itself very broad powers to deal with money and property, the second paragraph of its Articles of Incorporation did spell out with specificity that "None of the net income of the corporation shall be paid out to any of its members, or used for any purpose other than the assistance, maintenance or support of persons deserving of financial assistance, and the assistance, maintenance and support of institutions or corporations engaged in works of charity."[318]

Whether or not taxes played a role in the decision to set up the Helping Fund is not known. Although the Department of the Treasury would later claim (unsuccessfully) that the foundation was a sham to improperly shelter family assets from the IRS, Henry's and Ellen's decision appears to have been genuinely philanthropic in nature. The problem was that foundations were rare at the time, and the body of law interpreting them was just evolving. And so, the couple seems to have unintentionally created several traps for themselves based on the way the charitable foundation was set up. One of those traps was caused by the close control that the Bothin family exercised over foundation assets. Its initial trustees were Henry, Ellen, and Genevieve, all three of whom were designated as trustees for life. By so doing, Henry and Ellen gave the Treasury Department an opening: they claimed that since the donor had total control over the foundation, it was, in effect, their alter ego, and should be disregarded for tax purposes. The resulting dispute caused a bumpy start to what has since become a very highly regarded leader within the philanthropic community of the San Francisco Bay Area.

The problems began, according to a lengthy memorandum from attorney William Thomas (the attorney who incorporated the Helping Fund) when Thomas received a visit in July, 1920 from C.C. Ward, a field agent for the Internal Revenue Department. Mr. Ward apparently expressed his suspicions to attorney, Thomas, based on the facts that (1) the foundation was totally controlled by family members and (2) its books and records were "not kept in proper order." After meeting with Henry, Mr. Thomas wrote to agent Ward, offering to reorganize the makeup of the board in order to remove control from the Bothin family and also to formalize the record keeping. When he heard no response, Mr. Thomas stated in his memorandum, he became nervous and decided to take matters into his own hands. Accordingly, in the latter part of 1920, he advised Henry to elect outside board members to satisfy the concerns of the IRS. Henry agreed, and five non-family members were forthwith elected to the Board.

The early minutes of the Helping Fund are, indeed, confusing on this topic as well as others. They suggest that three—not five— non-family directors were elected to the Board, *in 1918*, not 1920. One, the Reverend C.P. Deems, was the Rector of St. John's Church in Ross, the parish to which the Bothins belonged. A second was Mr. Thomas himself, and the third was Robert C. Bolton, a stockbroker and close friend, and the man who Henry and Ellen relied upon for advice on their non-real estate related investments. What is confusing is the documents that purport to be the minutes of the initial meeting of the Board on October 4, 1917, as well as those of the next three meetings, said to have been held respectively on August 29, 1918, February 18, 1920 and July 6, 1920. All are copies which were apparently created on December 10, 1920. Although Reverend Deems, who was the acting Secretary, attested to those copies as being true and correct duplicates "recopied from the original minutes of the meetings… [which are]… in the offices of the corporation [at] 301 Atlas Building, 604 Mission St., Suite 301, San Francisco, Cal," the question is why Rev. Deems felt the originals needed to be copied, as opposed to simply being themselves placed into the Minute Book. The answer to that is not at all clear, but it certainly suggests the possibility that the minutes may not have actually existed, at least not in presentable form, prior to December 1920 and, instead, may have been created later to reconstruct, as closely as recollections might permit, actions taken earlier. I say that not to criticize or accuse Reverend Deems in any way of wrongdoing, but rather to wonder whether he actually saw original minutes of those prior meetings or, instead, was going on what may have been abbreviated notes of meetings taken by others. If the latter, that would certainly be consistent with the assertion, made just six months earlier by the IRS agent, Ward, about the poor state of the corporate records, which Ward cited as one of the primary reasons for his suspicion that the Helping Fund was a sham. In Rev. Deems' and the Helping Fund's defense, the original minute takers would have first been J.D. Osborne, whose death was reported in the copy of the minutes of the August, 1918 meeting, and, thereafter, R.B. Girdwood who, after Osborne's death, was appointed temporary acting Secretary until his resignation on October 25, 1920. In other words, it is altogether possible, indeed probable, that Reverend Deems was asked to, and did, review notes taken by both Messrs. Osborne and later Mr. Girdwood, and he interpreted them as best he could in order to memorialize actions taken at meetings that occurred prior to his involvement.

The reasons for my raising the issue of the date of the election of outside directors are several. First, if outside directors had indeed been elected as early as 1918 (two years prior to Agent Ward's visit to the attorney, Thomas) then why would Ward have raised such a hullabaloo about the issue of control at all? Secondly, Reverend Deem's "copy" of the minutes of the meeting of July 6, 1920 shows that Messrs. Deems, Thomas, and Bolton, as well as Genevieve, were all absent from that particular meeting. In other words, if those are accurate copies from the originals, and if Messrs. Deems, Thomas, and Bolton were in fact Board members as of July 6, 1920, then Henry and Ellen (who were the only Board members shown in the minutes as being present at that meeting) would not have constituted a quorum, in which case the business recorded as having been transacted at that meeting would have been null and void. This is important since the business that the minutes of that particular meeting show was transacted included the election to the Board of Edward F.R. Vail (a friend and contiguous neighbor from Santa Barbara, about whom little else is known) and William T. Summers (who was the President of the Merchants National Bank of California, with which Henry had a solid banking relationship.) Messrs. Vail and Summers were the fourth and fifth outside directors who Mr. Thomas' memo suggests he, in late 1920, recommended be elected to overcome the IRS claim of absolute family control. Since those two directorships were the ones that put family control in the minority, that item of business would have been extremely important to the defense that was ultimately mounted against the IRS claims.

The IRS did indeed pursue a significant claim against Henry and Ellen with the goal of imposing an assessment against them for what they called an "excess profits tax." Against Henry they claimed an assessment of $777,145.25, and against Ellen they attempted to assess $45,050.82. The basis of the claims were, first, that the foundation had three, and only three, trustees "for life"; to wit, Henry Bothin, his wife Ellen, and his daughter, Genevieve. Since other trustees, even if elected, could, so the IRS alleged, be voted out of office, then the fund's assets were in reality the assets of the family members. Second, they claimed the Helping Fund's "corporate records were in a ludicrous state"; this, they claimed, supported the argument that it was set up as a sham. Third, the IRS took the position that by placing a portion of its assets (9,725 shares of Judson Manufacturing Co) into the name of the Bothin Real Estate Company "in trust" the Bothins intended to defraud the government of what should have been taxable income. In other words, they argued that the assets of the foundation had never been legitimately transferred to the Helping Fund, but remained held in the name of the Real Estate Company, whose charter did not authorize it to act as a trustee for a charitable purpose. Hence, they argued, the assets were held by an entity that could at any time return those assets to the family members.[319]

The first prong of the defense was to argue that the gifts to the foundation were absolute and that in the event the charitable corporation was ever dissolved, the assets could not be returned to the Bothins. Accordingly, Mr. Thomas' argument went, Henry and Ellen had no ability to recover those assets because they had been irretrievably conveyed in trust for the public good. It followed, Mr. Thomas argued, that since those gifts were irretrievable, the fact of family control created no benefit to the donor. Although the IRS initially ruled against the family on that argument, it ultimately proved persuasive on appeal. The second prong, an extension of the first, was that the IRS should not attempt to tax either Henry or Ellen on income they never had received and never could receive, since the underlying assets were in the public domain and thus out of their control.

After a prolonged fight, on June 12, 1923 the Frauds Division of the Internal Revenue Department upheld Henry's appeal and, in so doing, reduced the assessment against him from $777,145 down to $32,600 and against Ellen from $45,050 down to $1,300. It also reversed the charges of false and fraudulent returns, dropped the penalty and interest charges, acknowledged the integrity of the Helping Fund, eliminated the possibility of criminal charges, and, as an outcome of all of that, upheld the reputation of both Mr. and Mrs. Bothin and also of the Helping Fund.

Before describing the good practices and the obvious philanthropic intent of the Helping Fund, it bears mentioning that there was one other term contained in the corporation's original charter that would seem, at least when looking at it through today's filters, to constitute a questionable practice. Since the IRS did not include it in its claim, I can only conclude the practice was not improper under the laws then in existence. The policy I refer to is contained in Article VIII of the original Constitution and Bylaws:

Temporarily no more than one-half of the net income of the corporation shall be devoted to the objects of charity for which it is organized. The other half of the net income shall be by the Board used in the partial liquidation of such obligations as may be assumed by the corporation, in cases where gifts are accepted by it, subject to outstanding liens. Whenever all such obligations have been liquidated and the corporation is free of debt, one-half of the net income of the corporation shall be devoted to charitable purposes, and the balance of the income shall be reinvested and added to the principal, for a period of twenty-five years. Thereafter, all of the net income of the corporation shall be devoted to charitable purposes. In the distribution of the net income of the corporation the Bothin Convalescent Home shall be preferred.

On July 6, 1920, the Board approved an amendment to the Constitution and Bylaws to replace the language of Article VIII with even more restrictive language that stated: "Until further action by the Board of Directors, not more than one-quarter of the income of the corporation shall be devoted to the object of charity for which it is organized…The balance of the income not paid out in charities shall be devoted to liquidating the indebtedness of the corporation and reinvesting and adding to the principal…"

The problem that language raises is that it seemingly would permit Henry and Ellen to overleverage certain assets with debt, use the proceeds of the borrowing to free up other assets, and then give the overleveraged assets to the charitable corporation, which would be responsible for servicing the debt using tax free dollars to do so. That would clearly benefit the Bothins at the expense of both the foundation and taxpayers in general. Nonetheless, I have to conclude that the policy in question was perfectly legal and acceptable under the laws as they existed at the time. I say this for several reasons. First, the policy was incorporated in the original Constitution and Bylaws of the corporation, which had been drafted by attorney William Thomas. Secondly, Thomas was a member of the board of the Helping Fund in 1920, a time when he knew the IRS was actively preparing to contest the validity of the Helping Fund as a charitable corporation, and he voted to approve the motion amending the policy to reduce the charitable payout even further than had initially been established.

On December 6, 1920 the Board approved assumption by the Helping Fund of personal notes given by Henry in the amount of $200,000 to the California Wine Association, $50,000 to the Santa Barbara Commercial Trust and Savings Bank, and $20,000 to the Merchants National Bank of San Francisco (where trustee William Summers was President.) In the case of the Santa Barbara Commercial trust indebtedness, a case could easily be made that assumption of that obligation was entirely fair, since the underlying property against which that mortgage note had been taken out had been given to the foundation. In other words, there seems to be no foul in making that gift subject to whatever secured indebtedness was on it. As to the $20,000 note payable to the Merchants National Bank of San Francisco, I simply have insufficient information on which to base any opinion. But the last and largest of the notes—the $200,000 in notes payable to the California Wine Association (CWA)—is interesting. Ultimately, it would seem to have been entirely appropriate; however, arriving at that conclusion was not a straightforward process, and ultimately it requires a fair amount of trust placed in the judgment of attorney, Thomas, who voted in favor of the Helping Fund accepting responsibility for all three of those obligations.

Regarding the $200,000 in notes given by Henry to CWA, first, it should be noted that on August 29, 1918, Henry made a gift to the Helping Fund of 3,000 shares of CWA's stock. Its stock, on that date, was valued at $82 per share,[320] so the value of his gift was $246,000. Furthermore, on that very date, CWA declared a surprise dividend of $20 per share, after which it traded at $72, thereby in effect increasing the value of the gift by an additional $30,000. If that had been all there was to the event, the assumption by the Helping Fund of Henry's note, while effectively reducing the size of the gift, would not be notable at all. But, as it turns out, there is more to the story. First, Henry was a director of CWA. Therefore, his gift was made based on inside information; however, since the gift conferred a benefit on his foundation, it would be difficult to find any reason to complain. Again, that is not the whole story. The other part, which does potentially raise questions, is the timing of the notes he assigned to the Helping Fund, for that was done not in 1918 when he made the gift of 3,000 shares to the foundation, but rather in December of 1920. Unfortunately, there are no surviving records that show all the gifts Henry and Ellen made to the Helping Fund or when they were made, and therefore it is not known if Henry also made a second gift of CWA stock at the same time that he assigned the obligation in December 1920. It is indisputable that, by December 1920, the stock in CWA was significantly higher in value than it was when he made the first gift in 1918, so even if there had been no second gift, it could be argued that he was simply asking the Helping Fund to assume a part of his cost for that earlier gift of stock. However, that argument would seemingly fail, because he would have taken a charitable deduction in 1918 for the entirety of that gift, which would have been unencumbered when the gift was made. So, it seems to come down to whether or not Henry made a second gift of CWA stock to the foundation during 1920. Let's examine that more closely.

First, the $200,000 in notes Henry proposed the Helping Fund assume were dated January 13, 1920—two weeks after "Prohibition" went into effect and thereby severely jeopardized the company's future. Interestingly, however, on that very date (January 13, 1920), the company, which had substantial real estate holdings scattered throughout California, as well as owning a significant inventory of wine located outside the United States, and which also had a plan to move forward as a profitable operating entity despite Prohibition, had authorized the issuance of $10,000,000 of additional stock through a public stock offering. The fact that the $200,000 in notes given by Henry to CWA were dated the same date as the notice of the new stock offering make clear that Henry was using the note to secure his subscription for $200,000 in that new stock issuance.[321] In fact, by the date Henry assigned the $200,000 obligation, the stock of the company was still soaring based on published reports that valued CWA owned assets well in excess of the market value of all outstanding shares in its stock. Even as late as December 1921, the company was claiming its stock was worth $172 per share.[322] In other words, that stock purchase would seem to have been a smart move if one believed the representations made by management, and clearly Henry, who was part of management, believed what was being reported and was willing to put his money where his mouth was.

The next piece of information in the puzzle is that the inventory of property Henry owned at the time of his death included only a token ten shares of the stock of CWA. While it is altogether possible that Henry might have sold all the rest of his position in the company prior to his death, it must be remembered that he was still a director up to the time he died, and the company was still viable and its stock decently priced. Insider selling is a well-known flag to investors and certainly would have been discouraged, even if Henry were otherwise disposed to have done so. For those reasons, I consider that the odds seem to favor his having gifted the block of stock he bought in January of 1920 to the Helping Fund either concurrently with or at least within the same twelve month period as when he asked the Helping Fund to assume the obligation of the notes he incurred in buying the stock. If I am correct, then again no foul was committed.

Unfortunately, the minutes do not show such a gift; however, we already know the early minutes are suspect on a number of fronts because they were probably recreated from incomplete notes. Also unfortunately, the report of the CPA firm of Klink, Bean and Associates, who were retained in July, 1920 for the specific purpose of tracing back all donations made between September,1917 when the Helping Fund came into existence and July, 1920, cannot be found and appears to be lost. We do know from the minutes of the December 6, 1920 meeting that the Klink Bean report had been by then completed, and it had been made available to the directors prior to their vote to approve incurring the obligation of the notes in question. I simply cannot accept the premise that attorney, Thomas, would have voted to accept that $200,000 obligation without also accepting an offsetting gift from Henry of at least that same amount.

The final piece of the puzzle comes from a review of the Helping Fund's audited 1924 year end statement (the first audited statement for the foundation). That audit showed asset values in excess of $2,000,000. Although the audit is silent on individual stock holdings other than Judson Manufacturing Company, it also does not show any large block of stock amounting to $200,000 or anywhere near that, and, more importantly, it does not reveal a note payable to CWA. Hence, it seems appropriate to assume that Henry made a gift of stock in the company that offset the obligation and that, by year end 1924, most, if not all, of the stock of CWA had been sold and the note paid off.

As an epilogue to this story, ultimately, the California Wine Association went out of business in 1925, and the Helping Fund's annual audit for that year shows a modest write-off of approximately $13,000, representing the totality of its residual holdings in CWA. That seems to put the final nail in that particular coffin.

As indicated, the records of the Bothin Helping Fund do not reveal the source or amount of its initial capitalization. The first record of gifts appears in the minutes of a Board meeting held on August 29, 1918. That meeting, which may have been only the second meeting of the Board, memorializes a gift by Henry of those 3,000 shares of the capital stock of the California Wine Association. It also discloses gifts by Ellen from her own separate property of eleven bonds (face amount not known) of the Riverside Portland Cement Company and 150 shares of the California Wine Association.

Returning to the nuts and bolts of the early years of the Helping Fund's existence, Mr. Vail resigned his Board seat in January, 1923 due to an extended travel schedule, and his seat was assumed by Ida Sutter Maas (Henry's favorite niece and the mother of Ted and Carlos Maas). Several months later Elizabeth Ashe, the driving force behind the Bothins' philanthropy, was elected to the Board. Both those events took place prior to Henry's death on October 14, 1923. Just two weeks after Henry died, he was replaced by C.O.G. Miller, another non-family member who had been Henry's longtime friend and a witness at his and Ellen's marriage. Less than a month after Henry's demise, Genevieve's husband Edmunds was added to create an odd number of Board seats (nine). Thus, by 1918, non-family members filled three of the six Board seats; by 1920 non-family members held a five to three majority; and within a month after Henry died three years later, non-family members held five out of the nine seats that then existed.

The makeup of the Board, and specifically the addition of non-family members who, after 1918, have always held close to if not an equal number of seats than those held by family members, became very important as the fight with the IRS played itself out. As important as the policy was back then, it also began a long term trend, a tradition continuing to this day of inviting non-family members to hold seats on the Board of the Foundation.

Ida Sutter Maas   *C.O.G. Miller*

Elizabeth Ashe   *Genevieve Bothin Lyman*

Henry's niece, Ida, his close friend, C.O.G. Miller, his philanthropic inspiration, Elizabeth Ashe, and his daughter, Genevieve, all of whom served on the Board.

Edmunds Lyman, husband of Genevieve Bothin

Genevieve (Genie) Lyman Casey di San Faustino

Ranieri di San Faustino, Genie's second husband

Edmona (Mona) Lyman Miller Mansell

Genevieve's husband, Edmunds Lyman, her two daughters, Genie and Mona, and Genie's husband, Ranieri, served on the Board.

As a result, the foundation has greatly benefited from the experience and perspectives of a large number of highly qualified individuals from all walks of life. That continuous injection of outside blood is, in my opinion, one of the great strengths of the foundation, and it has served us extremely well and enabled us, for close to a century now, to remain a valuable player in Bay Area philanthropy.

Although the records of the Helping Fund do not show the amount of its original corpus, it was later appraised, as of the date of Henry's death on October 14, 1923, at $2,003,379.81. That sum included its initial funding plus gifts of stock and real estate made to it thereafter by both Henry and Ellen during the Helping Fund's initial six years of existence prior to Henry's death. That value included stocks valued at $943,330.95, of which $746,000 consisted of 11,350 shares of the common stock of Judson Manufacturing Company, valued at $40 per share, and 2,920 shares of Judson preferred stock, valued at $100 per share. The holdings also included bonds valued at $198,730 and real estate totaling $1,004,941.83. All of the real estate held by the Helping Fund was located in Santa Barbara and included a total of twelve properties, of which ten were improved.[323] These were, for the most part, located in the center of Santa Barbara's downtown district. Their location (despite the unfortunate damage they were to suffer in the 1925 earthquake) provides ample further proof of Henry's solid understanding of the old real estate adage: "location, location, location." The appraisal also showed debts totaling $147,899.64, of which $78,889.64 was owed to R.C. Bolton, one of the directors. It is assumed, since Mr. Bolton was Henry's stockbroker, that the indebtedness was either margin debt or, more likely, commissions on the purchase and sale of stock.

For the year 1923 (the first year when financial information is contained in the minutes) charitable donations from the Helping Fund included $25,231.55 to the Bothin Convalescent Center and approximately $7,200 to other charitable organizations both in the San Francisco Bay Area and in Santa Barbara. Those other charities included the San Rafael branch of the Red Cross, the San Francisco YMCA as well as the YWCA, San Francisco Salvation Army, Canon Kip Day Nursery, American Jewish Relief Organization, the San Francisco Association for the Blind, Arequipa Sanitarium, St. John's Church in Ross, Children's Hospital (San Francisco), The Hemet Boy Scouts, the Visiting Nurses Association, St. Vincent's Orphanage in Santa Barbara, St. Francis Hospital in Santa Barbara, Cottage Hospital in Santa Barbara, and others that no longer exist.

During its early years the Foundation may be rightly criticized for poor record keeping and a less than well-thought-out membership structure; however, the aggressiveness shown by the IRS in pursuing both Henry and Ellen in the way it did seems both on its face and in hindsight to have been totally unreasonable and uncalled for. I say that because the Helping Fund's charter clearly stated that assets given to it were irretrievably dedicated to charitable purposes—precisely the reason why in the end the Bothins prevailed. By choosing to take the hard line position it did, the IRS imposed huge financial risk and the obvious stress that came with it upon both Henry and Ellen. While the dollar value of the financial risk can be quantified, the stress and underlying emotional toll cannot be as easily measured. It would be pure speculation to suggest that the stress of the IRS claim may well have contributed to Henry's death of heart failure just four months after the favorable outcome on appeal; however, that certainly cannot be ruled out. Everything I have written about his generosity, his unfailing support of Nurse Ashe's various efforts on behalf of the downtrodden, his weekly trips to Hill Farm during those first years of its existence, his and Ellen's joint efforts to fund Arequipa, and a lifetime of generosity to his siblings and their children, all suggest a generous spirit and a true dedication to philanthropy. The fact that Henry refused to buckle under to the government's heavy handedness is a testament both the Henry's deep-seated belief that he had done no wrong and also to his own stubborn refusal to ever step away from a challenge.

28.
Commercial Real Estate in Santa Barbara

Two years after Henry's death, Santa Barbara, and particularly the downtown portion of town, was shattered by a large earthquake that destroyed a number of the buildings he had purchased in Santa Barbara and later sold to the Helping Fund. But before that story can be told, we need to look back a few years to Henry's arrival in Santa Barbara and to his immersion in the community in the only way he knew how through the acquisition of commercial real estate.

As though Piranhurst and *Mar y Cel* weren't enough to load on Henry's plate during the years he spent in Santa Barbara, he also lost little time after the purchase of Piranhurst in 1910 before going on another real estate buying binge. He ultimately bought, in either his own name or that of the real estate company, sixteen properties in downtown Santa Barbara, and then, after he set up the Helping Fund, he sold twelve of them to the foundation for his cost of $252,000.

Almost all the properties Henry bought in Santa Barbara were located on State Street, which remains to this day the main street of town. His first acquisition was on April 27, 1910, just sixteen days after Ellen bought Piranhurst. Five months later he bought another property, again on State Street, this time near the corner of Canon Perdita Street. He followed those with further purchases in June 1911, November 1912, January 1913, January 1914, December 1915, April 1916 (2 properties), May 1916, July 1916, April 1917, May 1917, June 1918, December 1919, and finally May 1920.

It turned out, and could only have been known by hindsight, that of all the parts of Santa Barbara where humans were building structures, nowhere was there a worse place to have built than State Street. Unfortunately, the science of soils engineering was only in its

1330-1340 State Street, Santa Barbara
immediately following the earthquake (below) and as rebuilt thereafter

infancy back then, and so he probably had no way of knowing that the soils under State Street were comprised of landfill as opposed to the more solid rock undersurface on which most of the rest of the city was built.

Unfortunately, the lack of knowledge about subsurface conditions beneath the Santa Barbara properties he bought would lead to a similar disaster to the one he suffered through in 1906 in San Francisco. For just as San Francisco was earthquake country, so too was Santa Barbara. Santa Barbara had been rocked by a very large earthquake in 1812 that was centered in the Lompoc Valley;

404-410 State Street, Santa Barbara immediately following the earthquake (below) and as rebuilt thereafter

it reduced Mission La Purisima to rubble and badly damaged Mission Santa Barbara and the Santa Barbara Presidio. It had also seen damage in 1857 from the huge earthquake called the Ft. Tejon Earthquake, an event said to have been probably the strongest earthquake to strike California in recorded history. That quake, centered in the San Andreas fault, has been estimated at 7.9 on the Richter scale and is said to have actually caused the Kern River to flow backwards for a time. And in 1902 another strong earthquake jolted the region, this time centered in the small town of Los Alamos in northern Santa Barbara County.[324] Still, and just as Henry had rebuilt in San Francisco after the 1906 quake, so too the Helping Fund rebuilt after the '25 quake.

All told, Henry accumulated, and had in his estate at the time of his death, approximately 440 acres of land in various parcels in and around the communities of Santa Barbara, Summerland, and the Cold Springs Canyon region of Montecito.[325] Those land holdings, of which *Mar y Cel* made up 340 acres, were in addition to the lots he had purchased in downtown Santa Barbara and had given to his foundation.

29.
Ongoing Business Affairs

Henry Bothin's real estate holdings had made him one of the largest, if not the largest, individual landowners in San Francisco.[326] However, the pace of his acquisitions slowed and actually went into reverse as he began, after the formation of his real estate company in 1906, selling properties he considered to be of lesser value or to have lesser location importance.

BOTHIN REAL ESTATE COMPANY

Although he remained at the helm of the company between the date of its creation in 1906 and 1920, increasingly he delegated day-to-day management decisions to his great-nephew, Ted Maas, and, by 1920, he and Ellen had voted Ted onto the Bothin Real Estate Company's three-person board. In September 1922 they together appointed Maas vice president and general manager of the company. Henry, who by then knew he had a serious heart condition, in essence gave up control. Since it was a part of his nature to place trust in members of his family, it was not surprising that he turned to the son of his favorite niece, Ida, to run the real estate company. Although he and Ellen retained ultimate authority on important decisions, he knew he was passing the torch regarding the portfolio he had so carefully built over a thirty-plus year period. Fortunately, Ted Maas proved a competent manager.

Still, and although Mr. Maas may have played a part in it, one of the most important decisions made regarding the portfolio was one Henry himself made scant months before his death. That decision was to raise cash to assure operations could continue after his death, without the complications of probate causing undue delays or standing in the way of management decisions that would have to be made. As much as that decision might have made business sense, and it clearly did, it also had the unfortunate side effect of attracting a suit from the taxing authorities. Thus, the case entitled *Bothin Real Estate Company v Commissioner of Internal Revenue*[327] provides a glimpse into Henry's commitment to his real estate empire. That case, which wasn't finally decided until fourteen years after his death, dealt with a tax issue; however, the facts giving rise to that legal issue are instructive. The court in that case found that in 1923 Henry was the sole owner of all of the stock in the Bothin Real Estate Company. Between 1920 and 1923 the company had expanded and had also invested in improvements to the buildings it owned and had taken on approximately $750,000 in debt in the process. Some of that debt came from loans made by Henry personally with money he had borrowed from his bank and for which he had, in turn, pledged as collateral a sizable block of stock he owned in the East Bay Water Company, stock he had bought in several blocks during 1917 and 1918. Then, on September 27, 1923, less than three weeks before he died and at a time when he knew he was seriously ill, Henry transferred ownership of that collateral to the Real Estate Company. He did that so that the Real Estate Company would have the flexibility it might need to deal with its debt and its liquidity needs without having to apply to the probate court and undergo the delays that inevitably plague that sort of process.

The case involved the tax basis on the capital gain from the sale of the stock; however, its importance here is twofold. First, in the six years he owned the stock, its value had increased from roughly $103,000 up to $372,000. It seems that his eye for stocks was as good as his eye for real estate. Second, the case further illustrates Henry's ongoing dedication to his business and the fact that he was always a couple of steps ahead in his thought process. Even as he dealt with his own impending death, he was making plans to assure that none of his real estate holdings would have to be sold at unfavorable prices to meet cash needs during probate.

As of October 31, 1923 (two weeks after his death) the Bothin Real Estate Company prepared a balance sheet that showed a net worth of $3,459,929. In 2013 dollars that would be approximately $46,813.000.[328] The balance sheet showed an asset value of nearly $4,900,000, and, on the liabilities side, it showed debts totaling approximately $1,512,000. Those debts included mortgages payable of $214,000, bonded indebtedness of $500,000 (secured by five properties only), notes payable of $140,000, and approximately $575,000 in personal loans made to the company by Henry. Furthermore, the company was a cash cow. As of November 30, 1923, a profit and loss statement prepared for the real estate company showed net income for the first eleven months of the year at $192,491 (which would be the equivalent of roughly $2,650,000 today.) In other words, the company was in excellent financial condition with a healthy asset base, a relatively conservative debt load, and substantial free cash flow.

Judson Manufacturing Company

In addition to his real estate company, Henry continued on as the primary shareholder of Judson Manufacturing Company. By 1920 (and possibly before that) he had let operational control go in favor of another great-nephew, Carlos Maas. Both Carlos and Ted were sons of Ida. Although he named Carlos to succeed him as the President and CEO of Judson, Henry's ownership in the company (of which he gave a significant percentage to the foundation he set up in 1917) continued up to the end of his life so that he remained the final arbiter of important decisions. Carlos did a good job; however ultimately problems arose with Judson during the late 1920s. Ultimately, they forced it into a merger with Pacific Rolling Mills, and began a downward slide from which it never recovered. Events leading to the ultimate demise of Judson were brought about by fierce competition, mainly from eastern steel companies who cut prices drastically in order to gain market share and, in so doing, brought all of the steel companies in the West, including Judson, to their knees. The other factor that contributed to Judson's decline was a failure to have maintained proper reserves for the replacement of aging equipment. Whether those problems might have been anticipated and dealt with had Henry remained active in management is anyone's guess.

OUTSIDE DIRECTORSHIPS; CALIFORNIA WINE ASSOCIATION

As we have seen, Henry was, prior to the earthquake and fire, much in demand to serve on the boards of directors of other companies. That trend continued after 1906 and was very much evident during his later years. Sometime prior to 1910 he joined the Board of Directors of the California Wine Association, a position that, as with many others of his commitments, he continued to hold until his death. The California Wine Association was an interesting company with a complex history. It began as a trust formed by the seven largest producing wineries in California, who created it to improve the production of wine, eliminate adulteration which had adversely affected the reputation of California producers, and create a marketing association with enough power to push sales both nationally and internationally.[329] By 1914, CWA controlled the output of nearly 85 percent of California's wine production and it owned over 12,000 acres of land throughout the state, as well as improvements and product related equipment. Unfortunately, CWA was stopped in its tracks following the passage, in 1919, of the Eighteenth Amendment to the United States Constitution, commonly known as Prohibition. Prohibition became effective on January 1, 1920, and lasted until 1933, when it was overturned by the passage of the 21st Amendment. Still, even after the onset of Prohibition, the company's assets, including significant inventories of wine located outside the country as well as local inventories of wines that were exempt from the ban of Prohibition, were such, and its business plan going forward was also such that in January of 1920 it successfully undertook a large stock offering that doubled its capitalization from $10 million up to $20 million. Of that, Henry committed to the purchase of $200,000 of the company's stock from the new offering. The company's stock continued to attract investors based on optimistic representations by management until well after Henry's death, but then, in 1925, it closed its doors.

OUTSIDE DIRECTORSHIPS; EAST BAY WATER COMPANY

In 1914 Henry was chosen, along with C.O.G. Miller and George H. Collins (both executives of Pacific Lighting Company) and bankers Phillip Bowles and W.W. Garthwaite to serve on a committee whose task was to study and come up with a plan for reorganizing the People's Water Company, which was an agglomeration of the Oakland Water Company, the Alameda Artesian Water Company, the Contra Costa Water Company and the East Bay Water Company. About three months later they came up with a plan to reorganize the entity as The Consolidated Water Company and to recapitalize its equity and bonded indebtedness in a way that was considered fair by the stakeholders.[330] Eventually, that company was re-organized as the East Bay Water Company, and, in 1916, Henry was elected as a director of that company, joining former committee members Phillip Bowles (Chairman of the Board of American National Bank of San Francisco) and C.O.G. Miller. (Miller, in addition to being an executive with Pacific Lighting Company was also Vice President of Mercantile Trust Company, as well as being the man who replaced Henry upon his death in 1923, as a director of the Bothin Helping Fund.) In addition to those gentlemen, the board of the East Bay Water Company included John S. Drum (President of Mercantile Trust Company of San Francisco), Stuart Hawley (President of Alameda Investment Co.), J.A. McGregor (Director of the Federal Reserve Bank), and W.T. Summers (President of Merchants National Bank of San Francisco) among others. It is worth noting that Mr. Summers was also Henry's principal banker and was one of the first outside directors of the Bothin Helping Fund, having joined that body in 1920.

The East Bay Water Company (the precursor to the East Bay Municipal Utility Company) was formed as a stockholder company. Shortly after its incorporation on January 1, 1917, Frank Havens, who had been the owner of the Peoples' Water Company, which then included all the smaller water service and delivery companies in the very rapidly growing East Bay, conveyed his water company and its nearly 30,000 acres of watershed lands to EBWC. The price paid for those assets was $17,040,000 and was subscribed privately through a combination of bonded indebtedness ($8,400,000) and capital stock ($8,640,000.)[331] The directors of EBWC spent the following seven years developing a plan to overcome the financial difficulties that had plagued the People's Water Company and to design the catchment, storage, and delivery system for all of the East Bay water into a coordinated system. They built the San Pablo Dam, the Upper San Leandro Dam, and the Lafayette Dam, and they attempted to lay out a distribution system. Ultimately, the entity lost the public's trust, and so, in 1927, the East Bay Municipal Utility District was formed. It represented the interests of the residents of nine cities in

Alameda and Contra Costa Counties who voted to approve bonded indebtedness of $26,000,000 to purchase the assets of EBWC from its private bondholders and shareholders. So, although the directors were not able to accomplish their ultimate goal, they did manage to obtain a significant profit to their investors, of whom Henry was one.

OUTSIDE DIRECTORSHIPS; NATOMAS CONSOLIDATED

Another company on whose board Henry served was the Natomas Consolidated Company of California. Natomas was the name given by the Maidu Indians to the area in the Central Valley within the watersheds of the Feather and American Rivers. It was, for a period of literally thousands of years prior to the Gold Rush, home to peaceful Indians who considered it, because of its mild climate and abundant food resources, a sort of paradise.[332] Back in the early decades of the 20th century, the company that had taken that Maidu name bore little resemblance to the idyllic landscape the name was meant to convey. Rather, The Natomas Consolidated Company of California was a worldwide mining and dredging company that owned vast lands in the Central Valley and was involved in the water delivery business, as well as land development, gold dredging, transportation, and a host of other endeavors. It was very much involved in construction of the levy system that was designed to control periodic flooding of the American and Sacramento Rivers and to open up large tracts of its floodplain for housing as well as agriculture. It is not known exactly when Henry became a director; however, he was on the company's board at the time of his death and had been for at least several years before.

30.
The Final Years

Henry died in Montecito on October 14, 1923 of what was diagnosed as a cerebral hemorrhage, compounded by arteriosclerosis, hypertension and chronic myocarditis.

For most of his life, Henry had enjoyed excellent health and was looking forward to a long life. An interesting chronicle of that appears in a brief submitted to the Bureau of Internal Revenue in connection with the estate tax audit. There Henry's counsel recited the following:

> Mr. Bothin always lived a very temperate and moderate life. At the time he executed the trust instrument[333] he had no known physical ailments or disabilities (nor had he ever had any serious illness); he was in excellent health, and he had no thought of death. He was actively engaged in his usual pursuit, the active management and conduct of the business of the Bothin Real Estate Company of which he was president; he was negotiating on behalf of the Bothin Real Estate Company, for the sale or purchase of several pieces of real estate, and he had several

large buildings in the course of construction—a program which would not be undertaken by any person who might be giving any serious consideration to death. He was actively interested in the conduct and affairs of two charitable corporations which he had organized and endowed, The Bothin Helping Fund and The Bothin Convalescent Home; he was making a 230 acre tract of property located near Santa Barbara, California, which he subsequently gave to the Bothin Helping Fund, into a tremendous park and garden by putting in miles of stone walled roads, numerous reservoirs, hanging gardens, cascades, fountains, an amphitheater, a swimming pool, shrubs and lawns. His program for the development of the park, which he expected to complete during his lifetime, was 10 to 15 years short of completion by the time of the execution of the trust instrument. He was visiting, dining with or entertaining friends; he was planning a trip to Europe as soon as he could arrange his business to be away a suitable period, and in every way he conducted himself in such a manner as to indicate that he considered death to be a matter in the remote future.

At the time Mr. Bothin executed the trust instrument he was sixty-seven years of age, and the circumstances of his daily life all tend to indicate that he believed he would be living at the termination date of the trust, namely October 14, 1939, on which date he would be 86 years of age. It is possible, even probable, that Mr. Bothin would have lived to be 86 years of age or more had he not, about a year after the date of the trust instrument, overtaxed his heart while supervising the moving of some bags of cement on the park property mentioned above. Becoming impatient of the slowness with which the work was proceeding, Mr. Bothin himself, moved some of the bags of cement. The work was too strenuous for him and as a result he strained his heart and probably thereby shortened his life by many years. Although Mr. Bothin recovered from the attack, the organic disability resulting from this overexertion caused his death about a year and one half later.

Mr. Bothin remarked many times during his lifetime to members of his family, and to friends that he would live to be an old man, because the members of his family had all lived to a very old age. Mr. Bothin's father died when he was 84, and his mother when she was 79...."

Following the incident where he overexerted and brought on a cardiac condition, Henry had in fact become aware that his heart was damaged and that his life expectancy was far shortened. Indeed it was those known heart problems that had caused him, just weeks before his death, to transfer a significant block of stock to the Bothin Real Estate Company in order to provide it with liquidity and in the expectation that his estate would be tied up in the courts for a protracted period.[334]

Henry left an estate that was valued at over $4,000,000[335] and a complex will, which became the subject of substantial negotiation among family members. Ultimately, his wife, Ellen, received 2/9th, Genevieve inherited approximately 50 percent, and the remainder was divided among his surviving siblings and their descendants. However, that did not come easily. The estate was audited, and the tax division claimed the estate had been underreported by nearly

$1,000,000, resulting in a claimed tax deficiency of some $99,000.[336] Regarding his assets, the largest single asset was 5,000 shares of stock, all owned by Henry, in the Bothin Real Estate Company. That stock was valued at $3,142,284, or about $628.45 per share. He also had a stock portfolio valued at approximately $1,225,000, and he had significant personal real estate holdings, primarily land located in Marin and Riverside Counties, that were not in the real estate company's list of properties. The real estate company had never paid any dividends, nor had Henry ever drawn a formal salary. Just how he compensated himself is not clear and not mentioned anywhere in the Real Estate Company's minutes; however clearly his lifestyle was supported by draws based on a formula or formulas which were both acceptable to his lenders and also easily affordable by the company.

Although he was the power behind the scenes at Judson until his death, the largest single shareholder of that company was the Bothin Helping Fund, which held 58.4 percent of the stock of the company. The Bothin Real Estate Company, and Henry as an individual, together owned 20.5 percent, Ellen owned 13.3 percent, and the balance of 7.8 percent was split among Edmunds Lyman, Carlos J. Maas (who succeeded Henry as president) and W.T. Summers.

The estate did not include the nearly $2,000,000 in total assets that Henry had earlier contributed to the Bothin Helping Fund in the form of cash, stock in Judson, and real estate properties he had purchased in Santa Barbara and sold to the foundation at cost. The foundation, whose only source of endowment to this day is what Henry and Ellen contributed to it during the final six years of his life, continues to thrive and to improve the lives of countless people who have benefitted from the nearly $41,000,000 in grants it has made as of March, 2012.

31.
A Life Well and Fully Lived

When Ernst and Rosa Boethin left their home in Prussia, they abandoned not only their family, neighbors, and friends, but they also abandoned a way of life that had defined them, not by what they might achieve in life, but rather by the accidental selection of the parents who gave them life, as well as the location where they grew up, the experiences which colored their early lives, their marriage, the raising of their children, and the way they toiled for a living. When they left their homeland, they had undoubtedly never heard of the Declaration of Independence, with its famous phrase: "We hold these truths to be self-evident, that all men are created equal…" Nor in their preparations to emigrate to America had they likely thought much about the words "freedom" and "liberty" that were so often written in the letters they and others relied upon for information about the country they were about to embrace as their own. But intuitively they understood that in America there were opportunities to improve upon the hand they had been dealt in Prussia, and the reward at the other end of the voyage seemed to them well worth the risks of the unknown they surely knew they faced.

The concept of "equality," a word our country's founders used as the cornerstone of their vision of democracy, is inextricably intertwined with the words "liberty" and "freedom." As Benjamin Franklin put it, "Where liberty dwells, there is my country." But for an immigrant couple wrestling with real world issues of survival in a new land, their rudimentary understanding of our language would have left them far less interested in the meaning of those words in the abstract and far more interested in the practical effect those words had on their lives. To them the words meant that they had the ability, if they wished, to take risks in the pursuit of happiness, but they also must assume the corresponding responsibility to face the consequences of bad choices—in other words, the right to walk the tightrope between success and failure without a safety net.

Ernst and Rosa chose to take risks, and by doing so they lived their American dream. If they are to be criticized it was for their poor choices where it came to their treatment of Henry, for they denied him both the opportunity of an available public education, and later his freedom to leave home on dignified terms.

Henry too was a risk taker. In the ultimate analysis, the question is whether or not at the end of his days he would have felt satisfaction and fullness from having pursued the paths he did, risky or not; or felt frustration and emptiness from the choices he made. I would argue that, like most of us, Henry would have answered that rhetorical question with a carefully hedged response. In some ways he was successful beyond his wildest imagination, while in one aspect in particular he would have vastly preferred a different outcome. As I look at his life as a whole, I, unlike both my grandmother and my mother, neither of whom could look past the divorce, see his life as one well and completely lived.

As a young man, Henry chose freedom over servitude and aggressively broke the yoke of his father's farm that was suffocating him. At that time in his life he had no plan other than to escape from one life and let the chips fall thereafter. Fortunately for him, his sisters took him in, and they and their husbands taught him a trade, and in the process he learned that he had a mind for business and the capacity to be entrepreneurial. He formed a business partnership with Albert Dallemand, and together they created a company that, largely by virtue of hard work and careful control of expenses, grew as a profitable enterprise and provided him with the opportunity to dream of bigger things.

During the mid-1880s, Henry blossomed in business, but he also made a choice in marriage that he would come to regret. In business, he learned about both iron and steel and their exciting and near limitless prospects; but most particularly steel as a material for ships, bridges, railroad equipment, and high rise construction. Refusing to be dissuaded by a lack of formal education or a lack of background in the product, he jumped in with both feet, buying Judson, learning the business along the way, and ultimately growing that company into a major regional player in that industry's formative years.

With the passion of youth, Henry saw, at the same time he was rushing headlong into Judson, no reason that he couldn't expand his dream by buying commercial real estate, and in a major departure from his frugal nature, he embraced debt, believing as he did that he could spot value and buy at bargain prices and also believing that the value of San Francisco properties, particularly ones purchased well, would grow far faster annually than the interest rate on the loans he needed to make that happen. It turned out he was right far more often than he was wrong in that regard.

Gaining expertise in two unrelated fields required his full-time attention; attention he was willing to give because by then he had clearly, in his own mind, defined success with dollar signs. Having done so, he set the stage for what was to become a very unsuccessful marriage. His and Jennie's life together began happily enough, but in time Henry's inability to understand Jennie's needs cracked the foundations of their marriage. Circumstances caused those cracks to widen into crevasses, and ultimately his marriage fell apart. With it, he also lost the love and affection of his only daughter, which he deeply regretted but lacked the ability to overcome.

Along the way, Henry, a largely self-educated farm boy turned successful capitalist, earned the respect of most of his business peers, and he was invited to serve on a number of corporate boards, all of which seemed eager to have his input and his loyalty.

But his greatest accomplishment, and Henry would probably have been the first to acknowledge it, was the work he did with Elizabeth Ashe and the financial support he provided to help her accomplish her good deeds, Whether he ever imagined his foundation would remain viable and important nearly a century after his death is anyone's guess, but certainly he intended that Miss Ashe's good work should not be brought to a halt by his death.

Finally, and for good measure, Henry followed a failed marriage with a highly successful one based on mutual respect and on a convergence of values. While he may have overindulged himself in free time and travels with Ellen, he also found in her a willing partner in both his philanthropic efforts and in the creation of a residential masterpiece in Montecito. In that last, he finally was able to build a home that someone liked and wanted to live in.

With the objectivity born of time, I can now say that it is time to celebrate all the good that Henry accomplished and to bury once and for all the enmity and frustration that both my grandmother and mother felt toward a man whose acts and legacies eased their own paths through life.

Henry is buried in Santa Barbara next to Ellen, who died in 1965 at the age of 99.

Epilogue

There are a number of loose ends that occurred after Henry's death and that, for different reasons, deserve to be mentioned in this story of his life.

JUDSON

Through the kindness of David Maas, a member of the Maas family who were related to Henry through his sister, Emily, some later records of Judson have been located. These include the financial books and records for Judson that were kept by Theodore Maas for the years 1924 (the year after Henry died) through 1928. These tell an interesting story of a march from financial health in 1924 (or at least the outward appearance of health) to a steady decline thereafter and ultimately the need, in 1928, to merge with the revitalized Pacific Rolling Mills in order to survive. In 1923, when Henry died, Judson was prosperous and highly profitable, as was the case the year after. Unfortunately, it had structural problems which, had Henry been paying closer attention to them during the last years of his life, may well have successfully been addressed. Those problems, which were due to inadequate reserves for the replacement of aging machinery and equipment, coincided with a strong competitive environment, and ultimately brought about Judson's demise as an independent company in 1928. Still, during Henry's lifetime, Judson thrived, as did most other businesses with which he became involved.

In 1924, and for several years before that, Carlos Maas, Henry's great nephew, was Henry's chosen successor to hold the position that would today be called CEO of Judson. He reported, that year, that the company was sufficiently strong, and had enough retained earnings in hand, to begin to consider disbursing its profits as dividends to investors during the following year. The records showed that the company's working capital, all secured from earnings, had risen from $76,346 in 1921, to $318,145 in 1922, to $511,465 in 1923 and, finally, to $616,629 as of the date of his 1924 report. Unstated, but later very much discussed, was the fact that the equipment, used to produce the product that was so profitable in the short term, was becoming obsolete, and it would ultimately tie the hands of the company when, in the following year, the steel business went into a tailspin.

In 1925, pricing pressure rose dramatically due both to foreign competition and to the decision by eastern competitors to slash prices in an effort to repel foreign competitors and prevent their getting a toehold into the American market. The foregoing was compounded for Judson by a strike at its Emeryville plant. It should be noted in this regard that the foreign competition was from Europe, a region of the world that had rich iron ore deposits and the ability to mine raw materials at a fraction of the cost US West Coast steel companies faced. Even with the added cost of transportation, they were able to undercut prices and still remain profitable at well under the breakeven point for producers like Judson. Neither Judson nor other West Coast steel producers were able to overcome these competitive forces. In 1926, the company tried to hold its prices in the face of continued price slashing in the industry; however, that strategy resulted in fewer sales and significant idle time at the plant, thereby placing further pressure on the balance sheet. Mr. Maas' report reflects industry-wide confusion and an inability of the company to solve its problems of falling sales and profit margins by either differentiating its products, temporarily shutting down unprofitable lines, or investing in more efficient and cost cutting machinery. Only later did those options come up for discussion; however, by then the shareholders (principally the Bothin Helping Fund) were not of a mind to invest further in the company in order to spend on new equipment; in any event, by then it may have been too late.

In 1928, The Judson Manufacturing Company merged its shop business with Pacific Rolling Mills Company, and the resulting new entity became known as Judson Pacific Company. It seems that the rolling mill and open hearth lines were simply liquidated. During the span of Judson Pacific's existence, that company fabricated steel (primarily rebar) for such projects as the approach structures for the main spans of both the Golden Gate and Bay Bridges, the hoists in the intake towers of Boulder Dam, the Pacific Telephone and Telegraph Building, many buildings in and around San Francisco's Civic Center, as well as buildings on the campuses of both Stanford University and the University of California. It was also active during the war years, contributing rebar to companies building weaponry and defense plants throughout the West Coast, as well as producing hundreds of mechanized landing craft for the navy.

Then, in 1945, Judson Pacific merged with the J. Phillip Murphy Corporation to become Judson Pacific-Murphy Corporation. That company had high hopes of continuing in the steel fabrication business, but it lasted only about thirteen years. Parts of it were ultimately sold in 1958 to Yuba Consolidated Industries, which, in turn, went bankrupt in the early 1960s. Judson Steel Company was purchased by Birmingham Steel Company in 1987. Birmingham Steel was in turn acquired in 2002 by Nucor Corporation, and Nucor has indicated it has none of Judson's records and has no idea if any survive.

As for the effect of a weakened Judson on either Henry's estate or the Helping Fund, both seem to have weathered the storm. The best description of the family's attention to their investment in Judson and its decline is contained in records of the Helping Fund. Henry had given the Helping Fund stock in Judson, which, as of the date of his death in 1923, consisted of 34.7 percent of the overall ownership of the company and was valued at $746,000.[337] The first reference in the minutes of the Helping Fund of any concern about Judson appears in the record of a December 4, 1925 meeting of the foundation's Board, where the Finance Committee and Edmunds Lyman (Henry's son-in-law and a Board member) were tasked with determining and providing the Board with their recommendations regarding the "final disposition" of the Corporation's investment in the Judson Manufacturing Company. No such report is contained in any follow-up meeting minutes, and it was not until 1930 that the matter was even further dealt with. The minutes of the meeting held on February 3, 1930 approved an exchange of the foundation's preferred stock holding in return for 11,680 shares of the Judson Pacific "A" preferred stock. There is no indication in the minutes as to whether the values were or were not equivalent. As to the foundation's common stock holdings, the minutes of the meeting of June 11, 1930 reveal that Carlos Maas, who was still the president of Judson's successor corporation and who was also the brother of the Helping Fund's Managing Director, Ted Maas (both were sons of Ida Sutter Maas, who was one of the Helping Fund's directors) had made an offer to purchase the Helping Fund's "remaining common stock holdings." On a motion by Mr. Bolton, which was seconded by director C.P. Deems, the offer was accepted. No terms or price are contained in the minutes. In the interim, and although there are no references to any sales of Judson stock between 1925 and 1930, the minutes do contain a number of references to other stock purchases and sales generally as recommended by Director Bolton, who was the family's and the foundation's stockbroker. The minutes also suggest that the charitable goals of the foundation were being pursued in seemingly uninterrupted fashion.

It seems, therefore, that the various transformations of Judson following Henry's death were ultimately disposed of within seven years of that event and did not lead to any serious adverse financial consequences to the family or the foundation.

BOTHIN REAL ESTATE COMPANY

Although Henry retained the title of President of the Bothin Real Estate Company until his death, in fact operational control had been turned over to his great nephew, Ted Maas, several years earlier. Just six months before Henry died, Mr. Maas arranged a private bond offering in the amount of $500,000 and consisting of two series. The first series was broken into 13 issuances, each carrying a total face value of $25,000. The second series consisted of just one issuance in the amount of $175,000. Those bonds each carried a coupon rate of 5.5 percent and were set to mature, beginning with the issuance of the first series in 1925 and thereafter one each year for the next twelve years until 1937. The $175,000 series contained one bond that fell due in 1938. They were secured by five properties all located in downtown San Francisco. Although unstated in the corporate minutes, the purpose of the bonds was to create liquidity for the company so that decisions did not have to be made in haste or in response to time limits imposed by a probate judge. In other words, the bonds were another piece of Henry's final planning effort to assure the viability of the Real Estate Company after his death.

Henry was remarkably competent when running the show; however, his frequent placement of family members into positions of management sometimes failed him. That trait first surfaced when he put his brother, J.C., in charge of the Bothin Manufacturing Co. in 1890. Within a year the company had dropped off the radar screen, never to be heard from again. Regarding the Bothin Real

Estate Co, his choice of Ted Maas to succeed him was wise; however, Henry failed to appreciate the impact of the family after his death. His will was controversial and the subject of much frenzied negotiation among family members, and one of the outcomes of those negotiations was that the Board of the Real Estate Company was expanded to six members. Two of the six were designated to represent the interests of Ellen (herself and Robert Bolton), two to represent the interests of Genevieve (herself and her husband, Edmunds) and two to represent the interests of the offspring of all of Henry's six siblings (Ted Maas and Charles Mitchell, who was their collective attorney.) Unfortunately, none other than Ted Maas and possibly Robert Bolton (who, as a stockbroker, at least understood investments and markets) had any qualifications to run an active real estate company that owned and managed over one hundred properties. As though that wasn't a sufficient recipe for assured mediocrity, the parties' agreement (which was duly ordered by the Probate Court) called for 75 percent of the net income of the Bothin Real Estate Company to be distributed quarterly to Henry's heirs. That provision, of course, effectively prevented any thought to the development of a long term business plan or to managing the properties with an eye to maximization of performance or enhancement of the long term value of the portfolio. As a result, within literally weeks of his death, the stage was set for the company to stagnate for nearly fifty years.

Edmunds died in 1964. Finally, in 1971, the Bothin Real Estate Company was sold. The purchaser was a partnership of investors led by general partners Leonard Kingsley and Al Schreck, who set up the purchasing entity under the name of KSW Partners. Among the investors in the venture was Genevieve, who took a part of the sale price back as a limited partner in KSW. The partnership purchased the company's real estate assets, which, at that point, consisted of seventy commercial properties, most in San Francisco. The real estate portfolio also included some properties located in Marin,

San Mateo, Riverside, and Santa Barbara counties. The price paid, nearly fifty years after Henry's death, was $11,000,000, of which $6,000,000 was raised from investors and $5,000,000 was debt.

KSW Partners did a masterful job of managing the real estate portfolio. They sold off some of the lesser properties, improved others, entered into joint ventures with developers on yet other sites, and proved very astute at maximizing rental income. After forty years of owning and managing the real estate portfolio, the partnership terminated under its terms, and the properties were sold. After all was said and done, those investors who had put up $5,000,000 to purchase Henry's portfolio of properties, had, over the forty year life of the partnership, received a double digit annual rate of return—a yield that even Henry would have enthusiastically congratulated them for attaining.

THE BOTHIN HELPING FUND

Early on the morning of June 28, 1925, a powerful earthquake struck Santa Barbara. The quake, which historians report measured 6.3 on the Richter Scale,[338] did little damage to local residences; however, its impact was dramatic on State Street, where nearly every commercial building was either totally destroyed or heavily damaged. The reason given for the rather selective areas of damage was that, unlike most construction in the area, which was built on solid ground, the area around State Street was landfill that didn't have adequate compaction values. In addition to the damage on State Street, probably the worst damage was done to the Sheffield Dam, located near Rattlesnake Canyon at the north end of the city, which, because it was built on sandy soil, cracked apart, sending a wall of water through parts of Santa Barbara and carrying trees, automobiles, and three houses all the way to the ocean. A total of thirteen people died in the quake, and the damage to property was estimated at $8,000,000. Ironically, the old adage of location, location, location that had served Henry so well during his lifetime ended up costing the Helping Fund approximately $300,000 to repair the damage to the ten well-located but unfortunate buildings it owned in the damage zone. The buildings, listed sequentially by the number they carried in the Helping Fund's records, as well as their addresses, appraised value, a description of damage suffered, and cost to repair is provided in the following endnote.[339]

The properties were repaired (at a total cost approximately equal to their pre-earthquake appraisal value), and they remained in the Helping Fund's investment portfolio until the 1960s and 70s, when most were sold in order to eliminate problems with distant management and to provide greater liquidity in the investment portfolio. Several of the properties were given to nonprofit organizations that had been their tenants. Unfortunately, the Foundation (of which the author was then, and still remains to this day, a board member) failed to anticipate the real estate boom of the 1980s and 1990s and, in that respect, undoubtedly made decisions that Henry might well have criticized had he still been alive. Certainly, Henry's zest for real estate accumulation, which was at his very core, has not been followed, at least as far as the Foundation's assets are concerned, by succeeding generations. Whether that has worked out to the Foundation's benefit or not is a good question, and good arguments might be raised on both sides.

The Bothin Helping Fund was incorporated at a time when there was not much oversight of charitable foundations. Although it has, to the best of the family's knowledge, always operated in a completely aboveboard manner, during the mid-1930s, it did become involved in one questionable transaction. Genevieve had, through inheritance from her maternal grandfather, Frank Whittier, obtained an interest in the Whittier estate. Apparently that interest was illiquid (since the estate was battling several lawsuits filed by landowners in Hemet), and so, needing cash, Genevieve turned to the Helping Fund to make a $90,000 loan to her and her husband, Edmunds. That loan (which today would be clearly inappropriate and would not even be brought up for discussion) was approved not just by the other trustees but also by counsel. The loan was secured by assignment of Genevieve's interest in certain Whittier estate assets, and both Genevieve and Edmunds resigned from the board of the Helping Fund as part of the arrangement. Nonetheless, it was an example of a self-serving deal, which is notable not so much for any wrongdoing as for the fact that transactions of that nature were apparently not, back then, thought to be out of line. That loan, incidentally, was ultimately repaid six years later through the assignment by Genevieve of equivalent value in shares of the Bothin Real Estate Company.

In any event, the assets of the Bothin Foundation (which consist entirely of what Henry and Ellen provided during his lifetime) have grown steadily and are currently in the range of $40 million. The Foundation (whose board consists of lineal descendants as well as outside directors) gives away approximately $2,000,000 annually to people and organizations in need within San Francisco, San Mateo, Marin, and Sonoma counties. All in all, Henry Bothin has left his imprint on future generations in ways he would most assuredly be proud of.

Endnotes

1 Ernst Bothin's wife was referred to by a number of names. Her birth name was "Anna Rosina." Per the custom of the day, the name "Anna" was given to many girls, but was rarely actually used, and in Rosina's case that custom appears to have been followed. She has variously been referred to as Rosa, Rosina, Rozena, and Rosalie; however, every reference to her in records in the United States, including census records as well as her tombstone, refer to her as "Rosa." And so I have chosen to follow that route and to call her Rosa in this book.

2 Ida Sutter Maas's "Letter" (or, probably more accurately, a story about her ancestry) dated December 20, 1940 (letter in the possession of Ida's great grandson, Garrett Walkup). Ida was the daughter of Emily (Emma) Bothin, one of the eight children of Ernst and Rosa Bothin. She came to know her uncle, Henry Bothin, very well, and, later in the quoted story, she described having an early recollection, when she was about five years old, of the huge white handkerchief Henry produced from his pocket when he visited her family in Wisconsin. Ida became an accomplished pianist as well as having an ongoing interest in her family's history, and Henry came to admire her greatly as witnessed by letters he sent to both her and her mother. Ultimately, Henry persuaded Ida and her family to move to San Francisco, where three of her four sons became very much involved in Henry's

business affairs. Ida herself became a member of the Board of Trustees of the Bothin Helping Fund, a foundation Henry set up in 1917.

3   "Poznan Project" on the website *The Poznan Project*, accessed April 20, 2014 http://poznan-project.psnc.pl/

The sources of this information include the Poznan Project, an effort by many, many volunteers who have attempted to chronicle and put onto the internet records of all marriages occurring in Posen (a region of Prussia back when Ernst and Rosa Boethin were first married), which has since then become a part of modern day Poland and been renamed Poznan. It is a donation supported service which can be searched for one's ancestors who were married in Posen province, Prussia between 1800 and 1884. I also relied on the research talents of Iwona Dakiniecicz, a Polish genealogist who did some additional research to confirm the accuracy of the records turned up by the Poznan Project and to develop further data which has been very helpful.

Actually, Ernst's full name was Michael Ernst Boethin. Just as the custom of the day with girls was generally to disregard the first name, so too that custom appears to have been followed in the case of boys. There is no record of Ernst ever using the name Michael. Ernst and Rosa, incidentally, followed that tradition themselves when they named their third born child Auguste Pauline Boethin. "Auguste," like "Anna," was a common first name for girls which, however, was rarely used as the given name. In the case of Pauline it seems never to have been used after she was christened.

Ernst's parents were Johann Boethin and Charlotte Frederike Charlottae Teschen. Ernst was the third or fourth of seven children born over a twenty-eight year span. The eldest was Anna Marie who was born in 1800, followed by three brothers, the eldest of whom was Gottleib Leberect Boethin who was born in about 1805. Next came Johann Christoph, who was born sometime between 1810 and 1812, and then came Ernst, born on

September 22, 1811, who could have been a year older, younger, or a twin of Johann Christoph. The next sibling was Caroline Friederike who was born in 1818. She was followed by August Ferdinand who was born in about 1819. The baby of the family was Ernestine Wilhelmine who was born in 1828. All the aforementioned were later married at the Protestant church in Czarnków.

4   Ibid. Once Posen was found to have been their birthplace, a search through the Poznan Project database using both the names Boethin and Lawrenz developed the information which enabled further research, and ultimately has since led to the understanding I have, sketchy though it may be, of Ernst's and Rosa's roots.

5   Ibid. As indicated above, one older brother of Ernst's was Gottleib Leberect Boethin. Another brother, Johann Christoph, was born within a year on either side of Ernst. The youngest brother was August Ferdinand Boethin whose birthdate was about sixteen years prior to Ernst's and Rosa's marriage. The fact that marriage records for all three exist, showing that each was married in Czarnków means that obviously all three survived to adulthood.

6   William J. Gilmore, *Reading Becomes A Necessity of Life, Material and Cultural Life in Rural New England, 1780-1835* (Knoxville, Tennessee: The University of Tennessee Press, 1989) p.20 ff.

7   The Gale Group, "Kindergarten" in *Encyclopedia of Children and Childhood in History and Society, 2008* on the website *Internet FAQ Archives*, accessed April 20, 2014 http://www.faqs.org/childhood/Ke-Me/Kindergarten.html.

8   Obituary of Pauline Bothin Lee, *Wisconsin State Register*, February 14, 1880. The *Wisconsin State Register* was a newspaper of general circulation at the time in Portage, Wisconsin. Pauline was, chronologically, the third born of the children of Ernst and Rosa. Her obituary provides the first solid evidence of where in Prussia Ernst and Rosa came from as well as the

date they and their family arrived in the United States.

9 Ibid. Since, as will later be seen, Ernst and Rosa always used the word "Prussia" as their place of birth, and were never more specific than that, it was not possible until recently to trace their ancestry to any specific region of Prussia. Pauline's obituary was discovered, thanks to the efforts of Anna Mae Axness, a researcher in Portage to whom the author is greatly indebted for much of the material in this and later chapters relating to the family's life in Portage. Its discovery opened doors to begin the search for a narrower geographic region in Germany which Ernst and Rosa originally called home. Of all of the obituaries of Henry Bothin's siblings, Pauline's is the only one which proved helpful in that regard. It gave her place of birth as "Chodusen, province of Posen, Prussia." Although the name "Chodusen" does not exist, that clue led ultimately to the discovery of "Chodziesen" (the German name for the town currently located in northwest Poland and now known as Chodzież). From there it was only a matter of time to connect the dots.

10 Poznan Project, *ut sup.*

11 "Province of Posen," on the website *Wikipedia*, last modified February 21, 2014, accessed April 20, 2014 http://en.wikipedia.org/wiki/Province_of_Posen

"Partitions of Poland," on the website *Wikipedia*, last modified March 2, 2014, accessed April 20, 2014 http://en.wikipedia.org/wiki/Partitions_of_Poland

"November (1830) Uprising," on the website *Wikipedia*, last modified March 2, 2014, accessed April 20, 2014 http://en.wikipedia.org/wiki/November_Uprising

"Greater Poland Uprisings of 1848," on the website *Wikipedia*, last modified February 4, 2014, accessed April 20, 2014 http://en.wikipedia.org/wiki/Greater_Poland_Uprising_%281848%29

"Congress of Vienna," on the website *Wikipedia*, last modified February 19, 2014, accessed April 20, 2014 http://en.wikipedia.org/wiki/Congress_of_Vienna

"Duchy of Warsaw," on the website *Wikipedia*, last modified March 2, 2014, accessed April 20, 2014 http://en.wikipedia.org/wiki/Duchy_of_Warsaw

"Grand Duchy of Posen," on the website *Wikipedia*, last modified January 16, 2014, accessed http://en.wikipedia.org/wiki/Grand_Duchy_of_Posen.

12   Helmut Schmahl, "Transplanted But Not Uprooted: 19th Century Immigrants from Hesse Darmstadt in Wisconsin" (unpublished manuscript Center for the Study of Upper Midwestern Culture at the University of Wisconsin), http://csumc.wisc.edu/mki/Resources/Online_Papers/proceedings/schmahl.html.

13   Tyler Anbinder, *Nativism and Slavery: The Northern Know Nothings and the Politics of the 1850s* (New York: Oxford University Press, 1992), 7-8.

14   Ira Glazier and William Filby, *Germans to America—Lists of Passengers Arriving at U.S. Ports*, volume 1, (Wilmington, DE: Scholarly Resources, Inc., 1988), x-xii.

15   Schmahl, *Transplanted But Not Uprooted*," *ut sup*. Although discussing people from a different part of Germany, this dissertation is instructive on how letters from America helped make easier the decisions of many Germans to leave their homeland and to join fellow Germans in America.

16   Richard H Zeitlin,. *Germans in Wisconsin* (Madison, Wisconsin: Wisconsin Historical Society Press, 1977), 13-14.

17   Glazier and Filby. *Germans to America*., *ut sup*. This work is a controversially-researched multi-volume set of books which is, so they claim, continually updated and lists hundreds of thousands, if not millions, of German immigrants to this country between the years 1850 and 1893. The sources of the names listed come mainly from passenger lists of vessels and the listings contain the names of the immigrant head of household as well as family members traveling with him or her. I searched through all

volumes which contained entries for Germans who came to this country between 1850 and 1853. Unfortunately, the Boethins are not mentioned under any spelling which I could think of. Since their fifth child (and first son), Julius, was born in Prussia in about 1850, and since 1850 is the earliest year covered in the set, I started with volume 1. I ended with 1853 since we know that Henry was born in the United States on July 17, 1853. I also checked multiple spellings, including Buchin (which is how their names were spelled in the 1860 census), Bothier (which is how their names appear in the 1870 census), Böthin (which is how I understand their name was spelled in the old country) and a number of other possible spellings, all to no avail. Given also that Pauline's obituary lists August, 1852 as a date of arrival in this country, it seems reasonable to limit the search to that date range. From their absence in this work, one might conclude that most probably the ship they arrived on has simply not yet been added to the database. Another less complimentary possibility also exists, if the criticism by Professor Antonius Holtmann is valid. Professor Holtman, in his paper, *Germans to America—50 Volumes That Are Not to be Trusted*, first published in *The Palatine Immigrant* (1997), claims that this source is untrustworthy for a number of reasons, including, but hardly limited to the assertion that many legitimate German immigrants were excluded when, for instance, they arrived at smaller ports such as Galveston, Texas, and/or where they arrived on ships where fewer than 80 percent of the passengers were German.

18 Obituary of Pauline Bothin Lee, *Wisconsin State Register*. That obituary gives her date of birth which has been independently confirmed on the website *Family Search, accessed April 20, 2014* https://familysearch.org/pal:/MM9.1.1/NPT9-T3V. *Family Search* also provides the name of the town where she was born and grew up which, although misspelled in the obituary, has been independently confirmed at Chodziesen, province of Posen, Prussia.

19 Zeitlin. *Germans in Wisconsin.*

20   Consul Wilshire Butterfield, *The History of Columbia County, Wisconsin, containing an account of its settlement* (Chicago: Western Historical Company, 1880), 878-879.

21   Zeitlin, *Germans in Wisconsin.*

22   See Ernst's *Declaration of Intent to Become a U.S. Citizen* which was signed in Madison Wisconsin on November 8, 1853. See also Ernst's obituary in the *Wisconsin State Register* which reports that he had been a resident of Portage for 43 years as of the date of his death on March 29, 1896. Both those documents place him in Portage as of 1853. They conflict with the biographical sketch which was published in 1880 and appears in Butterfield. *History of Columbia County, Wisconsin.* That short sketch says he moved to Portage in 1855. I have accepted the earlier date primarily since I cannot account for his presence anywhere else in Wisconsin between 1853 (when we know from his application for citizenship that he was within 30 miles of Portage) and 1855. Since the topic is not central to this manuscript, I have been content to made an editorial call but with the caveat that it may be incorrect.

23   More specifically still, Portage is situated geographically at a point where the Fox and Wisconsin Rivers flow less than two miles apart from one another. Portage takes its name from the act of transporting boats and cargo from one of those rivers to the other—generally from the Fox which meanders slowly north to Green Bay but is easily paddled south against its light current, and the Wisconsin which flows south to the Mississippi. This combination of two nearly adjacent rivers enabled fur traders and other travelers to transport their goods all the way from the St. Lawrence Waterway and the Great Lakes down to the Gulf of Mexico. Near Portage the Wisconsin River also contains drop-offs resulting in a 42' elevation change, drop-offs which provided a natural source of water power which was used by early settlers to operate saw and grist mills and to foster industrial development which was primarily timber related. It is

also a geologic transition point between the granite bedrock to the north, the sandy central plain to the south, and the glacial activity to the east. As such, it is a highly bio-diverse and heavily wooded region of the state.

24 Michael J Goc, *Portage, a Sesquicentennial History* (Wisconsin, New Past Press, 2008) 11.

25 This newspaper article was quoted in Michael Goc's book, *Portage, a Sesquicentennial History*, 117. The quotation is re-printed as it appears in the book and not in its original form from the newspaper.

26 Goc,. *Portage, a Sesquicentennial History, ut sup.* 122 ff ; Malcolm Rosholt, *Photos from Wisconsin's Past*, (Wisconsin, Rosholt Housepages, 1986) 56-69.

27 Chapter 6, "Portage Crafts and Industry," in Joyce McKay, *An Intensive Historical Architectural and Historical Survey of the City of Portage, Columbia County, Wisconsin* (Portage Wisconsin: Portage Area Chamber of Commerce 1993) 126.

28 Ibid.,134-135.

29 Interestingly, Ernst himself loaned money to others and took back security which was generally land. Indeed, one loan that he made was to Carl and Emily Maas who were the parents of Theodore Maas who married Ida Sutter Maas. Ida was the niece of Ernst and Rosa who, as a teenager, listened to Rosa and later wrote the story about Ernst and Rosa's early life which has been referred to earlier.

30 Ida Sutter Maas' typed story dated December 20, 1940 *ut sup.*

31 Rosholt, *Our Story; Portage County, Wisconsin , ut sup.* 113.

32 Synder, Van Vechen & Co. *Columbia County, Wisconsin Maps and Written History, Wisconsin(as of 1878)* (Wisconsin: Synder, Van Vechen & Co. 1878).

33 Ida Sutter Maas' typed story dated December 20, 1940 *ut sup.*

34 Emil Bothin (Emily's son) to Ida Sutter Maas (his sister),

1877-1890, (collection in the possession of Garrett Walkup (Ida's great grandson)).

There are several references in these letters to the family's hope that Julius, the favorite of the senior Bothins, might be able to get back to Portage to see his parents before they died.

35   Sarah Kershaw, *"The Psychology of Moving,"* on the website of the *New York Times*, February 28, 2010 www.nytimes.com/2010/02/28/realestate/28cov.html.

36   Ibid. Citing psychologist Elizabeth Stirling, a psychologist in Santa Fe, New Mexico.

37   Butterfield, *The History of Columbia County, Wisconsin, ut sup.*, 878-879.

38   It seems that tragedy continued to befall Pauline's family even after her death. Thus, their son, Frank, was killed in a buggy accident when he was 38, leaving a wife and eight year old daughter, Ethel.

39   Ida Sutter Maas's typed story dated December 20, 1940 *ut sup.* Ernest and Rosa had 8 children. The first five were born in Germany. The following is an excerpt from that family summary and is largely unchanged (except for italicized notes inserted by the author to correct or add to the summary). The same single generation tree is redone and augmented in a later endnote based upon information discovered by the author. According to Ida:

Otillia was the eldest. She married a man named Mau, and they had seven children [*as to whom there is some detail provided in the memo*];

Amelia was born in 1845. She married a Mr. Kaufman, and was the mother of Frank, Emma, Meta and Harry. [*Ida's information is incomplete. In fact the Kaufmans had ten children, and her family is also discussed in a later endnote*];

Emily was born in 1847 and died in 1893. [*Actually, Emily was born on March 9, 1845 and was named Ernestine Amalie Boethin at the time of her birth*]. She married Joshua Sutter (1839-1897) whose father, Andrew Sutter was a brother of John Sutter who settled Sacramento. Emily and Joshua had three children, of whom Emil and Alvin both died childless in their early twenties and Ida (born 1871), married a man named Maas and bore Theodore A. Maas, Carlos J. Maas, Donald S. Maas, and Henry Bothin Maas. [*Theodore was one of the executors of Henry's estate, Donald was an officer of Henry's real estate company, and Carlos was an officer and later, the President, of Henry's steel company, Judson Manufacturing Company. Further information about this side of the family has been developed (largely with the help of Ida's grandchildren, Ted and David Maas and Barbara Walkup, and one of her great grandchildren, Garrett Walkup.]*

Pauline Bothin Lee. [*Pauline is listed by Ida as the fourth child of Ernst and Rosina. She was actually the third. Her birthdate was December 12, 1841, and her birth name was Auguste Pauline Boethin.]* She had one child, Frank, who in turn had two daughters. [*In fact, Pauline married twice and had two children, one from each marriage. Her first marriage was to John Harmon of Portage. Mr. Harmon went off to fight in the Civil War and attained the rank of Corporal. He died in the war on September 30, 1863. He and Pauline had a son from that marriage who died at about four years old. Pauline remarried Alfred Lee, also of Portage, and she and Alfred had one son named Frank. Pauline who died in 1880 of tuberculosis.]*

Willimina (Minnie) Bothin married Frank Sadler, and they had three children, Irwin (who died as a youth), Agnes who married a man named Schnakenburg, and Hermann. [*Actually, the name of Willimina's husband was Hermann Sadler.]*

Julius was the sixth of the Bothin children. He married and had one daughter, Lulu who apparently married a man named Craig and had a son named Carvel.

Henry was the seventh child.

Mary was the last of the Bothin children. She died unmarried in Wisconsin at age 17.

As recited in the will of Henry Bothin, dated October 15, 1922, all his siblings except Willimina (Minnie) had died before that date. Provision was made in his will for Willimina as well as for the children of Otillia, the children of Amelia, the child of Pauline, the child of J.C. (Julius), and for Ida Sutter Maas (the only surviving child of Emily).

40 Ida Sutter Maas' typed story dated December 20, 1940 *ut sup.*

41 Goc, *Portage, a Sesquicentennial History, ut sup.* 97.

42 Ibid., 97.

43 Maas, Ida Sutter.typed story, *ut. sup.*

44 J.I. Case Threshing Machine Company v. Haven, 1884, 21 *Northwestern Reporter*, 677.

45 For a good description of farm life, and particularly the life of a farm wife, see Sara Brooks Sundberg, "A Farm Woman on the Minnesota Prairie; The Letters of Mary E. Carpenter," *Minnesota History Magazine*, Volume 51(Spring, 1989) 186-193.

46 According to his obituary in *Pacific Service Magazine* (the monthly newsletter put out at the time by Pacific Gas and Electric Co, of which he had been a founding director in 1906), Henry worked as a clerk for several years when he first arrived in San Francisco. Presumably his employment with Chartres was in that capacity.

47 This memorandum was, apparently, prepared in response to the request by *The National Cyclopedia of American Biography* for further information about Henry in connection with the biography which they were preparing for inclusion in their many biographies of notable individuals. As earlier indicated, the author has been unable to actually find any biography published by that entity (or, for that matter, any other source either).

48 See end note #2 above.

49 Emil Sutter, letter to "The Folks at Home," October, 1889 (in family collection). Although Emil's letter is undated, it was

written on his 21st birthday. Not knowing his exact date of birth, the best I can do to date it is to say that it appears chronologically immediately following one dated October 1, 1889 and before another dated October 16, 1889. Therefore, I have assumed it was written sometime in October of 1889.

50   Ibid.

51   Genevieve Bothin Lyman was the only child of Henry and Lottie Jane (Jennie) to survive to adulthood. After Henry and Jennie went through their highly publicized divorce in the middle of the first decade of the twentieth century, Genevieve suffered cruel comments from friends and felt ostracized. She never got over it and could never bring herself to say a kind word about her father. See infra for more information about both Genevieve and the divorce.

52   *Early Navigation on the Upper Mississippi River* on the Gateways to Commerce website of the Army Corps of Engineers, accessed July 31, 2014, http://www.nps.gov/history/history/online_books/rmr/2/chap1.htm.

53   David A. Pfeiffer, "Bridging the Mississippi: The Railroads and Steamboats Clash at the Rock Island Brid*ge*," *Prologue Magazine*, Vol. 36, No.2 (Summer 2004).

54   Ibid., 4-7.

55   Mississippi and Missouri Railroad company v Ward, 1863, 62 U.S. 485.

56   William Issel and Robert W. Cherney, *San Francisco, 1865-1932: Politics, Power, and Urban Development* (California, University of California Press, 1986) 23.

57   Ibid., 26.

58   Ibid.

59   Undisclosed author and undated short essay entitled "Black History in Wisconsin" found on the website of the *Wisconsin Historical Society, accessed April 20, 2014* http://www.wisconsinhistory.org/topics/blackhistory/.

60   Rockwell D. Hunt, "Slavery and the Admission of California into the Union" *San Francisco Chronicle*, September 9, 1900and republished under the title *How California Came to be Admitted*, on the website *The Virtual Museum of The City of San Francisco*, accessed April 20, 2014, www.sfmuseum.org/hist5/caladmit.html.

61   California Constitution of 1849, Section 18.

62   Rudolph M. Lapp, "Negro Rights Activities in Gold Rush California," *California Historical Society Quarterly* (March, 1966) and re-printed in the *Virtual Museum of the City of San Francisco ut sup.*

63   "California in the American Civil War" on the website *Answers.com*, accessed April 20, 2014 www.answers.com/topic/california-in-the-american-civil-war.

In California, Lincoln won just 32.3 percent of the popular vote. 31.7 percent went to Stephen Douglas (the Democratic nominee who favored retaining slavery where it existed and leaving it to states to decide their positions on the issue), and 28.7 percent went to John C. Breckenridge (the candidate of the Southern Democrat party which obviously favored the extension of slavery wherever possible). The thin Republican Party majority gave them all of California's electoral votes; however, it also raised the hopes of many Southern California slavery sympathizers who seriously considered splitting off from Northern California and creating a separate territory.

64   Ward v. Flood, 1874, 48 Cal 46.

65   Brown v Board of Education, 1954, 347 U.S. 483.

66   Word of the discovery of gold in California made its way, via trading vessels, to Kwangtung Province where many Chinese, whose economy was in decline and where famine was widespread, saw opportunity and came to California in search of wealth. By 1852, the number of Chinese working in the mines in California had reached 25,000, and they were writing home

with glowing reports. The Chinese who came were typically young, single, uneducated males interested only in finding quick riches and returning to China. They had no interest in assimilating into the population, and they tended to congregate into enclaves of Chinese. Their habit of hard work was seen by many as giving them an unfair advantage, and soon anti-Chinese fever was at a high pitch. That anti-Chinese sentiment was given legitimacy by the case of People v. George W. Hall, A California Supreme Court decision in 1854, in which defendant Hall, an admitted bigot, was convicted in the lower court of murdering a Chinese gold miner. The Supreme Court determined that the laws preventing blacks and other minorities from giving testimony against whites included Chinese. Since all the testimony against the defendant came from Chinese witnesses, all of whose testimony was thereby excluded, the Supreme Court overturned the lower court's conviction, and Mr. Hall got off scott free.

67   "A History of Chinese Americans in California: The 1870s" on the website of the *National Park Service* , accessed April 20, 2014 http://www.nps.gov/history/history/online_books/5views/5views3d.htm.

68   Henry Kittridge Norton, *The Story of California from the Earliest Days to the Present,* 7th Ed., (Chicago, A.C. McClurg & Co., 1924) Chapter XXIV, 283-296.

69   *The Chinese*, on The Virtual Museum of San Francisco website, accessed July 31, 2014, http://www.sfmuseum.net/hist6/chinhate.html.

70   "A History of Chinese Americans in California: The 1850s" on the website the *National Park Service*, accessed on April 20, 2014 ttp://www.nps.gov/history/history/online_books/5views/5views3b.htm.

71   "Are We in Danger from Earthquakes?*"The San Francisco Real Estate Circular (April, 1872)* and reprinted on the website *The*

Virtual Museum of the City of San Francisco, accessed April 20, 2014 http://www.sfmuseum.org/hist1/1872.html.

72 "Danger from Fire—A New Sensation" *The San Francisco Real Estate Circular* (May, 1872)and reprinted on the website *The Virtual Museum of the City of San Francisco*, accessed April 20, 2014 http://www.sfmuseum.org/hist1/may1872.html.

73 Ibid.

74 Robert Wilson, "The Great Diamond Hoax of 1872" on the website *Smithsonian* (June, 2004), accessed April 20, 2014 http://www.smithsonianmag.com/history-archaeology/The_Great_Diamond_Hoax_of_1872.html.

75 "Civil War and Industrial Expansion, 1860-1897." *Gale Encyclopedia of U.S. Economic History*(Independence, KY: Cengage Learning, 1999).

76 Michael Barga, "The Long Depression (1873-1878)," on the website the *Social Welfare History Project*, accessed April 20, 2014 http://www.socialwelfarehistory.com/eras/the-long-depression/.

77 Nathaniel C. Nash, "Persuading Americans to Save," *New York Times* (December 17, 1989) on the website *N.Y. Times*, accessed April 20, 2014 http://www.nytimes.com/1989/12/17/business/persuading-americans-to-save.html?pagewanted=all&src=pm.

78 Samuel H. Williamson, "7 Ways to Compute the Relative Value of a U.S. Dollar Amount—1774 to Present." on the website *MeasuringWorth.com*, accessed April 20, 2014 http://www.measuringworth.com/uscompare/.

79 *The Great Boston Fire of 1872* on the Boston Fire Historical Society website, accessed July 31, 2014, http://www.bostonfirehistory.org/firestorygreatfireof1872.html.

80 The company name was not changed to reflect Albert Mau's absence until 1888; however, it is noteworthy that he was not present at the 1886 wedding of Henry and Lottie Jane Whittier.

Since both Otillia and their son, William were present, one has to assume that either Mr. Mau had died prior to that date or was ill and unable to leave home.

81 *The San Francisco Blue Book 1889*, accessed March 3, 2015, http://www.cagenweb.com/santaclara/books/TheSanFrancisco bluebook1889.pdf.

82 Cook County, Illinois Deaths Index, 1878 to 1922, on the website *Ancestry.com*, accessed April 20, 2014 http://www.ancestry.com/.

83 *Sacramento Daily Record-Union*, January 24, 1882, 3.

84 *City Directory of San Francisco*, 1887.

85 This trade journal was compiled by J.A. Miller and published by Bay City Publishing Co. It can be found at the offices of the San Francisco Historical Society.

86 *Kern County Californian*, March 8, 1884, p.4. There are many other newspapers where this material also was broadcast in prominent print advertising, including the *Sacramento Daily Union* (Volume 18, No. 56) October 26, 1883, p. 3, as well as numerous other editions of that newspaper as well appearing frequently in various editions of the *California Daily Alta* and the *San Francisco Call*.

87 Ibid.

88 Ibid.

89 *Sacramento Daily Record-Union*, March 15, 1884, p. 5 and numerous other editions of that same newspaper during 1884 as well as other newspapers including those cited above with respect to GIANT Baking Powder.

90 Richard A. Walker, "Industry Builds Out The City: The Suburbanization of Manufacturing in the San Francisco Bay Area, 1850-1940" in Robert Lewis, *The Manufactured Metropolis* (Philadelphia, PA: Temple University Press, 2004) 92.

91 "Denis Kearney and the Anti-Chinese Campaign," on the website

HarpWeek, accessed April 20, 2014 http://immigrants.harpweek.com/ChineseAmericans/2KeyIssues/DenisKearneyCalifAnti.htm.

92 Walker, "Industry Builds Out The City." *ut sup.* 93 and citing 93. Issel and Cherney, *San Francisco, 1865-1932 ut. sup.* 25, 54. R. Elgie,, *The Development of San Francisco Manufacturing, 1848-1880* (M.A.thesis, University of California, Berkeley 1966); N. Shumsky, *Tar Flat and Nob Hill: A Social History of Industrial San Francisco During the 1870s* (PhD dissertation, University of California, Berkeley, 1972) 22-24. Richard Walker, *Another Round of Globalization in San Francisco Urban Geography* (unpublished paper, U.C. Berkeley, 1996) 60-94.

93 Walker, Industry Builds Out The City, *ut sup.*

94 Daniel G. Volkmann, a booklet entitled *For the interest of the founder's descendants herein is presented a brief history of A. SCHILLING & COMPANY 1881-1947.* (privately printed for Daniel G. Volkmann by Lawton Kennedy, San Francisco, California, 1959). Found at www.allelementsdesign.com/schilling/company/spices/65years.

95 Ibid.

96 Ibid.

97 Enrico Caruso, "The 1906 Earthquake" was first published in London in *The Sketch*, later re-printed in *The Theatre Magazine*, Vol. VI, No. 65 (July 1, 1906) and now appears on the website of the *Virtual Museum of the City of San Francisco*, accessed April 20, 2014 www.sfmuseum.org/1906/ew19.html. Briefly, the article recounts how Caruso, who had sung in *"Carmen"* the night before, awoke at 5a.m. on April 18th (actually it would have been at 5:18a.m.) to feel his bed rocking as though he was on a ship at sea. He got up and looked out the window from his 5th floor suite to see buildings toppling, large pieces of masonry falling, and heard the cries and screams of men, women and children. He called in his valet, and, as plaster was crumbling from the ceiling all around him, he got himself dressed and ran down the

stairs to the street. Then, as his valet went back into the hotel to gather up all his trunks and other baggage, Caruso tried to fend off a thief who was trying to steal those of Caruso's pieces of luggage which the valet had brought down. Ultimately, a policeman was called and "makes the man who takes an interest in my baggage 'skiddoo' as Americans say." He made his way to Union Square where he found several other artists and singers, but refused their invitation to come indoors, preferring instead to stay out on the streets where he didn't have to worry about being in a building which might collapse. He tried to flee, but soldiers prevented his passing, and so that night he was forced to sleep "on the hard ground in the open." The next day his faithful valet managed to find a man with a cart who agreed to drive them and the luggage to the Oakland ferry, from which he made his way to Oakland and then to a train which he took to New York. Although Mr. Caruso's account rejects the commonly recounted story that, half crazed with fear, he ran out of the hotel, sat down on his valise and wept, nonetheless, his own account does nothing to dispel the image of a spineless egotist.

98 William Ralston was a victim of his own dreaming and incurable optimism. Through his bank (The Bank of California) he, probably more than any other banker or businessman in San Francisco, enthusiastically backed and financed the city's growth from the mid-1850s until his death in 1875. His name, more than probably any other, is associated with the dreams of San Francisco becoming a world class business and cultural center. Unfortunately, his brashness and headstrong attitude, which are obviously polar opposites of the traits one typically associates with a good banker, and his willingness to gamble with the money his shareholders had invested in his bank, were seemingly the causes of his undoing. The panic of 1873 (brought on by the failure of the banking house of Jay Cooke and Company and then exacerbated by a chain of other bank failures) resulted in huge stock market losses for Ralston. Other losses followed, and the final straw was his failure to secure approval from the

San Francisco Supervisors for his effort to sell the Spring Valley Water Company, a company he had borrowed heavily to purchase and was then trying to sell to the City at a hugely inflated price. He failed in his efforts to secure a bailout from his erstwhile friend and partner, William Sharon, and that effort (which became public) resulted in a run on his bank which forced it to close its doors. He was forced to resign, and the next day he went for his usual swim in the bay and was seen thrashing about. While the cause of his death was often attributed to a stroke, many feel he committed suicide.

99 Charles Fraccia, "Palace Hotel," on the website the *Encyclopedia of San Francisco*, accessed April 20, 2014 http://www.sfhistoryencyclopedia.com/articles/p/palaceHotel.html.

100 "A City Within a City," *San Francisco Newsletter and California Advertiser* (May 27, 1876) on the website the *Virtual Museum of the City of San Francisco*, accessed April 20, 2014 www.sfmuseum.org/hist11/citywithin.html.

101 *Sacramento Daily Record-Union*, July 25, 1883.

102 Mary E. Whitney, Valley, River and Mountain: Revisiting Fortune Favors the Brave: A History of the Hemet Lake Water Company (Hemet, CA:L The Hemet Area Museum Association, 1999); Mary E. Whitney, *Whittier, Fuller & Company* (Hemet, CA:L The Hemet Area Museum Association, 2000); and Mary E. Whitney, *Vignettes of the Valley* (Hemet, CA:L The Hemet Area Museum Association, 2003); Marsha Holm, *A Brief History of William Franklin Whittier* (San Francisco: California Historical Society, 1978) I have written extensively about Frank Whittier, but intend those writings to be part of a family history which will not be widely dispersed beyond family members. What I have included in this brief biographical sketch of Frank Whittier (as well as his wife, Charlotte) is taken from Marsha Holm's book which, itself, is heavily end noted.

103 *The Morning Call*, August 7, 1866. That article lists Henry's Best Man, Edward Wilson, as well as Groomsmen, Albert Stetson,

Frank D. Wiley, Walter Kenney, and William Fuller (the latter being the eldest son of Frank Whittier's business partner, William Parmer Fuller). The Maid of Honor was the bride's younger sister, Mattie, and the Bridesmaids were Otillia Mau (Henry's niece), Laura Pike, Nellie Stetson and Lizzie Dillman (of Los Angeles). Ernst and Rosa Bothin had been invited, but their names do not appear on the list of attendees. Prominent guests attending the wedding have been named in the body of this work and will not be repeated here.

104 Genevive Bothin de Limur in an interview with Carla Ehat, April 24, 1982, (transcript at the Ann Thompson Kent California Room at the Marin County Library, San Rafael, CA). According to Genevieve, the house was given to Jennie and Henry as a wedding present by her father, Frank Whittier. That is assumed to have been an accurate statement. The fact that he had no investment in the house might in part explain Henry's reluctance to spend money to replace it after the Earthquake and Fire which was to occur eighteen years later.

105 James B. Stetson, *San Francisco During the Eventful Days of April, 1906; Personal Recollections (Charleston, SC: Nabu Press, 2010)*. This 29 page essay comprising Mr. Stetson's recollections of the 1906 earthquake and fire shortly after its occurrence and while it was fresh in his mind is a very valuable resource. His home was across the street from the Bothin home and his recollections of the fire and of what happened to the Bothin home are very specific. Neighbors, whose homes were in the path of the fire and who his recollections include, were, among others, Mr. and Mrs. Charles Holbrook, Jonathon Merrill, Mr. and Mrs. J.B. Stetson, the Claus Spreckles, and the Schwabachers.

106 Solberg, *Gunyard, Hill Farm and Arequipa*, a publication of the Fairfax Historical Society, California, (San Rafael, CA: Marin County Printing Office, Spring 1997) 8-9.

107 Joseph S. Spoerl, "A Brief History of Iron and Steel Production," an undated paper published on the website *Saint Anselm College*,

accessed April 20, 2014 www.anselm.edu/homepage/dbanach/h-carnegie-steel.htm.

108   Ibid.

109   Norman Kelso, *A Romance of Steel in California* (San Francisco: Clathering Press, 1946) (An unpaginated book compiled by The Judson Pacific-Murphy Corporation as its seventy-eighth anniversary souvenir book).

110   Ibid.

111   Ibid.

112   Ibid.

113   Ibid.

114   "The Museum Gazette: James B. Eads and his Amazing Bridge at St. Louis" on the website the *National Park Service*, accessed April 20, 2014 http://www.nps.gov/jeff/historyculture/upload/eads.pdf.

115   "Big Business: Steel and Oil," on the website *Cliffs Notes*, accessed April 20, 2014 http://www.cliffsnotes.com/more-subjects/history/us-history-ii/industrial-america/big-business-steel-and-oil.

116   J. A. Miller, *1887 Illustrated Review; San Francisco, Its Commercial Progress and Importance*, (San Francisco: Bay City Publishing Co., 1887) It can be found at the offices of the San Francisco Historical Society.

117   Kelso, *A Romance of Steel in California, ut sup.*

118   Sherwood D. Burgess, *The Water King: Anthony Chabot, His Life and Times* (Davis, CA: Agaccess, 1992) 146. Note that sources for this information also include Smith, Gertrude and the children of the 6th grade of Anthony Chabot School, Oakland, CA, 1930, *Life of Anthony Chabot* and also Memorial Records at the Society of California Pioneers, Vol 13 "Antoine Chabot" (San Francisco, 1888).

119   *How Much Is That Worth Today?* on the website of Hofstra

University http://people.hofstra.edu/alan_j_singer/Gateway SlaveryGuidePDFFiles/1.Introduction/6.ActivitySheets/2. CostinthePast.pdf.

120   *Kelso, A Romance of Steel in California, ut sup.*
121   Ibid. The book is not paginated, and there are few references to Judson in the text. The book does, however, contain the following sentences: "At that time [1895] Henry E. Bothin, who had been a director and Executive Vice President since 1889, was elected President and General Manager. The business grew under his direction and fabricated some of the largest steel structures on the Pacific Coast—the Oakland City Hall as an example."
122   See PG&E obituary, *ut sup.*
123   Emil Sutter, letter collection (in possession of Garrett Walkup with copies in possession of the author). Emil, the brother of Ida Sutter Maas, spent about eighteen months during 1889 and 1890 working for Henry in the Emeryville offices of Judson. His letters home, of which the October 16th letter is one, are enlightening.
124   *The Morning Call,* October 5, 1890.
125   Theo. Maas, "A. Statement of the Financial Condition of Judson Manufacturing Company as of June 1st 1928" (unpublished document in the possession of David Maas) According to this unpublished document Theo A. Maas (brother of Judson's then President, Carlos Maas, and himself a board member, as well as the then President of the Bothin Real Estate Co). shows the ownership of Judson as being comprised of (1) Bothin Helping Fund, a corporation—68.4 percent; (2) Bothin Real Estate Co. & Henry Bothin—20.6 percent, (3) Ellen Chabot Bothin—13.3 percent, and (4) Edmunds Lyman, Carlos J Maas, and W.T. Summers—7.8 percent.
126   Kelso, *A Romance of Steel in California, ut sup.*
127   A copy of stock certificate number 823, dated February 16, 1891,

in the amount of 50 shares, and bearing Henry Bothin's signature as President of Judson is displayed on one of the unpaginated pages of the book, *A Romance of Steel in California, ut sup.*

128 One interesting apparent contradiction to the foregoing is an article appearing in the *Morning Call,* December 7, 1898, which discussed a large explosion the day before at the gelatin plant of the Judson Powder Works, an explosion which killed Superintendent, Charles Kennedy as well as five Chinese workers. That article includes a quote from a Mr. Lukens who is referred to as the president of the company. It is probable that the Judson Powder Works and Judson Manufacturing Company were two separate and unrelated entities (since one dealt with explosives while the other dealt with steel fabrication); however, unfortunately, there seem to be no records to either confirm that theory or offer an alternative.

129 *Business Successes* (January, 1911) An advertisement in which Judson is featured lists, among its officers, H.E. Bothin (President); H.J. Sadler (his brother in law), Vice President; J.D. Osborne (the Secretary also of the Bothin Real Estate Company), Secretary; F.D. Parsons (plant manager); and H.W. Gallet, (sales manager).

130 "History of the Steel Industry," on the website *Wikipedia,* last modified February 8, 2015, accessed March 3, 2015, wikipedia.org/wiki/History_of_the_steel_industry_(1850-1970).

131 Ibid.

132 John R. Waite, "Carnegie (Cranberry) Furnace" on the website *johnsondepot.com,* accessed April 20, 2014 http://www.johnsonsdepot.com/tweetsie/furnace.pdf.

133 Joseph Daniels, "History of Pig Iron Manufacture on the Pacific Coast," *Washington Historical Quarterly,* Volume 17, No. 3, (1926).

134 Ibid., 174-175.

135 James Moore Swank, *Statistics of the American and Foreign Iron Trades: Annual Statistical Report of the American Iron and Steel*

Association, 1910 (Philadelphia: The American Iron and Steel Association, 1910) 85, 128.

136 *Daily Nevada State Journal,* November 19, 1892.

137 *Oakland Tribune,* June 22, 1895. *Berkeley Gazette,* July 24,1895.

138 *Logansport Pharos,* October 31, 1896. The *Pharos* was a newspaper published in Logansport, Indiana.

139 *Oakland Tribune,* October 8, 1905.

140 *Oakland Tribune,* June 5, 1911.

141 Annual Number," *Oakland Tribune,* January, 1912.

142 *Kelso, A Romance of Steel in California, ut sup.*

143 F.W. Taussig and W.S. Baker, "American Corporations and their Executives: A Statistical Inquiry," *The Quarterly Journal of Economics,* 40, no. 1, (1925).

144 Katherine M. Savarese, "Perverting Civilization" or Pursuing Dreams? Economic Arguments about Executive Compensation Practices in the United States, 1890 to 1940" (working paper, Harvard University, 2010).

145 "What Would $10,000 in 19XX Be Equivalent to Today?" on the website *Observation* http://observationsandnotes.blogspot.com/2011/05/what-10000-in-19xx-equal-today.html.

146 The Grantor/Grantee Index for San Francisco real estate purchases and sales is on microfilm at the Main Branch of the City Library. There are no records prior to 1885, quite probably because they were lost in the 1906 calamity. The microfilm records from the Index between 1885 and 1888 have been reviewed but contain no entries for Henry (or H.E.) Bothin. Although it is certainly possible that he could have purchased a piece or two of property prior to 1885, I have assumed he probably did not. This assumption is based in large measure on the frequency with which his name begins to appear after 11/23/1888. Thus, a lapse of nearly four years between any earlier purchases and the purchase from Mr. Byrne would seem contrary to his

pattern, and that is why I have assumed that he made no purchases prior to 1888. The first record of any purchase appears to be of a property, the former owner of which was J.M. Byrne. The Index refers the reader to Deed Book #1329, page 35. Unfortunately, all Deed Books prior to 1895 have been lost, so no details about this initial purchase are available.

147 "Elevator," on the website *Wikipedia*, last modified April 18, 2014, accessed April 20, 2014 http://en.wikipedia.org/wiki/elevator. In 1852, Elisha Otis invented a device to prevent the fall of the cab if the cable broke. The article above reported that "a governor device engages knurled roller(s), locking the elevator to its guides should the elevator descend at an unsafe speed. He (Elisha Otis) demonstrated it at the New York Exposition in the Crystal Palace in a dramatic, death-defying presentation in 1854. Then in 1874, a patent was issued to J.W. Meaker for a method which permitted elevator doors to open and close safely. That was followed in 1887 by Alexander Miles' invention of automated doors which would close off the elevator shaft.

148 Ibid.

149 "Home Insurance Building" on the website *Wikipedia, ut sup.*

150 "The Home Insurance Building" on the website *Chicago Architecture Information*, accessed April 20, 2014 http://www.chicagoarchitecture.info/Building/3168/The-Home-Insurance-Building.php.

151 Joseph Korom, Jr., *The American Skyscraper 1850-1940: A Celebration of Height* (Wellesley, MA: Branden Books, 2008), 95.

152 Marten Kuilman, "4.1.4.2. The Future City," Quadralectic Architecture, accessed July 8, 2014, http://quadralectics.wordpress.com/4-representation/4-1-form/4-1-4-cities-in-the-mind/4-1-4-2-the-future-city/.

153 Kelso, *A Romance of Steel in California, ut.sup.*, "Antoine Borel, who in 1884 formed a syndicate to purchase Leland Stanford's interest in the California Street Cable Railroad, was also a

considerable stockholder in the Pacific Rolling Mills Company. In fact, during these years nearly every prominent industrialist or investor in San Francisco owned shares in the company. Listed among its Directors and Officers were such highly regarded businessman and investors as D.O. Mills, William Alvord, John Parrot, James Fair and William Ralston.

Records of the company for 1891—when quarterly dividends of $1.50 per share were paid regularly—show that James G. Fair, with 7,120 shares, was the largest shareholder and that other big name owners of its 20,000 shares were Louis McLane, Daniel Meyer, Calvin Paige, Abby M. Parrot, George Whittell, J.C. and E. Coleman, N. Luning, and James Rolph whose son was to become a famous Mayor of San Francisco and Governor of California."

154 Korom, *The American Skyscraper 1850-1940; A Celebration of Height*, ut.sup., 36.

155 Ibid., 24.

156 Frederick Baumann, *The Art of Preparing Foundations for All Kinds of Buildings, with Particular Illustration of 'The Method of Isolated Piers' as Followed in Chicago* (Chicago: J.M. Wing, 1873).

157 Amy Nutt, "The History of Steel Reinforced Concrete" on the website *Ezine @rticles*, accessed April 20, 2014, http://ezinearticles.com/?The-History-Of-Steel-Reinforced-Concrete&id=795044.

158 "Definition: Manufactured Gas" on the website *Business Dictionary*, accessed April 20, 2014, http://www.businessdictionary.com/definition/manufactured-gas.html.

159 "Electricity" on the website *Wikipedia*, accessed April 20, 2014, http://en.wikipedia.org/wiki/Electricity.

160 "Electrification" on the website *Great Engineering Achievements of the 20th Century*, accessed April 20, 2014, http://www.greatachievements.org/?id=2949.

161 "War of Currents" on the website *Wikipedia*, last modified

April 15, 2014, accessed April 20, 2014, https://en.wikipedia.org/wiki/War_of_Currents; "The Practical Incandescent Light Bulb, on the website *Edison Museum*, accessed April 20, 2014 http://edisonmuseum.org/content3399.html; "How Did Thomas Edison Make the Light Bulb" on the website *20-20 Site*, accessed April 20, 2014, http://www.2020site.org/history/How-Did-Thomas-Edison-Make-the-Light-Bulb.html; "Electric Power Transmission," on the website *Wikipedia* , last modified April 16, 2014, accessed on April 20, 2014, http://en.wikipedia.org/wiki/History_of_electric_power_transmission; "The Inventions of Thomas Edison," on the website *About.com*, accessed April 20, 2014, http://inventors.about.com/library/inventors/bledison.htm;"Thomas Alva Edison" on the website *ThomasEdison.com*, accessed April 14, 2014, http://www.thomasedison.com/enlightened.html; "Edison's Light Bulb," on the website *The Franklin Institute*, accessed on April 20, 2014, http://www.fi.edu/learn/sci-tech/edison-lightbulb/edison-lightbulb.php?cts=electricity.

162 *San Francisco Call*, April 15, 1906.

163 The letter, which has not been independently viewed, was discussed in a Journal on the Callaway family which is found at "The Butte Daily Miner, July 11, 1881" on the website *The Callaway Family Association*, Vol. I, no. 7 (July, 2005), accessed April 20, 2014 www.callawayfamily.org/cfanet/cfanet0705.htm.

164 Property number 106 which is listed as having an address of 225 Sacramento St., between Davis and Front Streets.

165 Dunn v Dunn, 1902, found at 137 Cal 51.

166 Bancroft Whitney Company v. McHugh, 1913, 166 C 140.

167 *San Francisco Call*, November 12, 1907, p.1.

168 As a pure aside, it was reported in the *Daily Alta California*, August 6, 1890, that Henry had been impaneled as a member of the 1890/1891 San Francisco Grand Jury. In California, grand juries have historically performed a civil role of oversight over

local government. Panelists are generally selected from among a group of applicants as opposed to petit jurors who are usually selected at random from voting records and other databases and are required to perform service for a specific trial or period of time. Grand jurors typically serve a one year term, and service can often be quite time consuming and involve investigation into various branches and departments of local government in order to assure taxpayers of the integrity and efficiency of their elected and appointed officials and departments. Whether Henry had applied for service and just how much time he spent during his term will never be known, nor can one speculate whether his jury service might have been a factor in delaying his becoming President of Judson.

169   The author served as a member of the Marin County Grand Jury during the period July, 2001 through June, 2002 and has been active in training subsequent jurors regarding the scope of their authority and the history of the Grand Jury process. California is one of only two states (the other being Nevada) which retain the Civil Grand Jury as an oversight body, and its function today is largely unchanged from the way it functioned back in 1890.

170   *Daily Alta California*, Volume 83, Number 171(December 18, 1890). A seven page summary of the report of the 1890 Grand Jury's findings and recommendations.

171   "The Panic of 1893" on the website *Wikipedia*, last modified April 20, 2014, accessed April 20, 2014, http://en.wikipedia.org/wiki/Panic_of_1893.

172   Kelso, *A Romance of Steel in California, ut sup.*

173   John King, "S.F. Downtown Plan at 25: Foresight and Futility," *SFGate*, last modified July 26, 2011, accessed July 8, 2014, http://www.sfgate.com/bayarea/place/article/S-F-Downtown-Plan-at-25-foresight-and-futility-2353281.php.

174   Neil H. Jacoby and Raymond J. Saulnier, *Business Finance*

and Banking (New York, NY: National Bureau of Economic Research, 1947), 133.

175   Ibid., 132.

176   *San Francisco Call*, January 11, 1903.

177   Walton Bean, *Boss Ruef's San Francisco* (Berkeley: University of California Press, 1952).

178   According to the Alameda branch of the 1908/09 *Attorneys and Bankers Directory of California*, Henry was no longer then listed as a Director of the bank (see page 59 of that Directory).

179   *San Francisco Call*, April 22, 1903.

180   *San Francisco Chronicle*, April 30, 1906.

181   The company took out a paid advertisement in the *Oakland Tribune*, December 22, 1906, in which it listed its officers and directors (which included Henry E. Bothin) and in which it announced, among other things, the following: that as of the day prior to the earthquake and fire it had assets of $456,000, of which $390,000 constituted surplus available for the protection of its policy holders; that as a result of the fire it lost most of its records, including the entire contents of its vault; that 3 weeks after the conflagration it announced in the press that it would pay all losses in full despite its inability to confirm accurately its obligations; that four months after the fire its stockholders unanimously voted to pay the $1,328,000 in confirmed losses to policyholders at one hundred cents on the dollar (presumably by assessing stockholders); and that, as of October 15th, the company had in fact adjusted and paid 595 claims totaling $1,548,367 "without discount or compromise."

The foregoing has been confirmed by Greg Clark, "1906 San Francisco Earthquake and Fire Panorama Photograph," on the website *Mirror-Pole.com*, last modified August, 2008, accessed April 20, 2014, http://mirror-pole.com/sfeq/background/sfp_background.html. The article, written by Greg Clark (a son of an insurance agent who apparently had some knowledge about

The California Insurance Company), notes that the company "...made the unusual decision to cover losses from the earthquake, even though it was not obligated to. It was the only insurance company that did this. Besides providing an important kick-start to the rebuilding effort, the gesture brought new customers." Mr. Clark was discussing a large panorama photograph which the insurer had commissioned photographer, R.J. Waters & Co. to take and to surround by copies of cancelled checks showings payments made to cover the losses. [Note: it is not known what Mr. Clark might mean by his statement that the company paid losses it was not obligated to pay. The fact that it lost its records might well excuse inaccuracies in its adjusting efforts; however, I am aware of no facts to support a legal excuse for non-payment of legitimate losses. What is unique about this particular insurer was its apparent cooperation with its insured customers and its commitment to pay losses at one hundred cents on the dollar rather than contesting claims, offering low ball settlements, drawing out payments, forcing claimants into time consuming litigation, and otherwise attempting to circumvent its obligations as so many other insurers did].

182   *Oakland Tribune,* November 17, 1906. That article briefly mentions the laws of California which establish unlimited liability on the part of shareholders of insurance companies and, having so stated, reports the appreciation of the San Francisco business community and citizenry over the responsible way in which claims adjusting and payment were handled, particularly given the fact that the company's records were all destroyed in the fire. In the article it is mentioned that six assessments had thus far been levied on shareholders in order to come up with the money to cover the insured losses. The article quotes from a letter from one satisfied policy holder, in particular, who stated his strong appreciation of the California Insurance Company's claims handling, noting that it had taken the efforts of the finest attorneys in the City to extract as much as $.30 to $.40 on the dollar from

other insurers with whom he had also had to deal with respect to other insured losses in his business.

183 *San Francisco, CA Ferry Boat Collision, Nov 1901*, on the GenDisasters website, accessed July 31, 2014, http://www3.gendisasters.com/california/3703/san-francisco-ca-ferry-boat-collision-nov-1901.

184 Bob Battersby, et. al., *Ross, California, The People, The Places, The History* (Ross, CA: The Ross Historical Society, 2008).

185 Lincoln Fairley, *Mount Tamalpais, a History* (San Francisco: Scottwall Associates, 1987).

186 I began running in 1970 after reading a book by Colonel Kenneth Cooper entitled Aerobics. Living at the time in San Francisco, I would jog down to the Marina Green—a 1.6 mile circuit around a large open park near the bay—and I would typically see three to four other runners. Now there are typically fifty to one hundred runners out at that time of day. When I first signed up for the Bay to Breakers run in 1971 there were 1,250 entrants. The following year 2,500 entrants ran the race, and it has since ramped up to a high of nearly 100,000 runners.

187 Barry Spitz, *Marin: A History*, (San Anselmo, CA: Potrero Meadow Pub Co., 2006) 104, 105, 116-199.

188 Ibid., 116.

189 Ibid., 162.

190 In 1972, the author and his wife, Jeanie, bought a home on Glenwood Avenue just a stone's throw from Henry's Ross properties. We lived in that house for twenty-one years and raised our three girls in it. We purchased that home before we knew anything about Henry Bothin's life in Ross. My first recollection of knowing anything about a family connection in Ross was of hearing my grandmother, Genevieve Bothin Lyman, recalling, as we drove her to our house one day, the various homes which had belonged to her childhood friends along Lagunitas Road. To say I was surprised is a bit of an understatement. Our home was

located less than 100 yards from the house my grandmother spent so much time in as a child. For reasons later made clear, I cannot say she grew up in Ross because it would appear she lived more with her mother at their home in San Francisco (her mother and Henry having separated at about the time the Ross home was built).

191 Oral History of Genevieve Bothin Lyman deLimur, *ut sup.*

192 Ibid.

193 Ibid.

194 Gary Scales, "A History of the Lugunitas Club" (unpublished, California Room of the Marin County Library); Named Henry Sachan, Rev. Eeffler, Roger Kent and Mrs. Stanley Arnold as members of the Lagunitas Club. "Clubs in Marin (c. 1930s)" (unpublished, California Room of the Marin County Library in a file regarding clubs and bearing number MC-504).

195 Scales, *A History of the Lagunitas Club, ut sup.*

196 "History" (article, appearing in the front of the Roster of the Lagunitas Club). The article indicates that the property on which the Pink Saloon had been built was purchased, sometime during the 1880s, by investors who included Albert Dibblee, Henry F. Allen, Abner Dobie, E.J. McCutchen, the Berry Brothers, E.L. Griffith and James Coffin, most of whom are well known names in the town to this day and many of whose descendants continue to live in Ross and its environs.

197 In 1889 the ranch, then owned by A.P. Hotaling and Warren Dutton, had been sold to Irwin C. Stump of San Francisco. Mr. Stump intended to subdivide the property into "villa and homestead lots and beautify it for settlement." Then, in December, 1893 the ranch was sold in its entirety to Phoebe Apperson Hearst. *The Marin Journal* reported that, on September 18, 1902, Mrs. Hearst sold it to James Tunstead who intended to re-sell it in smaller subdivided parcels. Two months later, on November 27, 1902 *The Marin Journal* reported that Henry Bothin was now the owner. Whether Mr. Tunstead even closed escrow or,

alternatively, simply sold his contract is not known.

198 "'Gentleman' Jim Corbett," on the website *The Cyber Boxing Zone Encyclopedia*, accessed April 20, 2014 www.cyberboxingzone.com/boxing/corbett.htm. See also an article authored by Lionel Ashcroft and published by the Fairfax [CA] Historical Society in the August, 1990 edition of its bulletin, *Fair Facts*; that article is reprinted in its entirety as footnote 1 to its publication Fairfax Historical Society, *Hill Farm and Arequipa* (Fairfax, CA: Fairfax Historical Society, 1997).

199 Jack Mason and Helen Van Cleave Park, *The Making of Marin*, (Inverness, CA: North Shore Press, 1980), 130.

200 *Nicasio, a Valley in Transition*, Marin County Planning Department (1970).

201 Mason and Park, *The Making of Marin*, *ut sup.*, 130-131.

202 *Marin Journal*, November 27, 1902. This article pre-dates the close of escrow on the property, but was presumably written shortly after it had become public knowledge that Henry was in contract to buy it from Phoebe Hearst. Its reference to speculation that Henry intended building a large home on it for himself is clearly in error since Henry was, at that time, also in the process of purchasing the large plot on Lagunitas described supra.

203 For more information on Elizabeth Ashe the reader is directed to a book entitled Elizabeth Ashe, *Intimate Letters from France and Extracts from the Diary of Elizabeth Ashe 1917 to 1919* (Whitefish, MT: Kessinger Publishing LLC, 2005), 228 pp.. The book, which contains a series of unedited letters and diary entries written by Miss Ashe during her service as a nurse in the Red Cross during the First World War, was copywritten in 1931 by Elizabeth Ashe and published in that same year by Bruce Brough Press. It contains an introduction signed A.G. which is believed to have been her friend and lifelong co-activist, Alice Griffith. That introduction provides a glimpse of Miss Ashe's character and stubborn pursuit of good deeds, describing, as it

does, her efforts to serve as a nurse in France as early as 1914, well before the United States was drawn into the Great War. Although she was initially turned down, once America entered the war, she again volunteered for service and, despite being over the age limit, was able to successfully plead her case and ultimately spent two years in the midst of the conflict.

204   *Hill Farm and Arequipa, ut sup.* 6.

205   Elizabeth Ashe, "Memo" (memo in the files of the Bothin Helping Fund, undated).. It appears in the files of the Bothin Helping Fund; however, its source is not identified. The memo provides further information about little Tony Garcia, his surgically repaired hip, his reluctance to try to walk, and his use of crutches to try to walk during that summer of 1905. She went on to remark at how Tony had later developed an interest in photography, how he had ended up in the employ of professional photographer, Gabriel Moulin, and how pleased and astonished she was to see him years later when he rode his motorcycle up to her cottage and told her that he was then a captain in Broemmel's motor delivery service.

206   Mary E. Whitney, *Valley, River and Mountain, ut sup.*

207   The building still stands as of the date of this writing in 2014. It has gone through different ownerships and is now known as the Nevins Building.

208   Whitney, *Valley, River and Mountain, ut sup.* 189.

209   Ibid., 189.

210   Mary E. Whitney, *Vignettes of the Valley, ut sup.*, 87.

211   Gladys Hansen "San Francisco Earthquake History 1769-1879," on the website *The Virtual Museum of the City of San Francisco,* accessed April 20, 2014 http://www.sfmuseum.org/alm/quakes1.html and http://www.sfmuseum.org/alm/quakes2.html.

212   Ibid. The first large earthquake to hit the City occurred, eerily, nearly 50 years to the hour before the 1906 event. Thus, at 5:23

AM on February 15, 1856, a severe shock, "preceded by a heavy rumbling noise…" caused property damage and also caused the water in the bay to rise several feet, hold that height for several minutes, and then to fall two feet below its ordinary level.

A quake in 1858 caused large cracks to appear in the Merchant's Exchange, to shake off several cornices from the U.S. District Courthouse, to shake off plaster at City Hall, and to ring a number of bells throughout the area.

On October 8, 1865 an earthquake is reported to have "wrecked … much of San Francisco" and specifically to have destroyed Popper's Building at the corner of Battery and Washington Streets, rendered a firehouse at Market and Sansome Streets uninhabitable, knocked Stoddard's warehouse on Beale Street off its foundation, broken windows throughout the city, broken water and gas pipes as well as lamp posts, and opened a nearly one inch wide fissure on Howard St. from 7th St. to 9th St.

On October 21, 1868 a large earthquake caused four people to lose their lives after being hit by falling cornices and chimneys, and a fifth to be killed by a falling masonry wall. It wrecked several buildings, caused some buildings near the bay to sink by anywhere from six inches to several feet, and created numerous fissures measuring up to six inches wide.

On March 30, 1898, an earthquake, lasting forty seconds, twisted chimneys, broke chandeliers, collapsed at least one building and damaged many others, and caused at least $350,000 in damage to the Naval Base at Mare Island.

213 This, greatly simplified, is my understanding of Professor Henry Fielding Reid's theory of elasticity. Being no geologist, I have tried to express it in lay terms and in few words, and hopefully I have not done Professor Reid too much of a disservice. To the extent my explanation is not fully accurate, I accept responsibility and apologize.

214 Mark Twain, *Roughing It* (Hartford, CT: American Publishing Co., 1872).

215 John Muir, *Our National Parks* (Boston and New York: Houghton, Mifflin and Company, 1901), 261-267.

216 "The Annals of San Francisco," on the website *The Virtual Museum of the City of San Francisco* www.sfmuseum.org/hist1/fire.html, accessed April 20, 2014. The first major fire occurred on December 24, 1849 and did over $1,000,000 of damage (using 1849 dollars). That fire destroyed the Plaza adjacent to Dennison's Exchange as well as the whole line of buildings on the south side of Washington Street between Montgomery and Kearney Streets.

Six months later, on May 4, 1850, a fire consumed three blocks of "the most valuable buildings in the City" at a cost of $4,000,000.

One month later, on June 14, 1850, a fire took out everything within a rectangle enclosed by Clay, Kearny, and California Streets and the bay.

A fourth large fire broke out on September 17, 1850 and did damage totaling only about $250,000. The reason for the more modest damage estimate is that the area involved had already been burned over and, so, had little remaining property to destroy.

On December 14, 1850, a fifth great fire started, doing damage estimated at yet another $1,000,000.

Finally, the sixth great fire occurred on May 4, 1851 (a year to the day after the second). That fire did more damage than the combined total of the earlier five. Starting in a paint and upholstery store, it generated hurricane force winds, was allegedly visible 100 miles out to sea, and ended up burning between 1,500 and 2,000 houses as well as destroying everything within the eighteen block main business district of the City. The burned area extended ¾ mile from north to south and 1/3 of a mile from east to west, and damage was estimated at $12,000,000.

217 "1906 Earthquake and Fire" on the website *Guardians of the City*, the website of the San Francisco Fire Department, accessed April 20, 2014, http://guardiansofthecity.org/sffd/fires/great_fires/1906.html.

218 "The Great 1906 San Francisco Earthquake and Fire" on the website *Historynet.com*, accessed April 20, 2014, http://www.historynet.com/the-great-1906-san-francisco-earthquake-and-fire.htm.

219 "1906 San Francisco Earthquake" on the website *Wikipedia*, last modified April 19, 2014, accessed April 20, 2014.

220 James B. Stetson, *Personal Recollections During the Eventful Days of April, 1906. ut sup.*

221 Wayne Bonnett, *Victorian Classics of San Francisco* (Sausalito, CA: Windgate Press, 1987), ix. An explanation is in order about Genevieve's name. After Edmunds Lyman's death in 1964, his widow, Genevieve, remarried Andre deLimur. Hence her name as it appears in the quote.

222 I highly recommend that the reader search out and read James Stetson's account. Not only is it masterfully written (given that it was undoubtedly meant, when written, as an account to be seen by family and friends only), but it also contains a beautifully written account by his grandson who was at school in Belmont and who managed to come back to the city in search of family.

223 Oral History of Genevieve Bothin Lyman deLimur. *ut sup.*

224 "1906 San Francisco Earthquake" on the website *Wikipedia*, last modified April 19, 2014, accessed April 20, 2014.

225 At the risk of diverting attention from Henry Bothin, I feel I must respond to the conclusion of Wikipedia's authors. What follows in this endnote is only my opinion and is not presented as fact. I personally believe that San Francisco's loss of primacy had as much, if not more, to do with other issues. In large part, the change reflects the strong effort by Los Angelinos to attract people and industry to their part of the state. People

were drawn by climate, beaches, cheap land, and by a far friendlier business climate than was the case in San Francisco. Those attractions were brought about because of aggressive actions by Los Angeles businessmen to bring water to their city from the Owens Valley, 250 miles to the north, and by subsequently enlarging on those flows by virtue of the Peripheral Canal. The movie industry became a huge draw, as did the wartime aviation industry. Finally, another draw was the annexation of the San Fernando Valley which, in combination with the development of major freeways, caused an explosion of growth in the suburbs. That growth continued to accelerate after the end of WW II, and the later growth was fueled in part by massive influxes of people from all over the world. As noted by Kevin Starr in a speech to the Los Angeles World Affairs Council on May 5, 2003, Los Angeles has the largest native-American population in the United States as well as the nation's largest pool of immigrants from Korea, Mexico, Armenia, Iran, Ethiopia, and China.

To the contrary, San Francisco has lost much of its allure for business. What began with the longshoremen's' strikes on the San Francisco waterfront during the mid-1930s (which badly tarnished its port's attraction to business) has continued with an anti-business political tilt which remains today.

226 Many sources were reviewed in preparation of this section on the earthquake and fire. They include the following: "San Francisco Earthquake, 1906" on the website *National Archives*, accessed April 20, 2014 http://www.archives.gov/legislative/features/sf/; "The Great 1906 San Francisco Earthquake" on the website *USGS*, accessed April 20, 2014 http://earthquake.usgs.gov/regional/nca/1906/18april/index.php; "The San Andreas Fault" on the website *USGS*, accessed on April 20, 2014 http://pubs.usgs.gov/gip/earthq3/safaultgip.html; "The 1906 San Francisco Earthquake and Fire—Enduring Lessons for Fire Protection and Water Supply" on the website *Earthquake Spectra*, accessed April 20, 2014 http://earthquakespectra.org/doi/abs/10.1193/1.2186678?journalCode=eqsa; "Jack London

and the April, 1906, San Francisco Earthquake" on the website *UCSB Projects*, accessed April 20, 2014 http://projects.eri.ucsb.edu/understanding/accounts/london.html; "Charles Darwin and the February 20, 1835, Concepcion, Chile Earthquake" on the website *UCSB Projects*, accessed April 20, 2014 http://projects.eri.ucsb.edu/understanding/accounts/darwin.html; "Mark Twain and the October 8, 1865, San Francisco Earthquake" on the website *UCSB Projects*, accessed April 20, 2014 http://projects.eri.ucsb.edu/understanding/accounts/twain.html;

"1906 Great Earthquake and Fire" on the website *Guardians of the City*, ut sup.http://guardiansofthecity.org/sffd/fires/great_fires/1906.html; "The Navy and the Earthquake and Fire of 1906" on the website The California Military Museum, accessed April 20, 2014 http://www.militarymuseum.org/PerrySFEarthquake.html. "The Great 1906 Earthquake and Fire" on the website *Historynet.com*, ut sup. http://www.historynet.com/the-great-1906-san-francisco-earthquake-and-fire.htm.

227 "Seven Ways to Compare the Relative Value of a U.S. Dollar Amount—1774 to Present" on the website *MeasuringWorth.com*, accessed April 20, 2014, http://www.measuringworth.com/calculators/compare/ There are five different ways to calculate the relative value of a U.S. dollar over time. The most conservative, the CPI, places the value of a 1906 dollar at $22.40 as of 2005. The other values range upward from there to as high as $402.40. Using the latter benchmark (based on the relative share of GDP), the total damage would be over $500,000,000,000.

228 *San Francisco Chronicle*, June 2, 1906.

229 *San Francisco Examiner*, April 22, 1906.

230 Gladys Hansen and Emmet Condon, *Denial of Disaster: The Untold Story and Photographs of the San Francisco Earthquake and Fire of 1906* (Petaluma, CA: Cameron & Company, 1989), 124. (source attributed to Chairman Atwood of the Fire Underwriters' Adjustment Committee).

231 Ibid., 127.

232 George W. Brooks, *The Spirit of 1906* (Whitefish, MT: Kessinger Publishing, 2004). Mr. Brooks, in his forward, noted that he hoped his reminiscences would convey some indication of "…the character of the men who composed the directors and stockholders of the California Insurance Company, who acted well their part, who fought the good fight and held the faith, whose stern sense of duty and heroic courage led them to lay upon the altar of their idealism the financial sacrifices which they made." He went on to say "Theirs is the honor achieved. They neither faltered nor hesitated in upholding and protecting their own individual good name…[and]…the fair name of the Company…"

233 Ibid.

234 Ibid.

235 "Letter dated May 2, 1906 from Henry Bothin to P.N. Myers," (letter in the Lake Hemet Water Company Papers (LHWCP), Hemet Public Library, 904.75).

236 "Letter dated May 15, 1906 from Henry Bothin to P. N. Myers," (letter in the Lake Hemet Water Company Papers (LHWCP), Hemet Public Library, 904.75).

237 Interestingly, it would appear that Mr. Osborn had initially been on Frank Whittier's payroll in Hemet and that Whittier released him during a shakeup but recommended him to Henry as a good secretary.

238 George D. Squires was Henry's attorney (who would later represent him in his divorce from Jennie). Hugh T. Roberts was a "bookkeeper" (per census data) for Judson Steel Co.—probably Henry's chief financial advisor. J. (John) D. Osborne appears in census data to have been the Secretary of Judson Steel Co. Hence he was presumably Henry's secretary. Harry J. Kaufman was Henry's nephew—the then twenty-seven year old son of his sister, Amelia. Interestingly, Kaufman would later alienate family members and Henry too because of a failed mining venture (Churchill Mining Company) into which he persuaded

Henry and Henry's wife, Ellen, to invest $2,000 each and in which Henry, in turn, persuaded other family members to invest as well. The venture failed, and, although apparently remorseful about his debts, Kaufman was unable to repay any of the family members any part of their investment. Ultimately Henry, who had lost his own investment, was pressured by some of his family members, primarily his sister, Minnie Sadler, to repay their lost investments as well. This became a bone of family contention for some time, and it is not known what ever became of Harry.

239 At his death, the list of properties owned by Henry Bothin and/or the Bothin Real Estate Company included the following:

1 NW corner of Battery & Merchants St. (437 Battery St), SF—3 story + basement Class C brick building erected in 1907.

2 SE corner of Green & Polk St. (2224-54 Polk St.), SF—4 story + basement, Class C2 brick building known as Avondale Apartments & consisting of 42 three-room apartments and seven stores.

3 2222 Polk St.—Two story Class "A" building housing a machine shop.

4 SW corner of Howard & 8th St.—one story + basement reinforced concrete Class "C" building.

5 SW corner of Van Ness Ave. & Lombard St. (2760-62 Van Ness Ave., with a 2 story frame flat dwelling.

6 661-7 Howard St. (between 3rd & Hawthorne St.) with 2 story + basement Class "C" building.

7 30-40 Natoma St. (between 1st & 2nd St.) with 3 story + basement Class "C" brick building.

8 48 Natoma St. (between 1st & 2nd) with Class "C" 2 story concrete building.

9 57-65 Clementina St. (between 1st & 2nd St) with an old corrugated iron shop.

10 65 Clementina St. (between 1st & 2nd St) with old four room frame cottage.

11   530 Folsom St. (corner of Folsom & Ecker) with 4 story plus basement Class "C" brick building.

12   33-7 Clementina St. with 3 story + partial basement Class "C" brick building.

13   63-73 Minna St. (between 1st & 2nd St.) with 3 story + basement Class "C" brick building.

14   144-52 Second St. (between Minna & Natoma St) with 3 story Class "C" brick building.

15   NE Corner of 8th and Clementina Streets between Howard and Folsom, known as 251 8th St., with 2 story reinforced concrete Class "C" factory building.

16   1932-49 Polk St. & 1589 Pacific Ave. which together had a frame and corrugated iron garage building with cement floor.

17   580 Folsom St. (between 1st & 2nd St.) with 3 story concrete Class "C" building.

18   79 Clementina St. with a one story corrugated iron shop.

19   Property known as Marin Ranch, consisting of two pieces, one @482 acres and one @570 acres. [Note, these are the residual pieces of the Hearst Ranch after the gifts to the Bothin Convalescent Home and Arequipa].

20   NE corner of Sansome & Jackson St. known as 700-10 Jackson St. with one story brick building with steel truss roof.

21   537 6th St. (between Bryant and Brannon St) with 2 story Class "C" brick building.

22   541 6th St. with 2 story brick building.

23   561 6th St. with one story brick warehouse.

24   612-24 California St. (between Grant and Kearny) with 3 story + basement Class "C" brick building.

25   602-6 Mission St. (between New Montgomery & 2nd St.) with 10 story + basement brick, concrete and steel office building.

26   15 lots in Sausalito containing a total of 152 acres.

27   SE corner of Van Ness & Olive St. (between O'Farrell & Ellis St.) known as 928 Van Ness Ave. with single story + basement &

mezzanine reinforced concrete building.

28 325-35 Pacific Ave. (between Battery & Sansome St.) with 3 story Class "C" brick building.

29 61 Natoma St. (between 1st & 2nd St.) with one story + mezzanine reinforced concrete building.

30 67 Natoma St. (between 1st & 2nd St.) with two story Class "C" reinforced concrete building.

31 546-48-50 Howard St. (between 1st & 2nd St.) with two story + basement Class "C" brick building.

32 552-4 Howard St. with 3 story + basement reinforced concrete Class "C" building.

33 910 Harrison St. (between 5th & 6th St.) with one story & mezzanine reinforced concrete building under construction.

34 228-34 Fremont St. (between Howard & Folsom St.) with 3 story + basement brick building.

35 236 Fremont St. with one story brick building.

36 SE corner of Polk & Jackson St. with a large two entry brick building entered from both 1591 Jackson and 1840 Polk St.

37 1836 Polk St. with a Class "C" single story & part basement brick building.

38 471-477 Clementina St. (between 5th & 6th St.) with a one story and mezzanine Class "C" reinforced concrete building.

39 1174-98 Howard St. (NE corner of Howard & 8th St.) with single story & part mezzanine Class "C" reinforced concrete building.

40 807 Montgomery St. (between Pacific & Jackson St.) with Class "C" two story + basement brick building.

41 1379 Sutter St. (between Van Ness & Franklin St.) with 3 ½ story frame residential building used as a rooming house.

42 42 Natoma St. (between 1st & 2nd St.) with one story brick shop building.

43 46-8 Natoma St. with one story + basement brick & corrugated iron building.

44 54 Natoma St. with two story + basement brick building.

45 60 Natoma St. with two story + basement brick building.

46 260-66 Spear St. (between Howard and Folsom St.) with older 1 story brick building.

47 461-463 Haight St. (between Fillmore & Webster St.) with 2 story + basement frame store and flat.

48 471-73-75 Haight St. with one story + basement furniture store building.

49 39-41 Tehama St. (between 1st & 2nd St.) with 1 story galvanized iron shack in poor condition.

50 500-516 Howard St. (NW corner of Howard & 1st St.) with 5 story + basement Class "B" reinforced concrete building.

51 39 Natoma St. with one story + mezzanine Class "C" reinforced concrete building.

52 611-15 Mission St. (between 2nd & New Montgomery St.) with 6 story and basement reinforced concrete Class "B" building.

53 Vacant lot at SW corner of Van Ness & Bay Streets.

54 201-8 Eighth St. (corner of 8th & Howard St.) with 2 story + part basement Class "B" reinforced concrete building.

55 Vacant lot on south side of Howard Street between 5th and 6th St.

56 NW corner of 1st & Tehama Streets with old corrugated iron shack on lot.

57 243-7 Fremont St. and 255-65 Fremont St. (between Howard & Folsom St.) with two story + basement Class "C" brick building in three units.

58 Vacant Lot on Mission Street between Julia and 7th St.

59 Vacant lot on Bay Street between Franklin and Van Ness St.

60 Vacant lot at the NE corner of Polk and Greenwich St.

61 Vacant lot on Polk Street between Lombard and Greenwich Streets.

62 1208-18 Howard St. (between 8th & 9th St.) with Class "C" reinforced concrete one story + mezzanine building.

63 2954 Van Ness Ave. (between Francisco & Chestnut St.) with 2

story frame and stucco house.

64 2912 Van Ness Ave. (between Francisco & Chestnut St.) with 2 story frame and plaster house.

65 Vacant lot on Howard Street between 6th and 7th Streets.

66 1868-90 Lombard St. and 3302-10 Buchanin St.—3 two story frame buildings of four flats each.

67 SE corner of Webster and Lombard Streets with two story frame house and small shack.

68 Vacant lot on 3rd St. south of Bryant.

69 SE corner of Brannan & Ritch Streets with two story + basement Class "B" reinforced concrete building under construction.

70 2450-80 Lombard St. (between Scott & Divisadero) with 2 two story shingle & frame building containing four flats.

71 2576-98 Lombard St. and 3102-4 Broderick St. (corner of Lombard and Broderick) with 2 two story shingle and frame buildings, each containing four flats.

72 2508-22 Lombard St. and 3201-7 Divisadero (NW Corner of Lombard and Divisadero St.) with 3 two story shingle and frame buildings of four flats each.

73 2511-25 Lombard St. (between Divisadero & Broderick St.) with 2 two story frame and shingle buildings of four flats each.

74 Vacant lot on north side of Lombard between Divisadero and Broderick St.

75 Vacant lot on SE corner of Greenwich and Broderick St.

76 Vacant lot on SW corner of Greenwich and Divisadero St.

77 Vacant lot of Ritch St. south of Brannan St.

78 1444 Green St. (between Van Ness and Polk St.) with single story reinforced concrete building.

79 Vacant lot SW corner of Ritch and Brannan St.

80 3141-7 Buchanan St. & 2001-29 Greenwich St. (corner of Buchanan & Greenwich) with 3 two story frame and shingle buildings, each containing four flats.

81 1433 and 1439-43 Greenwich St. (between Polk and Van Ness with a frame residence and a framed building with 3 flats and a basement.

82 Vacant lot on west side of Van Ness Ave. between Chestnut and Francisco Streets.

83 Vacant lot on Ritch Street 200' north of Brannan St.

84 Vacant lot on Zoe Street north of Brannan.

85 Vacant lot on Bay Street between Gough and Franklin Streets.

86 Vacant lot on Tehama St. west of 2nd St.

87 Vacant lot on SW corner of Ritch and Bryant Streets.

88 Vacant lot on north side of Lombard St. between Webster and Fillmore Streets.

89 1612-16 Pacific Ave. (between Van Ness and Polk) with 2 story frame store and flat.

90 333 7th St. (NE corner of 7th and Cleveland St.) with two story Class "C" reinforced concrete and steel building.

91 Vacant lot on south side of Tehama St. 150' east of 6th St.

92 230-38 Eighth St. (SW corner of 8th and Tehama St.) with two story Class "C" brick building.

93 Vacant lot on Stillman St. west of 3rd St.

94 281-83 Second St. (near Folsom St.) with single story + basement corrugated iron shop building.

95 Vacant lot on Minna St. 315' west of 8th St.

96 Vacant lot on Guerrero St. 200' north of 16th St.

97 "Old Hibernia Brewery" Property on Howard between 8th and 9th St. with old 3 story brick building and obsolete brewery equipment.

98 732-46 Brannan St. (NE corner of Brannan and Boardman St.) with two story Class "C" brick building.

99 Vacant lot on 6th St. north of Brannan.

100 509 and 512 Howard St. (between 1st & 2nd St.) with three story + part basement Class "C" brick building.

101   208-10 First St. with 3 story + basement brick building.

102   527 Mission St. (between 1st & 2nd St.) with three story Class "C" brick building.

103   521 Mission St. (between 1st & 2nd St.) with three story + basement Class "C" brick building.

104   613 Sansome St. (between Washington & Jackson St.) with two story + basement Class "C" brick building.

105   Two story concrete garage building known as #2 Hunt St. and 175 Natoma St. sitting on "L" shaped lot located at the end of Natoma St. near New Montgomery St.

106   225 Sacramento St. (between Davis and Front Streets) with single story + basement brick building.

107   809 Folsom St. (between 4th and 5th St.) with one story + mezzanine Class "C" reinforced concrete building.

108   817 Folsom St. with one story concrete building with steel truss roof.

109   819-21 Folsom St. with an "L" shaped single story + mezzanine galvanized iron warehouse building.

110   408-10-12 Valencia St. (between 15th and 16th St.) with a single story + basement Class "C" reinforced concrete store building.

111   25-31 Fremont St. (between Market and Mission St.) with a four story + basement Class "C" brick building.

112   1440 Broadway (between Polk and Larkin St.) with a reinforced concrete garage building.

113   Property known as "Bothin Park" consisting of a 12.6 acre subdivision in Fairfax in Marin County and containing 28 unsold lots and six lots under purchase contracts.

114   Home in Ross (corner of Glenwood and Lagunitas Road) and consisting of approximately 2.8 acres (note: this may be an error on the low side of acreage).

115   9.2 acre parcel of land in Ross immediately east of the Lagunitas Club and extending from Hazel Ave. (now Duff Lane) up the hill to the southern corporate limits of the town of Ross.

116 535 Sacramento St. and 136-8 Liedesdorff St. (corner of Sacramento and Liedesdorff) with three story and basement brick loft building.

117 Four parcels of land in Hemet, of which two were improved with two story brick and concrete buildings.

118 Ranchlands near Hemet in Riverside County, consisting of approximately 157 acres improved with apricot, peach and orange orchards.

119 Approximately 430 acres of land on and around Park Hill (a subdivision of Hemet) and comprising 29 lots averaging nearly 15 acres each—essentially most of the lands in that part of Hemet—and including water rights thereto as represented by water certificates issued by Hemet Water Company (Frank Whittier's company).

120 Approximately 440 acres of land in various parcels in and around Santa Barbara, including Montecito, Summerland, and Cold Springs Canyon.

240 *San Francisco Chronicle*, June 2, 1906.

241 Henry Bothin's PG&E obituary, *ut sup.*

242 *San Francisco Call*, September 2, 1906 reported that Mrs. William Irwin, Mrs. William Hinkley Taylor, and Mrs. George Boyd played bridge often but the Miss Jennie Blair, Mrs. Henry Bothin, and Miss Lillie O'Connor were experts at the game.

243 *San Francisco Call*, October 9, 1907.

244 Gabriel Moulin, *Gabriel Moulin's San Francisco Peninsula: Town & Country Homes, 1910-1930* (Sausalito, CA: Windgate Press, 1985), note 78 p.201.

245 *San Francisco Call*, October 5, 1907, reported: "At Ross, Mrs. Henry E. Bothin is easily the champion, although the Misses Coffin, Mrs. Ed Schmeidell and some of the other women of the Ross colony are far past the A,B,C of horsemanship." That article went on to explain Jennie's familiarity with horses and her recognition of the features which distinguish a good horse from one not so good. The reporter wrote: "She knows a horse

too, from hair to hoof, and she doesn't go by the studbook either. The Bothins have great pride in their stables—not just for how many dollars the horses stand for, but how few. They like a horse for his style, not for his blood, and the best stepper and highest-headed horse of the four is one Mrs. Bothin discovered one day hitched to a butcher-boy's cart. The purchase price was just $15, and the Bothins are not ashamed of it. The horse had good stuff in him, and a banged tail, good feeding, and proper grooming did the rest. Which may mean that horses with pedigrees had better look to their laurels now that women have taken to the whip."

246 "Gossip from the San Francisco Weeklies," *Oakland Tribune*, June 12, 1909.

247 *Oakland Tribune*, October 8, 1907, p.9.

248 *San Francisco Examiner*, January 11, 1908.

249 Children's Hospital was founded in 1875 by three physicians, Dr. Charlotte Blake Brown (the mother, incidentally, of Dr. Philip King Brown who started Arequipa), Dr. Sara E. Brown, and Dr. Martha E. Bucknell. Among other firsts, it was the first training school for nurses west of the Rockies. During its first several decades of existence its primary goals were to provide medical care for women and children, to further the advancement of women in medicine, and to serve as a center for training and education of nurses. Although Jennie Bothin was never, to the author's knowledge, a member of its Board of Directors, she certainly was highly supportive of the hospital, and both she and Henry were financial contributors all during their married lives.

250 *San Francisco Call*, January 14, 1905.

251 *Oakland Tribune*, October 8, 1907.

252 "Tracing Donna Baumrind's 3 Parenting Styles Through History! The Essence of the Dominant Child Rearing Paradigms" on the website *Positive-Parenting-Ally.com*, accessed

April 20, 2014 www.positive-parenting-ally.com/parenting-styles.html.

253   Oral History of Genevieve Bothin Lyman deLimur. *ut sup.*

254   Oral History of Genevieve Bothin Lyman deLimur. *ut sup.* The following colloquy appears:

Ehat: "Tell me, what brought your Father from Ohio in about 1875. What brought him to California?

Genevieve: I haven't the slightest idea.

Ehat: Did he ever tell you why?

Genevieve: I haven't the slightest idea and I know nothing about his mother and father. I just know that he came to San Francisco and then I don't know whether he lived here long or not and then he married my mother in San Francisco.

255   Ibid.

256   Genevieve died when she was just two months shy of her eighty-ninth birthday. She was born on December 17, 1894, and she died on October 23, 1983.

257   "Letter from Frank Whittier to J.W. Crump, manager of Hemet Lake and Water Company, dated June 12, 1908"(in the files of the Hemet Lake and Water Company).

258   "Letter from William Weir to Will Whittier dated February 13, 1919." (Part of the LHWCP papers found in the Hemet Public Library).

259   Marin County Superior Court action number 3062. See schedule of real estate owned at Henry's death which is a part of the inventory of his assets as it appears in the probate records.

260   Burgess, *The Water King, ut sup.*, 29-32.

261   The town of Standish was named after Mayflower passenger, Miles Standish. It is, today, a suburb of Portland, lying less than 20 miles outside Portland. Interestingly, it is only about 80 miles away from Vienna, Maine, where Henry Bothin's first wife's family (both paternal and maternal) were all born and raised.

262 Burgess, *The Water King, ut sup.*, 67-70.

263 Ibid. Ellen Hasty Chabot's twin sister, Emily, was married to Daniel Comstock, a miner. They had two boys, Frank and Harry. According to the 1870 census, the boys were, respectively, approximately six and three years older than baby Ellen.

264 Burgess, *The Water King*, chapter 11, 124-138. Lake Chabot's capacity for water storage was 5,000,000,000 gallons.

265 Ibid., 95.

266 Ibid., 142.

267 Ibid., 151.

268 Ibid., 171-172.

269 Ibid., 174.

270 Terry Carter (the granddaughter of Felix Rubalcava who was the head groundskeeper at Piranhurst from 1941 until his death in the late 1980s), interview with the author. Terry's mother, several uncles (including Isador Gonzalez), and aunts all worked for Ellen, and Terry's comments reflected the sentiments of all the family members who she contacted. In terms of attention to detail, Terry's mother told Terry about the requirement that all the gravel be freshly raked every day, that the children not walk or play on the gravel after it was raked, that it was not enough to prune the potted orange trees but that they also had to be dusted, and that in general she (Ellen) expected everything to be properly arranged and in its place.

271 Ibid.

272 David Heerfield (a close friend and confidant of Genevieve's during her later years) in an interview with the author during the 1980s. Mr. Heerfield explained a great deal about Genevieve, her dislike of her father, her lack of self-confidence, her insecurity, the reasons she married the man she did, and a great number of other insights into what made her the person she was.

In this regard, Genevieve Bothin Lyman was one of the funniest people the author has ever met. She was silly, and she saw humor everywhere and made people laugh uproariously. And yet, she was stifled in her marriage to Edmunds Lyman, a man who she married mainly because he was the first person who, according to Mr. Heerfield, ever told her she was beautiful. After Edmunds died, she married Andre de Limur, a widower with whom she spent probably the happiest years of her life. During those last few years of her life, she blossomed, and one could see how happy he made her feel. The family has always appreciated the fact that she had those years of joy.

273 *Marin County Tocsin*, July 31, 1909, a local weekly newspaper.

274 *Marin County Tocsin*, September 18, 1909.

275 Marin County Superior Court action number 3062. See schedule of real estate owned at Henry's death which is a part of the inventory of his assets as it appears in the probate records.

276 KSW Properties purchased the assets of Bothin Real Estate Company in 1971. They in turn began taking steps to develop the property around Richardson Bay, which led the Trust For Public Land, in 1975, to purchase an option to buy the property for $195,000. The property is now owned by the Marin County Open Space District and was renamed by them the Bothin Marsh to honor Henry's memory. See Barry Spitz, Open Spaces: Lands of the Marin County Open Space District (San Rafael, CA: Marin County Open Space District, 2000), 75.

277 Minutes of the Lagunitas Club, 1916.

278 "Report to Members by President, Lloyd Baldwin," in the Minutes of the Lagunitas Club, 1922.

279 That trophy, incidentally, has been given, ever since 1920, to the winners of the annual Bothin Mixed Doubles Tennis Tournament. It is still considered by many to be the most prestigious event of the Lagunitas Club tennis season.

280 The guest fee resolution (to charge nonmember guests a fee of

$.50 for use of the courts during the week and $1.00 per use on weekends) initially passed but was brought back up later on a motion to rescind. Following discussion, the weekend fee was rescinded and the weekday fee was allowed to stand. So, on that effort, he was able to at least score a partial victory.

281 Fairfax Historical Society, *Hill Farm and Arequipa*, ut sup., 15.
282 Dr. Philip King Brown's mother was Dr. Charlotte Blake Brown, his sister Dr. Adelaide Brown, his son Dr. Cabot Brown. Charlotte Blake Brown is of particular interest inasmuch as she was the founder of Children's Hospital in San Francisco, a hospital on whose board our family has a long history of involvement. Jennie Whittier Bothin was a founding member, and my grandmother and my mother have both had lifelong associations with the hospital.
283 *The Independent*, January 24, 1911. The size of Henry's second gift of land was 50 acres.
284 *The Independent*, September 24, 1911.
285 *San Francisco Chronicle*, September 1, 1911.
286 *San Francisco Chronicle*, September 3, 1911.
287 "Arequipa" on the website *Wikipedia*, last modified April 19, 2014, accessed April 20, 2014. The name "Arequipa" (the name given to what is now the second largest city in Peru) does not exist as a word but is thought to derive either from the local words "ari quepay" (meaning "yes, stay") or from words in the Aymaran language which translate to something like "near the mountain." Harvard University maintained an observatory at Arequipa around the turn of the 20th century. It may well be that Dr. Philip King Brown studied there and proposed its name for his sanatorium given Arequipa's elevation (about 7,600 feet above sea level) and proximity to the Andes, all of which suggests abundant fresh air.
288 William Sagar (Fairfax historian) "Unknown San Francisco Newspaper—September 3, 1911" (copy typed from an original

and given to the author by Mr. Sagar on January 14, 2009, as part of a packet of clippings.

289 Ibid. The article about Arequipa by Ida Brooks is found in an unknown newspaper (presumably one of the Marin weeklies). It was provided to me by Fairfax historian, William Sagar, on January 14, 2009 along with numerous other newspaper clippings regarding Arequipa, Hill Farm and other aspects of the life of Henry Bothin. Mr. Sagar, who re-typed the article for easier reading since it was not well preserved on microfilm, is entitled "Wooing Life Anew at the Potters Wheel." According to Mr. Sagar's attribution, it was published in "UNKNOWN NEWSPAPER-Oct. 1912."

290 Ibid. This article was also provided to me by historian, William Sagar. It contains original photographs and is obviously a copy of a published document; however, the only attribution available is a footer which appears at the bottom of page one and says: "Reprinted from The Survey of December 7, 1912. Whether there was at that time a medical periodical entitled "The Survey" is not known. The article was apparently found and copied by Mr. Sagar's predecessor at the Fairfax Historical Society, and that individual did not provide its source.

291 *Los Angeles Times*, March 2, 1913; *The Independent*, July 21, 1914; *Marin Journal*, February 4, 1915 (this article was re-printed from an undated edition of *The Building and Engineering News*).

292 The Oakland Museum of California houses the largest known permanent collection of Arequipa pottery and tiles, consisting of over one hundred pieces. Most of these were given to the Museum by Phoebe Hearst Brown, the daughter of Dr. Philip King Brown.

In addition, and ironically, some 8,750 ceramic tiles, all made by patients at Arequipa, were used in the construction of the lower great hall and the upstairs corridor of Casa Dorinda, a 65 room Spanish Colonial mansion in Montecito which was built by Mr. and Mrs. William Bliss. Mrs. Bliss, nee Anna Dorinda, met Dr.

Philip King Brown on a trip to Alaska and described her project to him and her quest for just the right floor tiles. Dr. Brown described the pottery being made at Arequipa, and the Bliss' then commissioned the production of 8,750 tiles for their home. That mansion is now a retirement home, and its Admission Director, Lorraine Darrow, confirms that the tiles are all still in place and that the upstairs tiles (which are covered in carpet) remain in excellent condition. Thus, in a totally unexpected way, the best surviving examples of Arequipa tiles, made possible in the first place by the generosity of Henry Bothin, are, by pure coincidence, located in Montecito, the very community in which he maintained a summer residence, spent considerable time later in life, and ultimately died.

293 *San Francisco Chronicle*, August 7, 1928.

294 "History of Santa Barbara, California" on the website *Wikipedia*, last modified April 12, 2014, accessed April 20, 2014 http://en.wikipedia.org/wiki/History_of_Santa_Barbara,_California.

295 Charlie Chaplin is reputed to have been among the stars of the silent film era who settled in Santa Barbara; however, that has not been confirmed and remains a rumor which many locals doubt.

296 History of Santa Barbara" on the website *Visit Santa Barbara: The American Riviera* , accessed on April 20, 2014 http://www.santabarbaraca.com/experience-santa-barbara/history-of-santa-barbara/.

297 "Santa Barbara's Grand Hotel—The Potter" on the website *edhat Santa Barbara*, accessed on April 20, 2014 http://www.edhat.com/site/tidbit.cfm?id=3534.

298 Myrick, *Montecito and Santa Barbara: Volume 2, The Days of the Great Estates*, *ut sup.*, 294.

299 Ibid.

300 Unknown local newspaper article, dated March 14, 1910, (among materials sent, on November 12, 1997, to William

Sagar, Fairfax historian, and in turn, provided to the author in 2009) The article announced the purchase of the property by the Bothins.

301 Unknown local newspaper article, dated July 12, 1902. in Ibid.

302 Myrick, *Montecito and Santa Barbara, ut sup.*, 295.

303 Ibid., 283.

304 Dreyfus v Richardson, 20 Cal Ap Reports, 800ff.

305 See a copy of the deed which is located in the Santa Barbara County Recorder's office at 1100 Anacapa St., Santa Barbara, and can be found in the Book of Deeds, Book 127, page 239).

306 Dreyfus v Richardson, *ut sup.*

307 Kathryn Masson and James Chen, *Santa Barbara Style* (New York, NY: Rizzoli, 2001), 32-45.

308 Myrick, *Montecito and Santa Barbara , ut sup.*, 296.

309 Masson and Chen, *Santa Barbara Style, ut sup.*, 32-45. According to the authors (and undoubtedly learned by them from research done by the current owners) St. Piran was the patron saint of tin miners. However, a check of Wikipedia reveals that St. Piran was more than that. He was a 6th century Cornish abbott of Irish origin, about whom legend has it that the heathen Irish tied a mill stone around his neck and rolled him over a cliff into a stormy sea. The sea immediately became calm, and St. Piran floated safely over the water to land upon the sandy beach of Perranzabuloe in Cornwall. In other words, the name is associated with calm and serenity, a far more likely descriptive theme.

310 *Oakland Tribune*, May 9, 1915.

311 *Wall Street Journal*, March 5, 1990.

312 Minutes of the Bothin Helping Fund, July 11, 1924.

313 Hattie Beresford, "Bothin's Tea House and Water Gardens," *Montecito Journal*, November 20-27, 2008.

314 *Santa Barbara Magazine*, May/June 1993.

315 "The Voice of the Village," *Montecito Journal*, November 20-27, 2008.

316 David Brainard, "Forgive Us Our Trespasses," in an undated edition of the *Gold Coast Montecito Journa*l This article appears next to a larger article in the same edition of that magazine which is entitled "Piranhurst—A Great Old Dowager Awaits Uncertain Future."

317 "Tea Fire," on the website *CalFire*, last modified November 17, 2008, accessed April 20, 2014 http://cdfdata.fire.ca.gov/incidents/incidents_details_info?incident_id=307.

318 "Articles of Incorporation of the Bothin Helping Fund" (document located in the Bothin Foundation Archives located at 1660 Bush Street, San Francisco, CA 94109).

319 William Thomas, "Undated Statement" c. 1923-1924 after the death of Henry Bothin) and "Opinion Letter to Henry Bothin, November 5, 1921" (letters located in the Bothin Foundation Archives located at 1660 Bush Street, San Francisco, CA 94109).

320 *Standard Corporation Service, Daily Revised* (New York, NY: Standard Statistics Company, 1918) 70.

321 H. D. Walker, *Walker's Manual of California Securities and Directory of Directors* (San Francisco: H.D. Walker, 1915) 138.

322 *Weekly Commercial News*, Vol. 64, no. 1 (January 7, 1922).

323

    1. Vacant lot. Location not known.

    2. 6 lots (#19, 20, 21, 22, 23 and 25) with 200' of frontage on State St. near Gutierrez, extending 261' deep. Improved with an auto dealership (El Camino Real Motor Car Co.).

    3. Lots 12 and 12A with 100' of frontage on State St. between Gutierrez and Haley, extending 200' deep. Improved with a mechanic shop (Vincent E. Wood Garage).

    4. Lot 14—a corner lot 90' square on the corner of State and Montecito Streets. Improved with the Savoy Hotel.

5. Lot 9—an "L" shaped lot containing 100' of frontage on State St. and extending around he corner lot to include about 100' of frontage on Canyon Perdido St.—improved with the Bothin Building.
6. A building fronting Canyon Perdido St. and extending back behind the Bothin Building. Leased to Western Auto Supply Co., Ferguson Furniture Co. and Libke Children's Shop.
7. Lots 7 and 8 at the corner of State and Sola Streets. 100' of frontage along both State and Sola Streets and improved with Blake Motor Car Co.
8. Lot 14 with 25' of frontage on State St. between Gutierrez and Haley Streets. Improved with an old building of marginal value.
9. Lot 10. Immediately adjacent to lot 14 above. Building leased to Western Machine and Foundry Co.
10. Lot 9—very valuable lot in the heart of downtown with 83.5' of frontage on State St. and facing City Hall Plaza to the rear near De La Guerra St. Improved with an older building which was well constructed.

324 "Santa Barbara Earthquake History," on the website *UCSB Projects*, accessed April 20, 2014 http://projects.crustal.ucsb.edu/sb_eqs/.

325 Marin County Superior Court action number 3062. See schedule of real estate owned at Henry's death which is a part of the inventory of his assets as it appears in the probate records.

326 An article in *The Knave* (undated) suggests that the city's largest landowner in terms of total acreage owned may well be a Swede named Carl G. Larsen who owned large tracts south of Golden Gate Park and extending into the Ingelside District. However, in terms of real estate wealth, the listed property owners include Henry Bothin, James and Jenny Flood, the Crocker Estate, James Phelan, Miss Abbie Parrott, and the Sutro and Sharon estates.

327 Bothin Real Estate Co. v Commissioner of Internal Revenue, 1937, 90 F.2nd 91.

328 "CPI Inflation Calculator" on the website *Bureau of Labor*

Statistics, accessed April 20, 2014 http://146.142.4.24/cgi-bin/cpicalc.pl.

329   James Simpson, *Creating Wine: The Emergence of a World Industry, 1840-1914* (Princeton, NJ: Princeton University Press, 2011), 204.

330   Oakland Tribune, July 13, 1914, p.1 and November 5, 1914, p. 2.

331   East Bay Water Co. v McLaughlin, 1938, 24 F.Supp. 222.

332   "Natomas History," on the website *Natomas Community Association, Inc.*, accessed April 20, 2014 http://www.natomas-community.org/?q=node/5.

333   The trust instrument referred to was the trust in favor of Henry's granddaughter, Genie, who was born on October 14, 1919. Henry created a trust in her favor on August 20, 1920 and funded it with a building on Fremont Street in San Francisco. The tax auditor attempted to claim that the value of the trust assets should be brought back into his estate, basing the claim on an argument that the trust had been established in contemplation of death and therefore constituted an effort to avoid paying tax. The brief was filed in opposition to that position, and ultimately the tax division reversed itself and allowed the trust to stand as a completed gift not made in contemplation of death.

334   Bothin Real Estate Co. v Commissioner of Internal Revenue, 1937, 90 F.2nd 91.

335   Using the CPI (the most conservative measurement for comparison of values), that estate would be worth $45,000,000 in 2005 dollars.

336   Darien B. Jaconson, Brian G. Raub, and Barry W. Johnson, "The Estate Tax: Ninety Years and Counting" on the website *IRS* http://www.irs.gov/pub/irs-soi/ninetyestate.pdf. The estate tax was progressive, rising from a low of 1 percent on the first $50,000 of assets up to a high of 10 percent on estates valued at over $5,000,000.

337 "Minutes of The Bothin Helping Fund," January 14, 1925. This meeting's minutes contains the auditor's valuation of the Fund's assets as of October 14, 1923. The Judson holdings consisted of 11,350 shares of Judson's common stock which were valued at $40 per share and 2,920 shares of Judson preferred which were valued at $100 per share.

338 "Historic Earthquakes: Santa Barbara, California" on the website *USGS*, accessed April 20, 2014 http://earthquake.usgs.gov/earthquakes/states/events/1925_06_29.php. The USGS has a page on its website which provides information about this earthquake, and on that page it is said to have actually measured 6.8. See. While it is tempting to accept the word of the United States Geologic Survey, it is noteworthy that the agency's page which describes the event also states that it occurred on June 29th, a day later than when we know it happened. Therefore, I'm going with the generally accepted estimate of 6.3.

339 Property #1, 121-123 State Street, known as Richelieu Hotel; appraised value $20,000. Brick veneer essentially all around needed replacing as did the interior plaster, plumbing, and the sidewalk. This property was a "cheap hotel," and the cost to repair was estimated at $4,509.90 which was estimated to be recoverable over time based on an assumed increase in rent from $100 per month up to $250.

Property #2, 318-330 State Street, known as the El Camino garage and Hotel; appraised value for this property with 200 feet of State Street frontage was estimated at $190,000, of which the building was valued at $90,000. The front of the building collapsed, leaving the standing portion unsafe. The structure would have to be totally replaced. Cost to rebuild was estimated at $59,575. It was recommended that the building be rebuilt, but as a four story building rather than two story, using steel frame construction. The top three stories would be available as a hotel, while the street level would be available as a garage as before.

Property #2-A, 20 Gutierrez Street, known as Montecito Van

and Storage Co. This property had just been purchased by the Helping Fund at a cost of $15,250. Its location value was principally to provide a side street exit for property #2. Steel trusses collapsed because they were not properly anchored. The steel roof fell into the building but was felt to be able to be repositioned once the supporting columns were properly installed. Estimated cost to repair was $7,850, for which amount, the building would be a single story glass front structure suitable for an auto dealership and for which about $200 per month rent could be obtained.

Property #3, 404-406 and 408-410 State Street. Appraised value $90,000, of which $40,000 represented the pre quake structure value. Damage was nearly total, with the roof collapsing into the structure. Cost to rebuild in original condition was estimated at $11,000. The recommendation was to spend $15,400 to improve the office space as well as the ramps for vehicle use up to the second floor, at which point rent of $1,000 per month could be expected.

Property #4, 435 State Street—California Billiard Parlor and OK Lunch Diner. This building largely escaped damage.

Property #5, 232, 236, 240 and 242 State Street—Savoy Hotel. The building was totally shattered and needed to be torn down and rebuilt. This building was uneconomical before the quake, and the estimate of $70,000 to rebuild it would call for a steel framed, class 3, three story structure containing 50 rooming hotel rooms on the upper stories and four retail spaces on the ground floor. Total expected rent would be on the order of $1,100 per month.

Property #6, the Bothin Building located at 905, 907, 909, 911 and 913 State Street. This property was appraised at $175,000, of which the structure was valued at $53,800. The front wall was torn from its anchors and was leaning 5 inches into the building, and the rear wall was leaning dangerously outward. Possible repairs, if one wanted to replace the space, included removing the top two stories and rebuilding them at a cost of $47,500. However, the report suggests the architectural style was old fashioned and the construction poor. The recommendation was to tear down the building and replace it with a two story structure consistent with the City's goal to emphasize Spanish design characteristics and to create more efficient office and retail space.

Property #6-A, West Canon Perdido Street buildings, consisting of three buildings located at 12, 16, and 18 West Canon Perdido St. Appraised value of the three was $76,500. All three buildings were totally destroyed. In this case, First National Bank wanted to purchase approximately 1/3 of the total 86' of street frontage in order to expand the depth of their own building. The recommendation was to entertain an offer and use the proceeds toward the overall cost to replace property #6 whose footprint would then include the remainder of property #6-A. If that were accomplished, it would decrease the cost of replacing the building to a net of about $15,000 and would result in significant efficiency.

Property #7, 1330-1340 State Street—Blake Motor Car Company. This was an old building at the corner of State and Sola Streets. It was in poor condition before and was effectively destroyed in the quake. The appraised value of the structure was $30,000 and the cost to replace it with a new single story steel framed structure was estimated at $32,000.

Property #8, 424—426 State Street—2 buildings. The one at 420-424 State Street had minimal damage which the lease required the tenant to repair. The second building was an old two story brick structure whose second floor had burned to the point of making it uninhabitable prior to the earthquake. The recommendation was to remove the old structure and rebuild it as a modern one story store at a cost of $5,025.

Property #9, 740, 742, 744, and 746 State Street—known as the McKay building.

INDEX

A

ABC Fence 135
Active 241
Alameda Artesian Water Company 365
Alameda Investment Co. 366
Alaska 63, 211, 440
Alcatraz Island 211
Alers, August 101
Allen v. Railroad Commission 119
Alta California xxx, 321
Alvord, William 127, 128
American Jewish Relief Organization 356
American National Bank of San Francisco 366
American River 367
American Wire Nail Company 146
Anderson, Elizabeth J. 307
Anderson, Minnie 333
Anthony Chabot Regional Park 286
Anthony, Susan B. 96
Anti-Saloon League 96
Apache 120

Aquitania 290
Arequipa iv, xxv, xxvii, xxxii, 309–319, 313, 332, 341, 356
Arizona 30, 78, 129
Arnold, Philip 78, 79
A Romance of Steel in California 127, 130, 146, 148, 154
Arsenal Island 59
A. Schilling and Co. 109
Ashe, Elizabeth vi, xxv, xxxii, 223, 224, 225, 226, 227, 271, 276, 302, 305, 306, 307, 308, 309, 310, 311, 314, 315, 352, 353, 356, 376
Ashe, Mrs. R. Porter 306
Ashe, Richard Porter 223
Asheville, North Carolina 223
Asia 65, 71
Atchison, Topeka and Santa Fe 179
Atherton, California 264
Atlantic Ocean 12, 290
Atlantic States 76
Atlas Building 146, 149, 151, 181, 182, 198, 250, 256, 343
Atlas Coffee 100, 101

Australia 117, 206
Awberry Plant of the Southern California Edison Company 155

B

Babcock, Julia 290
Babcock, William 290
Bacon Block 147
Baker City 130
Baldwin, Maine 284
Baltimore and Ohio Railroad 56
Bancroft Whitney Co 175
Bancroft Whitney Co v McHugh 175
Bank of America 280
Bank of California 63, 78, 111, 128, 345
Bank of Italy 280
Batcheller, Mary Ann 285
    See Chabot, Mary Ann Batcheller
Battle of Mobile Bay 223
Baumann, Frederick 166
Bay Area 144, 204, 292, 321, 337, 342, 355
Bellows Garage Building 155
Benz, Karl 120
Berkeley Gazette 145
Bermuda 290
Berry, Thomas C. 307
Bessemer, Henry 126, 127, 130, 131, 154, 161
Biddle, Mrs. 323
Big Four 65, 119, 127, 133
Bigler, John 71
Birmingham Steel Company 379
Blacks 9, 68, 69, 70, 72
Board of Health 178
Board of Supervisors 178, 185, 201, 203

Boethin, Johann xvii
Boethin, Michael Ernst xvii, 388
Bolinas, California 214
Bolton, Robert C. 343, 344, 355, 380, 382
Booth, Mr. 279, 280
Borel, Antoine 128
Boston, Massachusetts iv, xxvi, 15, 85, 114, 315
Bothier *See* Bothin
Böthin *See* Bothin
Bothin, Amelia *See* Kauffman, Amelia Bothin
Bothin Building 230
Bothin Convalescent Home 306, 307, 308, 309, 310, 311, 317, 341, 347, 355, 370
Bothin Dallemand 93, 94, 95, 97, 98, 99, 100, 102, 134, 195
Bothin Dallemand and Company 93, 94, 134
Bothine *See* Bothin
Bothin, Ellen Chabot v, ix, xxv, xxvi, 39, 47, 135, 136, 139, 218, 265, 268, 278, 281, 283-301, 304, 305, 306, 307, 321, 322, 323, 324, 329, 330-338, 342, 343, 344, 345, 346, 347, 349, 352, 355, 356, 358, 361, 371, 372, 376, 382, 385
Bothin, Emily "Emma" *See* Sutter, Emily "Emma" Bothin
Bothin, Ernest xv, xvi
    See also Bothin, Ernst
Bothin, Ernestine Gloksin 22, 33, 34, 389, 396
Bothin, Ernst xiv, xvii, xviii, xix, xx, xxiv, xxv, 1, 2, 3, 4, 6-31, 33, 34, 40, 41, 42, 43, 45, 46, 49, 51, 54, 55, 91, 97, 373, 374

Bothin Foundation v, xii, xxxii, 278,
    341, 384, 385
Bothin, Frank Whittier 121, 214, 215,
    265, 276, 299
Bothin, Genevieve *See* Lyman,
    Genevieve Bothin
Bothin Heights 253
Bothin Helping Fund v, ix, xii, 148,
    278, 322, 333, 341, 342, 343,
    344, 345, 346, 348, 349, 350,
    351, 352, 355, 356, 357, 360,
    366, 370, 372, 379, 380, 383,
    384, 385
Bothin, Henry Ernest
  BIRTH 23
  CHILDHOOD 18-57
  COMPANY DIRECTORSHIPS
    201-206, 364-367
  DEATH 369-373
  DIVORCE FROM JENNIE
    WHITTIER 259-275
  EARLY BUSINESS EXPERIENCES
    86-93
  MANUFACTURING BUSINESSES
    BOTHIN DALLEMAND 93-101
    BOTHIN MANUFACTURING
      COMPANY 95-103
    JUDSON MANUFACTURING
      COMPANY 123-156,
      363-364
    PACIFIC IRON AND NAIL
      COMPANY 108
  MARIN COUNTY 209-218,
    299-304
  MARRIAGE TO ELLEN CHABOT
    283-294
  MARRIAGE TO JENNIE
    WHITTIER 113-122
  PARENTHOOD 275-282
  PHILANTHROPY 219-227,
    305-319, 341-356

  REAL ESTATE INVESTMENTS
    HEMET 229-232
    PROPERTIES, SAN FRANCISCO
      19-21 Fremont Street 188
      25 Fremont Street 188
      30-40 Natoma Street 190
      30 Beale Street 188
      37 Clementina Street 190
      39-41 Tehama Street 190
      39 Natoma Street 190
      42 Natoma Street 190
      46 Natoma Street 190
      48 Natoma Street 190
      54 Natoma Street 190
      57-65 Clementina Street 190
      60 Natoma Street 190
      61 Natoma Street 190
      63-67 Minna Street 190, 197
      67 Natoma Street 190
      79 Clementina Street 190
      112 Fremont Street 280
      144 Second Street 190
      206 First Street 189
      222 Second Street 189
      225-227 Sacramento Street 197
      228-234 Fremont Street 190
      236 Fremont Street 190
      333 Market Street 185, 188
      341 Market Street 188
      500 Howard Street 185, 187,
        190
      530 Folsom Street 197
      546-550 Howard Street 190
      546 Howard Street 197
      552-554 Howard Street 190
      554 Howard Street 197
      580 Folsom Street 190
      615 Mission Street 185
      2240 Polk Street 184
    SAN FRANCISCO 159-200,
      233-258, 295-297, 361-363

SANTA BARBARA 321–340,
   357–360
RELATIONSHIP WITH PARENTS
   24–56
Bothin, Jennie Whittier viii, ix, xi,
   xxxii, 113, 114, 115, 117,
   119, 120, 121, 122, 157, 163,
   172, 173, 174, 177, 209, 211,
   214, 215, 216, 217, 218, 229,
   230, 231, 232, 243, 247, 254,
   259–275, 277, 281, 282, 283,
   292, 293, 294, 297, 302, 375
Bothin, Julius xix, 12, 23, 28, 30, 39,
   42, 93, 123, 124, 163, 164, 176,
   179, 281
Bothin. Julius "J.C." 39, 41, 93, 94,
   123, 310, 381
Bothin, Lulu 30, 281
Bothin Manor 222
Bothin Manufacturing Company 95,
   100, 101, 102, 108, 109, 110,
   123, 124, 171, 176, 381
Bothin Marsh 302
Bothin, Mary vii, 13, 23, 31, 32, 34,
   42, 43
Bothin, Otillia
   See Sadler, Otillia Bothin
Bothin, Pauline
   See Lee, Pauline Bothin
   Harmon
Bothin Real Estate Company 148,
   183, 189, 254, 255, 281, 295,
   296, 345, 361, 362, 363, 369,
   371, 372, 381, 382, 383, 385
*Bothin Real Estate Company v.
   Commissioner of Internal
   Revenue* 362
Bothin Reservoir 333
Bothin, Rosa xiv, xv, xvi, xviii, xix,
   xx, xxv, 2, 3, 4, 7-13, 15, 16, 17,
   18, 20, 22, 23, 24, 26, 27, 28,
   29, 30, 31, 33, 34, 42, 43, 45,
   46, 49, 51, 91, 373, 374
Bothin, Willimina "Minnie"
   See Mau, Willimina "Minnie"
   Bothin
Botine *See* Bothin
Boulder Dam 379
Bourn, William 204
Bowles, Phillip 365, 366
Boyd, John F. 307
Boyd, Louise 290
Brainard, David 325, 338, 340
Bremen, Germany 109
Breuner Furniture Warehouse 155
Brodrick, R.G. 311
Brooklyn Wire Nail Company 146
Brooks, George W. 251
Brooks, Ida L. 311, 312
Brown, Philp King 307 -311, 313,
   314, 315, 318
Brown v. Board of Education 70
Buchin *See* Bothin
Buffalo 15, 142
Buffington, Leroy 162
Bureau of Internal Revenue 369
Burlingame, California 209, 264, 272
Burlingame Country Club 264
Burnet, Edgar 154
Burton, William P. 241
Butler, Charles 138
Butler, George 211
Byrne, J.M. 159

C

Cabot, Richard C. 313, 314, 315
California xxv, xxix, xxxii, 28, 41, 45,
   47, 48, 51, 56, 68-78, 103, 104,
   106, 107, 114, 128, 129, 135,
   142, 143, 177, 192, 193, 248,
   255, 261, 283, 321, 350, 360

California Constitutional Convention, 1879 106
California Engine Works 107
California Gold Rush vi, xxv, xxix, xxxii, 223, 227, 271, 302, 306, 314, 352, 353, 376
California Historical Society 114
California Insurance Company xxxii, 205, 206, 251, 252, 296
California Jute Mill Company 153
California National Guard 240
California Northwestern Railroad 222
California Pacific Medical Center 270
California's Supreme Court 176
California State Legislature 70
California Theatre 238
California Victor Mower 134
California Wine Association xxxii, 96, 348, 349, 350, 351, 352, 364, 365
Call Building 130
Calloway, Nellie 174, 175
Canada 290
Canal Zone 193
Canary Island Date Palms 339
Canon Kip Day Nursery 356
Cape Horn 193
Capital Flour Mills 107
Carnegie, Andrew 129, 131, 133, 142, 143, 144, 149, 323
Carolan, Mrs. Francis J. 310
Carter, Terry xxvi, 287, 288, 292
Caruso, Enrico 111
Cascade, California 154
Case Thresher 42
Casey, Maurice 119
Catron, John 62
Cazadero, California 221

Central Pacific Railroad 57, 107, 110, 117, 127, 129
Central Tower 130, 153
Central Valley 367
Chabot, Anthony 135, 136, 139, 140, 283, 284, 285, 286
Chabot College 286
Chabot, Ellen Hasty 284
Chabot, Mary Ann Batcheller 285
Chabot Observatory 286
Chamberlain, Mrs. Joseph C. 310
Charleston 130
Chartres Coffee and Spice Company 47
Chicago xxviii, 57, 58, 59, 84, 98, 103, 142, 161, 162, 166, 214, 224, 315, 322
Chicago, Milwaukee, St. Paul and Pacific Railroad 57
Children's Hospital (San Francisco) 270, 356
China 12, 68, 71, 117
Chinese 70, 71, 72, 73, 74, 104, 105, 106, 221
Chodusen, Poland. *See* Chodziesen, Poland
Chodziesen, Poland xix, xxiii, 1, 2, 12
Chodzież, Poland xix, xx, 1, 2, 3, 4 *See* Chodziesen, Poland
Choynsky, Joe 219
Chronicle Building 130
Cincinnati 100, 179
City and County Hospital of San Francisco 314
City and County of San Francisco 178
City and County Treasurer 178
City Hall (Oakland) 146, 147, 149, 153
City Hall (San Francisco) 105, 130, 203

City's Master Plan 185
Civil Grand Jury 177, 178
Civil War 9, 27, 35, 62, 68, 82, 83, 96, 223
C.J. Capwell Building 147
C.J. Heeseman's 147
Claus Spreckels Building 153
Claus Spreckels Mansion 243
Clay Street 244
Cleveland, Grover 120
Cleveland, Ohio xx, xxi, 11, 15, 16, 35, 120, 142
cloud scraper 162
Coffin and Hendy 65
Coffin, James 211, 306
Coffin, Mrs. James 306, 310
Coinage Act of 1873 85
Cold Springs Canyon 360
Cold Springs Reservoir 333
Coleman, Edward 310
Coleman, John C. 310
Coleman, Persis 310
Cole, R. Beverly M.D. 101
Collier's, The National Weekly 237
Collins, George H. 365
Colston, Walter 69
Columbia 12, 19, 24, 193, 212
Columbian government 192
Colwell, Jesse 220
Compromise of 1850 70
Comstock Lode xxix, 46, 127, 128
Congress, United States 18, 62, 66, 214
Consolidated Steel and Wire Company 146
Contra Costa Water Company 284, 365
Coppee, Miss 306
Corbett, Jim 219
Cornwall 325
Corte Madera 213

Cottage Hospital 356
Council Bluffs, Iowa 57, 58, 59
Cowdery, J.F. 138
Crocker, Mr. and Mrs. Charles 119
Crocker, Mrs. W.H. 310
Cross Country Club 212
Crystal Springs 238
Cushing, S.B. 138
Cutler, A.D. 205
Cuyahoga County, Ohio xxi
Czarnków, Poland xx, 3

D

Daily Alta California 108
Daily Nevada State Journal 145
Dallemand, Albert 93, 94, 95, 97, 98, 99, 100, 102, 108, 119, 123, 134, 138, 171, 195, 375
Dallemand and Co 94
Dallemand, Mr. and Mrs. Albert 119
Daniels, Joseph 142, 143
Davenport, Iowa 59
Da Vinci, Leonardo 40
Davis, Jefferson 58, 59
Dean, W.E. 251
Declaration of Independence 373
Deed Book, San Francisco 159, 181, 197
Deems, C.P. vi, 343, 344
DeForest, Elizabeth 338
de Lesseps, Ferdinand Marie 192
Denicke, E.A. 205
Department of the Navy 130
Department of the Treasury 342
Des Moines, Iowa 58
Detroit, Michigan 142
Diamond Drill Company 78
Dibblee, Albert 213, 419
Dibblee, Mrs. Benjamin 311
Dillman, Lizzie 115

Dipsea Race 212
di San Faustino, Genie Lyman Casey 255, 262, 269, 270, 274, 280, 281, 287, 304, 354
di San Faustino, Ranieri 354
Donahue, James 168
Donahue, Michael 168
Donahue, Peter 127, 134, 167
Donner Summit 63
Doolittle, Mrs. Jefferson 317
Douglass, W.A. 101
Downtown Plan 185, 190
Drexler, L.P. 152, 153, 177, 180
Dreyfus, Louis 323, 324
Dreyfus v. Richardson 323
Drum, John S. 366
Duncan Mills 221
Dunn v. Dunn 175
Dutton, William J. 204

E

Eads Bridge 131, 132
Eads, James Buchanan 131, 132, 133
Eagle Rock 236
Earthquake and Fire, 1906 xxxi, xxxii, 41, 111, 120, 130, 149, 159, 175, 182, 194, 196, 204, 205, 206, 207, 216, 226, 233, 238, 242, 245, 246, 247, 249, 253, 257, 295, 297
East Bay xxxii, 114, 141, 155, 204, 241, 362, 365, 366
East Bay Masonic Temple 155
East Bay Municipal Utility Company 366
East Bay Municipal Utility District 366
East Bay Water Company xxxii, 362, 365, 366
East Coast xxix, 57, 100, 129, 145

Eaton, Charles 332, 333
Eaton, Mrs. Charles 324
Edison, Thomas 40, 169, 170
Effie Afton iv, 59, 60, 61
Einstein, Albert 40
Eldridge Grade 212
El Mirasol 338
Embarcadero 3 174
Emeryville 134, 137, 139, 150, 155, 156, 204, 206, 293, 308, 378
Emigrant Pass 63
Emperor Norton 67, 68, 74, 75. *See also* Norton, Joshua
Empire Gold Mine 204
Emporium 130
England 2, 26, 38, 84, 101, 114, 125
Esberg, Mrs. M. 306
Ettler, John A. 256
Eureka 107, 248, 285
Eureka Foundry 107
Europe viii, xviii, xxiii, 1, 2, 5, 18, 83, 84, 100, 115, 129, 144, 260, 290, 292, 337, 370, 378

F

Fabiola Hospital 286
Fairbanks, Douglas Jr. 321
Fairfax, California iv, viii, xxv, 213, 219, 220, 221, 222, 225, 226, 276, 302, 305, 306, 310
Fairfax Ranch viii, 219
Fair, James G. 127, 128
Faraday, Michael 169
Farmers and Merchants Bank of Los Angeles 230
Farragut, David Glasgow 223
Feather River 367
Federal Reserve Bank 366
Fillmore Street 204

Fireman's Fund Insurance Co. 204
First Congregational Church 286
First National Bank of Oakland 135
Florida Avenue, Hemet, California 230
Folsom, Frances 120
Folsom Street, San Francisco 190, 255
Foreign Miner's License Law 71
Fort Armstrong 59
Fort Point 210
Foster, A.W. 222
Foundry Square III 189
Franklin, Benjamin 168, 374
Freeman, Frederick N. 239, 241
French American Bank of Savings 296
Ft. Tejon 360
Fugitive Slave Law 70
Funston, Frederick 239, 240

G

Gallet 148
Garcia, Tony 226
Garlock, Nevada 155
Garthwaite, W.W. 365
George Caswell Company 255
George Simmons and Company, 97
German xiv, xvi, xviii, xix, xxxi, 1, 3, 4, 6, 7, 13, 15, 16, 17, 24, 26, 27, 28, 85, 114, 296
  See also Germans, Germany
German Consulate 114
Germans xxiv, 4, 6, 7, 38, 68, 109

German Savings and Loan Society 296
Germany xiv, xviii, xix, 4, 5, 6, 10, 11, 20, 27, 83, 93, 96, 109, 114
Geronimo 120, 219, 220, 221

Gerstle, Mark L. 251
Ghirardelli Chocolate and Coffee 107, 205
Ghirardelli, Domingo 66, 205
GIANT Baking Powder 100, 101, 402
Gillette, William 322
Girdwood, R.B. 344
Glenwood Ave., Ross 213, 214, 215
Goat Island 241
Goff, Vivian 317
Golden Eagle Hotel 110, 111
Golden Gate xiii, 65, 101, 209, 210, 243, 379
Golden West Plating 107
Gold Rush xxix, 46, 103, 283, 367
gold standard 85
Goodall, Nelson and Perkins 65
Grace Cathedral 223
Grant, Mrs. Joseph D. 310
Grantor/Grantee Indices 159, 196
Gray Brothers 224
Great Chicago Fire 1871 57, 84, 161
Great Diamond Hoax 77, 80
Great Lakes 17, 129
Great Western Iron Works 142
Greeley, Horace xxix
Green, F.M. 154
Griffith, Alice 223, 224, 307
Griffith, Millen 211
Griffith, Mrs. Edwin L. 306
Gunst, Moses 310

H

Hallidie, Andrew 129
Hammet, Dashiell 184
Harmon, John 27, 28, 36
Harpending, Asbury 78
Harper's Bazaar 329
Harrmon, Frank 28
Harry Kaufman 281

Harvard Avenue, Hemet 230
Harvey, Downey 204
Hasty, Betsy Fitch 284
Hasty, William 284
Havana 290
Havens, Frank 366
Hawaii 145, 206
Hawaiian Gazette 206
Hawley Brothers Hardware 65
Hawley, Stuart 366
Hearst, George 219
Hearst, Phoebe 219, 221, 222, 302
Hearst, William Randolph 219
Hellman, Elias 230
Hellman, Isaias 66
Hemet Boy Scouts 356
Hemet, California viii, 119, 229, 230, 231, 232, 252, 253, 254, 255, 281, 282, 296, 303, 356, 385
Hemet Dam 119
Henry Bothin v. Cal Title Insurance and Trust Co 176
Henry Miller 135
Henry P. Drake Reservoir 336
Henry Street Settlement House 224
Herron, William 174
Hibernia Bank 63, 173, 194
Hibernia Savings and Loan Society 296
Hill Farm iv, xxv, xxxii, 226, 227, 228, 271, 305, 306, 307, 308, 309, 310, 315, 317, 341, 356
Holbrook, Charles 205
Holbrook, Merrill and Stetson 205
Holden House 111
Holmes, Sherlock 322
Holonson, Knute 42-45
Holton, Mrs. L. H. 310, 311
Home Insurance Building 161, 162
Hooker, Osgood 204
Hoover, Hattie 281

Hopkins, Mark 65, 119
Hopkins, Mr. and Mrs. Timothy 119
Hospital for Children and Training School for Nurses 270
Hotaling, A.P. 143
Howard, Charles Webb 135, 139
Howard Street, San Francisco 197, 256
Howe, Louis 311
Hudson, F. Garvin 324
Hull House 224
Huntington, Collis 65
Huntsman, O.D. 220
Hurd, John 61
Hurd v. Rock Island Railroad Company 61
Hyde, Ricky 340

I

Iller, Mrs. H.M.A. 306
Illinois 58, 59, 146, 322
I*llustrated Review: San Francisco, Its Commercial Progress and Importance, 1887* 98
Indiana Wire Fence Company 146
Indian country 78
Indian wars 63
infantile paralysis 121, 214, 225, 299
Internal Revenue Department 342, 346
Iowa 17, 18, 28, 57, 58, 59, 90
Ireland 26, 83, 96
Irish 6, 15, 17, 38, 68, 70, 224, 442
IRS 342, 343, 344, 345, 346, 348, 352, 356
Italian 224, 324, 331
Italy 96, 280

J

Jackson Street, San Francisco 114, 216
J.A. Folger Coffee Company 107, 109
J.A. McGregor 366
Janin, Henry 79
Japan 117
Jay Cooke & Co 85
Jayne Building 165
Jenney, William Le Baron 161
J.I. Case Co 42
Johnson, Frank S. 307
John's Restaurant Building 184
Johnston, William 304
Jordan, James C. 311
Jordan, Mrs. J.C. 310
J. Philip Murphy Corporation 148, 379
Judson, Egbert 134, 135, 136, 138, 139, 141, 143, 144, 146, 147, 151, 152, 177, 180, 206, 285
Judson Horse Nail Company 134
Judson Manufacturing Company viii, xxxi, 90, 107, 123, 124, 134, 137, 143, 147, 150, 152, 153, 279, 285, 337, 351, 355, 363, 379, 380
Judson Pacific-Murphy Corporation 148
Junior League 317

K

Kaiser Hospital 286
Kansas 281
Kansas City, Kansas 162
Kauffman, Amelia Bothin 12, 23, 28, 29, 30, 28
Kaufman, Harry J. 254
Kaufman, J.J. 307
Kearney, Denis 90, 105
Keller, George Frederick 72
Kentfield 213, 214
Kent, William 214, 307
Kern River 360
King City, California 248
King, Clarence 79
King, Homer S. 204
Kingsley, Leonard 255, 382
Kittle, Harriette de Witt 307
Kittle, John 310
Kittle, Mrs. John 225
Klink, Bean and Associates 351
Kohl, Mrs. Frederick 310
Korom, Joseph Jr. 165
Koshland, Marcus F. 310
KSW Partners 183, 382, 383
Kuangtung Province 71
Kuznica Czarnkowska 2

L

LaBoyteaux 299
Ladies' Relief Society 286
Lafayette Dam 366
Lagunitas Club xxvii, 214, 215, 301, 302, 303, 304
Lagunitas Creek 221
Lagunitas Road 212, 213, 214, 293, 301
Lagunitas Tennis Club 302, 303
Lake Chabot 285, 286
Lake Superior 142
Lake Temescal 284, 286
Langford, E.A. 220
La Société Internationale du Canal Interocéanique 192
Lawrenz, Anna Rosina Schroeder 2
Lawrenz, Philipp Jacob 2
Lawrenz, Rosa 2. See Bothin, Rosa
Lawson, Andrew C. 248
Lawson Report 248

Lee, Alfred 12, 27
Lee, Frank 28, 32
Lee, Pauline Bothin Harmon xxiii, 12, 13, 23, 27, 28, 32, 34, 308
Lee, Robert E. 58, 59, 61
Leslie 241
Levy, Fanny 310
Lewiston, Wisconsin xxiii, 20, 22, 24, 25, 26, 28, 29, 30, 31, 39-46, 49, 50, 68, 91
Liedesdorf Street 256
Lincoln, Abraham 9, 58, 61, 62, 70
Livermore Valley 286
Liverpool 290
Lombard Street, San Francisco 247
Lompoc Valley 359
London 78, 79, 234, 237
London, Jack 234, 237
Long Beach, California 155
Long Depression 85
Loop District 161
Lord's Prayer 75
Los Alamos 360
Los Angeles 104, 155, 230, 247, 315, 333
Lux, Mr. and Mrs. Charles 119
Lyman, Edmunds vi, 279, 280, 352, 354, 372, 380, 382, 385
Lyman, Genevieve Bothin v, vi, ix, x, xi, xii, xxvi, 54, 120, 121, 174, 214, 216, 231, 244, 247, 255, 262, 265, 266, 267, 269, 270, 272, 273, 274, 275, 277, 278, 279, 280, 281, 287, 289, 293, 294, 300, 302, 317, 342, 344, 345, 352, 353, 354, 371, 382, 384, 385
Lynn, Massachusetts 285

M

Maas, Carlos 153, 180, 352, 363, 364, 378, 380
Maas, David 377
Maas, Ida Sutter vi, xiv, xv, xvi, xvii, xviii, xix, xxiv, xxv, 10, 22, 27, 29, 41, 47, 48, 49, 51, 52, 75, 89, 90, 311, 352, 353, 361, 364
Maas, Ted 47, 352, 361, 362, 377, 380, 381, 382
Mace, Louis S. 311
MacLaughlin, Maurice 304
MacLean, John 59
Madison, Frank D. 307
Maidu Indians 367
Maine 113, 114, 260, 284, 285
Manor/Lyman House 307
Manor Subdivision, Fairfax 302, 307
Mansell, Edmona (Mona) Lyman Miller 255, 354
Mare Island Naval Base 241
Margie 115
Marin Art and Garden Center 225
Marina, San Francisco 247
Marin County, California viii, xxv, xxvii, 209, 210, 211, 212, 213, 215, 218, 220, 222, 225, 254, 264, 265, 266, 273, 295, 299, 302, 311, 336, 372, 382, 385
Marin County Open Space District 302
Marin County Water Company 222
Marin Municipal Water District. 222
Market Street, San Francisco 130, 146, 163, 183, 185, 188, 190, 194, 202, 237, 242
Mark Twain xxx
Marlborough House 111
Martin, John 211, 306, 310
Martin, Mrs. John 306

Mar y Cel iv, ix, xxvi, 292, 331, 332, 333, 334, 336, 337, 338, 339, 340, 357, 360
Mason, Jack 220
Matson Lines 206
Mau, Alice 281
Mau Family 108, 281
Mau, Henry 48, 92
Mau, Mrs. Will 51
Mau Sadler Company 92, 93, 94, 99, 100
Mau, William 92, 108
Mau, Willimina "Minnie" Bothin xxx, 12, 23, 28, 30, 40, 41, 42, 45, 46, 48, 49, 50, 55, 75, 76, 91, 92, 148, 281, 333
McAllister, Hall 211
McCutchen, Edward J. 204
McCutchen, Olney & Willard 204
McGregor, J.A. 366
McLaughlin, D.E. 143
McLaughlin, Mrs. Charles 119
McNear, Bessie 288
McNear, Mrs. Seward 306
McNear, S.B. 215
Mead Dry Press Brick Machine Company 139, 201
Meares, J.L. M.D. 101
Mercantile Trust Company 296, 366
Merchants Exchange Bank 63
Merchants National Bank 345, 348, 366
Metcalf, Honorable and Mrs. Victor 288
Methodist Episcopal Church 23
Mexican border 63
Mexico 17, 69, 72
Midwest xxix, xxx, 56, 81, 82, 142
Miller and Lux empire 107
Miller, C.O.G. vi, 167, 288, 307, 352, 353, 365, 366

Miller, Harry 288
Miller, Joaquin 212
Miller, Mr. and Mrs. C.O.G. 288
Miller, Mr. and Mrs. Henry 119
Mills Building 130
Mills College 114
Mills, D.O. 128, 129
Mill Valley 212, 302
Milwaukee Road Railroad 57
Minnesota 18, 162
Mission District 242
Mission La Purisima 360
Mission Santa Barbara 360
Mission Street, San Francisco 181, 182, 185, 250
Mississippi and Missouri Railroad 59
Mississippi River iv, 1, 17, 56, 57, 58, 59, 61, 62, 131, 210
Missouri Compromise 69
Missouri River 57, 58
Mitchell, David 382
Moffitt, Mrs. James 310
Moline, Illinois 59
Monteagle, Louis F. 204, 205
Montecito, California iv, xxv, 278, 288, 290, 293, 296, 299, 322, 323, 324, 330, 331, 333, 336, 339, 360, 369, 376
Montecito County Water District 333
Monterey, California 69, 120, 329
Montgomery Street, San Francisco 111, 127, 130
Moody, V.D. 135, 138, 139
Moreno 230, 254
Morgan, C.R. 138
Morgan, J. Pierpont 133
Morrison, Alexander 211
Mountain Drive 331
Mountain View Cemetery 286
Mr. McFeeley 138
Mrs. Mill's Cream Yeast Powder 94

Mt. Tamalpais 210, 212, 213, 214
Muir, John xxxi, 234, 235
Muir Woods 214
Murphy, Daniel T. 204
Murphy, Grant & Co 204
Murphy, Honorable and Mrs. J.D. 119
Murray, Hugh 73
Musician's Union 202
Myers, P.N. 253, 254, 255, 282
Myrick, David 324

N

Napoleon 1, 2
National Academy of Engineering 169
National Flor Mills xxxi, 63, 107, 135, 169, 195, 237, 240, 339, 345, 348, 366
National Ironworks 107
Native Americans 63, 70, 120
Natomas Company xxxii
Natomas Consolidated Company of California 367
Netzkrug, Poland 1, 2
Nevada xxix, 63, 128, 129, 145, 155, 177, 230, 248, 281
Nevada Bank 230
Nevada Central Railroad 129
New England 38, 101
New Orleans 210
New York 15, 26, 27, 57, 76, 85, 86, 114, 162, 193, 205, 210, 224, 290, 315, 324
New Zealand 206
Nicaragua 193
Nicasio, California 220
Niles Canyon 110
Nob Hill 243
Noble Electric Steel Company 143

Nordhoff, Charles 321
North Beach, San Francisco 194, 204
Northeast 82, 198
Northern Pacific Railway 85, 179
North Pacific Coast Railroad 213, 220, 221
North Shore Railroad 221, 222
Norton, Joshua 66
    See also Emperor Norton
Norway 27, 83
Norwegians 68

O

Oakland 57, 67, 106, 110, 134, 135, 137, 140, 145, 146, 147, 149, 153, 155, 156, 252, 268, 270, 283, 284, 285, 286, 288, 289, 290, 292, 293, 365
Oakland City Hall 146, 147, 149, 153
Oakland Tribune 139
Oberfelder Brothers 99
Oberfelder, Max 94, 95, 99
Oberfelder, Tobias 94, 95, 97, 99
Oceanic Steamship Company 206, 207
Ohland, N. 138
Older, Fremont 239
Olema, California 220, 221
Oliver Wire Company, 146
Olympic Club 219
Omaha, Nebraska 57
Omnibus Cable Company 130
Oregon 104, 142
Orient 100, 179
Orizaba 129
Osborne, J.D. 148, 254, 344
Owl Drug Store 185, 186

P

Pacific Coast 65, 98, 134, 138, 142, 143, 145, 146, 147, 154, 213, 220, 221
Pacific Coast Steamship Company 65
Pacific Gas and Electric xxxi, 137, 155, 167, 204, 205, 206, 249, 256
Pacific Gas Improvement Company 168
Pacific Hardware and Steel 107
Pacific Iron and Nail Company 108, 138
Pacific Lighting Company 167, 365, 366
Pacific Ocean 206, 212
Pacific Rolling Mills 128, 129, 130, 134, 140, 143, 144, 145, 148, 149, 151, 163, 364, 377, 379
Pacific Telephone and Telegraph Building 379
Page, Mrs. George 306
Palace Hotel 111
Panama iv, 192, 193, 290, 315, 319
Panama-Pacific Exposition in San Francisco 315
Panic of 1873 58, 85, 105
Panic of 1893 180,
Pardee, George 248
Park, Helen Van Cleave 220
Park Hill, Hemet 230, 253, 281, 282
Parrott, John 128
Parsons, F.D. 148
Payne Bolt Works 205
Payne, George L. 205
Payson, Albert 204
Pediatric Department of the University of California 308
Peninsula 108, 211, 212, 264
Pennsylvania Railroad Company 131
People's Water Company 365, 366
Perry, Alfred 101
Phelan, James D. 119, 202, 203
Phelan, Mr. and Mrs. James 119
Philadelphia and Reading Railroad 179
Pickford, Mary 321
Pierce, Franklin 58
Pierce, Henry 284
Pilarcitas, California 238
Pine Street 134
Pinkard, Mrs. George 306
Pink Saloon 214, 419
Pioneer Ironworks 107
Piranhurst iv, ix, xxv, xxvi, 288, 290, 292, 301, 321, 322, 323, 324, 325, 328, 329, 330, 331, 332, 336, 340, 357, 358
Pittsburgh, Pennsylvania 162, 323
Placer County, California 143
Plant, Carl S. 301
Poles (Polish) 4, 68
Poppe, Mr. 174
Portage, Wisconsin iv, xiv, xix, xxiii, xxx, xxxi, 11, 12, 13, 16-39, 42, 51, 55, 57, 68, 90, 91
Portola, Gaspar de xxx
Posen, Grand Duchy of 4
Posen, Poland xxiv See also Poznan, Poland
Posen Province, Poland 2
Potter Hotel 322, 323
Poznań 2
Poznan, Poland xx, xxiv, 4
Prairie Du Chien, Wisconsin 17, 28, 42, 90
Preble 241
Presbyterian Hospital 224
Presidio 239, 240, 243, 247, 360
Price, Thomas 101
Prohibition 96, 349, 350, 365

Promontory Point, Utah 57
Prussia xvii, xviii, xix, xxiii, 3, 4, 9,
    10, 12, 23, 27, 31, 54, 56, 373
Psychological Care of Infant and Child
    275
Pt. Reyes Station 220, 221
Puget Sound 143
Purchasing Agents Association of
    Northern California 155

R

Racine, Wisconsin 42
Railroad Bridge Company 59
Ralston, Mrs. W.C. 119
Ralston, William 78, 79, 111, 119,
    128
Rancho Canada de Herrera 219, 302
Rand McNally Building 162
Rattlesnake Canyon 383
Red Cross 356
Redlands, California 229
Remington, Mrs. E. 306
Reminiscences of the Outdoor Life 214
Republican Party 202
Rhead, Frederick 311, 313
Richardson Bay 212, 302
Richardson, Daniel 322, 323, 325
Richardson, Julia M. 322, 323, 324,
    325
Richter Scale 247, 360, 383
Ripley, Mr. 324
Risden Ironworks 107
River Dee 125
Riverside, California 383
Riverside County, California 282
Riverside Portland Cement Company
    352
Roberts, George 78
Roberts, Hugh T. 254
Rochester, New York 162

Rock Island Bridge iv, 59, 60
Rock Island, Illinois 58, 59
Rock Island Line 58, 59
Rock Island Railroad 61
Rocky Mountains xxx, 98, 145, 146
Rolph, James 128, 140, 141, 152
Rolph, James Jr. "Sunny Jim" 140
Roosevelt, Theodore 193
Rosenbaum & Friedman 93
Ross ix, xxvii, 209, 211-222, 225, 231,
    247, 262, 264, 265, 266, 278,
    289, 290, 293, 296, 298, 299,
    301, 302, 314, 324, 343, 356
Ross Improvement Company 214
Ross, James 213
Ross Valley 209, 211, 213, 214, 221,
    222, 262
Roughing It xxx
Rubalcava, Felix 288, 437
Ruef, Abraham 202, 203, 239

S

Sacramento, California 57, 63, 66, 89,
    93, 94, 100, 106, 110, 111, 115,
    156, 197, 201, 256, 284, 367
Sacramento Street, San Franciso 256
Sadler Family 42, 48, 50, 92, 93, 94,
    99, 100, 108, 148, 281
Sadler, Hermann 42, 92, 108, 148,
    281,
Sadler, Otillia Bothin xxx, 12, 23, 28,
    30, 41, 42, 45, 46, 47, 50, 53,
    75, 76, 91, 92
Sadler, R. 108
Sadler, William 45
Sais, Domingo 219
Salvation Army 96, 356
San Andreas Fault 233, 248, 360
San Anselmo, California 213, 300,
    301

San Anselmo Fire Department 300, 310
San Diego, California 110, 130, 156
San Diego Oil Company Building 156
San Francisco Association for the Blind 356
San Francisco Bay 65, 321, 342, 355, 403
San Francisco Board of Health 101
San Francisco Bulletin 239
San Francisco, California xii, xiii, xxix, xxx, xxxi, xxxii, 30, 41, 42, 45, 46, 47, 48, 49, 51, 55, 57, 63, 64, 65, 66, 67, 68, 71, 74, 75, 76, 77, 78, 81, 87, 90, 91, 92, 93, 100, 103, 104, 105, 106, 107, 108, 110, 111, 113, 114, 115, 117, 119, 120, 121, 124, 127, 128, 129, 133, 134, 143, 144, 146, 150, 151, 153, 155, 156, 159, 163, 167, 168, 173, 174, 175, 179, 180, 183, 184, 192, 193, 194, 196, 197, 198, 202, 204, 205, 207, 209, 210, 211, 213, 216, 221, 223, 224, 229, 230, 233, 234, 237, 241, 246, 247, 250, 253, 254, 255, 257, 263, 264, 265, 266, 269, 270, 271, 280, 283, 284, 285, 290, 293, 295, 308, 310, 311, 315, 343, 359, 360, 361, 375, 381, 382, 385
San Francisco Chemical Works and Sulphur Powdering Mill 139
San Francisco City Directory 47, 86, 93, 108, 141, 402
San Francisco City Directory, 1868 93
San Francisco City Directory, 1875 47
San Francisco City Directory, 1876 86
San Francisco City Directory, 1879-1880 93
San Francisco Fire Department 178, 237
San Francisco Gas Company 167, 168
San Francisco Hospital 153
San Francisco Illustrated Wasp 72
San Francisco Opera House 286
San Francisco Public Library 153
San Francisco Real Estate Circular 76, 77
San Francisco Salvation Army 356
San Francisco Savings Union 296
San Francisco Stock and Bond Exchange 155
San Francisco Transit Center District Plan 190
San Francisco Water Company 197, 198
San Francisco YMCA 356
San Geronimo 219, 220, 221
San Jacinto Mountains 119
San Leandro, California 286
San Leandro Creek 285
San Mateo, California 383, 385
San Mateo Polo Club 264
San Pablo Dam 366
San Quentin Prison 135
San Rafael, California 211, 290, 300, 301, 307, 356
San Rafael Fire Department 300, 301
Santa Barbara, California iv, ix, xxv, xxvi, 277, 287, 290, 292, 301, 321, 322, 323, 324, 329, 331, 332, 345, 348, 355, 356, 357, 358, 359, 360, 370, 372, 376, 383
Santa Barbara Presidio 360
Sausalito, California 211, 213, 221, 225, 302

Savings and Loan Society 296
Schilling, August 109
Schmeidell, Mrs. E.G. 215
Schmiedell, Edward 211
Schmitz, Eugene 202, 203, 212, 239, 240
Schreck, Al 183, 382
Scott, Irving 130, 143
Seattle, Washington 104, 110, 129
Second Industrial Revolution 81, 106
Sempervirens Club 212
Sentinel Rock 235
"separate but equal" 70
Serra, Father Junipero xxx
S.F. Gas and Electric Board 204
Sharon Estate 176
Shasta County, California 143
Shaver's Grade 212
Shepard, John L. M. 139
Shore Valley Railway Company 204
Siberia 117
Sierra Nevada 63
Sightseers Club 212
Silver Lake Cemetery 12, 34
Silver Spoon Bikini Baking Powder 94
skyscraper xxviii, 146, 161, 166, 250
Slack, John 78, 79
S. Newman Building 156
Snyder, A.J. 135, 139
Sonoma, California 385
Sonoma County, California 221
Sotomoyo 241
South America 65, 145
Southern California xxv, 119, 155, 168, 173, 229, 230, 247, 321
Southern Pacific Railroad 110, 202, 204
South of Market, San Francisco 185
Spreckels, Claus 65, 66, 119, 153, 243
Spreckels, Mr. and Mrs. Claus 119

Spreckles, Rudolph 203, 204
Spreckles Sugar 204
Spring Valley Water Company 135, 204
Squires, George D. 254
Standish, Maine 284
Stanford, Senator and Mrs. Leland 119
Stanford University 379
State Bar of California 202
State Earthquake Investigation Committee 248
State of California 135
State Street, Santa Barbara 357, 358, 359, 383
Statue of Liberty 120
Stetson, James B. 243, 245
Stetson, Mr. and Mrs. J.B. 119
Stevens, Lucy 322, 333
St. Francis Hospital, Santa Barbara 356
Stinson Beach, California 212
St. John's Church, Ross 356
St. Johns Evangelical Church, Portage 12
St. John's Lutheran Church, Portage 23
St. Louis, Missouri 59, 76, 131
St. Luke's Church, San Francisco 243
Stockton and Copperopolis Railroad 129
Stockton, California 110, 129
Stone House 306, 308
Stowe, Harriet Beecher 9
St. Piran 325
Strauss, Levi xxvii, 66
St. Vincent's Orphanage, Santa Barbara 356
Suez Canal 192
Sullivan, Dennis T. 238, 239
Summerland, California 360

Summers, William T. 345, 366
Sunnyside Train Station, Ross 212
Superior Barb Wire Company 146
Sussman, M. 310
Sutro, Adolph 130
Sutter, Emil xxv, 27, 51, 52, 53, 87, 91, 137, 139, 308
Sutter, Emily "Emma" Bothin xiv, 23, 28, 29, 30, 33, 34, 39, 40, 41, 42, 49, 51, 89, 91, 120, 123, 156, 157, 163, 164, 171, 172, 174, 179, 196, 281, 377
Sutter, John 42,
Sutter, Joshua 51
Sutter's Mill xxix
Syndicate Bank 204
Sypher, Leigh 272

T

Tacoma Building 162
Taiping Rebellion 71
Tamalpais Club 212
Tay Bridge Disaster 125
Telegraph Hill Neighborhood Center 225
Telegraph Hill Neighborhood House 225
Telegraph Hill, San Francisco 224, 225, 271, 305
Telephone Exchange Building 156
Temescal Creek 284
The Bothin Helping Fund v, ix, xii, 278, 341, 370, 383, 384
The Commercial Hotel 111
The Consolidated Water Company 365
The History of Columbia County 12
The Independent 315
The Making of Marin 220
The Maltese Falcon 184

The National Gold Bank and Trust Co 63
The People v. George W. Hall 73, 74
The Willing Circle 223
Third Street, San Francisco 234
Thomas, William 342, 343, 344, 345, 346, 348
Thurston, W.W. 303
Tiffany, Charles Lewis 79
Tillman-Bendels 107
Tishman Speyer 189
Tomales Bay 221
Tongs 74
Tower Building 162
Transbay Bus Terminal 190
Transcontinental Railroad xxix, 56, 65, 81, 106, 193, 284
Transit Tower 190, 191
Tubbs Hotel 285
Twain, Mark xxx, 234

U

Uncle Tom's Cabin 9
Union Iron Works 107, 127, 130, 134, 143, 167
Union Labor Party (ULP) 202
Union Pacific Railroad 57, 58, 179
Union Savings Bank Building 147
Union Square 242
United Railroads 203
United States xviii, xix, 1, 2, 9, 10, 15, 18, 56, 59, 62, 63, 66, 67, 81, 83, 104, 117, 145, 147, 192, 193, 205, 210, 286, 289, 350, 365
United States Board of Engineers 210
United States Supreme Court 62
United States v. The Rock Island Bridge Company 59
University of California 202, 248, 379

Upper San Leandro Dam 366
U.S. Circuit Court for Northern
    Illinois 59
U.S. Navy 223, 238, 239
U.S. Patent Office 82
Utah 57, 142

V

Vail, Edward F.R. 322, 345, 352
Van Ness Avenue 121, 244
Van Trees, Frank 181, 256
Veterans Home in Yountville 286
Victoria Luise 290
Victorian Classics 244
Victor Mowing Machine 135, 148
Viel, Harry P. 311
Vienna, Maine 113, 114
Visiting Nurses Association 356
Volkmann, Daniel 109
Volkmann, George 109
Volta, Alessandro 169, 170
Von Lawrence, Rosena xv
    See Bothin, Rosa

W

Wagner, P.A. 108, 138, 139
Waldron, W.B. 174
Walnut Creek, California 48, 75
Ward, C.C. 342, 343, 344
Ward, D. Henshaw 138
Ward, James 62
Ward v. Flood 70, 399
Washington, D.C. 70, 130, 142, 179, 286
Washington State 286
Watson, John Broadus 275
Weir, William 282
Wells Fargo and Co 63, 204, 230
West Coast 50, 57, 63, 65, 117, 129, 130, 134, 142, 143, 144, 145, 149, 151, 153, 155, 168, 212, 296, 378, 379
West Coast Life Insurance Company 296
West Indies 290
Westinghouse Factory 155
West Marin xxvii, 213
Westmont College 338
Whipple, John 322
White's Hill xxvii, 219, 220, 221
Whitney, Mary 117, 173, 252
Whittell, George 128, 412
Whittier, Charlotte Robinson 113, 114, 115, 116, 120, 259, 260
Whittier, Frank 113, 114, 116, 117, 119, 120, 163, 172, 173, 215, 229, 230, 253, 254, 255, 259, 260, 268, 282, 384
Whittier, Frank Jr. 113, 215
Whittier Fuller and Company 115, 117
Whittier, Jennie   *See* Bothin, Jennie Whittier
Whittier, Martha "Mattie" Smith 114, 282
Whittier, Nancy Edith 114
Whittier, William Robinson 114, 282, 292
Wilder Building 162
Wilkinson, Elliott, J. 322
William Parmer Fuller Paint Company 117
Williams, Henry 138
Wills, Helen 304
Windgate Press 244
Wisconsin viii, xiv, xix, xxiii, xxx, 5, 7, 12, 13, 15, 16, 17, 18, 19, 20, 23, 24, 28, 35, 36, 37, 38, 42, 45, 46, 47, 48, 63, 65, 67, 68, 75, 87, 89, 90,

Wisconsin River 17, 19, 20, 24, 36, 37, 38, 65,
Wm. T. Wenzell & Co 101
Women's Christian Temperance Union (WCTU) 96
Women's' Sheltering and Protection Home of Oakland 286
Woodacre, California 221
Woodside, California 209, 264
"Wooing Life Anew at the Potter's Wheel" 312
Workingman's Association 105
Workingmen's Party 106
World War I 154, 315
World War II 114, 288
Wormser, Mrs. Samuel 306
W.R. Grace Company 175
Wright, William 108
W.W. Garthwaite 365
Wyoming 79

Y

Yale 79
Yerba Buena Island 241
Yosemite Valley 235, 236
Young Mens' Christian Association 147
Yuba Consolidated Industries 379

www.ingramcontent.com/pod-product-compliance
Lightning Source LLC
Chambersburg PA
CBHW071850290426
44110CB00013B/1093